P9-ARN-090

DATE DUE

323.4 FAC V2 1967

Facts on File.
Civil rights, Volume 2,
1967-68.
Civil rights, Volume 2, 1967-68.

BCCC

a31111000799294n

DEMCO

CIVIL
RIGHTS
Volume 2
1967-68

CIVIL
RIGHTS
Volume 2
1967-68

Compiled by Steven D. Price

FACTS ON FILE, INC.   NEW YORK, N. Y.

L. W. NIXON LIBRARY
BUTLER COUNTY COMMUNITY JUNIOR COLLEGE
Haverhill Road at Towanda Avenue
EL DORADO, KANSAS 67042

© Copyright, 1973, by Facts on File, Inc.

All rights reserved. No part of this book may be
reproduced in any form without the permission
of the publisher except for reasonably brief
extracts used in reviews or scholarly works.
Originally published as an Interim History paperback.
Published by Facts on File, Inc.,
119 West 57th Street, New York, N.Y. 10019.

Library of Congress Catalog Card Number 73-166438
ISBN 0-87196-246-2

9 8 7 6 5 4 3 2
PRINTED IN
THE UNITED STATES OF AMERICA

323.4 FAC V2 1967

Facts on File.
Civil rights, Volume 2,

ii

INTRODUCTION

T HIS VOLUME, A CONTINUATION of *CIVIL RIGHTS 1960-66,* records developments in what is sometimes called the "black revolt" as well as in the American Negro campaign for equality during the years 1967-8.

Among many diverse events, 2 major elements appear in the civil rights movement: (1) efforts of Negroes working within the system and (2) activities of those operating outside it.

The former continued what has become traditional methods of seeking equal rights: peaceful demonstrations and campaigns, application to courts and administrative agencies, and organizational drives to persuade fellow citizens to back their goals. Efforts in these channels achieved varying degrees of success. For example, the Poor People's March in Washington, D.C. apparently spurred Congressional action on welfare legislation; desegregation suits resulted in school integration gains, and federal agency regulations made it possible for black Americans to find employment opportunities they had seldom before enjoyed.

Violence, however, made a more profound impression on the country. "Long hot summers" of racial rioting, murders of civil rights leaders and battles between police forces and militant groups seemed to persuade growing numbers of white Americans —from those in "the Establishment" on down—that more must be done to satisfy justified demands of the black community.

In some instances, it appeared, the 2 rival courses of action interacted to bring positive results. For example, the slaying of the Rev. Dr. Martin Luther King Jr., followed by a nationwide wave of rioting, was considered a major factor in Congress' passage of civil rights legislation that nonviolent activists had been advocating. Smoldering cities torn by riots, looting and arson provided a catalyst for the examination of the causes of racial tension and unrest.

The struggle for civil rights was also affected by generational influences. Older Americans, both black and white, seemed more willing to accept the *status quo* than were their children. It was, in fact, young people whose actions galvanized many of the critical episodes of this period. Raised in ghettos, deprived of edu-

1

cational and economic advantages, growing numbers of black youths viewed the society in which they lived with anger and distrust. Dismayed by the slowness and apparent non-productivity of their parents' methods, they expressed themselves through civil disorders.

The Black Panthers became the most noted—or notorious— of the militant organizations. Founded in 1966 by (among others) Eldridge Cleaver and Bobby Seale, the Panthers advocated guerrilla warfare tactics against the "system." They held that there can be no neutrality in what they and other black-power groups saw as a civil war; as Cleaver expressed it: "If you're not part of the solution, you're part of the problem."

Young members of the more traditional NAACP (National Association for the Advancement of Colored People) and National Urban League also called for more militancy. Black students in universities across the country agitated for black studies courses as expressions of pride in their Afro-American heritage. Another demand was for open admission to colleges, so that disadvantaged students would be given the opportunity of college education regardless of their previous scholastic attainments.

In many instances white youths and adults were deeply involved in the struggle for equality—despite a growing tendency on the part of many younger Negroes to reject all whites as beyond redemption. A complicating factor in some of the militant activity was the antiwar movement, which often involved the same people and similar tactics (marches, sit-ins, riots, etc.) as the battle for racial justice.

The civil rights movement was able to record some degree of success in 1967-8. States that traditionally separated the races began to acknowledge that school integration was indeed the law of the land. Important steps were taken against housing and job bias, particularly through federal and state participation. Courts played an important role in all of the movement.

This book is based on material that appeared in FACTS ON FILE. Despite the controversial nature of the subject, extreme care was taken to record these events without bias.

1967

Racial rioting shook many cities across the U.S during 1967. 26 people were killed in Newark, at least 40 in Detroit, scores more in other cities. Reaction to the disorders came in the form of proposed legislation and the establishment of a Presidential commission to investigate underlying causes of the riots. Civil rights organizations were beset by internal agitation to adopt more militant stances. Thurgood Marshall became the first Negro appointed as a U.S. Supreme Court justice. Open-housing and equal employment campaigns were mounted in the North and South. There were slight gains in school desegregation, primarily through the implementation of court decisions. The Justice Department filed a record 105 suits against discrimination in fiscal 1967 (the 12 months ended June 30). During the fiscal year more than 175,000 persons registered to vote in the 5 states where the Voting Rights Act of 1965 had its main thrust—Alabama, Georgia, Louisiana, Mississippi and South Carolina.

An unprecedented wave of racial disturbances took place in cities across the U.S. during 1967. As in previous summers, the violence was precipitated by allegations of police brutality and by charges of discrimination in employment and housing facilities. Although Newark, N.J. and Detroit received most attention because of the severity and duration of their riots, few areas of the U.S. escaped 1967's "long hot summer."

At an impromptu news conference in New York Apr. 16, the Rev. Dr. Martin Luther King Jr., head of the Southern Christian Leadership Conference and the U.S.' foremost black leader, had warned that at least 10 cities could "explode in racial violence this summer." He described the cities as "powder kegs" and said that "the intolerable conditions which brought about racial violence last summer still exist." The cities he named were Cleveland, Chicago, Los Angeles, Oakland, Calif., Washington, Newark and New York. He said that the other cities, which he did not name, were in the South.

NAACP Executive Director Roy Wilkins, at a press conference in New York Apr. 20, denounced King's warning of summer violence as "dangerous." But he declared: "The conditions of the ghetto are responsible, the poor schools, poor housing and lack of jobs in the slums. These are responsible for riots, not what Dr. King says."

FBI Director J. Edgar Hoover May 31 charged civil rights leaders with issuing an "open invitation" to violence in naming cities where summer violence was expected. In an article in the June issue of the *FBI Law Enforcement Bulletin,* Hoover said that although civil rights leaders "claim to support nonviolence," their warnings were "more like an open invitation to hotheads and rabble rousers . . . to move into action on cue."

King had confirmed May 25 that he planned to "stir up trouble" in major American cities that summer. Speaking in Chicago, King said that demonstrations would be for "righteous" causes, and he insisted that they would be "an alternative to violence."

26 Die in Newark Rioting

The worst outbreak of racial violence since the 1965 summer rioting in the Watts section of Los Angeles erupted in Newark, N.J.

July 12-17.   In 6 days of rioting, 26 persons—24 Negroes and 2 whites—were killed; more than 1,500 persons were reported injured; 1,397 persons were arrested.   More than 300 fires, 12 of major proportions, were reported.   Property damage was estimated at $15-$30 million.   At its height, the rioting spread to 10 of the city's 23 square miles.

Newark, according to observers, was a city that had become ripe for racial turmoil.   Its black community had grown from 17% of the city's population in 1950 to 34% of the total in 1960, the year of the last census.   According to current reports, Negroes made up 52% to 60% of Newark's estimated 1967 population of 405,000. The city's unemployment rate, 7.2%, was reported to be nearly double the statewide New Jersey rate.   According to 1965 statistics of the Eagleton Institute of Politics, median annual incomes of $14,000 were reported for some of Newark's suburbs, compared with $5,454 for metropolitan Newark.   (The *N.Y. Times* reported July 15 that average annual household income for Newark proper was $6,890, for the suburbs $11,394.)   The city's public schools reportedly were 80% black.   Newark had received $25 million in federal anti-poverty funds in the past 3 years.

The rioting began July 12 in Newark's black ghetto, the Central Ward, after policemen arrested a black taxi driver, John William Smith, 40, for an alleged driving violation.   A brief scuffle between Smith and police officers outside the 4th Precinct station house was witnessed by a score of residents of a nearby housing project. About 25 taxi drivers loaded black bystanders into their cars and converged on the police station after they heard a report, later proved false, that Smith had been beaten to death.

As the rumor of Smith's death spread through the community, the mob swelled to 200-250 persons, who began throwing rocks and bottles at the station house, smashing its windows.   5 policemen reportedly were hit by stones.   Gangs of black youths then spread through the district and into Newark's downtown area.   They set false alarms, smashed windows, looted stores and threw merchandise on the sidewalks.   Several carloads of Negroes drove to City Hall to protest police brutality.   Order was not restored until 3:00 a.m.

Newark Mayor Hugh J. Addonizio met with about 20 of the city's black leaders early July 13 and promised to appoint a 10-member committee to investigate charges of police brutality.

(Although black leaders contended that police brutality had

been the immediate cause of the rioting, citing many complaints lodged in recent months, they said that a series of other incidents had added to tension in the black community. One of these was Addonizio's recent appointment of City Councilman James T. Callaghan, a white, to the $25,000-a-year post of secretary to the local school board. Black leaders had sponsored Newark Budget Director Wilbur Parker, a Negro, whose academic and professional training, they contended, better qualified him for the job. After a June 27 protest at City Hall, the school board had decided not to accept the resignation of its current secretary. A 2d issue centered on the city's selection of a 50-acre Central Ward site for the construction of a planned New Jersey College of Medicine & Dentistry. Negroes had opposed the plan on the ground that it would displace at least 1,800 low-income persons; they wanted the site used for housing.)

Violence erupted again at 7:35 p.m. July 13 in front of the 4th Precinct station house after about 200 Negroes gathered to protest Smith's alleged beating. Although the marchers reportedly started out in good spirits, the mood changed when one youth tossed a bottle over the crowd and hit the station house. About 150 teenagers then joined in tossing rocks and bottles at the building. After waiting for 45 minutes, Public Safety (police) Director Dominick A. Spina dispatched about 60 police, who pushed the mobs to the housing project near the station house.

The disturbance spread to surrounding streets and began moving toward the downtown section of Newark and in the opposite direction as well. An additional 90 policemen were called in to contain bands of marauders. Shortly after midnight, at 12:30 a.m. July 14, snipers had opened fire on police, shooting from cars and rooftops in the West, East and Central Wards. An estimated 3,000 Negroes roamed a 20-block area on Springfield Ave., smashing windows and looting stores. Debris from liquor stores, appliance and toy stores was scattered on the sidewalks. A toy store was set on fire by a Molotov cocktail and the flames spread to 2 adjoining stores.

At 1:00 a.m. July 14, Mayor Addonizio and Public Safety Director Spina abandoned their policy of limiting police to containment of riot-torn areas and ordered police to "return fire if necessary." 30 minutes later, as the violence spread, Addonizio ordered the city's 1,400-man police force on full alert. Police armed with shotguns were sent to guard firemen fighting a blaze sweeping several stores near Broad and Market Streets. Hundreds of persons were taken into custody by police although only about 75 were formally arrested. At least 4 of the 300 persons listed as injured were treated at Newark City Hospital for gunshot wounds. 3 persons, all of them Negroes, were killed during the night.

At 2:20 a.m. Addonizio telephoned New Jersey Gov. Richard J. Hughes and asked him to send National Guardsmen and state troopers to the city. Within 10 minutes Hughes summoned the state police and placed New Jersey units of the National Guard on "state alert" (they were not federalized nor was Newark placed under martial law). Guardsmen and troopers, under the command of Maj. Gen. James F. Cantwell, commander of the New Jersey Army and Air National Guards, and Col. David B. Kelly, superintendent of the New Jersey State Police, began arriving in Newark by 5:00 a.m. July 14. As they went through white sections of the city of the Central Ward they were met by small groups of whites who shouted "Kill the bastards" and "Shoot the niggers."

Gov. Hughes arrived in Newark at about 5:00 a.m. July 14. After setting up emergency headquarters in the Roseville Armory, he toured the city. He telephoned Pres. Lyndon B. Johnson later in the morning to say that federal aid was not necessary then.

At a news conference later July 14 Hughes said that "the destruction is unbelievable." He said he was "shocked and horrified" at the "holiday atmosphere [in riot-torn areas of the city]. . . . It's like laughing at a funeral." He charged that the rioting was a "criminal insurrection" that had "nothing to do with civil rights." "People who burn and loot and kill are not concerned with civil rights," he declared. "I think Negroes in the main are just as ashamed of this as I am. This is the work of the criminal element."

By the afternoon of July 14, 3,000 Guardsmen, 375 state troopers and nearly all of the city's 1,400 police had formed a perimeter around the riot area, a 10-square-mile section bounded by Bergen, Washington and Orange Streets and Chancellor Avenue (about ⅓ of the city). Barbed-wire barricades were put up to seal off the city from the suburbs. Guardsmen and state troopers armed with pistols, rifles and shotguns patrolled the streets in cars, jeeps and trucks. There were reports of sporadic gunfire between snipers and police through the day. Looting continued with rioters forming human chains to move stolen merchandise.

Mayor Addonizio July 14 imposed a 10:00 p.m.-to-6:00 a.m. curfew on vehicular traffic (except food trucks) and an 11:00

p.m.-to-6:00 a.m. curfew on pedestrians. The mayor, appearing at an early evenings news conference with Gov. Hughes, declared: "Up to early this afternoon, I thought it was unorganized and the work of just the criminal element. But I have just met with about 35 clergymen, and they indicated to me that it might be controlled possibly by people from outside." Hughes said the situation was "deteriorating." "The line between the jungle and the law might as well be drawn here as any place in America," he asserted.

Guardsmen, police and Negroes exchanged gunfire at a Central Ward housing project early in the evening of July 14 while fires raged in adjacent buildings. Frederick W. Toto, 34, a Newark police detective, was killed in the battle. Police and Guardsmen sprayed the upper stories of the building with bullets as Negroes hurled bottles and stones from the roof. The fighting ended when 24 Guardsmen rolled up to the entrance of the building in an 11-ton armored personnel carrier with a mounted machine gun. When they took control of the building, however, the snipers had disappeared.

Sporadic fighting continued through the night. One policeman was wounded in a battle at 7th and Wood Streets. Police engaged Negroes in a running gun fight at 18th St. and Springfield Ave. Before dawn July 15, firemen answering a fire alarm on Springfield Ave. were attacked by sniper fire. One sniper fired 6 shots into the crowded emergency room at the City Hospital.

By early morning the death toll had risen to 15. All the victims but one, the detective, were black. The injured totaled nearly 1,000, including 5 policemen who were treated for gunshot wounds. By the afternoon, Gov. Hughes said that 1,012 persons (including 121 women and 176 children under 16) had been arrested, among them the black playwright LeRoi Jones, who was charged with possession of 2 loaded .32-caliber pistols. Hughes declared: "It was plain and simple crime and not a civil rights protest." "Most of them," he said, had prior criminal records. Hughes said at a news conference that the city "looks like an atom bomb fell on our streets," but he added that the situation was "in control except for snipers."

Hughes met later July 15 with Mayor Addonizio and black and white citizens who had formed a Committee of 5 to work out ways to restore order and open communication between the city's white and black communities. The committee said it would recruit volunteers to walk through the streets and urge people "to cool it." The committee's statement said:

We have been in constant contact with the governor and the mayor and are working jointly with them to create a climate where we can work out and solve the problems that exist in our community.

We are working jointly with the governor and the mayor to provide food, medicine and other needed services for all the people.

We are also working jointly with the governor, the mayor and the business community to provide jobs for thousands of youths and adults in the city who are unemployed.

We are appealing to all Newarkers to set an example by remaining at home and keeping their youngsters off the street.

We urge you to play it cool and let's work together to build a better Newark and a new day.

(The committee said July 16 that its efforts to calm the rioting had failed due to harassment by the National Guard and state police.)

It was disclosed later July 15 that Gov. Hughes had met secretly with black leaders for 4 hours the previous night at the home of Oliver Lofton, administrative director of the Newark Legal Services Project. Lofton said the discussion had centered on the underlying problems of the black community in Newark. He said Hughes had agreed to urge Mayor Addonizio to immediately appoint a Negro as acting police captain in the 4th Precinct and to urge merchants in the area to reopen their stores to provide food and other essentials for the community. Lofton also said that the county prosecutor, Brendan Byrne, had agreed to open a grand jury investigation into charges of police brutality.

Vice Pres. Hubert Humphrey phoned Hughes July 15 to renew an offer of federal help in coping with the Newark unrest. Hughes declined the offer, declaring that he was satisfied with the police and National Guard actions to deal with what he again called a "criminal insurrection." But the Rev. Robert L. Pierson of Newark's St. Barnabas Episcopal Church, former son-in-law of N.Y. Gov. Nelson A. Rockefeller, criticized Hughes' use of the National Guard. "I don't think it was helpful," Pierson said. "It's just like Vietnam; the more we pour in, the tougher it's going to be."

Heavy sniper fire continued through the night of July 15 and into the daylight hours of the next day. By afternoon July 16, 9 more persons had been killed, bringing the total to 24 slain. 2 policemen were overcome by tear gas as they tried to force a sniper from a building. Police also began firing at each other. At 10:30 p.m. July 16 the police radio network warned police to "Hold your fire. You're shooting at your own men." Snipers continued firing at the city hospital for the 3d night, forcing a black-out of the building at 9:30 p.m.

The emergency distribution of food was begun in central Newark July 16. (At the peak of the rioting, food deliveries had been curtailed by suppliers, and stocks of black- and white-owned stores had been depleted by looters or had been sold out. Many ghetto residents had not been able to procure food for 5 days.) Thousands of Negroes, guarded by armed militia, lined up to receive food rations provided from Agriculture Department surplus stocks. 8 distribution centers were in operation in housing projects and community centers. 5 supermarkets, closed at the outbreak of violence, had reopened, as had some others in response to Hughes' pleas. Hughes asked other business to remain closed, but he voiced hopes for an early resumption of critical services such as garbage collection.

Members of an *ad hoc* committee organized by Dr. Reynold E. Burch, a black obstetrician, met with Hughes the afternoon of July 16 to protest "excesses" allegedly committed by National Guardsmen and state troopers sent to Newark. The 40-member group produced photos and statements by witnesses to document its charges. Included in the testimony taken by the committee was a statement by Mrs. Nancy Ferguson, a black storeowner, who described how state troopers allegedly shot out the windows of her store and of stores owned by 17 other black merchants in the neighboring 5-6 blocks. Only stores bearing the sign "Soul Brother," designating black ownership, were affected.

The group sent to Pres. Johnson a telegram requesting "fully integrated federal troops" to replace police and National Guardsmen, who, it said, had committed "wanton destruction of property" and "murders." Many Negroes, the telegram said, had been killed or wounded by "indiscriminate firing." It assailed Hughes and Addonizio for what it said were "inflammatory statements" that had brought the formation of white vigilante groups on the edges of the black ghetto.

Hughes contended July 16 that the charges of police brutality were based on "hearsay" and "mostly 2d-hand information." He said he was assessing the situation and promised that "justice will be done" as soon as the facts were clear. He said Guardsmen and state troopers would remain on duty, however, until order was restored and all snipers, whom he called "unregenerate criminals," were arrested. At a news conference early July 16, Hughes had offered executive clemency to any of the 1,650 riot prisoners who volunteered information leading to the conviction of snipers. He estimated that at least 25 snipers were still battling with police in the ghetto area. He said he had been informed that some of the snipers came from outside the city. He said that although he had no evidence of a conspiracy, "the rather expert sniping, the jumping from place to place—the cruel and despicable efficiency with which this sniping occurred, indicate some organization and some coordination between those criminals participating in it."

(Atty. Gen. Ramsey Clark, interviewed on the ABC-TV program "Issues and Answers" July 16, said there was "very, very little evidence of intercity activity to deliberately activate" the Newark rioting. He added that there was "very little the federal government can do" to implement law enforcement in riot-stricken cities.)

In the afternoon of July 16, 40 white businessmen and 10 Negroes attended a meeting called by the Newark Legal Services Project to express "concern in the black community of indiscriminate suppressing of disorders." The group adopted resolutions, calling on Hughes for (1) a reduction of militia in the city; (2) a change in bail policy to permit those charged with minor crimes to be released on personal recognizance; (3) a more severe policy toward white vigilantes; (4) an independent investigation of the rioting by an outside group.

Hughes announced July 17 that "the rioting and looting are over." He said: "The restoration of order is accomplished. While sniping incidents continue, it is grinding to a halt." Hughes announced the withdrawal from the city of all but a few of the 3,000 Guardsmen and 375 state troopers. A small force was to remain to assure order and assist in the distribution of food. Hughes curtailed most emergency restrictions by 3:00 p.m. July 17 and lifted the city's curfew. (His action was bitterly denounced by many Newark whites as "premature." Police headquarters reported more than 100 phone calls protesting the withdrawal of the Guardsmen.)

Sanitation trucks were sent into the ghetto to begin cleaning up riot debris and garbage, which had accumulated and was becoming a health hazard. Hughes asked all businesses except bars and liquor stores to reopen the next day.

The city's 25th riot victim, Michael Pugh, 12, a Negro, had been shot to death early July 17 while emptying a garbage pail outside his home. The 26th victim, Raymond Gilmer, 20, a Negro, was killed later in the day while allegedly looting a store. Police said that 25 cases of looting were reported during the night of July 17.

(The Newark City Hospital's medical director, Dr. C. Richard

Weinberg, said July 18 that some 700 persons had been treated during the rioting; 58 persons, most of them black, had been admitted to the hospital; 75% of them had suffered gunshot wounds.)

At a news conference July 18, Addonizio ascribed the racial violence to "years of discrimination and bigotry of generations," which were "fueled by the rash of wild and extremist statements and behavior of the past 10 or 12 weeks in our city." "Some outsiders were arrested who have participated in the riot," he said. "We're convinced also that this was a planned situation."

An interracial group of 60 community and civil rights leaders July 18 formed a Committee of Concern to study problems stemming from the riots. Malcolm Talbott, a white and vice president of Rutgers University, and Oliver Lofton, a Negro, were elected co-chairmen. The committee issued a statement calling for an independent commission to investigate charges of "violence and terror visited upon the vast majority of the Negro citizens who were in no way involved in the rioting and were shot, beaten and brutalized by military and police forces without regard to wrong-doing." The statement continued: "A large segment of the Negro people is convinced that the single continuously lawless element operating in the community is the police force itself in its callous disregard to human rights."

Hughes July 19 appointed 6 men to a "blue ribbon" committee to investigate charges of police brutality, and to determine the causes of the rioting. The committee was also instructed to consider Newark's housing, unemployment and education problems. Robert Lilley, president of the New Jersey Bell Telephone Co., was named chairman of the committee. The other members were ex-N.J. Govs. Alfred E. Driscoll (R.) and Robert B. Meyner (D.); Catholic Bishop John J. Dougherty, president of Seton Hall University; Bishop Prince Taylor, a Negro, presiding bishop of the Methodist Church in New Jersey; Ray Brown, a black lawyer and member of the State Board of Control. Ex-State Supreme Court Justice William A. Wachenfeld and Joseph J. Gibbons, president of the N.J. Bar Association, were added to the committee July 21.

In a copyrighted interview in the July 31 issue of *U.S. News & World Report* (reported July 23), Hughes conceded that he had no evidence that outside agitators had played any role in the Newark rioting. "Many things are said by people throughout the country which are inflammatory in nature, but so far as a conspiracy from outside moving into Newark—I couldn't say that happened," he admitted. Hughes asserted that while less than 2% of the city's population had participated in the rioting, the nation could "not permit criminal elements who are burning and maiming and killing and looting to hide behind the shield of 'civil rights.' "

The U.S. Marshal's Office in Newark reported Aug. 8 that 90% of those arrested during the rioting lived in Newark and that nearly 50% of them were over 25 years old. About 75% of the indictments were for breaking and entering, larceny, or possession and receipt of stolen goods.

In the aftermath of the Newark rioting, 18 Negroes sued in U.S. District Court in Newark Aug. 24 for a federal receiver to take over and run the Newark Police Department on the ground that police consistently discriminated against Negroes. The defendants named in the suit were Newark Mayor Addonizio, Public Safety Director Spina and Police Chief Oliver Kelly. The suit was announced at a press conference at the N.Y. City offices of the American Civil Liberties Union. The plaintiffs charged that Newark police had engaged in a systematic pattern of "violence, humiliation and intimidation" and thereby had denied blacks their constitutional rights. It charged that the Newark police, the New Jersey State Police and the National Guard had intentionally destroyed black-owned property and had used "massive and unlawful deadly force against members of plaintiffs' class when said force was unnecessary" during the rioting.

The suit was signed by 22 lawyers representing 5 cooperating agencies in the case: the American Civil Liberties Union (ACLU), the National Association for the Advancement of Colored People (NAACP), the Newark Legal Services Project, the Law Center for Constitutional Rights and the Scholarship Education & Defense Fund for Racial Equality.

At a Senate Labor & Public Welfare subcommittee hearing in Washington July 19, Sen. Winston Prouty (R., Vt.) had said that Spina had telegraphed OEO (Office of Economic Opportunity) Director Sargent Shriver May 25 to protest the use of antipoverty funds for "fomenting and agitating against the government and agencies of the City of Newark." According to Spina, the antipoverty officials had rented cars "to agitate against the [Newark] Planning Board" and had pressured employes of the UCC (United Community Corp., Newark's antipoverty agency) to picket. Shriver said the cars were used to move chairs.

The OEO's Northeast Regional Office asked the UCC Aug. 1 to suspend Willie Wright, 35, a member of the UCC executive board and president of the United Afro-American Association, pending an investigation of charges that he had made inflammatory statements after the July riot. Wright reportedly said at a Negro rally that it was his "firm conviction that complete chaos will have to prevail in the streets of American cities and blood will have to flow like water before the black man will become an accepted citizen of this society." He was reported to have told Negroes to arm themselves for "the next time the while man walks into the black community." The UCC refused to suspend Wright since he was "not an employe of the UCC but a duly elected board member." The OEO withdrew its demand Aug. 4 pending the Aug. 17 board meeting of the UCC, and the full UCC membership voted unanimously Aug. 17 against suspending Wright.

The Newark Office of Economic Development Aug. 15 reported $10,251,200 in business damages in the rioting—$8,284,-060 in stock losses and $1,967,140 in property damages. Liquor stores suffered the most: 151 had $141,745 in property damages and $1.8 million in stock loss. 80 clothing stores suffered $322,-550 in building damages and $1,412,375 in stock losses; 72 furniture stores had building damages of $232,000 and stock losses of $1,173,659. The report said: "Of the 889 businesses whose stores were damaged, 2.8%, or 25 stores, were completely demolished while another 15.4%, or 136 stores, were heavily damaged. The remaining 728 stores were either lightly or moderately damaged." P. Bernard Nortman, director of the Economic Development Office, said that altogether, 1,029 stores were damaged or looted or both in the riots.

Gov. Hughes July 25 had appointed an 8-member cabinet-level, interdepartmental panel to work out programs for easing New Jersey's urban problems. The governor July 28 announced extensive reforms in training programs for state and local police; the reforms included courses in riot and sniper control, use of weapons and police equipment, law enforcement communications, police relations with the public and police relations with constitutional issues of due process and arrest and search and seizure. Hughes Aug. 16 announced a drive to recruit 700 Negroes and Puerto Ricans for the New Jersey National Guard. He said the state would also try to recruit more blacks in the State Police; only 5 Negroes were members of the 1,200-man force. The N.J. Defense Department announced Sept. 15 that 87 Negroes had joined the state National Guard. (Before the special recruitment drive, there had been 251 blacks in the state's 14,733-man Army National Guard and 50 in the approximately 2,500-man Air National Guard.)

Hughes and Dr. Carl L. Marburger, state commissioner of education, announced Aug. 15 the establishment of a New Jersey Urban Education Corps to recruit qualified men and women to fill nearly 1,650 vacancies in the state. The "greatest need," Marburger said, "is for teachers who are highly skilled in the education of the disadvantaged and eager to help solve the urban crisis that confronts the nation."

The Roman Catholic Archdiocese of Newark Sept. 20 announced that it would sponsor a nonsectarian housing and rehabilitation program in the Newark archdiocese (Bergen, Essex, Hudson and Union Counties; population: almost 3 million persons). Nearly $50 million in state and federal funds was to be used to finance low- and middle-income housing during the next 2 years and to provide counseling and guidance services. The program would be directed and sponsored by the Mount Carmel Guild, the church's social service and rehabilitation agency.

John W. Smith whose arrest had set off the riot, filed a $700,-000 damage suit against the police in the U.S. District Court in Newark Aug. 11, He charged that policemen had arrested him "without cause" and beat and injured him. The arresting officers —Patrolmen Vito Pontrelli and John DeSimone—said Smith had been tailgating their police car, that when they stopped him he was abusive and attacked them. They denied beating him. Smith had been indicted July 25 on charges of assault and battery of the 2 policemen. Public Safety Director Spina, Police Chief Kelly and the 2 arresting officers Sept. 7 filed a $16½ million slander suit in U.S. District Court in Newark against Smith and 7 other unidentified persons involved in the incident. They charged Smith with fighting the arresting officers "with intent to do grievous bodily harm." They alleged that the defendants had made false statements about police and that the 7 unidentified persons had conspired to have "malicious false statements" published and reported on TV and radio.

Smith was found guilty of traffic violations charges Sept. 12; he was sentenced to a 60-day jail term and fined $40 but was released on $300 bail Sept. 13 pending appeal.

Mob Kills Plainfield (N.J.) Policeman

A white policeman was shot and beaten to death by a mob of black youths in Plainfield, N.J. July 16. National Guard units were sent to the city after violence had swept through its black neighborhoods, but order was restored only after 4 days of looting and vandalism. More than 100 persons were arrested, and 10 were reported to have been injured during the disorders.

The disorders took place in a community not previously considered a prime target for racial strife. Negroes comprised about ⅓ of Plainfield's population of 50,000. According to the city's Chamber of Commerce, the unemployment rate in the area was only 2%. Average annual family income for the city was reported to be $7,200. Plainfield's affluence in large part was attributed to the fact that 10,000 of its residents commuted to work in New York.

The Plainfield unrest broke out July 14 when a gang of 40 black youths threw rocks at police cars and store windows. They dispersed when additional police arrived. Looting and firebombing began in Plainfield's West End section at 10:00 p.m. July 15 and continued until 3:00 a.m. July 16. Molotov cocktails were tossed at several stores, and a fire truck was hit and destroyed by a fire bomb. One fireman suffered minor burns. 38 persons, including 10 white motorcyclists and 3 white men carrying baseball bats, were arrested during the disorders.

Rioters began stoning cars driving through the black section July 16. A few police patrol cars and the fire chief's car were damaged. By the evening of July 16, more than 300 black youths were rampaging through a 14-block area of the neighborhood, smashing store windows, looting and throwing Molotov cocktails and stones. Snipers shot at a fire station.

A mob converged on the corner of Front Street and Plainfield Avenue, where Patrolman John V. Gleason Jr., 36, was on traffic duty. It swept through the area and began to pursue some young whites who had tried to stop a black looter. When Gleason attempted to stop the looter, he was attacked by a crowd of about 30 Negroes. According to witnesses, Gleason drew his gun and fired into the mob, wounding a black youth, Bobby Williams, 7. Members of the crowd then wrested the gun from Gleason, and one of them shot him with it. A witness, David Hardy, a reporter for *The Plainfield Courier-News,* said: "It was really brutal. They got shopping carts and threw them on him. They beat him and stomped him. He was raising his hand and they just kept kicking him." When others tried to intervene, members of the mob attacked them with rocks and bottles. Gleason was dead by the time help arrived. (Gail Madden, 22, and George Merritt Jr., 24, both Negro, were convicted in Elizabeth, N.J. Dec. 23, 1968 of first-degree murder in the killing of Gleason. 2 other defendants were acquitted; 6 others had been acquitted previously. During the trial, witnesses testified that Merritt had attacked Gleason with a butcher knife and that Miss Madden, who weighed more than 250 pounds, had jumped up and down on him. The jury recommended life imprisonment rather than the death penalty.)

Shortly after Gleason's slaying, at 11:15 p.m. July 16, Leo F. Kaplowitz, Union County prosecutor, announced that 100 National Guardsmen had been sent to Plainfield at the request of Mayor George S. Hetfield. 60 police reservists were added to the city's 75-man force to deal with the rioters, many of whom carried rifles and automatic weapons; it was reported late July 16 that 46 semiautomatic rifles and ammunition had been stolen from the Plainfield Machine Co. in Middlesex, N.J. The Guardsmen formed a perimeter around the riot area. A 10:00 p.m.-to-6:00 a.m. curfew was imposed, and the mayor ordered all liquor stores and taverns closed.

Looting and sporadic sniper fire continued July 17, though with lessened intensity. State troopers moved into the city and were joined by another 30-man unit of National Guardsmen July 18.

Black leaders and youths held a closed meeting the evening of July 17 with Mayor Hetfield, State Atty. Gen. Arthur J. Sills, New Jersey Community Affairs Commissioner Paul N. Ylvisaker and Col. David Kelly, superintendent of the State Police.

Sills announced early July 18 that white and black leaders had agreed on a peace plan under which National Guardsmen, state troopers and police would withdraw from the West End riot area and black leaders would assume responsibility for maintaining order in the district. Sills said that efforts would be made to expedite bail procedures by reducing fines and to promptly investigate Negro charges of police brutality.

300 heavily-armed National Guardsmen and state troopers conducted a house-to-house search for the stolen Middlesex weapons in the 128-unit West End Gardens public housing project and 14 other "selected spots" in Plainfield July 19. They acted without search warrants under Gov. Richard J. Hughes' proclamation of "a state of disaster and emergency" in Plainfield. The proclamation had been signed July 17, but its disclosure had been withheld while city officials negotiated with black leaders. (Earlier July 19, 12 black youths had been released on their own recognizance on condition they asked other Negroes to return the stolen rifles.)

Due to what was termed a misunderstanding, 4 armored personnel carriers started moving into the riot area before the search. They were stopped by Paul Ylvisaker, who sprinted to the middle of an intersection shouting: "Stop Stop! . . . This is a peaceful community. This will be an orderly search." The heavy equipment was withdrawn, and 20 jeeps and 12 trucks brought in the searchers.

Crowds gathered, however, to protest the search procedure used by the Guardsmen and troopers. Doors and windows reportedly were broken, beds were torn apart and clothes and linens were said to have been strewn on floors. The search, conducted like a military operation, continued for more than 2 hours. Many Negroes whose homes were searched complained of serious damage to their property.

The Plainfield Human Relations Commission and the state branch of the American Civil Liberties Union July 19 issued formal protests denouncing the search. The ACLU group said the search was "an unconscionable violation of the constitutional rights of the Negro community" and "a deliberate attempt to provoke rioting." State Police Col. Kelly conceded that there had been a "misunderstanding" about the search techniques to be used; he said that when this became known, the search was ended. 3 guns were found during the search; one had been found earlier. New Jersey ACLU Director Henry DiSuvero said July 21: "Gov. Hughes' action in Plainfield is nothing more than the discredited Southern doctrine of interposition of state laws against the federal Constitution. Gov. Hughes cannot decide to abolish, even for a minute, the 4th Amendment and its rule against unreasonable searches and seizures."

The Union County prosecutor said July 19 that the search had not been expected to produce the stolen weapons. "The search," he said, "is a symbol of law and order, and it is vitally important for this community to see that symbol."

Plainfield remained calm July 20. Several hundred policemen from 50 northern New Jersey communities attended funeral services for Patrolman Gleason. While police were absent from the riot area, "talk squads" of young Negroes patrolled in an effort to prove that order could be maintained without the presence of white police. All National Guard units were withdrawn from Plainfield July 21. All but administrative personnel and one operational unit of the state troopers were removed. The curfew was lifted and liquor stores and taverns were allowed to open.

Other New Jersey Violence

Racial disorders soon spread from Plainfield and Newark to several other New Jersey communities. Among major incidents reported:

Englewood—A suburb of New York City just 2 miles from the George Washington Bridge, Englewood was torn by 3 nights of racial violence July 21–23. The disorders began early in the evening of July 21 in the 4th Ward, where nearly all of the city's 12,000 Negroes (40% of the population) lived. Rock- and bottle-throwing mobs raced through the streets and smashed store windows. Little looting was reported, but 8 policemen suffered minor injuries in the outbreak. The riot was brought under control by local police reinforced by policemen from nearby communities. 5 Negroes were arrested, and several were reported to have been injured.

Violence flared again the next evening when several stores were looted and small fires were set. Shotgun-carrying police, sealing off the riot district, fired on one sniper but reported no serious injuries. 8 Negroes were arrested. After meeting with ghetto residents July 22 and 23, Mayor Austin N. Volk characterized their grievances as "not momentous." A white-owned grocery store was set afire by a Molotov cocktail July 23, but otherwise the town remained quiet.

(Federal housing officials revealed July 25 that the government had turned down plans for 2 urban-renewal projects in Englewood after the city had refused to take steps to integrate the projects. Black leaders had cited dilapidated housing as a major grievance in the ghetto.)

New Brunswick—False fire alarms, looting incidents and sporadic rock- and bottle-throwing broke out July 17 in New Brunswick, the site of Rutgers University. 50 persons were arrested. The City Commission imposed a 10 p.m. curfew July 18 and asked bars and taverns to close by 7 p.m. Police said that about 50 store windows had been smashed.

Elizabeth—Racial violence erupted July 17 in Elizabeth, a city of 113,000 bordering on Newark. Police officials reported that a mob of 200 black youths had smashed store windows and thrown fire bombs before being dispersed. Minor fires were set, and fewer than a dozen stores were looted. There were no arrests and no injuries.

Jersey City—Sporadic firebombing and rock throwing was reported in Jersey City July 15-17. One man, a Negro injured when a fire bomb was thrown into the taxi in which he was riding, died from his burns July 17. At least 50 persons were arrested in the disorders, which included sniper activity.

Passaic—Gangs of young Negroes ran through the streets of Passaic July 27–28, smashing store windows and tossing fire bombs. Most of the property damage was suffered by 2 looted liquor stores. About 50 youths were arrested, but most of them were quickly released by the police.

40 Killed in Detroit Riots

At least 33 Negroes and 7 whites were killed in racial violence that swept Detroit, the nation's 5th largest city, July 23–30. According to some figures, the death toll was 43—or 45—as reports of fatalities continued into mid-August.

Rioting, looting and arson reached a scale unknown in a U.S. city in the 20th century and brought the dispatch of federal troops to aid local and state forces in suppressing the disorders. (This was the first time in 24 years that U.S. troops had been used to quell civil strife. The previous use of federal force against urban disorders also had been in Detroit, during racial rioting in 1943 in which 34 persons died.)

The 1967 Detroit violence left more than 2,000 persons injured. 5,000 persons were homeless as a result of fires that gutted large parts of the city's ghetto areas. 1,442 separate fires were reported to have been set during the rioting, and they caused damage estimated to total $250–$500 million. At least 5,000 persons were reported arrested before the disorders were halted.

Prior to the outbreak, Detroit had not been considered a particularly likely scene of serious racial strife. According to the 1960 census, blacks comprised 29% (487,000) of the city's 1.67 million inhabitants. However, the Michigan Civil Rights Commission reported July 24 that the city's population had dropped 10% to 1½ million while the black population had increased to 537,000 —about 33% of the total. The black unemployment rate in Detroit was 6% to 8%—approximately double the national average. While the city had only one black councilman, it was the only city in the country that had 2 black Congressmen: Rep. John J. Conyers Jr. (D.) and Rep. Charles C. Diggs (D.). The Aug. 4 issue of *Time* magazine reported that 40% of Detroit's black inhabitants owned their own homes. Detroit had been considered one of the most progressive U.S. cities in its efforts to deal with poverty and racial tensions.

The violence erupted shortly before 4:00 a.m. July 23 when police raided a "blind pig" (after-hours drinking club) on 12th Street on Detroit's West Side, and arrested 73 Negroes and the bartender. A crowd gathered outside the building. Rumors spread that policemen had beaten a man and kicked a woman. Bystanders then began throwing stones at the police. Following the departure of the policemen and prisoners, a Negro threw a stone through the window of a clothing store, and 50 persons began looting the shop. The police drove by again but failed to stop or return, and the looting then spread. Within an hour dozens of stores in a 16-block area had been plundered and set on fire.

The looting and arson continued to expand swiftly. The police estimated that at least 5,000 persons, black and white, were soon roaming through the West Side and moving into the East Side neighborhoods of the city. The violence spread speedily along 3-mile and 4-mile sections of Grand River and Woodward Avenues and 12th Street in the downtown section of Detroit and ranged to as far as 6 to 7 miles toward the edge of the city.

An initial force of 600–700 National Guardsmen, 200 state troopers and 600 Detroit police officers sealed off large areas of the city but was unable to disperse the crowds or contain the violence. Gov. George W. Romney placed 7,000 National Guardsmen on standby alert, and city police were ordered to 24-hour duty.

Snipers opened fire on police in the West Side, but the police were ordered to hold their fire in hopes of reducing antagonism and avoiding a major conflagration. Firemen who tried to contain fires, by then consuming a 15-block area, were attacked by mobs with rocks and bricks; at times they were forced to lay down their hoses and retreat.

On several occasions, whites and Negroes, armed with shotguns and rifles, were reported to have stood guard for firemen attempting to control the fires. At nightfall July 23 a mob of 3,000 rampaged through Detroit's East Side, looting and throwing firebombs, ignoring a 9:00 p.m.-to-5:30 a.m. curfew imposed by Detroit Mayor Jerome P. Cavanagh. Firebombing and looting spread to almost every section of the city and into the suburbs of River Rouge and Highland Park and the enclave of Hamtramck.

By evening, Romney conceded that the situation was "out of

control" and declared a state of public emergency. Romney said: "It's a case of lawlessness and hoodlumism and apparently not organized. Disobedience to the law cannot and will not be tolerated in Michigan. I will supply whatever manpower the city needs to handle the situation." Liquor stores and taverns were closed; gatherings of 5 or more persons were prohibited. 7,000–8,000 National Guardsmen on standby in Grand Rapids since early in the day were called to the city. Police helicopters equipped with floodlights and submachine guns combed the city in search of rooftop snipers.

In the first day of rioting July 23, 20 persons were injured, 15 of them policemen. At least 650 persons were arrested. With at least 150 fires reported, the city lay under a heavy cloud of smoke.

Before dawn July 24, U.S. Atty. Gen. Ramsey Clark informed the White House that Romney was preparing to ask for federal troops for Detroit. At 10:56 a.m. Pres. Johnson received Romney's telegram requesting "the immediate deployment of federal troops into Michigan to assist state and local authorities in reestablishing law and order in Detroit." "There is reasonable doubt," the telegram said, "that we can suppress the existing looting, arson and sniping without the assistance of federal troops. Time could be of the essence."

Within 6 minutes, on Johnson's directions, Defense Secy. Robert S. McNamara ordered 4,700 airborne troops flown to Selfridge Air Force Base, about 30 miles outside of Detroit. The paratroopers, the 3d Brigade, 82d Airborne Division at Ft. Bragg, N.C. and the 2d Brigade, 101st Airborne Division at Ft. Campbell, Ky., were under the command of Lt. Gen. John L. Throckmorton, 54, former deputy commander in Vietnam.

The President sent a personal representative, ex-Deputy Defense Secy. Cyrus R. Vance, to Detroit to assess the situation. Vance was accompanied by Deputy Atty. Gen. Warren Christopher, John Doar, Assistant Attorney General in charge of civil rights, and Roger Wilkins, chief of the Community Relations Service in the Justice Department. When they arrived in Detroit, they met with Romney and Cavanagh and then toured the city.

While the troops were being moved to Selfridge Air Force Base, the rioting grew worse. Businesses closed; baseball games were canceled, and several airlines canceled flights over the city because of the danger of sniper fire. By the evening of July 24 the death toll had reached 15. More than 1,800 persons had been arrested, and at least 800 people had been injured. 100 new fires were reported. Property damage from firebombing and looting reportedly had risen beyond $150 million.

With nightfall, sniper fire increased. Police were then given orders to shoot. Military barricades were erected to limit entry to the city. The border to the neighboring Canadian city of Windsor was sealed off. Romney and Vance toured the city again early in the evening, and at 10:00 p.m. Vance ordered 1,800 troops to the Michigan State Fairgrounds, within the city limits. He declared that the soldiers "will be promptly available to provide assistance and support . . . if they are needed," but he did not order them into active service. Cavanagh reportedly sharply disagreed with Vance's assessment of the situation. He said: "I would certainly like to see the troops in the community at this point." Noting the gravity of the use of federal troops, he added that he "understood the traditional federal desire not to get involved in this type of dispute." "With more and more cities getting involved in riots," Cavanagh continued, "the government is asking: 'How involved can we get?' "

At 10:31 p.m. July 24, on the recommendation of Vance, Pres. Johnson signed a proclamation calling on "all persons engaged in such acts of violence to cease and desist . . . and to disperse. . . ." At 11:25 p.m. Johnson issued an executive order instructing Defense Secy. McNamara to "take all appropriate steps to disperse all persons engaged in acts of violence" and to "restore law and order." He also authorized McNamara to call "any or all units" of the Michigan National Guard into federal service. Later that night the President ordered federal troops sent to Detroit; he announced his action in a TV address to the nation just before midnight. The President's executive order authorizing the use of federal troops and a Presidential proclamation commanding all citizens to desist from acts of violence were issued before he spoke to the nation.

In his address, Johnson described the sequence of events that had led him to order troops to be flown to the Detroit area and, finally, to be deployed to the riot-torn city. Johnson said: Gov. Romney had informed U.S. Atty. Gen. Ramsey Clark in the early morning of July 24 "of the extreme disorder" existing in Detroit; a telegram from Romney requesting federal troops was sent at 10:46 a.m. and received by the President at 10:56 a.m.; the President issued orders at 11:02 a.m. for the initiation of the troop movement, and about 5,000 troops were on their way to Detroit by plane within a few hours. Cyrus R. Vance, acting as a special assistant to the Defense Secretary, was sent to the city for on-the-spot observation and talks with Romney and local officials. Lt. Gen. Throckmorton, in charge of the federal troops involved, reported in the afternoon "that the situation might be controlled" without the use of the federal troops assembling at Selfridge Air Base, northeast of Detroit, but at "approximately 10:30" p.m. Vance and Throckmorton reported "it was the then unanimous opinion" of state and federal officials in Detroit that the use of federal troops was "imperative" and that "the situation was totally beyond the control of the local authority." The President then had "forthwith issued" the orders necessary to use the federal force in Detroit.

Johnson told the nation: He had taken the step "with the greatest regret, and only because of the clear, the unmistakable and the undisputed evidence that Gov. Romney . . . and the local officials . . . have been unable to bring the situation under control. Law enforcement is a local matter. It is the responsibility of local officials and the governors of the respective states. The federal government should not intervene, except in the most extraordinary circumstances. The fact of the matter, however, is that law and order have broken down in Detroit. . . . And the federal government in the circumstances . . . had no alternative but to respond, since it was called upon by the governor of the state, and since it was presented with proof of his inability to restore order in Michigan. We will not tolerate lawlessness. We will not endure violence. It matters not by whom it is done, or under what slogan or banner. It will not be tolerated." "With few exceptions" the people of Detroit, Newark, Harlem and all U.S. cities "deplore and condemn these criminal acts," and "the vast majority of Negroes and whites are shocked and are outraged by them." "All of our people in all of our cities" should "firmly . . . show by word and by deed that riot, looting and public disorder will just not be tolerated."

Federal paratroopers reconnoitered the area before 2 a.m. July 25 and then moved into the East Side of the city, armed with rifles, machine guns and tear gas. They set up barbed-wire barricades across the streets as snipers continued firing. National Guardsmen were ordered to the city's West Side. 1,200 federal troops were held in reserve at the fairgrounds.

2 police stations came under massive sniper attack early in the morning July 25, and 100 National Guardsmen were trapped temporarily.

The violence subsided temporarily later in the day. Gov. Romney announced that he was sending National Guardsmen to quell outbreaks of rioting in other Michigan cities: Flint, Pontiac and Grand Rapids. He made an appeal for law and order and said he would ask Washington to declare Detroit a federal disaster area.

After touring the city in the afternoon, Mayor Cavanagh announced that in view of food shortages, he would provide guards for delivery trucks to replenish supplies. He said that garbage collection would be resumed. A ban on gasoline sales was temporarily lifted for several hours during the afternoon, and businesses were allowed to reopen. 700 refugee centers were opened during the day to care for families that had fled from the rioting or had been left homeless by fires. Cavanagh met with 15 black leaders later in the day to discuss the causes of the violence and to find ways "to pick up the pieces again." He suggested that a private investigation of the disaster be made. He rejected demands made by the Malcolm X Society, a black nationalist organization, which had claimed that it could restore order if troops were immediately withdrawn and prisoners were released.

By evening July 25 the death toll had reached 26 (21 Negroes and 5 whites), 900 persons had been injured and 2,700 were under arrest. More than 950 buildings had been destroyed or seriously damaged by fire, and more than 1,500 others had been looted. Fire Chief Charles J. Quinlan said that 10 new fires were being reported every hour.

After 10:00 p.m. snipers and National Guardsmen fought a gun battle on the West Side. The Guardsmen fired machine guns at the snipers from Sherman tanks and armored personnel carriers.

Cavanagh and Police Chief Ray Girardin came under sharp attack July 25 for not stopping looting and disorders with firmer police policy at the onset of the violence. A banner headline in the city's black newspaper, *The Michigan Chronicle,* read: "It Could Have Been Stopped." The newspaper said that "if the police had stopped looting when it centered on one 12th Street block early Sunday [July 23], when the mood was allowed to become a Roman holiday, the riot could have been prevented."

At news conferences early July 23, Girardin and Cavanagh had said they had ordered police to use "restraint" in order to avoid indiscriminate shooting that might have led to "guerrilla warfare." (At a news conference July 27, Girardin defended his policy of using the police as a "containment force." "I still believe in putting human lives above property," he declared. But he conceded:

"They hit us when we were the lightest. We don't have many men out on Sunday morning.")

Gun battles between snipers and National Guardsmen continued through the night of July 25 and into the daylight hours of July 26. Snipers fired on firemen fighting new blazes and launched an attack on a police command post at the Herman Keifer Hospital. Armed helicopters continued flying low over buildings in efforts to flush out the snipers. Guardsmen in tanks sprayed rooftops and buildings with barrages of machine-gun fire. There were several reports of bullets hitting innocent persons sitting out the violence in their darkened apartments.

The death toll climbed to 36—29 blacks and 7 whites—during the afternoon of July 26. It thus exceeded the 34 deaths recorded in the 1965 rioting in the Watts section of Los Angeles. Property damage, already believed to be the largest from civil disorder in the nation's history, rose to an estimated $200 million. The number of people arrested had reached 2,665; 1,163 fires had been reported; more than 1,000 persons had been injured.

Police said that the pattern of gun fire indicated that snipers might be organized in bands of 5 to 6 persons. But earlier in the day Vance had said the riot "is not highly organized." He estimated that there were about 100 snipers in the city. He said that the rioting had followed a "cyclical" pattern and that the first phase —looting and burning—had ended and had been followed by the sniping phase, which would probably continue for another 24 hours. Vance asserted that the East Side, patrolled by federal troops, was "under control." The West Side, where National Guard patrols were operating, continued to be the source of most of the continued violence. (During the day the local offices of U.S. Rep. John J. Conyers Jr. were sacked.)

The Common Council of Detroit met in emergency session July 26 and passed an ordinance prohibiting the sale of food at prices "greater than retail prices existing prior to the emergency." It was reported that 3 loaves of bread, which usually sold for 90¢, were being sold for $1.30. In some areas milk reportedly was being sold at $1 a quart. During the day 10,000 persons received food distributions at emergency centers.

Gov. Romney and Mayor Cavanagh telegraphed Pres. Johnson July 27 to request that Detroit be declared a disaster area and be given emergency federal aid. Describing the devastation as a "disaster by any reasonable definition of that term," they declared: "It simply does not make sense not to commit federal assistance to the city of Detroit in view of what has happened there in recent days." Johnson did not immediately accede to their demands, but he ordered a regional officer of the Office of Emergency Planning to meet with Romney. He said that he was making available surplus food commodities and was asking hospitals to release emergency drug supplies for use in the city.

Vance declared the morning of July 27: "It's pretty close to over." Romney lifted the curfew, but later in the day reimposed it to curtail an influx of sightseers into riot areas. City cleaning crews with bulldozers and cranes began removing debris and knocking down the walls of gutted buildings. Soldiers were ordered to sheathe their banyonets, although many reportedly disobeyed the order. By July 27, arrests had reached more than 3,400; more than 1,500 persons had been injured; 1,700 stores had been looted. Sporadic reports of sniper fire continued, and 2 more persons were killed during the day, bringing the total slain to 38.

Cavanagh and Romney met with 150 white and black community leaders July 27. Cavanagh called on them to unite in "building the city from the ashes of the present tragedy." Romney told the group that what had happened in Detroit was "national in scope." He declared that the rioting, however, was different from the racial riot in Newark. He promised to review the high bail bonds that had been set to permit pretrial release of some prisoners. (Bond had been set at as high as $200,000 for accused snipers and $25,000 for accused looters.)

Walter P. Reuther, president of the United Auto Workers, told the group: "We can take very little comfort and it does us no credit to be the very first city in America to achieve integrated looting." He said: "What we suffered, any city in America can suffer any day of the week. . . . We have left some Americans behind. They are the 'have nots' of America. Ugly economic facts feed their frustrations and their sense of hopelessness, which makes them strike out. If you expect them to act as part of our society, you are kidding yourselves." He told the group that 600,000 union members had pledged their own time to help clean up the city. He asked industry to volunteer the necessary bulldozers and trucks for the removal of debris.

300 state policemen and 600–800 National Guardsmen were withdrawn from the city July 28, but 13,000 to 14,000 troops,

Guardsmen and police remained on duty. Romney said that police and military officers assured him that "the city is now secure." Cavanagh said July 28 that the city would issue at least $12 million in emergency bonds to pay for overtime for police, firemen and city employes. Romney said the State Legislature would provide funds if legally possible to help pay for cleaning and rebuilding the city. Romney later eased the curfew from 9:00 p.m. to 10:00 p.m.

(It was reported July 28 that an estimated $100,000 in loot had been recovered. Police said they were accepting the return of stolen goods without questioning those who returned them.)

Cyrus Vance returned to Washington July 29 to report to the President. After their meeting, Vance told reporters that law and order had been restored in Detroit. He announced that Pres. Johnson had directed the administrator of the Small Business Administration to declare those sections of the city ravaged by rioting "areas that have been hit by disaster and therefore eligible for appropriate assistance to home owners, and businessmen under the Small Business Act," and to make available 3% loans for up to 30 years for rebuilding homes and small businesses. The President, however, did not act on Romney's request that Detroit be declared a disaster area.

Romney July 31 accused Johnson of having "played politics in a period of tragedy and riot" in his version of events leading to the use of federal troops in Detroit. Romney made the charge at a news conference called, he said, to counter a "purported chronology" from the White House of the actions leading up to the use of federal troops. The chronology was reported by Max Frankel in the July 30 *N.Y. Times.*

According to the Frankel article, the President and his advisers contended that Romney had shown "vacillation for nearly 20 hours about the need for the troops." The President's staff reportedly conceded there was "an underlying tension between the President and the governor," a leading GOP Presidential contender, but the White House officials insisted that the President's primary concern was over the legal basis for the use of troops and the precedent it formed for White House intervention in future riots. The officials also reportedly regretted the President's "having belabored," in his July 24 TV address, Romney's apparent inability to control the situation without federal troops.

The Frankel report said Romney had repeatedly called Atty. Gen. Clark in the early hours of July 24 but had kept "changing his mind about whether to call for the Army and make the legally necessary admission that events were beyond his control." The President's special adviser in Detroit, Cyrus Vance, reportedly informed Washington at 7 p.m. July 24 that use of the troops would be premature at that time. This view, he said, was shared by Romney and most Michigan Congressmen but not by Mayor Cavanagh and other local observers, who urgently wanted the troops used. This split between Romney and Cavanagh reportedly was evident at a news conference at 8:15 p.m., when, according to Vance, Romney publicly noted he was not then "requesting" federal troops. According to Frankel, Romney, even after 10 p.m. July 24, "was said to be expressing doubt again about his ability to control events but would not make the official finding that they were out of control." By 11:22 p.m., however, state and federal officials were agreed on the need for troops and Johnson signed the necessary order.

At his news conference July 31, Romney denied that he had shown vacillation about his decision to ask for the troops. He blamed the delay on Washington's changing position on the type of request that would be necessary. Romney said he had sought the troops through Clark and had understood that Army men would be sent, but "quibbling" developed in later conversations over the wording of the request. "I had the impression generally that he [Clark] was making more of a political request than a legal request" about the wording, Romney said. Romney indicated that while he had not wanted to say the situation was out of control, he was willing to say it could not be controlled without the Army. Romney reportedly also was reluctant to apply the phrase "civil insurrection" to the situation, partly because it might validate escape clauses for insurance. After Vance's arrival in Detroit, Romney said, he and many others had told Vance "as forcefully as we could that we need" the troops. (In a TV address July 30, Romney had said the riot "was caused more by national conditions than Detroit conditions" and "unless we take the proper course the nation in the years ahead could be plunged into civil guerrilla warfare.")

At a news conference July 31, Johnson was asked about Romney's criticism. He said: "I don't think anything is to be gained by trying to justify or explain" his actions on the recommendations for troops and their deployment. (Johnson added that he thought the U.S. was "rich enough" to both carry on the war in Vietnam and deal with its domestic responsibilities.)

Atty. Gen. Clark, at a news conference Aug. 1, said it was "absolutely" untrue that the President had "played politics" in the Detroit situation. He said that "the first communication that we had that indicated his [Romney's] firm decision that he wanted federal troops present [in Detroit] was when we received the telegram at the White House at 10:56 a.m." July 24. Clark said that at 8 a.m. July 24, after 2 nights of rioting, some 3,000 Michigan National Guardsmen were still uncommitted although he had informed Romney that all local and state forces should be used before federal troops were called. Clark also said it was his opinion that an oral request from a governor was sufficient to request federal troops but that the governor had to "request" their use, and the word "insurrection" had to be applicable to the situation. (Section 331, Chapter 15, Title 10 of the U.S. Code covered the use of federal troops at local request. It read: "Whenever there is an insurrection in any state against its government, the President may, upon the request of its legislature or of its governor if the legislature cannot be convened, call into federal service such of the militia of the other states in the number requested by that state, and use such of the armed forces as he considers necessary to suppress the insurrection.")

Speaking specifically about Detroit, but with implications for other areas where local law-enforcement agencies were insufficient to quell rioting, Johnson asserted Aug. 3 that he had "tried to be very careful" in deciding whether to order federal troops to Detroit. 3 "elements" had to be present, Johnson said, before a President could order troops to intervene and put down "civil disorder": (1) a request from a state legislature or a governor, (2) "certification of insurrection or domestic violence" and (3) "demonstration of a clear inability of state and all local authorities to control the situation despite the use of all law enforcement resources which can be brought to bear." The President said that he had been notified at 2:30 a.m. July 24 that "there was a problem . . . which might necessitate troops" in Detroit. He had "momentarily alerted" the troops, Johnson said. He had received the telegram requesting troops at 10:56 a.m. and had ordered the units to move at 11:02 a.m. Certification that a state of insurrection or domestic violence existed was made at about 11 p.m. by Lt. Gen. John L. Throckmorton, in charge of the federal troops on the scene, and by Cyrus Vance, the Presidential representative in Detroit. Johnson said that "when they made that certification, the

President, in the same conversion ordered the deployment" of the troops.

(At a news conference June 13, the President had been asked about racial violence in the cities and had said: "We want to keep these incidents to a minimum but we will have to rely primarily on the good judgment of the people themselves and the local authorities to try to work out solutions to the problems as they arise." "We are trying to do everything we can in cooperation with the cities, the counties, the states and the private employers to minimize the tensions that exist," he said.)

The President spoke of his role in the Detroit events while meeting with newsmen at the White House to introduce Throckmorton and Vance, who had just reported to him that order had been restored in Detroit and law enforcement responsibilities had been returned to local authorities. Johnson said that none of the 4,800 federal troops sent to Detroit had been wounded or injured and that only one person had lost his life at the hands of the troops.

The reported death toll rose to 43 as of Aug. 5, but Detroit police asserted Aug. 7 that the count was only 41, holding that 2 of the deaths had not been connected to the rioting. A 42d death was reported Aug. 9 and a 43d Aug. 14.

2 white Detroit policemen were charged Aug. 7 with the murder July 26 of 2 black youths at the Algiers Motel during the riot. The bodies of 3 black youths had been found at the motel, a mile from the scene of the most serious rioting. Police said the Negroes had died in an exchange of gunfire between policemen and snipers. But residents at the motel said the youths had been deliberately killed by policemen who were raiding the motel for snipers. Patrolman Ronald August, 28, was charged with the murder of Aubrey Pollard, 19, a Negro; Patrolman Robert Paille, 32, was charged with the murder of Fred Temple, 18, a Negro. No one was charged in the death of the 3d black youth, Carl Cooper, 17. The officers pleaded not guilty. In a formal statement made by August July 31 and read to the court Aug. 17, the policeman said he had shot Pollard in self-defense after Pollard grabbed his shotgun. Recorder's Court Judge Robert DeMascio Aug. 17 ordered August to stand trial for the murder of Pollard. The charge of murder against Paille was dismissed.

Paille, Patrolman David Senec, 23, a prosecution witness at the examination hearing, and Melvin Dismukes, 24, a Negro, were charged Aug. 23 with conspiracy to "beat, abuse and intimidate a number of people" in the Algiers Motel. August was named as co-conspirator but not as a defendant since he already faced trial on a murder charge. Dismukes had also been charged with felonious assault in the beating of 2 blacks at the motel.

The *Detroit News* and the *Detroit Free Press* July 31 had published reports from eyewitnesses in the motel. According to the witnesses, about 16 Guardsmen and state and local policemen had invaded the motel and had cursed, beaten and threatened Negroes and 2 white teen-age girls. Both newspapers reported that the victims were each shot at least twice. The *Free Press* said that a pathologist it had hired had said that the shots were "fired at close range, from no more than 15 feet away, probably less."

The *Free Press* charged Sept. 3 that most of the deaths could have been prevented. A 24,000-word, copyrighted article by Gene Goltz, 37, William Serrin, 28, and Barbara Stanton said that after interviewing more than 300 persons and reading hundreds of documents, the reporters had reached the "inescapable" conclusion that "a majority of the riot victims need not have died." The article said: "18 of the 43 riot victims were shot and killed by Detroit police, and of that number, 14 have been confirmed as looters. . . . The other 4 are a sniper, a possible but unconfirmed arsonist and 2 of the 3 men shot and killed in the Algiers Motel. At least 6 of the victims were killed by the National Guard, 5 of them innocent, the victims of what now seem to be tragic accidents. In 5 more cases, both police and National Guardsmen were involved. . . . 4 of these victims were innocent of any wrongdoing. 2 more persons, both looters, were shot and killed by storeowners. 3 more were killed by private citizens; murder warrants have been issued in 2 of those cases. . . . And 2 looters died when fire swept the store from which they were stealing. 2 victims, one a fireman, the other a civilian, were killed by electric power lines. 5 deaths remain. They are a 19-year-old boy killed accidentally by an Army paratrooper; a 23-year-old white woman shot by an unknown gunman; a Detroit fireman killed by either a hidden sniper or a stray National Guard bullet; a policeman shot as a fellow officer struggled with a prisoner, and the 3d victim of the Algiers Motel slayings, whose assailant is not known. . . . Both the number of snipers active in the riot area and the danger that snipers presented were vastly overstated. . . ."

The Records Bureau of the Detroit Police Department reported Aug. 28 that 7,207 persons had been arrested during the rioting. 3,595 of those arrested had criminal records, but the records in-

cluded such minor offenses as traffic law violations. 3,365 of those
arrested were charged with felonies, including 7 charges of murder.
95 were charged with assault with intent to commit murder; police
listed 26 of the latter, including 5 women, as snipers. 255 persons
were arrested on charges involving weapons or explosives. It was
reported that more than 90% of those arrested were from Detroit.
According to police statistics, a composite picture of the "average
rioter" showed him to be a male Negro, aged 20 to 28, arrested on
a charge of looting, with a 50-50 chance of having a criminal record.

Bernard Decoster, Detroit fire marshal, had reported Aug. 4
that 477 buildings had been destroyed or badly damaged in fires
during the rioting. He said that an estimated $50 million in losses
could be attributed to fires. The *Wall St. Journal* had reported
Aug. 3, however, that the Detroit fire department maintained that
fire damage totaled $250 million. It said that the arson did not ap-
pear to be organized, that most of the damaged businesses were operated by whites and that furniture and grocery stores were the most
frequent targets. The General Adjustment Bureau, Inc. said Aug.
11 that insurance losses from the rioting would total about $85
million. The Bureau reported that 538 business establishments
had been destroyed and 549 others seriously damaged. Thousands
of smaller losses were also reported. 12 apartment buildings were
seriously damaged, 12 destroyed. A Dun & Bradstreet survey revealed that about 600 of an estimated 1,200 damaged businesses
had reopened during the first week after order was restored; Dun &
Bradstreet estimated that the average damage suffered per business
in Detroit was $23,063, compared with $12,000 in the Newark
riots.

A hearing on the handling of the riots was held Aug. 22 by the
House Armed Services Committee. Witnesses were Throckmorton,
Army Undersecy. David F. McGiffert and Maj. Gen. Charles P.
Stone, Throckmorton's deputy in Detroit. Throckmorton said he
had given orders to the federal troops to unload their weapons and
fire only if ordered by an officer. "I was confronted with a group
of trigger-happy, nervous soldiers in the National Guard," he said.
"I had no intention of seeing those soldiers shoot innocent civilians
or children." He said that paratroopers used in Detroit had obeyed
the order "without difficulty" but that the Guardsmen had not.
Stone said he had personally checked 500 Guardsmen after the
order, and 90% of them had loaded weapons. Several committee
members took exception to the testimony. Rep. Porter Hardy Jr.

(D., Va.) accused Throckmorton of "casting aspersions" on the Guard and called his order to unload weapons "preposterous." Chairman F. Edward Hébert (D., La.) said that he did not see how a Guardsman could be expected to "take cover if fired upon and await the arrival of an officer."

Gov. Romney had lifted the state of emergency from the Greater Detroit area at noon Aug. 6. He said: "Recent days and nights have indicated a return of normalcy in the metropolitan area." Romney July 31 had eased the curfew and the prohibition of the sale of gasoline and liquor but had maintained a ban on the sale of guns and explosives. The curfew was ended Aug. 1. The federal paratroopers had been withdrawn from patrol duty July 30 but were ordered to remain in the city temporarily. About 2,000 men of the 101st Airborne Division left Detroit Aug. 1, and the last of the 7,000 National Guardsmen were removed from the city Aug. 6.

Romney and Mayor Cavanagh Aug. 3 appointed a 37-member New Detroit Committee to plan the rebuilding of the city. The committee, headed by Joseph L. Hudson Jr., department store operator, was composed of 14 businessmen and industrialists, 3 labor leaders, several civic leaders and 9 Negroes, 3 of them black nationalists. Included on the committee were Henry Ford 2d, chairman of the Ford Motor Co., James Roche, president of the General Motors Corp., Max M. Fisher, Jewish philanthropist, and Walter P. Reuther, president of the United Auto Workers.

Nearly 400 militant Detroit Negroes met Aug. 9 and formed a 60-member New Black Establishment Committee. The Rev. Albert Cleage Jr., militant leader of the group, said that Detroit officials had failed to "get the message" from the riots. He said: "The Hudson committee will take orders from us." Clyde Cleveland, local CORE chairman, said: "There should have been a black man to head the Hudson committee. . . . If the community is to be rebuilt, this community will decide what's to be built." Hudson said Aug. 10 that his committee "recognized, welcomed and encouraged" the New Black Establishment Commitee. "We want to work with them as quickly as possible," he said. "We're not playing games. We're deadly serious about working with this group."

(Romney, a prospective GOP Presidential contender, toured 17 areas in 12 states Sept. 11–30 to get first-hand information on urban problems. At the end of his tour Romney Sept. 30 issued a statement in which he said: "Time is running out for those who have responsibilities for the tranquility of our nation." "As I have rubbed elbows with those who live in the ghetto, as I have listened to the voice of revolt, I am more convinced than ever before that unless we reverse our course, build a new America, the old America will be destroyed." "The seeds of revolution have been sown. They cannot be rooted out by force. While we must maintain law and order, we must either achieve orderly progress or change will be inflicted with mortal wounds. Either we shall join hands, hearts and minds and march together on paths of fulfillment for all, or we shall find ourselves torn asunder.")

Disorders in Spanish Harlem

Rioting and anti-police disorders took place July 23–25 in the East Harlem ghetto of New York City known to its Puerto Rican residents as *El Barrio*—The Neighborhood. The 3 days of rioting spread through 125 blocks of the community—famed as the first stop for Puerto Ricans arriving in the U.S. 2 persons were killed, stores were looted, cars were over-turned and set afire, 36 persons were injured and 13 persons were arrested.

The violence began at 12:30 a.m. July 23 when an off-duty patrolman shot and killed Renaldo Rodriquez, 25. Rodriquez, wielding a knife, had allegedly lunged at another off-duty policeman when the officer attempted to arrest him after finding him standing in the street over another Puerto Rican, knife in hand.

News of the killing of Rodriquez spread quickly, and crowds began to converge on the area. Bottles and bricks soon were being rained on passing squad cars. Although a few stores were looted and trash cans set afire, most of the crowd's hostility was directed at the police. At about 4 a.m., the city's white-helmeted Tactical Patrol Force—a special elite police unit often used for riot suppression—was given orders to clear the area. According to Puerto Ricans in the crowd and some newsmen who witnessed the melee, the police waded into the crowd swinging their nightsticks. Their first charge was turned back by a barrage of bricks and bottles, but their 2d charge succeeded in clearing the streets.

Mayor John V. Lindsay arrived in the neighborhood from his summer home shortly after 4 a.m. He wandered through a crowd of about 75 Puerto Ricans, listening to their complaints.

A meeting between Lindsay and 10 ghetto residents took place later that morning at the mayor's residence. Lindsay said at a news conference later that he would investigate charges of police brutality and would discuss the possibility of keeping the Tactical Patrol Force out of the Spanish Harlem area. (A delegate confirmed to newsmen later that a basic grievance was over the use of the special force. "However bad the precinct police might be," he said, "they know us.") Puerto Rican community leaders met with Police Commissioner Howard R. Leary and other city officials later July 23. After the meeting, a Lindsay assistant said the Puerto Ricans had been promised that there was "no intention of bringing in the Tactical Patrol Force at this time."

But the special force entered the district again late July 23 to break up a crowd throwing bottles at police cars. Minor cases of arson and looting were reported during the night.

The worst night of rioting began shortly after dark July 24, when roving bands of youths stoned police cars and looted stores. Police in the district opened fire on roof tops after reporting that they were under sniper fire. Flaming brands from a bonfire lit in the middle of 3d Avenue, a main thoroughfare, were used in a futile attempt to set a gas station afire. Crowds swarmed through the streets, overturning trash cans, smashing windows and setting small fires.

2 ghetto residents were killed during the July 24 rioting, both by .38-caliber bullets of the type used by the police. Police reported at first that one of the victims, a Puerto Rican boy of 16, had fallen from a rooftop and died of a broken neck and that the other, a 44-year-old woman found dead in her home, had been killed by a .22-caliber bullet. The reports were corrected after city autopsies were performed.

More than 100 *Barrio* residents and anti-poverty workers roamed the district's streets urging Puerto Ricans to return to their homes but largely to no avail. Rioting spread July 24 from Spanish Harlem to the heavily Puerto Rican slum in the nearby New York City area of south Bronx. The Bronx disturbances were confined largely to looting and the setting of small fires, although some sniper shots were reported. By the night of July 26, rioting in both areas had subsided.

After the disturbances, city and community officials began to seek ways to avert further rioting. The police July 26 were placed on a 6-day week to provide more men for riot duty during the evening hours. The director of the city's Neighborhood Youth Corps program announced July 26 that he was deploying the corps' 1,867 teenaged workers to East Harlem to spread a message to "cool it."

The Police Department July 28 ordered precincts in Spanish-speaking neighborhoods to assign one Spanish-speaking patrolman to each squad car.

The leadership of the Puerto Rican Community Conference July 27 blamed Lindsay and his administration for failing to act on a series of recommendations made by the city-sponsored conference in April. The group blamed poor police tactics and use of the Tactical Patrol Force for the outbreak and continuation of the violence. However, Bronx Borough Pres. Herman Badillo, a Puerto Rican, rebuked the conference July 30 for their statement. The Puerto Rican Bar Association July 30 praised the police for using minimal force in quelling the riots.

(About 200 black teenagers looted stores along New York's exclusive 5th Avenue shopping district July 26. The teenagers, who had attended a rock-'n'-roll concert in Central Park, swept through the theater district, jostling passersby. On reaching 5th Avenue, they smashed the windows of 2 men's clothing stores and a shoe store and took an estimated $26,000 worth of merchandise. Among the loot: $56 Alpaca sweaters regarded as a ghetto status symbol. The raiders fled as police arrived, but 22 youths were arrested. 4 later were revealed to be employes of city-sponsored anti-poverty youth projects.)

(Minor rioting and looting broke out July 29 in another New York City ghetto area, the Bedford-Stuyvesant section of Brooklyn. But order was quickly restored. The Police Department moved a large contingent of black patrolmen into the area July 30 and issued a set of instructions to police officers to use courtesy and restraint.)

H. Rap Brown's Oratory Precedes Violence

Violence in at least 3 communities—Dayton, O., Cambridge, Md. and East St. Louis, Ill.—took place shortly after H. (originally Herbert Geroid) Rap Brown, 23, the new chairman of the Student Nonviolent Coordinating Committee (SNCC), delivered inflamatory addresses in which he called on ghetto blacks to abandon peaceful protest and to adopt more forceful, militant methods. And a flareup in Chicago followed an SNCC rally that Brown did not attend.

The Dayton violence erupted in the predominantly black West Side June 12. Black youths set fires, smashed windows and looted

stores, and the police sealed off the area.   The violence began when
Negroes attacked a white man after a speech by Brown.   The rioting continued sporadically June 15 but ebbed after Dayton officials
organized a black "youth patrol" to keep peace.   The youths, wearing white helmets, began patrolling the ghetto by 8:00 p.m.

Although some officials attributed the Dayton outbreak to
Brown's inflammatory speech, others said the youths were "keyed
up" and that any other incident would have served to ignite the
rioting.   Black leaders met with city officials June 16 to work out
recreation and employment programs.

Fire swept through the black business section of Cambridge in
the early hours of July 25.   The fire, apparently set by arsonists
in the 50-year-old, all-black Pine Street Elementary School, raged
out of control after the city's white volunteer firemen refused to
take action against the blaze.   The fire and accompanying violence
followed a speech in which Brown had exhorted a crowd of 400
young Negroes in Cambridge the previous evening to "burn this
town down."   (Brown's alleged incitement of the Cambridge disturbances led to his arrest in Washington, D.C. 2 days later.)

Brown reportedly told the black Cambridge audience: "You
better get yourselves some guns.   The only thing honkies [whites]
respect is guns."   He singled out the Pine Street school as a "fire-
trap" and told the crowd that "you should've burned it down
long ago."

After ending his speech a few minutes before 10 p.m. July 24,
Brown gathered a group of about 40 men and began a march toward the white business center of Cambridge.   The marchers were
met by helmeted police who ordered them to halt.   When they
kept marching, the police fired shotguns loaded with pellets into
the crowd.   Brown received a minor wound, which was later
treated at a local hospital.   One other Negro received a super-
ficial wound.   The other marchers dispersed.

Violence then erupted along Pine Street at about 11:15 when
Negroes attacked a car driven by white youths.   The car returned
a few minutes later, and its occupants sprayed the street with
buckshot.   Black residents sought protection in doorways and
under porches.   About an hour later a city patrolman was wounded
by a shotgun blast as he sat in his parked car in the black section.

The fire began in the Pine Street school at about 2:15 a.m.
July 25.   It spread quickly to the unpainted wooden buildings
situated near it.   Cambridge Police Chief Brice G. Kinnamon kept

the volunteer fire department's equipment on fire-preventive duty in the white business district for 2 hours while a Negro church, stores and other black-owned buildings were consumed by the flames a block away. Kinnamon was quoted as telling a group of 30 Negroes who offered to operate a fire truck: "You shot one of my policemen. Don't give me that stuff." When the fire equipment finally moved into the black section 2 hours after the first alarm, many Negroes helped fight the blaze. Nearly 20 buildings were destroyed. Damage was estimated at $200,000.

Later July 25, Gov. Spiro T. Agnew toured the district and told newsmen that Brown was to blame for the disturbances. As Agnew spoke to local officials, 700 National Guardsmen took up stations in the town at his orders. This was the 2d time in recent years that the National Guard had been sent to the city of 13,000 (4,000 Negroes) to curb racial violence. (Cambridge, located in Maryland's Eastern Shore section, had been the scene of more racial violence than any other city in the state.) Police Chief Kinnamon said July 27 that he was "firmly convinced this eruption was a well-planned Communist attempt to overthrow the city of Cambridge." Agnew declared July 28, however, that Cambridge was a "sick city" in which "segregation is completely obvious."

Cambridge police officials announced July 27 that 2 men had been arrested for the shooting of a policeman during the July 24–25 violence. Each was held on $50,000 bond. A 3d suspect was arrested July 29, charged with inciting to riot, and was held on $25,000 bond. The 3d man arrested, Lemanuel Chester Jr., 21, was the leader of the militant Cambridge Black Action Federation. Newsmen reported that Chester had not made any statement at the rally July 24.

Brown was indicted by a Dorchester County grand jury in Cambridge Aug. 14 on charges stemming from the violence. Brown, indicted *in absentia,* was charged with arson, inciting a riot and acting in concert with others in disturbing the public peace. 5 others indicted were: Lemanuel Chester, on charges of inciting a riot and disturbing the public peace; Gladys Fletcher, about 30, and James duPont Fletcher, about 40, on charges of arson; James Lee Lewis, 30, and Leon Lewis, 25, on charges of assault with intent to murder a Cambridge policeman and simple assault. The 5 had been released from jail on bond.

Within hours after his Cambridge speech Brown had become a fugitive hunted by state police and the FBI as fleeing from Maryland charges of "inciting to riot" and "counseling to burn." The charges had been made and warrants obtained by William B. Yates, the county attorney of Dorchester County, Md. A federal fugitive warrant was obtained July 25, empowering the FBI to seize Brown for fleeing across a state border to avoid arrest.

Acting on a tip by an airport policeman, the FBI arrested Brown at the Washington National Airport July 26 as he was about to board a plane to New York. Brown told newsmen at the federal courthouse in Alexandria, Va. that he had been on his way to New York to surrender to the FBI under a deal worked out with the FBI by his lawyer, William Kunstler. The FBI denied that it had made any deal for Brown's surrender. After Kunstler arrived at the courthouse, the Justice Department, following a procedure often used to allow precedence to usual extradition processes, dropped the federal fugitive warrant. Meanwhile, Alexandria police had obtained a warrant and prepared to arrest Brown. After being ejected from the comparative sanctuary of the federal courthouse, Brown stood on the steps of the building, surrounded by fist-shaking black nationalists, and shouted to newsmen that "J. Edgar Hoover has held me all day on federal property so these peckerwood, honky cops here in Virginia can arrest me."

After Brown had declared he would not move off the steps, 4 Alexandria policemen dragged him into a waiting squad car. He was released on $10,000 bail at 1 a.m. July 27 after a hearing on his extradition to Maryland was set for Aug. 22. Speaking later July 27 in the heart of Washington's black ghetto, Brown repeated the advice he had offered in Cambridge: "You better get you a gun. The honky got respect for but one thing, a gun." He assailed Pres. Johnson as a "wild mad dog, an outlaw from Texas" who had sent "honky, cracker federal troops into Negro communities to kill black people." Brown told a SNCC-sponsored rally that evening: "There should be more shooting and looting." "If Washington, D.C. don't come around, Washington, D.C. should be burned down," he added. Brown predicted that "the rebellions will continue and escalate." "I say violence is necessary," he asserted. "It is as American as cherry pie."

Brown was re-arrested in New York at 2:30 a.m. Aug. 19 on a federal charge of carrying a gun across state lines while under indictment. He was taken into custody by agents of the Alcohol & Tobacco Tax Division of the Internal Revenue Service, which enforces the National Firearms Act. The complaint, filed in U.S.

District Court in New Orleans by Alcohol & Tobacco Tax agents
Wally Moll and Albert L. Klotz, alleged that Brown had carried
a .30-caliber "Enforcer" semi-automatic carbine on an Aug. 16
flight from New York to New Orleans and on a return flight to New
York Aug. 18.   Section 902 (e) of the Firearms Act made it "unlawful for anyone under indictment to transport a firearm in interstate commerce."   When a boarding agent at New Orleans International Airport asked Brown Aug. 18 whether he was carrying a
gun, Brown said he was and gave the weapon to the agent for transportation on the flight to New York.

Brown was arraigned before U.S. Commissioner Earle N.
Bishopp Aug. 19, bail was set at $25,000, and Brown was placed
in solitary confinement.   William Kunstler, Brown's attorney, denounced the bail as "excessive and outrageous" and a "political
maneuver" to keep Brown in jail.   At a *habeas corpus* hearing the
afternoon of Aug. 19, Federal Judge Inzer B. Wyatt rejected a
motion that the bail violated Brown's constitutional rights.

Kunstler Aug. 20 released a statement in which Brown charged
that he was "being held as a political prisoner."   "My confinement,
however, will not rebuild Detroit nor will it save America from its
due fate," he asserted.   "For, as America has bestowed on me in
my 23 years her extreme disfavor, she has also, through her inhu-
manity, racism, oppression, and exploitation of both black and
white, both domestic and foreign, made herself an enemy of mankind."   Late Aug. 21 U.S. District Court Judge Thomas F. Murphy
signed an order directing federal authorities to show cause why
Brown's bail should not be reduced.   Brown's attorneys had appealed to Murphy after U.S. Commissioner Bishopp had twice
refused to lower the bail.   Judge Murphy Aug. 22 ordered the
bail reduced to $15,000 in cash and certified checks, and Brown
was released at 5:20 p.m.   (New York bail bondsmen had refused
to furnish bail for Brown.)

After his release Brown addressed a crowd of about 100
Negroes from the top of the courthouse steps in Foley Square.   "It
was black power that got that bail reduced," he declared.   "We're
at war!   We are caught behind enemy lines, and you better get
yourself some guns."   Pointing to whites in the crowd, he said:
"That's your enemy out there.   And you better not forget, because
I ain't going to."

Virginia Gov. Mills E. Goodwin Jr. Sept. 7 signed an order
for Brown's extradition to Maryland.   Brown was released on

$15,000 bond in New Orleans Sept. 8 after pleading not guilty to charges of violating federal firearms laws, but he was then arrested in Alexandria, Va. Sept. 13. He spent 5 days in jail and was freed in Richmond, Va. Sept. 18 in custody of his lawyer, Kunstler, on $10,000 personal recognizance. U.S. District Judge Robert R. Merhige Jr., who ordered Brown's release, specified that except for court appearances, Brown could not leave the "district in which the custodian resides" (11 counties in the Southern District of New York). (Merhige Sept. 29 denied a petition to ease the bond restrictions on travel. Brown appealed to the U.S. 4th Circuit Court of Appeals in Richmond to release him from the restrictive bond terms. His attorney contended that the restriction was an infringement of Brown's right to free speech because it prevented him from keeping speaking engagements in the U.S. and England. The Appeals Court Nov. 28 refused to modify the bond's travel restrictions.)

In the 3d incident that followed oratory by Brown, violence broke out in East St. Louis Sept. 10 shortly after Brown told a cheering crowd of more than 1,000 Negroes there that "America has no use for Negroes" and urged them to "stop singing and start swinging." Reports of looting and arson continued Sept. 11–13. At least 5 persons were injured and more than 55 arrested.

40 county deputy sheriffs and 30 state troopers were brought to East St. Louis Sept. 10 to aid 60 city policemen in quelling looting and firebombing. Police barricaded a 3-block area of the city. The night police chief said that the vandalism was centered "in the commercial section of the colored district," where several stores and 2 cars were firebombed.

Roosevelt Young, 18, a black high-school dropout, was shot and killed by a policeman in East St. Louis late Sept. 10. Police said that the shooting occurred when the youth, being questioned about a stolen car, tried to grab a gun from a policeman and then fled. They denied that the incident was related to the disorders. But 30 young blacks shouting "black power" marched on police headquarters and the newsroom of the *Metro East Journal* Sept. 11 to protest the shooting. About 40 Negroes marched to City Hall to talk with Mayor Alvin G. Fields Sept. 12 and demanded the release of prisoners arrested during the disorders. Police dispersed the group after an hour but the blacks then marched to police headquarters and staged a sit-down demonstration in the lobby.

During the East St. Louis disorders, firemen in the area answered 58 calls Sept. 11–13, several stores were looted and a drug store was set afire. White motorists were pelted with bottles and bricks, and some of them were dragged from their cars and beaten. But Police Commissioner Russell Beebe asserted that only "1/10 of 1% of the Negro community" was responsible for the disturbances. 2 black youths were hospitalized Sept. 13 for burns and flesh wounds, and at least 6 Negroes were arrested on charges of disorderly conduct and suspected arson.

In the Chicago incident, violence flared for more than 5 hours on the city's South Side Sept. 14 following a Negro rally sponsored by the Student Nonviolent Coordinating Committee in protest against alleged police brutality. Speakers at the rally charged that police had kicked Corinne Roby, 18, a Negro, in the stomach when they arrested her Sept. 12. The police said that Miss Roby had tossed a bottle at them.

The Chicago violence began after black students at the nearby Forrestville High School were let out for the day. They joined the SNCC rally, and youths began smashing windows and throwing rocks and bottles. Police headquarters sent in tactical forces, and a 240-block area was cordoned off. The police, using bullhorns, urged people to go home and stay off the streets. All businesses were closed. Sniper fire began shortly after dark, and the police returned the fire with carbines and submachine guns. 11 persons were injured, 5 of them policemen. About 50 persons were arrested on charges of aggravated battery, mob action or disorderly conduct.

State Sen. Charles Chew (D.), a Chicago Negro, visited the scene of the disturbance and said: "Black agitators from Chicago and outside of Chicago are stirring them up."

Brown had said Aug. 6, at a rally of about 1,500 Negroes at the St. Albans ballroom in Queens (N.Y. City), that the 1967 summer's racial riots were only "dress rehearsals for revolution." He urged Negroes to arm themselves against a "honky [white] conspiracy of genocide." Brown said that both the late Pres. John Kennedy and Pres. Johnson, whom he called "lynching Johnson" and the "greatest outlaw in history," had "tricked black people." He declared that the U.S. was "escalating its war against black people," but he warned: "If you play Nazis with us, we ain't gonna play Jews." (At the start of the rally, several men had shouted "Out, Out, Out! Get the honky reporters out." The white press was given 5 minutes to gather their notes and leave.) Brown told his St. Albans audience to go to the Queens County Criminal Court Aug. 9 for a hearing scheduled for 17 Negroes indicted June 21 on charges of conspiring to murder moderate civil rights leaders. "It's important you go to the courtroom," Brown declared. "It's important you go with a show of force. That's black power. If they [the defendants] go on trial and they are the only black people in the courtroom, you know what kind of justice they are going to get."

Brown told a cheering crowd of about 3,000 Negroes in riot-stricken Detroit Aug. 27: "You did a good job here." But he said the riots in Detroit would "look like a picnic" when Negroes united to "take their due." "The honky is your enemy," he shouted. "Within 20 years we will be just like the buffalo. We're going to have to defend ourselves. The white man is not going to defend us." After the speech Negroes hurled rocks and bottles at 2 white TV newsmen, but both escaped unharmed.

Violence in Many Communities

The hot summer months of July and August 1967 brought racial violence to more than 3 dozen other urban U.S. communities. Violence had begun earlier in some communities, while in others, disorders were reported into the fall and later. Among developments:

Atlanta—One Negro was killed and 3 others were seriously wounded as unrest swept through black residential areas of Atlanta June 19–20. Stokely Carmichael, ex-chairman of the Student Non-violent Coordinating Committee (SNCC), had been arrested June 18 when he joined a crowd of 200–500 gathered in the black Dixie Hills section of west Atlanta. He was charged with failure to move when requested by an officer. 4 others were arrested and jailed with him. All 5 were released on $50 bond the next morning.

Early June 19 Douglas Richmond, 21, a Negro, was wounded by a black policeman. According to the police version of the incident, black policemen had been sent to investigate a burglar alarm at a grocery store in the Dixie Hills section. One of the policemen, Robert McKibben, said that Richmond started kicking the police alarm box and persisted despite the officer's order to stop. McKibben arrested Richmond for "malicious mischief"; but when he tried to take the youth into custody, the youth's friends interfered. Richmond reportedly struck McKibben with a broomstick, while the others hit him on the back and arms with rocks. McKibben then fired his gun at Richmond and wounded him in the thigh. Richmond was charged with drunkenness, disorderly conduct, cursing, resisting arrest and assault on an officer. According to SNCC, the policemen had sought Richmond's aid in stopping the alarm.

Violence erupted in the evening of June 19 after Carmichael told a crowd of about 350 blacks at a church near the Dixie Hills shopping center that "the only way these honkies [whites] and the honky lovers can understand is when they're met by resistance." "They've got everybody marked, ready to shoot," he declared. But "they've got us surrounded tonight, so we'll just walk around and play it cool." 100 policemen were sent to the area after the crowd began throwing rocks. They restored order in an hour. 4 policemen and 2 civilians were reported injured.

Georgia State Sen. Leroy Johnson, a Negro, organized a youth patrol in the area early June 20. But blacks assembled in the shopping center in the evening June 20 and began throwing rocks at policemen. The police ordered the crowd of several hundred persons off the streets and fired shots in the air to speed their dispersal. As the Negroes retreated, there was a series of explosions; Timothy Ross, 46, a Negro, who was standing in the doorway of a nearby apartment building, was killed. Catherine Duncan, 51, Marion Ward, 34, and Reginald Rivers, 9, all Negroes, were injured.

According to Police Superintendent J. F. Brown, neither of the 2 policemen standing a short distance from the doorway had fired in the direction of the Negroes. 2 black witnesses charged, however, that the police had opened fire after a gas bomb exploded near them.

Mayor Ivan Allen Jr. immediately went to the Dixie Hills area. He proclaimed a state of emergency and ordered a 9:00 p.m.-to-6:00 a.m. curfew in the section. State Sen. Johnson rushed to the area and urged everyone to stay off the streets. Later the curfew, denounced by Carmichael and others because of the hot weather, was lifted.

About 1,000 Negroes June 21–22 signed a petition indorsing "nonviolent, peaceful demonstrations as a method of obtaining our rights" and calling on "those persons who have caused or aided in causing turmoil in our community to leave and let the residents of this area restore peace in our community. . . ." The petition enumerated black grievances, including inadequate playground facilities and serious sewage problems, which, the petition said, must be "corrected without delay."

Carmichael and 2 associates, Donald Stone and Ernest Stephens, were convicted June 22 and sentenced to serve 50 days in jail or pay $53 fines.

9 black youths were arrested in Atlanta July 3 after a small crowd gathered and threw bottles at store windows and police. 2 policemen were injured slightly. Among the arrested was Willie Ricks, an SNCC organizer.

Birmingham, Ala. —More than 200 black youths smashed windows and looted stores in Birmingham July 22 after a white policeman had wounded a black burglary suspect. 400 National Guardsmen were called in to quell the rioting. 11 persons were reported injured and more than 70 were arrested. The National Guard was relieved of duty early July 23, but 100 state troopers remained on standby alert.

Boston—Violence erupted in Boston's predominantly black Roxbury district June 2–5. The outbreak was Boston's first large-scale racial rioting in recent years. 60 to 75 persons were injured and 75 to 100 were arrested.

The rioting began following a demonstration at a city Welfare Department building in the Grove Hall section of Roxbury. About 30 women, members of a group called Mothers for Adequate Welfare (MAW), staged a sit-in in protest against what they alleged was the department's termination of welfare payments without notice or investigation, the hostility of social workers and the rudeness of police on duty at the welfare center. At 5:00 p.m. the women padlocked the building's doors and locked themselves, 20 social workers and about 10 policemen in the center. As police reinforcements arrived with ladders and attempted to enter the building through a window, a crowd of black youths gathered and began throwing stones and bottles. Police inside the building formed a flying wedge and charged out of the center. They were bombarded by a volley of bottles, stones and rocks by the crowd outside. (The demonstrators in the building charged they had been assaulted by the police locked in with them.)

Black leaders arrived at the scene and tried to restore order, but the violence was quelled only temporarily. By 11:00 p.m. mobs raged through the district, setting fires, looting stores and throwing rocks and bottles from rooftops and side streets at policemen and firemen. Snipers fired shots from the rooftops.

1,700 policemen, some armed with bayonets and submachine guns, were mobilized to put down the estimated 1,000 rioters. A command post was established at the nearby Franklin Park football stadium.

At least 25 stores were reported looted; 2 multiple alarm fires were attributed to the rioting. Scores of people were injured, including about 30 policemen, firemen and newspaper reporters. A 15-year-old white girl, riding through the area in a car, was struck in the head and suffered a skull fracture. More than 40 persons were arrested, including 3 prominent black leaders. They were arraigned in special court sessions June 3 on charges ranging from assault and battery to trespassing.

Shortly after midnight June 3 when a degree of order was restored, black community and civil rights leaders met with Police Commissioner Edmund L. McNamara. The meeting was not reported to have produced tangible results. Mayor John F. Collins called an emergency meeting with black leaders June 3, but only the district's 3 state legislators showed up. The mayor issued a statement denouncing the rioting as "the worst manifestation of disrespect for the rights of others this city has ever seen." A black leader, the Rev. Virgil Wood, said, however, that "war was declared on the black people by the police force last night and in all likelihood this will happen again until the whole attitude of the administration changes." The Rev. James P. Breeden, a Negro and member of the Commission on Race & Religion of the Massachusetts Council of Churches, declared: "The people of Roxbury did not riot, the police did. The policemen inside the building roughed up the mothers, and those who arrived on the scene . . . panicked and began laying into bystanders."

Police cars patrolled the riot-torn section during the day. But rioting and looting resumed in the evening. The rioters littered the area with debris as they tossed bottles and stones, set fires and smashed windows. A fireman was shot in the wrist by a sniper when his crew responded to one of several false alarms. About 1,900 policemen were sent to the district to stem the rioting. They sealed off a 15-block area and by midnight order was restored. 68 persons were arrested.

Roving bands of black youths continued to set fires, smash windows and loot stores June 4.

Representatives of Mothers for Adequate Welfare presented the group's 10 demands to Mayor Collins June 5. These included: the removal of Welfare Administrator Daniel I. Cronin; the appointment of mothers on welfare to Welfare Department policymaking boards; the treatment of welfare clients "as equal human beings"; the elimination of aid cut-offs "based on hearsay evidence or malicious gossip." The group threatened "other action" if the mayor did not act within 48 hours.   The mayor scheduled a meeting for June 6, but he insisted: "Mr. Cronin will be welfare director as long as I am mayor." (The mother's group failed to appear for the meeting, but arrangements were made for closed negotiations with city officials.)

In accordance with an agreement among civil rights leaders, the mayor and the police commissioner, all uniformed police were removed from the welfare center in Roxbury by early June 5.   About ⅓ of the 100 employees did not report for work.

The Roxbury Tuesday Luncheon Group, an inter-organizational committee composed of members of civil rights, self-help and human relations organizations, organized a mass meeting June 6 for Roxbury teenagers (believed by many to have kept the rioting alive) at the district's St. Hugh's Church.   Roxbury youths were urged to come and "speak your piece" on the causes of the riots. The white press was barred.   200 teenagers attended the meeting, which lasted beyond 10:30 p.m.   There was no rioting that night. A 2d meeting was held June 7 and again there was no rioting.   The youths reportedly organized "safety patrols" and special committees to plan recreational facilities and jobs.

Buffalo, N.Y.—Negroes rioted in the predominantly Negro East Side section of Buffalo June 27–30, and 85–100 persons were reported injured.   205 alleged rioters were arrested.   Property damage was estimated at $100,000.

The disturbance began June 27 after a black youth reportedly threw a stone at a passing bus and hit a passenger.   Bands of young Negroes numbering 300–350 gathered, threw rocks and set fires in a 10-block area.   75 policemen were rushed to the scene, and 22 persons were arrested before quiet was restored at about 1 a.m. June 28.

Mayor Frank Albert Sedita, 60, met early June 28 with 40–50 city officials and black leaders, including representatives of the NAACP, CORE, SNCC and BUILD (Build Unity, Integrity, Liberty & Dignity), a federation of 143 Buffalo civil rights, community and church groups organized by social-action leader Saul D. Alinsky.   The mayor reportedly agreed to meet with the city's business leaders in an effort to find jobs for the city's 3,500 unemployed youths and avert further violence.

Rioting started again June 28 shortly after 7:00 p.m. despite patrolling by more than 400 policemen.   A white couple driving through the area were dragged from their car and beaten before the police could rescue them. Several other cars were overturned and other white persons in the area were beaten. Gangs of youths totaling more than 1,000 battled with policemen, who were armed with shotguns and tear-gas guns. The youths were temporarily disabled by tear gas, but they reassembled in a short time, and battling continued through the night. 4 or 5 Negroes were wounded, one seriously, by gunshots, at least some of them reported to be from snipers. Late in the evening 2 policemen were also reported shot. By 11:00 p.m. 40 persons, 11 of them juveniles, had been arrested. 35–40 persons were injured.

Sporadic incidents of rock throwing, looting, fire-bombing and gunfire were reported June 29 while store fronts remained barricaded and helmeted police patrolled the city, their car windows taped to prevent shattering. More than 100 persons were taken into custody by the police.

At a news conference at City Hall early June 29, Mayor Sedita charged that "out-of-towners are the cause of the trouble." He said that he had been told that a man had offered "impressionable" black youths a dollar for every window they broke. Later in the day, at a meeting called by the Youth Council of the NAACP, Sedita told about 200 black youths that he planned to meet with 150 of the city's business and industry leaders to work out a summer job program. His pleas to "give me a week's time . . . a chance to get the message across" were met with angry shouts of "You gotta do more for us," "We want jobs for everybody" and "If we don't get what we want we're gonna turn Buffalo into a living hell."

Rioting was renewed later that evening despite the mayor's plea. About 40 persons were reported wounded, many by shotgun pellets. Small crowds were dispersed by tear-gas bombs. Looting was reported, and 46 persons were arrested.

Temporary calm June 30 was broken shortly after 10:00 p.m. Looting, rock-throwing and sniper fire were reported. A police car was stoned. 100 additional policemen were brought into the area. 20–25 persons were reported arrested.

Gov. Nelson A. Rockefeller June 30 ordered his special assistant for urban affairs, ex-baseball star Jackie Robinson, to meet with Buffalo officials.

At an afternoon meeting of business and civic leaders June 30, black leaders presented Sedita with a list of Negro demands. These included: (1) "a minimum of 3,000 jobs to be provided youngsters from the Negro area"; (2) "immediate reduction of the number of police in the Negro community and the removal of such antagonistic and provocative shows of force as shotguns in hand and out of car windows and police dogs"; (3) the "immediate halting of the indiscriminate use of tear gas"; (4) reduction of bail for those arrested. The group also called for the reduction of overcrowding in schools, the upgrading of black teachers in the school system and an increase of low-cost housing in the black community. At the meeting, the Bethlehem Steel Corp. offered 100 summer jobs in its Lackawanna plant for youths 16–20 years old. The mayor announced that the finance committee of the Erie County Board of Supervisors had agreed to appropriate $294,000 to hire 600 youths for work in county parks. He said the Post Office and the Board of Education had promised 350 jobs. Robinson, accompanied by Milton L. Luger, director of the N.Y. State Youth Division, pledged state aid from Rockefeller. According to Ambrose Lane, head of the Community Action program, Buffalo's anti-poverty group, the jobs were "coming at a late date and were too few." "We have an official unemployment rate of 10.4% among Negroes," he said, but "it's really about 20%."

(60 black youths in Buffalo July 2 formed a "federation of young black adults to articulate our generation's anguishes and hopes." The group's spokesman, Melvin Erni, 29, director of the African Culture Center, said "the mayor and everyone else, gets a lot of bad advice and does not know what's really going on," because "the power structure always calls in a lot of preachers who are out of it" to find out what's going on in the black community.

(The Buffalo Urban League reported July 2 that 750 Negro youths had signed up for jobs during recruiting July 1–2.)

Cairo, Ill.—Gov. Otto Kerner ordered National Guard units to Cairo July 19 after 3 days of rioting in the city. The racial violence had begun July 17 after reports of the death of a 19-year-old black soldier in the city jail. Police claimed that the soldier had hanged himself with his shirt, but most Negroes in the city of 9,000 apparently believed that he was a victim of police brutality. That night arsonists burned down a warehouse and damaged 3 stores and an automobile.

Snipers opened fire the night of July 18 on a police car cruising outside the Pyramid Court public housing project, the home of about 1,000 of Cairo's 3,000 Negroes. During the same night, firebombs started blazes at a lumber yard and a cotton warehouse. About 100 Guardsmen took up stations in Cairo July 19 and an 8 p.m. curfew was declared.

Spokesmen for young Cairo Negroes warned Mayor Lee Stenzel and city officials July 20 that unless their demands for new job opportunities, more recreation facilities and an end to police brutality were met, there was likely to be a renewal of the firebombing. (Cairo, situated at the juncture of the Ohio and Mississippi Rivers, suffered from severe unemployment.) Following 2 days of meetings, city officials agreed July 23 to hire one black fireman and one more black policeman. They also agreed to help open up jobs in industry to Cairo Negroes.

Chicago—Scattered vandalism, firebombings and looting broke out on Chicago's South and West Sides July 26–Aug. 1. 2 persons died of bullet wounds in the violence, and at least 120 persons were reported arrested.

In the Hyde Park area of the South Side, Molotov cocktails set off fires in at least 6 stores July 26. Youths smashed windows in the Lake Meadows Shopping Center on the near South Side. A Chicago Transit Authority bus was pelted with bottles and rocks, and 5 persons were injured. Near the Comiskey Park stadium black crowds gathered and chanted "Black Power!" At least 10 fires were reported on the West Side. Firebombs were hurled onto the Eisenhower Expressway, and a mailbox was thrown into the path of a car. 250 policemen were called in, and they cordoned off portions of the West Side. At least 22 persons were reported arrested July 26, and 35 more were taken into custody July 27.

At a news conference July 27 Chicago Mayor Richard J. Daley said that he had been in contact with the National Guard, that it was "prepared to act immediately" and that it could have "thousands of men in the streets within the hour."

Herman Hancox, 31, a Negro, was shot to death July 28 by a black policeman who said Hancox had attacked him with a knife. Police exchanged gunfire with black youths July 29 after the youths had fired on a patrolman. No injuries were reported, and the police said they had brought the situation under control with a "minimum of force." During the night police officers sitting in their patrol cars on the South Side were fired on by snipers. No one was injured.

A store on the West Side was burned to the ground July 29 after 5 Molotov cocktails were thrown through the rear window. 9 black teenagers were arrested.

The *Chicago Daily News* Aug. 5 corrected rumors about the Aug. 1 shooting of Julius Woods, 40, a Negro, by Nicholas James Nicholaou, 34, a liquor store owner. According to the *News,* 2 black youths aged 12 and 14 broke the liquor store window July 31 while scuffling on the sidewalk. False rumors began to spread through the neighborhood that Nicholaou had had the youths arrested. The *News* reported that the next morning Woods, a transient with a minor police record, drank some beer and then went to the liquor store. Woods, who was not related to either of the boys, demanded to know why Nicholaou had the youths arrested and, according to one witness, told Nicholaou: "I'm going to kill you." Then, the *News* said, Nicholaou fatally shot Woods. A rumor circulated that Woods had been shot while trying to recover his son's bike. According to one widespread rumor, Woods had been shot by the police. Mobs gathered, and the police sealed off an 8-block area. Before the crowds were dispersed 54 persons had been arrested on charges of mob action, disorderly conduct and interfering with police performing their duties. Nicholaou was held in jail without bond; he was later indicted for murder and was released on $20,000 bond.

The Rev. Jesse L. Jackson of the Southern Christian Leadership Conference said Aug. 3 that he had asked Gov. Otto Kerner and Mayor Daley to declare the city a disaster area to forestall further rioting. "Chicago is sitting on a powder keg," he declared. "We have more evidence of the possibility of riots here than in other cities."

(Police and Negroes had clashed for more than 2 hours in Chicago May 21 following a memorial service for the late Black Nationalist leader Malcolm X. Participants said that police had been "harassing" the meeting after several whites had attempted to "invade" the service, attended by 500 Negroes. Police contended, however, that the Negroes had marched from the service to a busy intersection, causing traffic congestion and forcing police to disperse them. Stones and bottles were tossed at police as the crowds milled around in the street. 10 persons were reported injured. Police arrested 30 persons on charges of disorderly conduct, resisting arrest and inciting to riot.)

(Chicago Police Superintendent James Conlisk announced Dec. 28 that a year-long investigation had revealed that 6 patrolmen in the Chicago Police Department had been involved in Ku Klux Klan activity. Conlisk said the 6 would be disciplined.)

Cincinnati, O.—Rioting, looting and fires swept through black sections of Cincinnati June 12–15, and more than 300 persons were arrested before order was restored. Property damage was estimated at over $1 million.

The rioting began June 12 following a demonstration by about 300 persons at the Samuel Ach Junior High School in predominantly black Avondale, 2 miles northeast of downtown Cincinnati. They were protesting a death sentence given Posteal Laskey, 29, a Negro charged with the murder of a white secretary. Peter Allen Frakes, a Negro, carrying a sign reading "Freedom for Laskey," was arrested and charged with interfering with pedestrian and vehicular traffic. After the protest, marauding gangs of black youths formed in the area and battled with police for nearly 2 hours. 3 persons were slightly injured, and 7 were arrested.

Rioting erupted at about 7:00 p.m. June 13 in Avondale and spread to the Evanston and Walnut Hills sections, both integrated residential neighborhoods, and to Norwood and the Old West End —encompassing 5 or 6 square miles of the city. There also were reports of violence in Lockland, 18 miles northeast of the city. Police Chief Jacob Schott estimated that "thousands" of teenagers and adults were roaming through the city. By 9:00 p.m. more than 900 policemen were in the area. Shortly after 9:00 p.m., at the request of Mayor Walton S. Bachrach, Gov. James A. Rhodes sent in about 800 National Guardsmen armed with rifles and gas masks. Some arrived in jeeps with mounted machine guns. At least 13 persons were reported injured in clashes, and 47 arrests were reported.

Earlier June 13 the City Council had held a special session with black leaders and clergymen. The Negroes charged police with behavior that "served only to inflame an already tense situation." They also called for (1) the repeal of the city's no-loitering law, (2) the release of persons arrested and (3) employment opportunities for the city's youths. (The unemployment rate of Cincinnati's Negroes [about 150,000 of the city's 500,000 population] was reported as 13% to 15% compared with 3%–4% for whites; the black teenage unemployment rate was said to be more than 20%.)

Negroes walked out of talks with the mayor and City Council June 14. They charged that the National Guard had dispersed some of their group while they were waiting outside for their turn to testify. Black leaders insisted that the trouble could be traced to the failure of city officials to act on demands for new jobs, swimming pools and other recreational facilities. The Rev. Otis Moss Jr., a Negro, asserted that the violence was being spearheaded by "an active and militant minority" that was difficult to control.

Violence raged unabated in some parts of the city and suburbs

June 14. James Shirk, 15, a white youth, was shot and wounded by Negroes riding in a car.

Violence spread to the Cincinnati Workhouse June 15 on the arrival there of 12 Negroes who had been convicted of participation in the rioting and sentenced to a year in prison and $500 fines. The 409 Negro and white workhouse inmates fought with prison guards, police and National Guardsmen for more than 3 hours. Police fired tear-gas shells into the cell blocks to force the prisoners outdoors, but once outside they began ripping up bricks from a walk and attacking the guards. About 50 National Guardsmen were sent into the prison to quell the rioting.

Sporadic cases of gunfire and window smashing were reported in Cincinnati June 15 despite National Guard patrols. Firemen answered more than 45 fire alarms and extinguished more than 20 fires.

About 100 of the more than 300 persons arrested during the 3 nights of violence were tried June 15.

Chairman H. Rap Brown of the Student Nonviolent Coordinating Committee arrived in Cincinnati June 15. At a news conference he demanded the removal of the National Guard and the release of the 12 imprisoned blacks. He declared: "Cincinnati will be in flames so long as the honkie cops are here."

The executive director of the Cincinnati Human Relations Commission, David D. McPheeters Jr., a Negro, was suspended for 4 weeks June 17. Commission Chairman Robert Black noted that McPheeters had been away from the city during the "critical" situation.

The National Guard was removed from Cincinnati streets June 17 and withdrawn from the city June 18.

Violence erupted again in Avondale July 3. Gangs of black youths began roaming Avondale streets shortly after 9:00 p.m., smashing windows, looting stores, stoning cars and setting fires. 12 to 15 persons were reported injured. 26 fires occurred during the night, causing an estimated $1 million in damage. Order was restored by 5:00 a.m. July 4, but further outbreaks of firebombing and vandalism the night of July 4 resulted in 11 arrests.

Cincinnati Safety Director Henry Sandman swore in the city's firemen as special policemen July 6 and instructed them to carry shotguns in every truck for protection against snipers.

Violence broke out again in Avondale July 26, when black youths stoned firemen fighting a blaze in a housing project. The youths set fires and looted stores. Walter Evans, 46, a bystander, was accidentally wounded in the hip when police fired over the heads of the youths.

The formation of Jobs for Cincinnati, Inc., a new nonprofit corporation to help find jobs for the hard-core unemployed, was announced July 26 by the organization's executive director, Joseph Breiteneicher, as one method of fighting the conditions thought to have given rise to the racial turmoil in Cincinnati. 25% of Cincinnati's 500,000 inhabitants were black. The city's overall unemployment rate was about 3%, but the rate for Negroes in the city was close to 8% and the jobless rate for Avondale was nearly 13%. The average annual income for the city's white families was $6,800, while for black families it was about $4,100. 36% of the black families (17% of the white families) lived in "poverty" conditions —defined as an income of less than $3,000 annually. About 14% of the black families owned and 45% of the black families rented what was classified as "substandard" housing.

Cleveland, O.—Racial rioting flared in the Hough section of Cleveland Apr. 16. According to conflicting reports, the disorders started at or near a carnival. The disturbances spread along Superior Ave. from East 75th St. to East 105th St. Store windows were smashed and several stores looted. 2 youths were arrested while carrying furniture out of one store. 2 other youths were arrested after they tossed an empty soda bottle at a police car and cracked the rear window.

The Rev. Martin Luther King Jr. said at a news conference in Cleveland Apr. 26 that Cleveland was a racially "divided city" facing the possibility of increasing violence in the summer. He said: "Negroes are restricted to the East Side [the Hough section] and . . . confined in a mass of substandard housing in high density areas"; Cleveland's mayor, Ralph S. Locher, was "insensitive to the problems of the Negro" and was "more concerned with keeping the community divided to enhance himself politically than in helping to solve its citizens' problems." King criticized the police crackdown on black "looters and firebomb throwers." "A get-tough policy should mean getting tough against poverty, inferior education and rat-infested slums," he said.

(King announced May 16 that his Southern Christian Leadership Conference [SCLC] had chosen Cleveland for organized civil rights action during the summer. He said the conference would organize the black community in the same way it had in Grenada, Miss.,

Chicago and Louisville, Ky. The goals would include organizing black political and economic power, establishing collective bargaining by black tenants, open housing and a full-service bank for the Negro community. King announced June 14 that SCLC had chosen the city's bread industry for a selective buying campaign to press for more and better jobs for Negroes. The United Pastors Association, which originally had asked King to come to Cleveland for the summer, announced a campaign to raise $150,000 for SCLC's "Operation Breadbasket" project.

(Leaders of 9 civil rights organizations announced June 14 that they planned to work together during the summer and to make Cleveland the target of their combined efforts. The announcement followed a secret meeting in a Suffern, N.Y. motel June 13–14, sponsored by the Metropolitan Applied Research Center, an organization formed in March 1967 to deal with civil rights and urban problems. Among those who attended the meeting: the Rev. Dr. Martin Luther King Jr.; Roy Wilkins, executive director of the NAACP; Floyd B. McKissick, national director of CORE; Ivanhoe Donaldson, a representative of SNCC; Whitney M. Young Jr., executive director of the National Urban League; Dr. Kenneth B. Clark, president of the research center; Bayard Rustin, executive secretary of the A. Philip Randolph Institute; Jack Greenberg, director of the NAACP Legal Defense & Educational Fund, Inc.; Dorothy I. Height of the National Council of Negro Women.

(Clark, who served as spokesman for the group, said in New York June 14 that the "underlying causes of unrest and despair among urban ghetto Negroes, as well as clear indications of their grim, sobering and costly consequences, are found in classic form in Cleveland." He blamed Cleveland's Mayor Locher and the city's "inept police" for perpetuating the situation. He said that Cleveland's administration had "turned aside offers from the business sector and other parts of the community to help find ways to alleviate the situation." Clark said that rights organizations would work to ease racial tensions in Cleveland and to "wipe out inequality and injustice in employment, education, housing, health and welfare services, voting and the administration of justice."

(Reporting on the progress of the Operation Breadbasket program in Cleveland, King announced Nov. 28 that Pick-N-Pay Supermarkets, a division of Cook Coffee Co., had agreed to provide 300 jobs—including 6 as store managers—for Negroes. The jobs would produce more than $1,700,000 in annual income. Pick-N-

Pay also agreed to list job vacancies with agencies that dealt in minority employment, to advertise jobs in Negro-oriented newspapers, to deposit "a substantial amount of money" in the black-owned and -operated Quincy Savings & Loan Co., to stock products of black businessmen and to support the United Negro College Fund. The agreement was the 2d in the Operation Breadbasket drive. King had announced Aug. 8 the cancellation of a boycott against Sealtest Dairy Products, a division of National Dairy Products Corp., because Sealtest had agreed to provide "50 new upgraded jobs for the Negro and other nonwhite citizens of Cleveland," to deposit $10,000 in the Negro savings and loan firm and to advertise in the Negro press. At the close of a 3-day National Conference of Clergymen in Chicago July 12 King had called for national boycotts of National Dairy Products, the Kellogg Co. and the California Packing Co., makers of Del Monte brand foods, until they hired more blacks. King said that the drive would extend later to the drug industry and to General Motors. King disclosed in Cleveland July 29 that the Great Atlantic & Pacific Tea Co. had agreed to observe the Sealtest boycott, which King had announced July 9.)

Dayton, O.—Incidents of window-smashing and looting broke out in the predominantly black West End section of Dayton Sept. 19 following a demonstration of 500 to 600 persons protesting the fatal shooting Sept. 17 by a white off-duty policeman of Robert Elwood Barbee, 41, of Findlay, O., a black civil rights worker.

It was reported that Barbee was shot when he ran from detective R. S. Collier and another detective, who said they saw a pipe in his belt and thought it was a gun. The policemen had been working at a Shriners Convention. 131 persons were arrested, ⅓ of them juveniles, and more than 50 were reported injured.

Black and white officials had met in the evening Sept. 18 in an effort to ease racial tension, but the meeting was reported to have turned into a shouting contest.

(Additional policemen were put on duty Sept. 20, and sporadic rock-throwing and looting were reported throughout the day.)

Des Moines, Ia.—Police arrested 17 Negroes in Des Moines in a racial disturbance July 16. What was described as a "large crowd of young blacks" had begun a rock- and bottle-throwing melee at 2 a.m. Windows in several stores were smashed and a police patrol car was damaged. 17 persons were arrested before order was restored. 4 of those arrested were from Kansas City,

Mo. (7 black youths had been arrested after disturbances in Des Moines July 2.)

Durham, N.C.—Police and National Guard units were summoned to put down violence that erupted in the wake of Negro rights demonstrations in Durham July 19–20.

2 persons were injured July 19 when some 300 blacks began smashing plate glass windows in the downtown area of Durham following a demonstration at City Hall for desegregated public housing. It was reported July 20 that cars used in the protest were registered to Operation Breakthrough, the city's antipoverty organization. In Washington July 20, the director of the Office of Economic Opportunity, Sargent Shriver, reportedly condemned the use of the cars as an "inexcusable mistake in judgment."

300 Negroes conducted a 2d Durham protest march the evening of July 20 as police and 120 National Guardsmen called in by Gov. Daniel K. Moore lined the streets. Police arrested one white heckler. There were no serious incidents. Black leaders had warned the marchers earlier: "If just one person picks up a brick and hits one of those white people there's going to be shooting and somebody's going to be killed." "The only thing we can do is sing and clap hands."

At a special meeting July 20 the City Council voted to appoint a 5-member committee to study Negro demands for open housing. Black leaders had argued that the City Council's plans for further housing projects would merely extend the city's black ghetto. Early in the day Gov. Moore had dedicated a new low-income housing project in the black section of Durham. The City Council, meeting in emergency session July 21, agreed to accept 9 demands of the city's Negroes. These were for paved streets, grievance procedures, the extermination of rats in public housing and improved bus service. Black leaders agreed July 22 to suspend demonstrations for 5 days.

Duke University in Durham announced July 27 that it would take an active role in trying to work out racial problems in the city. The university proposed a program that would make 526 apartments in traditionally white sections available to Negroes. Duke Pres. Douglas M. Knight said that to his knowledge it was the first time a Southern university had been directly involved in such a project.

Elgin, Ill.—Firebombing and window-breaking were reported in Elgin Aug. 5 as bands of Negroes roamed the downtown area.

A fire was reported in the warehouse section of a Sears Roebuck & Co. store, causing more than $135,000 in damages. 3 Negroes were arrested and held under $50,000 bond. There were no injuries.

Erie, Pa.—Racial disturbances were reported in Erie July 11–12. Gangs of youths congregated at street intersections, blocked traffic and threw stones at cars. 8 Negro youths were arrested July 11 and 2 persons were injured. Police halted further disorders July 12 with the aid of police dogs. But Mayor Louis J. Tullio said July 13 that police dogs would not be used again and that he would try to find more jobs for the city's black youths.

Violence flared again in Erie July 18. 8 Negroes were arrested on charges of rioting and assault and battery. Mobs gathered to watch several fires that had been set, and began throwing rocks and smashing car windows. 3 persons were beaten before police could restore order. One fire was reported to have caused $150,000 damage. Mayor Tullio asked the city council July 19 to implement an Office of Economic Opportunity grant of $115,000, made the previous week, to rehabilitate a recreation center in the city's black neighborhood.

Flint, Mich.—Firebombings in the Detroit suburb of Flint July 24 resulted in the arrests of more than 100 young Negroes. Charges—ranging from arson and inciting riot to vandalism and disorderly conduct—were dropped the next day after the youths agreed to spread through the streets urging others to "cool it." The mayor of Flint, Floyd McCree, a Negro, began July 25 to speed action on a proposed open-occupancy housing ordinance.

Fresno, Calif.—Gangs of young Negroes smashed windows and set fires in Fresno July 16–17. Mayor Floyd Hyde met with Negro leaders July 17 to discuss ways of ending the disturbances. On leaving the meeting, the director of a federal job program in Fresno, Dennis Mathis, 27, was wounded by a black private patrolman, Spencer Carter, 66. Police said Carter told them he thought Mathis had thrown a bottle at him. The bullet ricocheted from the sidewalk and hit Mathis in the arm and side. Carter was booked on suspicion of assault with a deadly weapon. Minor disorders were reported the evening of July 17, and 8 youths were arrested.

Grand Rapids, Mich.—3 Negroes were wounded in racial violence in Grand Rapids, Michigan's 2d largest city (200,000 inhabitants), July 24–25. The wounded men were members of a task force attempting to cool tempers. They reportedly were shot by a sniper. Officials reported that about 40 fires were set, that more than 40 persons were injured and that more than 200 people were arrested during the disorders. Gov. George Romney proclaimed a state of emergency in the city July 25. Sporadic looting occurred July 26, but the city remained relatively calm. 250 National Guardsmen had arrived July 25, and a curfew had been imposed.

Hamilton, O.—One person was wounded in Hamilton July 29 when black and white gangs clashed.

Hartford, Conn.—Rioting broke out in Hartford July 12 after a Negro was arrested, allegedly for using derogatory language to a waitress in a luncheonette. An angry group of blacks gathered on the street as he was being driven off in a squad car. About 2 hours later rocks and firebombs were thrown through the windows of several stores reputed to have overcharged ghetto residents. Police broke up the disorders early in the morning of July 13.

A 2d wave of racial violence began in Hartford's black North End neighborhood late in the evening of July 13 but it was quickly contained as police sealed off the area. 2 dozen store windows, however, were broken by bricks hurled by crowds. Except for isolated incidents, calm returned to the North End July 14. There were no serious injuries and only about a dozen arrests during the disturbances. The lack of looting kept property damage at a minimum.

66 persons were arrested in Hartford Sept. 18–19 after racial violence erupted during a demonstration calling for stricter enforcement of the state's open housing laws. Some 150 demonstrators, mostly Negroes and Puerto Ricans, had started a scheduled 3-mile march from the North End late Sept. 18. They were heading for the South End, an almost entirely white middle-class neighborhood with a large number of European immigrants. But the march, led by black restaurant manager John Barber, 30, broke up about 2 miles from the planned destination when the marchers reached Hartford's new shopping and business center and began throwing rocks and bottles. Several policemen were injured, and about 24 store windows were broken. 25 marchers, half of them white, were arrested, mostly on charges of breach of the peace. A crowd of hostile whites awaiting the demonstrators in the South End then dispersed. Police Chief John J. Kerrigan said: "We had adequate protection for them [the demonstrators]—perhaps 250 men. But they became unruly and started throwing things, so we moved in and broke it up."

Policemen Sept. 19 used tear gas to disperse black youths who were pelting cars passing through the North End. 14 policemen, some guarding fire trucks answering false alarms, were injured; dozens of cars were damaged. During the day Mayor George B. Kinsella met with city officials at an emergency post at police headquarters. Later he asked parents to observe a "voluntary curfew by keeping their children off the streets of our city tonight and until the situation has been clarified."

(A group of militant Negroes called the Black Caucus met with city antipoverty workers Sept. 22–23 to discuss the militants' proposals for a new antipoverty program for the city. The caucus held that the city's antipoverty agency, the Community Renewal Team [CRT], had failed to reach the poor. John Barber, a caucus leader, said at a City Hall meeting Sept. 22: "Colonialism in antipoverty" must be ended; "what we propose is that the poor run their programs."

(It was reported that 30% of Hartford's 160,000 inhabitants were black. According to Douglas Andrews, the CRT housing supervisor, "no meaningful housing has been built in Hartford in the last 10 years." He said: "Urban redevelopment has not built one bit of residential housing in its 8 years of existence"; "business runs this town"; "Pratt & Whitney [aircraft engine manufacturers] determines what kind of housing gets built, and they want housing for white white-collar workers; they send blue-collar workers to me to find a place for them to live"; the worst areas in the North End had the highest rent; people on welfare were paying $110 to $200 a month for housing.)

Kalamazoo, Mich.—A disturbance involving about 200 Negroes was quelled by police July 23. The early morning disorder followed the wounding of a black girl by an unidentified gunman.

Kansas City, Mo.—Police used tear gas to disperse a rock-throwing mob of about 150 Negroes in Kansas City's Swope Park July 9. 11 persons were arrested and one was injured following a 2-hour clash with police. The violence began after 4 vice squad officers (2 Negroes and 2 whites) arrested 3 Negroes on a liquor violation. The mob attacked police cars and smashed windows. The 11 men arrested were fined $50 each July 10 for disorderly conduct and breaking the peace.

Lansing, Mich.—Police battled rock-throwing black youths for 4 hours in black neighborhoods of Lansing June 14–15. 17 persons were arrested June 15. 2 policemen were injured and several cars were reported damaged.

Long Beach, Calif.—Sporadic violence broke out in the black neighborhoods of Long Beach July 28. Bands of black youths set fires and threw rocks and bottles. At one point during the disorders, police sealed off about 400 youths in one part of the city. 2 policemen exchanged rifle fire with a sniper, and 2 other policemen were injured by flying glass. 14 Negroes were arrested.

Lorain, O.—Gov. James A. Rhodes sent 100 National Guardsmen to Lorain July 28 as a precautionary measure. Several fire-bombings had been reported July 26.

Marin City, Calif.—Sniper fire was reported July 28 during a 5-hour rampage by 25–30 black youths in predominantly black Marin City, 2 miles north of San Francisco's Golden Gate Bridge. 3 Negroes were wounded. Firemen trying to put out small fires were shot at until deputies were called in to protect them.

Memphis, Tenn.—Tennessee Adjutant Gen. Robert Akin ordered 4,000 National Guardsmen to Memphis July 28 as a "precautionary" measure in the face of racial tension in the city. Gov. Buford Ellington had put the Guard on standby alert the previous day after Memphis officials reportedly expressed concern over possible outbreaks of violence. Bands of Negroes roamed the streets early July 28, throwing rocks and smashing windows. Several small fires were reported in the evening. NAACP leaders canceled a planned demonstration against job discrimination to prevent increased tensions.

Milwaukee, Wis.—Rioting swept Milwaukee's predominantly black "Inner Core" neighborhood on the city's near North Side July 30–Aug. 3. A 24-hour curfew was imposed in the city, the nation's 11th largest, and Wisconsin National Guard units were called in. 4 persons were killed; at least 100 were reported injured, and 705 persons were arrested during the disorders. Property damage was relatively light.

The violence erupted at 9:30 p.m. July 30, when Negro gangs began setting fires, smashing windows and looting stores. There were exchanges of gunfire between police and Negroes. By 3:00 a.m., when a rainstorm began and forced the rioters to take cover, 2 persons, a policeman and an elderly white woman, had been killed. 83 persons were injured, including 12 policemen and a fireman; 145 to 180 persons were arrested. 28 fires were reported.

Mayor Henry Maier asked Gov. Warren P. Knowles to alert National Guard units at 12:40 a.m. July 31. Shortly afterwards, Maier notified the White House of the situation in the city and said: "I will not hesitate to demand a call of federal troops if necessary."

Finally, at 2:27 a.m. July 31, after 2 policemen had been wounded by snipers, Maier called in the National Guard. He proclaimed a state of emergency and ordered a 24-hour curfew for everyone except doctors, nurses, policemen, firemen and newsmen. The sale of liquor and beer, arms, ammunition and gasoline in containers was prohibited by the mayor.

Gov. Knowles immediately dispatched a force of 1,450 National Guardsmen to the city. The metropolitan area was sealed off and police barricaded areas of the downtown Inner Core, a 5½-square-mile section inhabited by most of Milwaukee's approximately 80,000 Negroes (about 10% of the city's population). All stores and public and private facilities were closed. Public and private transportation came to a halt. Mail deliveries were curtailed. 7:00 p.m. curfews were imposed on all Milwaukee suburbs, effective July 31.

By 10:20 a.m. July 31, 450 Guardsmen had established patrols in the main riot area in the Inner Core. Within the ghetto, they cordoned off a 105-square-block area. Some 1,000 Guardsmen were on standby in nearby staging areas. At noon, Maj. Gen. Ralph Olson, acting state adjutant general, called in an additional 2,400 Guardsmen to help the 1,900-man city police force. The troops were placed under the command of Maj. Gen. John A. Dunlap, commanding general of the Wisconsin National Guard Infantry Division.

Maier lifted the curfew from 4:00 p.m. to 6:00 p.m. July 31 to permit residents to leave the riot area to buy food. Guardsmen carrying loaded guns escorted milkmen into the riot areas to deliver free milk to residents. In the afternoon, the Rev. James E. Groppi, assistant pastor at the St. Boniface Roman Catholic Church, an adviser to the Youth Council of the Milwaukee branch of the NAACP, and 6 other members of the council were arrested and charged with violating the curfew. Groppi, who was released on bail, denounced the curfew as "foolish." (Groppi and the 7 Youth Council members were convicted Aug. 22 of violating the curfew. They were fined $5 each. He declared: "I blame this on the School Board, the Common Council, the police chief and the church. It's all white apathy." Groppi reportedly had warned the city's Common Council the previous week that a "holocaust" was inevitable unless an open-housing ordinance were enacted.)

During the night of July 31, policemen in 4 rented armored Brinks trucks responded to reports of sniper fire. Maier Aug. 1 lifted the curfew until 7:00 p.m. and limited National Guard activities to standby duty at the city's armories. In an interview Aug. 1 he told newsmen: "The curfew has been a good . . . cooling-off device." He said that only .005% of the city's Negroes had participated in the violence but that these were a criminal element "beyond the reach of any program now in existence."

Scattered sniper fire erupted again in the evening of Aug. 1 after Negroes attacked firemen fighting a blaze in the Inner Core. By Aug. 2 the death toll had risen to 4 and arrests had reached 539.

Groppi and 24 other civil rights leaders Aug. 2 denounced city officials for having failed to do anything to eliminate the causes of the rioting or alleviate Negro frustrations stemming from bad relations with the police and bias in employment, education and housing.

The withdrawal of the National Guard force—which had grown to 4,800 men—was begun Aug. 2. 3,400 remained in the city Aug. 3, 850 of them on duty, the rest on standby. Maier lifted the curfew at 5:30 a.m. Aug. 3 but announced 2 hours later that it would be reimposed at 9:00 p.m. because of reports of firebombings, vandalism and lootings. Later in the day the mayor asked businessmen to help solve the economic problems of the black ghetto. He appealed to them to provide summer jobs for unemployed youth.

Minneapolis—600 National Guardsmen were moved into Minneapolis July 21 to curb racial violence that had beset the Minnesota city for 2 days. The disorders began July 19 with an outbreak of street fighting and firebombing that resulted in 13 arrests and 9 injuries. Violence erupted again on the city's North Side the next night. More arrests and injuries were reported as the disorders grew to include car burnings and sniper fire.

Mayor Arthur Naftalin requested July 21 that 300 Guardsmen be sent to the North Side to aid Minneapolis police. But Gov. Harold LeVander sent 600 troops to the area, where most of the city's 12,000 Negroes lived. Despite the burning of a Catholic church that night, there was no major rioting and only 7 arrests were made, compared to 36 reported during the previous 2 days. Guardsmen patrolled the streets with fixed bayonets.

Black leaders blamed police brutality for the rioting, but Naftalin said that a major factor was the shortage of jobs for teenagers. Although there were no serious injuries during the rioting, Fire Department officials reported 22 confirmed cases of arson, which caused nearly $1 million in damages. The National Guard was withdrawn from the ghetto area July 25. Except for the firebombing of one tavern, all was reported to be quiet in the riot area.

Mt. Vernon, N.Y.—Rioting broke out in the black section of Mt. Vernon July 24–28. (Negroes comprised about 30% of the city's 72,000 population.) Mayor Joseph P. Vaccarella July 26 declared a state of emergency and imposed a 10 p.m.-to-6 a.m. curfew on the 5-to-6-block area. Liquor stores and taverns were closed. Police reinforcements were called from the neighboring cities of White Plains, Yonkers and New Rochelle.

Under terms of an agreement between black and white leaders of the community, police were withdrawn from the black neighborhood July 28. The curfew was lifted and black leaders consented to patrol the area and persuade youths to "cool it." The police also granted permission for an outdoor grievance meeting attended by 100 Negroes later July 28.

Labor Secy. Willard Wirtz sent Neil McArthur, deputy assistant U.S. manpower administrator, to Mt. Vernon July 29. At a meeting called by Rep. Ogden R. Reid (R., N.Y.), McArthur told county antipoverty officials, local aldermen, civil rights leaders, businessmen and residents that he would call on the Federal Employment Service to find jobs for residents. Mayor Vaccarella agreed to a proposal by Negroes that $250,000 be allocated for 200 new jobs for unemployed persons. But City Controller Nicholas Yannantuono rejected the proposal July 31, declaring the funds were not available for the program. Later July 31, Rep. Reid announced that the Labor Department had agreed to appropriate $215,000 to underwrite 409 new training jobs in Westchester County; 200 of the jobs were set aside for Mt. Vernon.

New Britain, Conn.—Scattered incidents of rock throwing were reported in New Britain July 22–23. Early July 23 a white man was dragged from his car by a mob of black youths, beaten and robbed. By midnight police and their auxiliaries had sealed off a 5-block area and dispersed the youths.

Newburgh, N.Y.— Bands of Negroes clashed with police, smashed windows and looted stores in Newburgh July 29–30. The violence began following a meeting of the National Renaissance Party, a neo-Nazi group, in the Orange County Courthouse. 42 Negroes were arrested July 29; 28 were arrested July 30.

New Castle, Pa.—Bands of black youths set fires, smashed windows and beat up a white man on New Castle's South Side July 29.

The city's entire police force was called to duty, but there were no arrests. 2 firebombs were exploded July 30, but no injuries were reported.

New Haven, Conn.—Sporadic violence flared in New Haven Aug. 19–23. Nearly 450 persons were arrested during 5 days of looting, arson and vandalism. But there were no serious injuries reported, and there were no shots fired at any time during the disorders.

The disorders took place in a city that had been trying to avert racial confrontation. It was estimated that of the 145,000 residents of New Haven, 30,000 were Negroes and Puerto Ricans. New Haven was reported to have the largest urban renewal grant per capita in the country—about $120 million in federal aid, or about $800 for every person in the city. The black unemployment rate in New Haven was reported to be 8%—double the rate for whites in slum areas.

According to Police Chief Francis McManus, the disturbances began late Aug. 19 after Edward Thomas, 31, a white restaurant owner, shot and wounded Julio Diaz, 35; Diaz allegedly had threatened Thomas with a knife. Within a short time bands of Negro youths were roaming the Hill and Dixwell sections of the city, both only a mile from Yale University. Looting broke out in a 4-block area. Police together with leaders of the Hill Parents Association, a community group, and Yale students, members of Students for a Democratic Society, urged the milling crowds to disperse. Police finally brought out riot sticks, shotguns and tear gas; but only one tear gas canister was fired. By midnight order was restored, and Public Works Department crews began clearing away the debris and boarding up broken store windows. 120 windows were reported broken. 50 persons were reported arrested.

The disorders resumed Aug. 20. That evening Mayor Richard C. Lee declared a state of emergency and imposed an 8 p.m. curfew. 200 state troopers were called in to augment the 400-man city police force. A 12-block area in a black and Puerto Rican neighborhood was sealed off and placed under heavy patrol. A 250-man National Guard unit was put on standby alert, and all bars were ordered closed. 68 persons were arrested during the evening. 100 windows were reported broken, 3 cars set afire, 2 stores burned and dozens of stores looted.

Sporadic violence was reported Aug. 21. Several dozen windows were broken. 27 fires, most of them confined to heaps of rubbish on sidewalks, were reported in the early hours of the evening.   The number of arrests rose to 263 by evening.

Mayor Lee conferred with black leaders and city officials throughout the day Aug. 21.   Negroes gathered outside the circuit court at City Hall, where black prisoners were being arraigned, and signed affidavits charging police brutality.   Black youths circulated a petition demanding "an immediate commitment by the city to a massive program of jobs, housing and educational programs to close the economic gap between blacks and whites."   40 black leaders met at the Zion Evangelical Church in the evening of Aug. 21. They issued a 2-page manifesto calling for the immediate lifting of the curfew, a million-dollar loan for rehabilitation of the area and an apology from police for alleged brutality.

Gangs of black youths roamed the city late Aug. 21 in defiance of the curfew.   Looting and vandalism continued, and 24 fires were reported.   11 persons were arrested, mostly on minor charges.

Police and state troopers continued to patrol the black neighborhoods Aug. 22.   More than 100 arrests, mostly on charges of breaking the peace by failure to observe the curfew, were reported during the night Aug. 21 and early Aug. 22.   Police arrested several carloads of white youths who, they said, were driving around with firearms "looking for trouble."   150 state police replacements arrived in the city the evening of Aug. 22.

Mayor Lee said Aug. 22: The disorders were "disorganized, sporadic, but there has been a good deal of it"; the curfew would remain in effect, and cars would be stopped and searched; "vigilante action will not be tolerated."   He added that "not one single shot" had been fired in New Haven since the disturbances began.

Lee relaxed the curfew Aug. 23 by delaying it until 11 p.m. He said, however, that police patrols would remain available "on a saturation basis."   About 130 persons were arrested Aug. 23.

Mayor Lee said Aug 23: "I am hopeful that the worst of our problems are behind us"; "New Haven is not a model city, and it never has been.   We've done a lot, but for every one thing we've done, there are 5 that we haven't."

Nyack, N.Y.—Minor disturbances were reported in Nyack July 19 when about 50 black youths ran through the town, smashing windows and taunting police.   There were no injuries; 18 Negroes including 2 women were arrested.   It was announced July 21 that the police had agreed to consider the reassignment of 2 policemen who reportedly had been in conflict with black youths.

Peekskill, N.Y.—200 black youths rampaged through the streets of Peekskill July 27 and early July 28, smashing windows and looting at least 44 stores. Several false alarms were reported, but no fires occurred. Police arrested 21 persons.

Peoria, Ill.—Police and snipers traded gunfire in a largely black housing project in Peoria Aug. 2 as the police attempted to direct traffic around a grocery store that had been set ablaze by a firebomb. According to witnesses, 3 Negroes and 2 white men had driven up to the store and tossed the firebomb in through a broken window. 2 persons were arrested for carrying concealed weapons.

Philadelphia—Mayor James H. J. Tate issued a proclamation of limited emergency July 27, on the 2d night of scattered disorders in predominantly-black South Philadelphia. Roving Negro gangs were reported to have stoned police cars and smashed windows. Several hundred police were reported to have been sent to quell the rioting.

The proclamation, issued by Tate on the advice of Police Commissioner Frank Rizzo and made effective until Aug. 14, prohibited groups of 12 or more persons from gathering at either public or private places for purposes other than organized recreation. Tate said he had issued the orders because the city "is now faced with the threat of an eruption similar to the violence that has flared in other cities throughout the country."

A biracial group of 150 civic leaders and gang representatives, called the Appeal for Reason Committee, issued a statement July 28 scoring the proclamation as "premature and an incitement to riot."

Special police riot squads were put on duty in undisclosed sections of the city July 28.

The Pennsylvania adjutant general, Maj. Gen. Thomas R. White Jr., said in Harrisburg July 28 that he had ordered special training in riot control for the state's National Guard units.

30 demonstrators protesting the limited state of emergency were arrested in Philadelphia July 30.

Police reported July 31 that 40 rifles and an unknown number of pellet guns and bows and arrows had been stolen over the weekend from a wholesale distributing company in the city.

250 Philadelphia businessmen attended a luncheon with Mayor Tate Aug. 3 and agreed to hire at least 1,500 unemployed persons. Tate told the group: "It would be very foolish indeed for us to pretend that the same tragedy could not strike Philadelphia again

. . . unless we, who have the most to lose, do something about it." "One of the major causes," he said, "is the frustration of a large number of our citizens—frustration arising from discrimination, lack of opportunity, boredom, crowded and unwholesome living conditions. One of the things that could go a long way toward alleviating the pent-up pressure is a job."

Phoenix, Ariz.—Black youths rioted, threw rocks and started fires in Phoenix July 25–26. Police sealed off a 9-block area July 26, and Phoenix Mayor Milton Graham imposed a night curfew on the black section. Several stores were looted in the melee July 26; fire destroyed a laundry, and several cars were destroyed. Black spokesmen met with Graham July 26 and presented him with demands for better jobs and recreation facilities, higher welfare payments, more respect from the police, better hospital care and better education. 48 persons were arrested in the evening of July 26 on charges of violating the curfew. The restrictions were not ended until July 30.

Pontiac, Mich.—2 Negroes were killed in racial disorders in Pontiac July 24–25. One of the dead was Alfred Taylor, 17, who was killed by a shotgun blast fired by Michigan State Rep. Arthur J. Law. Law said he fired the gun at a half-dozen black youths when they threw a trash basket through the window of his food market. A policeman was wounded by a sniper, and 87 persons were arrested. Pontiac, 25 miles northwest of Detroit, had 82,000 inhabitants, 15,000 of them Negroes.

Portland, Ore.—Gov. Tom McCall placed 500 National Guard troops on standby alert July 30 following an outbreak of rock-throwing, firebombing and vandalism in northeast Portland's Albina district, the home of 14,000 of the city's 18,000 Negroes. The disorders came after a meeting at which a speaker had blamed whites for poor conditions endured by Negroes. Firemen answered 26 alarms, half of them false alarms, 9 of them the result of fire-bombs. A black youth fleeing a firebombed store was shot and wounded by police. 47 persons—30 Negroes and 17 whites—were arrested. There were reports of sporadic rock throwing and firebombing July 31. But police restored order, and the National Guard troops were released.

Poughkeepsie, N.Y.—11 persons were arrested during disorders in the predominantly black downtown section of Poughkeepsie July 27. Police sealed off a 4-block area July 28 to prevent further outbreaks.

Prattville, Ala.—Ex-SNCC (Student Nonviolent Coordinating Committee) Chairman Stokely Carmichael was arrested June 11 outside a Negro church in Prattville after an argument with white police officers. He was charged with disorderly conduct for allegedly threatening to "take care of" the police and to "tear this town up." Police said they had gone to the church, where Carmichael was addressing a rally of 60 black youths, to investigate reports that a Negro had pointed a shotgun at white passers-by. Blacks said that as whites drove by the rally, they raced their car engines. One witness said the trouble began when Carmichael shouted "black power" at a police cruiser the 2d time it drove by. The police stopped, and an argument between Carmichael and Asst. Police Chief Kenneth Hill reportedly broke out. Carmichael was jailed without bond.

Snipers and police exchanged rifle fire that evening. After Carmichael's arrest, about 30 Negroes had gone to the home of Dan Houser Jr., a Negro, in the "Happy Hollow" section of Prattville and, according to police, had started shooting from inside the house. The Negroes reportedly charged that police had fired into the house first.

Within a few hours Gov. Lurleen B. Wallace sent 150 National Guardsmen to Prattville with orders to "shoot to kill if this be necessary. . . ." (In a June 14 editorial the *Alabama Journal* sharply criticized the state's *de facto* governor, George C. Wallace, for calling in the National Guard before receiving a request for help from local authorities. The paper asked: "Has the state administration now become so arrogant that it usurps local police functions without even bothering to tell the top officials?" "In short, has Alabama become a banana republic. . . ?")

The shooting ended around midnight when 25 Negroes filed out of the house. 10 were arrested. During the reported battle, 3 policemen and a black dog handler were injured. Houser claimed June 12 that no shots had been fired from his house, and his wife said the house had not been hit by bullets. Reporters could find no damage to the house from gun fire.

(Houser was hospitalized early June 12 for eye and facial injuries suffered in a beating. Prattville Police Chief O. C. Thompson said Houser had been questioned at City Hall early in the morning, but that he had been released unharmed. Houser June 15 filed a $100,000 damage suit against the Autauga County sheriff and 4 Prattville policemen for allegedly conspiring to deprive him of his civil rights by beating him.)

Armed with bayonets, the National Guard June 12 halted 300 Negroes marching in Montgomery to protest the arrest of Carmichael.

SNCC Chairman H. Rap Brown, speaking in Atlanta June 12, charged that Carmichael's arrest was a "declaration of war" by racist America" and "part of America's gestapo tactics to destroy SNCC as well as to commit genocide against black people." He said: "We are calling for full retaliation from the black community across America. We blame Lyndon Johnson." It appeared, he said, that "Alabama has been chosen as the starting battleground for America's race war."

$500 bond was set for Carmichael June 12. The other 10 arrested men were released on $500 bond after the charges against them were changed from inciting riot to unlawful assembly.

Carmichael June 13 led an evening march to within one block of the Alabama capitol in Montgomery in protest against white mistreatment of Negroes. Police accompanied the marchers. Protest marches continued in Prattville June 14–15, the 2d day without a permit.

Gov. Lurleen Wallace refused June 15 to meet with black leaders to discuss their 10-point list of grievances.

About 250–300 of Prattville's black youths marched June 19, again without a permit. Sporadic vandalism was reported after the marchers were stopped by police. 12 persons were reported arrested. Scattered incidents involving firebombings and looting were reported June 20.

Providence, R.I.—Negro and white gangs clashed in predominantly black South Providence July 31–Aug. 2.

350 police were called in to restore order July 31 after gangs of black youths threw stones at a white man who used a gun to defend his lemonade stand against mob attack. The stand was destroyed by the youths. 2 Negroes were shot in the melee, neither seriously. At least 4 persons were arrested.

Sporadic sniper activity was reported Aug. 1. Gangs of white youths shouting "White Power" tried to attack Negro gangs in the evening. 20 persons were injured as snipers and heavily armed police traded gunfire; 13 persons were arrested in the clash. Looting incidents were reported during the day, and 3 persons were injured in clashes resulting from them.

72 persons, most of them whites, were arrested in the early morning of Aug. 2.

A special session of the City Council Aug. 2 gave Mayor

Joseph A. Doorley emergency powers to handle the disturbances. Doorley imposed a 9:00 p.m.-to-6:00 a.m. curfew of the 100-block area where most of Providence's 15,000 Negroes lived.

50 antipoverty workers, most of them Negroes, wearing white helmets, aided police Aug. 2 in patrolling the streets but several fires were reported in the evening. Doorley maintained his "selective curfew Aug. 3. In a special TV appearance that day he thanked police, residents and "soul patrol" members for their cooperation in restoring order in the city.

Riviera Beach, Fla.—46 Negroes were arrested in Riviera Beach, Fla. July 31 in disorders that broke out simultaneously with fires in a lumber yard and a plastics and rubber plant. Police used tear gas to disperse a mob of 400 Negroes who threw rocks and bottles at firemen trying to contain the blaze. The police were reported to have angered the mob when they arrested 2 men after the fire broke out. Fire damage was estimated at about $350,000.

Rochester, N.Y.—Racial disturbances involving firebombing and looting were reported in Rochester July 23–25. The rioting broke out at 10 p.m. July 23 when 200 youths began throwing stones at a Public Works Department sprinkler truck that was watering down a street to prevent drag races. The disorders spread, and by early July 24, 400 members of the 562-man police force were called to duty. The police sealed off a 20-block area. At least 50 persons were arrested July 23–24.

In another part of the city 2 Negroes were wounded early July 24 when they were fired at by a group of whites in a passing car. They were not seriously injured. Thomas Lee Wright, 21, a Negro, was shot fatally when he tried to run a police barricade in the 3d Ward. (Another shooting later July 24 resulted in the death of one person, but the incident was not related to the racial violence.)

Rochester City Manager Seymour Scher, responding to demands for legal action against the policeman who killed Wright, said July 25 that the shooting was "an unavoidable by-product of lawlessness."

Rockford, Ill.—Police dispersed a rock-throwing crowd of 100 to 200 persons in a predominantly black district of Rockford July 29. 31 persons were arrested. 11 more persons were arrested July 30 after groups of Negroes threw firebombs into the streets and smashed windows. There were several exchanges of gunfire, but no injuries were reported. Police and firemen were ordered on standby alert July 31.

Saginaw, Mich.—Firebombing and looting broke out in Saginaw July 25–26, but order was restored after 70 persons were arrested. 8 persons were wounded in the shootings.

San Bernardino, Calif.—Sniping and firebombing were reported July 30–31 in the black and Mexican-American sections of San Bernardino, Calif. There were no injuries; 2 persons were reported arrested.

San Francisco—Mobs of black youths rioted in San Francisco July 27–28. 37 persons were arrested July 28. No injuries were reported. (Violence, looting and vandalism had been reported in San Francisco May 14–15. 29 youths, most of them Negroes, were arrested May 14 after a brawl at the Playland Amusement Park. 14 persons were injured in the fighting. Gangs of Negro youths stoned cars in the Hunters Point district and smashed store windows May 15. Earlier that day 2 white youths were assaulted by a mob of black youths and Molotov cocktails were thrown at a junior high school.)

South Bend, Ind.—Bands of black youths roamed the streets of South Bend July 25–28. The National Guard was called to standby duty by Gov. Roger D. Branigin July 26, shortly after South Bend Mayor Lloyd Allen had imposed a general curfew on the city. 7 black youths were wounded by police July 26 when disturbances broke out at a West Side recreation center. Black leaders charged that the violence had erupted when riot control police fired weapons without provocation and turned dogs on about 70 teenagers. Allen ordered an immediate investigation of the shooting. Firebombings were reported July 28, but no serious property damage was reported. The removal of the National Guard was begun July 29.

Springfield, O.—2 persons were injured in Springfield July 29 when firebombs were tossed into 2 homes.

Syracuse, N.Y.—Sporadic disorders took place in Syracuse Aug. 16–19. The disturbances were described as relatively minor —flurries of rock-throwing and window-breaking but little looting and few assaults. 100 persons were arrested, mostly for disorderly conduct, public intoxication and violating the curfew.

According to Bernard Schell, chairman of Crusade for Opportunity, the local antipoverty agency, the disorders were touched off by the arrest of a teenaged Negro Aug. 16 by black Patrolman James Mickel. The youth reportedly failed to respond to the officer's order to "move on." That evening protesting youths gathered outside the antipoverty agency's teenage club. As the agency's director, Theodore Lee, and one of the workers, LeRoy Glenn Wright, 25, a Negro, were trying to persuade the youths to go home, Patrolman Mickel came along and arrested Wright on charges of disorderly conduct. The disorders that ensued, Schell contended, were a direct result of "police brutality," specifically the actions of Mickel and Reilly Harrison, 2 of the 9 Negroes on the city's 380-man force. Lee said Mickel had used his nightstick to choke Wright.

During the night of Aug. 16–17 the police used tear gas to disperse a crowd of about 200 Negroes who stoned patrol cars near police headquarters. Incidents of rock-throwing and bottle-throwing were reported in the south and lower east sides of the city. 2 or 3 fires were reported. By morning 27 persons had been arrested.

In the afternoon Aug. 17 Mayor William F. Walsh imposed an 8 p.m.-to-6 a.m. curfew on the 2 affected sections of the city. 25 Onondaga County sheriff's deputies were called in to maintain order. About 90 deputies in 7 adjacent counties were alerted, and Gov. Nelson A. Rockefeller sent in several state police officials.

In the evening Aug. 17 the police used tear gas and fired gunshots in the air to disperse 100 to 200 Negroes who had gathered outside the curfew area. One policeman was hit in the head by a rock.

Mayor Walsh Aug. 18 announced a 4-hour reduction in the curfew. The city's new police chief, John F. O'Connor, met with 100 to 150 black youths for nearly 2 hours in the afternoon. (O'Connor was to have been sworn in Aug. 22, but he took office Aug. 17 because of the "serious situation.") At the meeting Wright told about his arrest, and O'Connor said he would investigate. Another youth suggested that closed circuit TV be installed in police headquarters to monitor any police brutality. O'Connor said he would request funds for it. The youths, however, rejected O'Connor's proposal to establish a youth patrol.

Walsh lifted the curfew Aug. 20 and said conditions "had returned to normal."

Tampa, Fla.—Violence broke out in Negro sections of Tampa June 11 shortly after police shot and killed a black robbery suspect. The violence, which continued June 12–13, was quelled after city officials enlisted the aid of 100 black youths from the ghetto neighborhoods. In 3 nights of violence a total of 65–80 arrests were reported.   Property damage was estimated at more than $1.5 million.

The outbreak began when Patrolman J. R. Calvert began chasing 3 youths he had discovered robbing the Tampa Photo Supply Co., near Central Avenue, a street of stores and nightclubs bordered by a public housing project.   According to Calvert, the youths refused to stop on command.   He fired 2 warning shots and then shot at one of them, Martin Chambers, 19, a Negro, and hit him in the back.   Chambers was pronounced dead on arrival at the hospital.

Less than 3 hours later crowds had gathered and violence had broken out on Central Avenue and in the housing project.   Policemen and rioters exchanged rifle fire.   The rioters set an entire block afire and looted stores.   A white man, Carl DeWitt, was dragged from his car, beaten and taken hostage by rioters.   Policemen, armed with guns and bayonets, moved with dogs into the area to restore order.   About 20 persons were arrested, 15 were injured; one policeman died of a heart attack.

Gov. Claude R. Kirk Jr. called 500 National Guardsmen to Tampa June 12.   Kirk visited the riot-torn area and asked Negroes to stay in their homes.   Rioting spread, however, June 12 to other black sections.   Firemen in the old Spanish section of Ybor City were forced to call for assistance from police when rioters hurled fire bombs at fire trucks.   Rampaging gangs of youths roamed the streets throwing rocks and setting fires.   Many buildings were entirely destroyed; houses owned by Tampa's Urban Renewal Agency were damaged.   There were reports of sniper fire.   The National Guard was shifted from the Central Avenue section to quell new outbreaks of violence in the Ponce de Leon and College Hill housing projects in the western section of the city.

Robert L. Gilder, president of the Tampa branch of the NAACP, June 12 attributed the rioting to Tampa's unemployment situation and to "police brutality."   (The unemployment rate for Tampa's Negroes, about 16% of the city's population, had remained steady at about 10% for the last 10 years.   The situation had been made worse by job competition from 10,000 Cuban refugees who had come to the city in recent years.)   Gilder said the rioters were anxious to meet with Mayor Nick Nuccio, but, he said, he had not been able to persuade the mayor to come to the area of unrest.

Jim Williams, an assistant football coach at predominantly-black Southern University at Baton Rouge, La., was flown to Tampa from Tallahassee, Fla. June 13. Blake, described as the "only man" with a strong influence over Tampa Negro youths, toured the area for more than 24 hours.

Mayor Nuccio met with black leaders June 13 and refused their demand for suspension of Patrolman Calvert. Tampa's prosecuting attorney ruled June 14 that the shooting of Chambers was justifiable homicide. Chambers' mother filed a $500,000 damage suit against the city and Calvert for her son's death.

Tampa's Commission on Community Relations, at Williams' suggestion, June 14 recruited about 100 black youths aged 15 to 20 to help prevent further violence in the city. The youths, clad in white helmets, patrolled the black residential areas June 14, and no further violence occurred. The Tampa City Council June 15 voted the members of the youth patrol a citation for their role in restoring peace. The National Guard units were sent home June 15. Gov. Kirk met with the youth patrol June 19 to commend its members for their work.

Violence, however, broke out again in Tampa less than 4 weeks later. Black youths roamed the city July 9, throwing firebombs, breaking windows and looting. The disturbances followed false rumors of a police shooting of a black robbery suspect. Mayor Nuccio July 9 imposed an 11:00 p.m. curfew on "anyone 17 years of age and under."

Toledo, O.—Racial disorders broke out in the black section of the near South Side of Toledo July 24–26. Although there were reports of scattered firebombings and vandalism, there were no serious injuries or deaths in the city of 450,000. A 300-man police force was put on duty to quell the disturbances, and 48 persons were arrested during the first night of unrest. About 20 fires were set, causing an estimated $75,000 in property damage.

Gov. James A. Rhodes July 25 ordered 500 National Guardsmen under the command of Maj. Gen. Erin C. Hostetler to standby alert in an armory at the edge of Toledo. The Ohio Highway Patrol set up roadblocks at the nearby Ohio-Michigan state line. Mayor John Potter imposed a 9:00 p.m.-to-6:00 a.m. curfew on all persons under 21 later that day. The sale and display of weapons was prohibited.

At least 7 firebombings were reported late July 25. About 37 persons were arrested. Firebombings and looting continued July 26 and police reportedly arrested 42 persons.

The National Guard units were relieved of standby duty near Toledo July 30.

Washington, D.C.—Arson, vandalism and looting were reported in the black ghetto of northwest Washington Aug. 1. 34 persons—21 adults and 13 juveniles—were arrested. About 50 store windows were reported smashed, and 11 minor fires were reported.

The disorders began at 12:30 a.m. Aug. 1 when firemen fighting a 2-alarm blaze were pelted with rocks and bottles by a crowd of about 400 onlookers. Gangs of youths then began roaming nearby streets, mainly in the Shaw Urban Renewal Area, a mile-square area 8 blocks north of the federal buildings on Constitution Ave. A white soldier was beaten and robbed of $5. The Police Department's Tactical Squad was called in, and order was restored by 5:00 a.m. The 34 arrested persons were charged with disorderly conduct or failing to obey police orders to move on. The Washington Urban League provided $25 bail each for the release of most of those arrested. Julian Dugas, director of the city's Neighborhood Legal Services project, said that the arrests were "inflammatory" because most of those taken were bystanders and not involved in the disturbances.

The city's governing body, the 3-man Board of Commissioners of the District of Columbia, issued a statement Aug. 1 congratulating "the vast majority of our citizens" for their restraint during the "relatively minor disturbance." The commissioners appointed a task force of city officials to study citizens' grievances. The group was headed by James C. Gilman, director of the Community Renewal Office. The commissioners met later the same day with Rufus Mayfield, 20, and a group of 40 other black youths to hear their grievances and demands for the release of those arrested.

The Labor Department Aug. 3 awarded a $300,000 grant to a black youth employment group called Pride, Inc., organized by Mayfield. Mayfield said that Pride, Inc. would hire some 900 youths at $56 a week for a month-long slum clean-up and rat control program in the 10 areas of the city covered by the antipoverty Neighborhood Development Program. (Rep. Joel T. Broyhill [R., Va.] charged Aug. 3 that the Labor Department was "guilty of a . . . deliberate affront to the House and Senate of the U.S. Congress in placing convicted felon Rufus Mayfield in a position of guidance and authority over 900 District of Columbia youths." Mayfield had served 27 months at the Lorton Youth Center for auto theft and a year at the National Training School.)

The city's Department of Sanitation said Aug. 3 that it would provide 434 jobs for youths under a $100,000 federal grant to the Neighborhood Youth Corps.

Waterloo, Ia.—Bands of black youths smashed store windows and set fires in Waterloo July 9 before being dispersed by police. The police quelled the disturbances by sealing off a 12-block area of the black section and imposing a 10 p.m. curfew for "all young persons" July 10. Negroes made up about 8% of the city's population of 75,000.

West Palm Beach, Fla.—Disorders broke out in a 9-block black district of West Palm Beach July 30–31. 2 National Guard units were mobilized to disperse roving gangs of black youths who hurled firebombs, smashed windows and fired shots at police. A firebomb exploded next to a police patrol car, but there were no injuries. One Negro was arrested on charges of carrying concealed weapons and conspiracy to commit arson.

Wilmington, Del.—Negroes rampaged through the West Side district of Wilmington July 28–29, setting fires, looting stores and firing guns. The violence lasted about 4 hours and was restricted to 6 square blocks in the black section. At 2:00 a.m. July 29 Wilmington Mayor John E. Babiarz imposed a 2:30 a.m.-to-6:30 a.m. curfew on the city. 80 to 100 persons, most of them aged 18 to 25, were arrested on charges of looting, disorderly conduct and possession of firearms. 7 injuries from gunshots were reported.

In a special session July 29, the City Council enacted 3 emergency ordinances prohibiting the gathering of 10 or more persons in a public place, the sale of gasoline or other inflammable liquids in containers and the manufacture, use or possession of Molotov cocktails. The police reported a return of order July 30.

Wichita, Kan.—19 persons were arrested in Wichita July 31 during a night of rock throwing and firebombing by bands of black youths. City Commissioner A. Price Woodward, a Negro, acting as mayor in the absence of Mayor Clarence Vollmer, imposed an emergency curfew at 1:00 a.m. Aug. 1. Order was restored by dawn, and the curfew was lifted during the day.

Violence flared again in northeast Wichita Aug. 3–5. 20 Negroes and whites were wounded by shotgun blasts from ambush early Aug. 4. 4 white youths were arrested Aug. 5 and charged with felonious assault for the shooting after 100 Negroes had

threatened to "burn this town down" unless the whites were apprehended. Despite the arrests, 300 Negroes rampaged through the
neighborhood at about 3:00 a.m. Aug. 5. Several policemen suffered cuts when mobs threw rocks and bottles at them, and 2 stores
were reported firebombed. After a special City Council meeting
Aug. 5, Mayor Vollmer imposed a 10 p.m.-to-5 a.m. curfew. A
sniper wounded a pedestrian Aug. 7 and minor fires were reported
throughout the day.

Winston-Salem, N.C.—Racial violence erupted in Winston-
Salem Nov. 2 after the death of a Negro who had been struck by
a white policeman. More than 250 persons were arrested Nov. 2–4
for reasons directly and indirectly related to the disturbances.

The disorders began after the burial of James Eller, 32, a Negro
who had been blackjacked by W. C. Owens, a white policeman.
Owens, who had arrested Eller for public drunkenness, said it was
necessary to subdue Eller by force when he became disorderly.
Owens was charged with murder and suspended.

Gangs of black youths, numbering nearly 500, roving the streets
in small bands late Nov. 2, began setting fires, throwing rocks and
bottles, overturning autos and looting stores. Policemen fired shots
in the air to disperse a crowd of about 100 Negroes who had gathered after dark between white and black sections of the city.

Gov. Daniel K. Moore Nov. 2 ordered 200 National Guardsmen to the troubled city, and a squad of state troopers were sent to
aid police. Nearly 50 persons, including 8 policemen, were injured,
and more than 100 people were arrested. Property damage was
estimated at $350,000.

The Board of Aldermen Nov. 3 granted Mayor M. C. Benton
Jr. emergency powers. At nightfall the mayor imposed an 11 p.m.-
to-dawn curfew. It was also announced that an additional 600 National Guardsmen had been sent to the city and had increased the
combined force of police and guardsmen to 1,200 persons.

Sporadic sniper fire, several trash-basket fires and same looting
were reported Nov. 3, and 20 persons were arrested for curfew violations Nov. 4. But, with order restored, half the National Guardsmen were withdrawn from the city, and the curfew was suspended
Nov. 5.

Wyandanch, N.Y.—Stoning and firebombing were reported to
have broken out Aug. 2–4 in predominantly black Wyandanch, L.I.
(Negroes comprised about 80% of the town's 7,000 residents.)
The fires damaged a car and the auditorium of a school. There

were no reports of gunfire or looting. One arrest was reported Aug. 3, and 7 youths were arrested Aug. 4 on charges of rioting.

Members of a local Young Adult Action Committee held a grievance meeting Aug. 2 with young Negroes who complained of an absence of public transportation and the lack of recreation facilities. Suffolk County Executive H. Lee Dennison met Aug. 4 with black youths to hear their demands for better jobs, education and recreation facilities and more black policemen.

Youngstown, O.—2 buildings were dynamited and 3 others were burned in Youngstown July 22. The destruction was accompanied by disorders in which 3 men were beaten. Of the 7 persons arrested, 2 were Negroes. Leaders of the black community July 27 presented the City Council with a list of demands which included the addition of 25 Negroes to the city's police and fire departments, the creation of a civilian police review board and improvement in city services in the "ghetto neighborhoods." A special City Council committee July 22 had agreed to recommend the demands to the full council.

Campus & High School Disorders

Several colleges and high schools were the scenes of racial violence during 1967. Among developments reported:

Nashville colleges—Negroes rioted in Nashville, Tenn. Apr. 8–10. More than 80 persons were reported arrested and 17 injured, 2 of them by gunfire. The rioting began near the predominantly black Fisk University in the early evening April 8 after police ejected a Negro from the University Dinner Club at the request of the Negro management. Within minutes black students began to picket the club and rioting broke out. The disorder quickly spread to the predominantly black Tennessee A & I State University campus and continued until dawn. Bands of roving youths—students and non-students—threw rocks and bottles at policemen and littered the 2 campuses.

The rioting started less than an hour after the departure of Stokely Carmichael, then chairman of the SNCC (Student Nonviolent Coordinating Committee). Earlier that afternoon Carmichael had attended a symposium at predominantly white Vanderbilt University with the Rev. Dr. Martin Luther King Jr. and Sen. Strom Thurmond (R., S.C.). Carmichael had told a predominantly white audience of about 4,000 persons that for the Negro, black power was the only real alternative to domination by a white society. He said: "Our Negro communities can become either con-centration camps filled with miserable people who have only the power to destroy or they can become organized communities that make a meaningful contribution to our nation. That is the choice." (In an impromptu speech at Fisk Apr. 7, Carmichael had said: "I am nonviolent right now, but if the white man tries to put his arm on me, I am going to break his arm." "If we don't get changes, we are going to tear this country apart.")

(Earlier in the week the *Nashville Banner* had urged Vanderbilt University to withdraw its invitation to Carmichael in view of its dependence on white philanthropists for support. The Tennessee State Senate, a Veterans of Foreign Wars post and 2 American Legion posts approved resolutions in support of the *Banner*'s position. But Nashville's morning *Tennessean* strongly defended Vanderbilt's invitation. It said, "Those who would ban Mr. Carmichael fail to understand the significance of the phenomena that give him stand-ing. . . . The problem is that more than a few people listen to him [Carmichael]. Society needs to find out why.")

Rioting resumed at dusk Apr. 9, and nearly 400 policemen were mobilized to quell the rioters. Negroes fired rifles at passing cars. Policemen were pelted with rocks and bottles, and at one point policemen exchanged rifle fire with snipers. A white-owned grocery store and 2 business buildings were set afire with Molotov cocktails. Roving bands of youths shouted "black power."

2 of Carmichael's aides—George Washington Ware of Atlanta and Ernest Stephens of Tuskegee—and 7 people who reportedly had no connection with SNCC were arrested on incitement charges.

At 4:00 a.m., several blocks away from the rioting, William Reagan, 21, a Negro, was shot and injured in the neck while driving home from a restaurant. Calvin Conners, 19, a student, was shot and injured in the neck during an exchange of gunfire between po-lice and Negro students on the Tennessee A & I campus.

Rioting broke out again at 7:00 p.m. Apr. 10 despite patrolling by student anti-riot squads at Fisk and A & I. Police fired tear gas into rock-throwing mobs of 200–300 A & I students. Quiet was restored by 11:00 p.m.

The Tennessee House of Representatives Apr. 10 adopted a resolution asking the U.S. Immigration & Naturalization Service to deport Carmichael. (Carmichael was born in Trinidad but had automatically become a U.S. citizen when his parents were naturalized.)

The Interdenominational Ministerial Alliance, an organization of black clergymen, called a meeting of police, city officials, ministers, university officials and students Apr. 11 to find ways of averting further violence. They issued a statement asserting that: Carmichael was not "the sole cause" of the rioting. "The real causes ... were in existence long before Carmichael was born."

Dr. James Lawson, acting president of Fisk, charged that most of the rioters were "outside agitators" brought to Nashville by SNCC.

Jackson State College—Negroes rioted on the campus of the all-black Jackson State College May 10–11 in Jackson, Miss. The National Guard was called in and martial law was imposed. One Negro was killed and 2 others were wounded before the rioting ended.

According to Kenneth Dean, director of the Mississippi Council on Human Relations, the rioting began late May 10 "[when] 2 Negro policemen arrested a speeder on the campus and students began pouring from their dorms." He said: "The students seemed to have all of the traditional grievances of Mississippi Negroes but were not rioting over any specific grievance." Police said that 1,500 students, including some from nearby Tougaloo College, joined the rioting. Calm was restored by daybreak.

Jackson Mayor Allen Thompson visited the campus May 11. He succeeded in dispersing a mob of about 500 students after promising to withdraw police from the campus. Earlier in the day, at Thompson's request, Mississippi Gov. Paul B. Johnson Jr. alerted the National Guard.

Minor incidents continued throughout the day, and serious rioting broke out again at about 8:00 p.m. About 100 rioters built a bonfire on Lynch Street, the main street through the campus. Shouting "Hell no! We ain't going!" they rushed a barricade police had set up to seal off the campus. They retreated, throwing rocks and bottles, and hit a state highway patrol investigator on the head. They charged a 2d time, and as they retreated again, the police fired shots into the crowd. Benjamin Brown, 22, a black delivery man, was shot in the back of the head and the lower part of the back. He fell on the sidewalk within 60 yards of the policemen. About 50 Jackson policemen stood by without aiding Brown for more than 10 minutes. Finally Brown was carried away from the scene by Negroes. He was taken by ambulance to the University Hospital, where he died at 5:00 a.m. 2 other Negroes were wounded but not seriously. (The Delta Ministry said May 12 that its investigation showed that Brown was on his way to a restaurant in the area when he was shot.)

Calm was restored with the arrival of 1,200 to 1,400 National Guardsmen.

19 students from Millsaps College marched May 12 from their campus to the City Hall with signs that said "White Students Protest the Murder of Benjamin Brown." More than 300 Negroes marched from a Methodist Church to City Hall in the evening May 12 in protest against the shooting. Black ministers and civil rights leaders said the march had been organized to substitute "nonviolent protest" for the rioting of the past 2 days. Earlier, at a rally at the church, SNCC (Student Nonviolent Coordinating Committee) leaders had urged students to boycott the march and answer violence with violence. At City Hall, however, Charles Evers, Mississippi NAACP director, told the marchers they didn't need SNCC in Jackson and would not gain anything by violence.

Jackson State College Pres. John Peoples said May 12 that 90% of the rioters were "unscrupulous outsiders," not students. Student leaders also attributed the rioting to "intruders—people who have come in and distorted the movement."

The National Guard was removed May 13.

Texas Southern University—One policeman was killed and 2 policemen and a student were wounded in Houston May 16–17 when police and students exchanged rifle fire at Texas Southern University, a predominantly Negro school. 488 students were arrested; 5 of them were indicted June 2 for the slaying.

Sporadic incidents of violence had preceded the rioting. Students had disrupted classes Mar. 28 by barring doors to buildings to protest the administration's refusal to recognize Friends of SNCC as an on-campus organization and to protest the firing of the group's faculty sponsor.

19 Texas Southern students demonstrated May 16 outside the Norwood Junior High School in protest against allegedly unequal punishment meted out to 14 white and black students who had been fighting. The black students reportedly had been suspended for the remainder of the school year, while the whites had been suspended for only 3 days. The Texas Southern students were arrested, fined $1 each and were released.

Another student demonstration was held May 16 at the city garbage dump, situated near a black neighborhood. The pickets said the dump was a health hazard. 45 students were arrested.

About 120 students held an evening rally May 16 on the university campus. More students were asked to picket the Norwood school. Tension was heightened by a rumor, later proved false, that a member of the Ku Klux Klan had shot a black child. During the rally a watermelon was hurled at the car of 4 policemen standing nearby. The policemen arrested a student, Douglas Waller, 21, who, they said, was carrying a pistol.

As the 4 officers drove from the campus, they became the target of stones and bottles. They stopped, and were met with gunshots reportedly fired from Lanier Hall, a freshman dormitory. Patrolman Robert G. Blaylock was wounded in the leg and another policeman, Allen D. Dugger, was wounded in the cheek. Within an hour there were more than 600 policemen in the area and the campus was sealed off.

Members of the crowd hurled bottles of gasoline and set fire to barrels of tar in a street going through the campus. They tried to erect a barricade across the avenue with pieces of metal from a construction site nearby. At this point Police Chief Herman Short conferred with Houston Mayor Louie Welch, who ordered him to clean up "this damned mess." Police then began shooting into Lanier Hall. Press reports indicated that 2,000 to 3,000 shots were fired.

The shooting lasted about 40 minutes, and at about 3:00 a.m. 100 police rushed the dormitory. Louis R. Kuba, 24, a rookie policeman, was shot in the forehead and died 7 hours later. Morris English, 22, a student was wounded in the back.

Police began arresting students and searching the dormitory for arms. They were reported to have totally wrecked the building's interior and furnishings. Mrs. Mattie M. Harbert, Lanier Hall house mother, charged May 17 that police had stepped on her and smashed her personal belongings. The police found one shotgun, a rifle and a pistol. Later May 17 they searched the rooms in the girls' dormitories.

Felony charges were filed May 17 against 5 students for Kuba's death, and bond was set at $10,000. They were indicted June 2. 472 of the arrested students were released after questioning May 18.

Ohio CSU—The Ohio National Guard was called in Nov. 13 to quell violence on the predominantly black campus of Central State University in Wilberforce, O. The school was closed Nov. 14. Before classes were resumed Nov. 27, Dr. Harry E. Groves, 46, a Negro, had announced his resignation as president of the university (effective in 6 months at the expiration of his contract).

The disturbances began Nov. 13 when Michael Warren, 23, a black senior, returned to the campus. He had been suspended Nov. 9 after allegedly threatening to kill Dr. Rembert Stokes, the black president of predominantly black Wilberforce University nearby. Warren had gone to Wilberforce University Nov. 2 to recruit students for a CSU demonstration and reportedly had told Stokes: "When the revolution comes, I will kill you."

When policemen attempted to arrest Warren later Nov. 13, about 30 to 50 students barricaded the entrance to the building in which the youth was attending classes. About 100 sheriff's deputies were sent to the campus but failed to disperse the students. Greene County Sheriff Russell Bradley was summoned to the campus by Dean Charles Flowers, and students squirted a fire extinguisher in his face. Bradley then called for the aid of the National Guard and the Ohio Highway Patrol.

Violence broke out that evening after a student rally. About 100 to 200 students from the rally began throwing bricks and rocks at the police, and 9 policemen were injured. Policemen arrested more than 90 students, many of whom they reportedly dragged kicking and screaming from the dormitories. The students were charged with disorderly conduct and released on bond.

Sidney Davis, president of the county chapter of the NAACP, accused the police Nov. 14 of brutality. He said he saw police "use clubs on students" but didn't intervene because "we can't fight police."

Although "black power" advocates called for a class boycott Nov. 14, the majority of the 2,600 students (80% Negro) reportedly attended classes. 2 students were arrested Nov. 14, one for carrying a concealed weapon, the butt end of a pool cue in his sleeve, and one for failure to produce school identification according to a new Ohio law.

Later Nov. 14 Dr. Groves announced that the deans, the board of trustees and National Guard and Highway Patrol leaders had agreed to close the school until further notice to avert further violence. By 9 p.m. 60% to 70% of the students had left. Groves said Nov. 22 that members of Unity for Unity, the militant black power group that officials blamed for the disorders, would not be expelled from the university because "the university does not wish to suppress legitimate thought." (Groves, announcing his resignation Nov. 25, said he was "prepared for the larger battles" but "disgusted by the trivia." "In this hour of genuine institutional crisis, brought about by elements determined to destroy the university," he said, "I find many students, parents, alumni and faculty members not discussing improvement in developments of the university, or even the really basic issues threatening the life of the institution, but calling upon me to defend an allegation that I changed the route of march for graduation ceremonies and such equally inane charges.")

Philadelphia high schools—More than 3,500 students from 10 predominantly black high schools clashed with more than 400 policemen in Philadelphia Nov. 17 during a demonstration outside the Board of Education's administration building. At least 22 persons were injured, and 57 were arrested.

The students had marched on the building in protest against the "white policy" of the board. Earlier in the week 12 to 16 students had been reported suspended from a technical-vocational high school for participating in a demonstration calling for the inclusion of black history courses in the school curriculum. A Board of Education spokesman said Nov. 17 that they had not been suspended and that the board had promised to start the courses requested.

The students gathered Nov. 17 outside the administration building while a delegation of 30 presented demands that included overall improvement in education, more black teachers and principals and the teaching of black history. At one point policemen attempted to arrest a youth who was standing on top of a car. Students surrounded the policemen, and the disorders followed.

School Board Pres. Richardson Dilworth blamed police for the outbreak. Originally, he said. the police had agreed that only plainclothesmen would be assigned to the demonstration. The trouble began with the arrival of 2 busloads of uniformed policemen, he said. Then, for more than an hour, gangs of youths roamed the streets, smashing car windows, throwing rocks and assaulting passers-by. Newsmen, clergymen, office workers and others said that policemen used nightsticks on the youths.

At a rally Nov. 19, the NAACP called for the removal of Police Commissioner Frank L. Rizzo, 46, for allegedly improper police actions in quelling the rioting. Community Legal Services, Inc., a federally financed legal aid group, filed suit Nov. 21 against city officials on charges that black youths had been deprived of their rights. The suit proposed that the police department be placed in the hands of a receiver. Mayor James H. J. Tate pledged Nov. 22

to support Rizzo. He appointed a 3-man committee to investigate racial unrest and charges of police brutality.

8 adults and 3 juveniles sued in U.S. District Court Nov. 24 for an injunction to bar Tate, Rizzo and other officials from arresting participants in the rallies. They asked the court to order the defendants to halt the "harassment of the plaintiffs and all others in their class who seek to improve the quality of education and the dignity of public school students in Philadelphia."

The Pennsylvania Human Relations Commission Dec. 20 ordered the Philadelphia Board of Education to integrate faculties in the city's 275 public schools by Sept. 1969.

Chicago schools—Fighting between white and black students broke out in the cafeteria of the Waller High School in Chicago's Near North Side Nov. 21. The clashes spread to 2 other schools. At least 12 persons were injured and 84 arrested. The fighting reportedly followed a false rumor that white youths had pushed a black youth into the path of an elevated train. Fighting spread to the school's corridors and outside to the playground areas. Within an hour school officials closed the school. Some rioters then marched to 2 nearby schools, hurling bricks and stones and setting off fire alarms as they went. Police reinforcements were sent in to stop the more than 2,000 rioting students. Order was restored by 8 p.m.

Bombings & Arson

Bombs and fire were also used in violent racial incidents during 1967. In one of the year's first such incidents, fire destroyed a Negro church in Collins, Miss. Jan. 21. The church had been used in the federal Head Start Program. The Vincent Chapel A.M.E. Church, a black church in Grenada, Miss., was damaged by fire Mar. 4. It had served as headquarters for the Southern Christian Leadership Conference. Grenada Police Commissioner Paul McKelroy said the fire was "definitely not" arson.

Wharlest Jackson, 36, a black active in civil rights, was killed in Natchez, Miss. Feb. 27 when a bomb exploded in his truck as he was driving home from work at the Armstrong Tire & Rubber Co. plant. This was the 2d bombing aimed at a black employe of the Natchez plant. (Pres. George Metcalfe of the Natchez NAACP had been injured Aug. 27, 1965 by a bomb in his car.)

The explosion, which occurred shortly after 8:00 p.m., about 3 blocks from the plant, destroyed the truck. Jackson, the father of 6 children, a Korean War veteran and treasurer of the Natchez chapter of the NAACP, had been employed at the plant since Jan. 1955. Recently he had been promoted to mixer, a job held previously only by whites.

(A protest rally was held in Natchez in the afternoon of Feb. 28 as anger at Jackson's murder mounted, and Mississippi NAACP field director Charles Evers threatened a national boycott of Armstrong tires. He charged that the company had "harbored" members of the Ku Klux Klan "for a long time." He said that since his brother Medgar had been murdered in 1963, 41 Negroes had been killed in Mississippi. Nearly 2,000 Negroes demonstrated without incident outside the Armstrong plant gates the evening of Feb. 28. Demonstrators marched from a nearby church to a paved parking lot outside the gates Mar. 1 during a shift change. About 25 Natchez policemen formed a line between the workers who filed in and out of the plant and the demonstrators. Evers and local ministers led about 1,600 Negroes in a silent protest march through Natchez the evening of Mar. 1.

(White Natchez community leaders including Adams County Sheriff Odell Anders, Natchez Mayor John J. Nosser and Natchez Police Chief J. T. Robinson met with about 700 Negroes at the Beulah Baptist Church Mar. 2 to inform them of the progress of their investigation. Nosser said the murder had brought the people of Natchez together for the first time in biracial meetings, and he called this "the beginning of a new era."

(Evers led about 1,000 Negroes in a 2d silent march through Natchez Mar. 4, and NAACP executive director Roy Wilkins Mar. 5 led a motorcade of 25 cars 125 miles from Jackson, Miss. to Natchez to attend Jackson's funeral. At a news conference later Mar. 5, Wilkins said moderation was becoming "noticeable" in rural Mississippi: "These killings are the tail end, we believe.")

Fire destroyed a former Episcopal church in Hayneville, Miss. Mar. 12. The building had served as headquarters for the Lowndes County Christian Movement for Human Rights, Inc., an antipoverty organization.

The Head Start office in Liberty, Miss., serving 3 counties in Southwest Mississippi, was severely damaged by a bomb explosion Mar. 13.

The Macedonia Baptist Church, a Negro church in Fort Deposit, Ala., was destroyed by fire Mar. 13.

A bomb exploded in Montgomery, Ala. Apr. 25 outside the home of Mrs. Frank M. Johnson Sr., mother of U.S. District Court Judge Frank M. Johnson Jr. Judge Johnson was a member of a 3-judge panel that had ordered the statewide desegregation of Alabama schools by the fall. Mrs. Johnson, an elderly widow, was not injured. The blast loosened the foundations of a car port and knocked out windows. Gov. Lurleen Wallace Apr. 26 offered a $5,400 reward for aid in catching the bombers.

STRUGGLE AGAINST VIOLENCE

The President, Congress, federal and local officials, black leaders and troubled citizens throughout the U.S. expressed deep concern at the racial violence battering the nation's cities. Action on various levels was started to provide means of halting riots, to make such outbreaks less likely and to correct the inequities that many believed to be the major cause of violence. In specific cases, however, observers indicated a belief that a preoccupation with politics was the basis for efforts to assess blame for the disturbances.

Pres. Johnson went Mar. 2 to Howard University in Washington, where he told students and teachers that he had "come back . . . [to the university] to renew my commitment," the pledge he had made in a June 1965 speech at Howard to work for equal opportunity for Negroes. Appearing unannounced at Howard's 100th anniversary celebration, the President said: "Tomorrow's problems . . . will not be divided into 'Negro problems' and 'white problems.' There will be only human problems, and more than enough to go around."

Legislative Action

An omnibus civil rights bill entitled the Civil Rights Act of 1967 was sent to Congress with a special message by Pres. Johnson Feb. 15. In what appeared to be an effort to win passage of at least part of the President's proposals, Congressional leaders divided the omnibus plan among several separate bills so that each group of proposals could be judged and acted on according to its merits. Despite this maneuver, no major part of Johnson's program won Congressional approval during 1967. When the year ended, most of the bills were still tied up in committee.

In his Feb. 15 message, Johnson said the goals of his proposed rights act would be to end housing bias by 1969, to strengthen "existing federal criminal laws against interference with federal rights," to prevent discrimination in the selection of juries, to authorize the Equal Employment Opportunity Commission to issue cease-and-desist orders, to extend the life of the U.S. Commission on Civil Rights and to increase appropriations for the Community Relations Service by 90%—from $1.4 million to $2.7 million in fiscal 1968.

The housing proposals would have imposed an immediate bar against discrimination in the 3% or 4% of the nation's homes already covered by federal executive orders. The anti-bias ban would be extended Jan. 1, 1968 to real estate developments and large apartment houses (30% or 40% of all homes). The ban would be extended Jan. 1, 1969 to cover all housing. Under the proposed act, the Housing & Urban Development (HUD) Secretary would be required to seek voluntary solutions in cases of discrimination. But administrative hearings would be held on complaints, and cease-and-desist orders could be issued in case of continued violations. Federal suits could be initiated to break up suspected patterns of discrimination.

The act would make it a federal crime to interfere with anyone exercising a civil right guaranteed by federal law. It would also bar violence or threats to keep anyone from exercising a civil right. Victims would be permitted to institute civil suits for damages or for relief by injunction.

(Prior to the submission of the message, the President, HUD Secy. Robert C. Weaver, Health Education & Welfare Secy. John W. Gardner and Acting Atty. Gen. Ramsey Clark had conferred with civil rights leaders at the White House Feb. 13. The rights leaders included Clarence M. Mitchell of the NAACP; Whitney M. Young Jr., executive director of the National Urban League; the Rev. Walter E. Fauntroy of the Southern Christian Leadership Conference; the Most Rev. Patrick A. O'Boyle, Roman Catholic archbishop of Washington; the Rev. Theodore M. Hesburgh, president of Notre Dame University and member of the U.S. Civil Rights Commission; Mrs. Dorothy Height, president of the National Council of Negro Women; Andrew Biemiller of the AFL-CIO. In a Lincoln's Birthday address at the Lincoln Memorial in Washington Feb. 12, Johnson had hailed the "commanding clarity in Lincoln's belief that no man can truly live in creative equality when society imposes the irrational spiritual poverty of discrimination on any man.")

A major group of anti-riot proposals was incorporated in a non-Administration bill (HR421) to make it a federal crime to cross state lines or to use interstate facilities to incite a riot. HR421 was passed by the House July 19 and sent to the Senate by 347–70 vote (167 D. & 180 R. vs. 66 D. & 4 R.). The Senate Judiciary Committee held hearings on the measure Aug. 2–30, but the Senate took no action on the bill during 1967.

HR421 would provide penalties of up to $10,000 fine and 5 years in prison, or both. Rep. William C. Cramer (R., Fla.), author of the bill, said it was "aimed at those professional agitators" who traveled from city to city to "inflame the people . . . to violence and then leave the jurisdiction before the riot begins." Many similar speeches were delivered in an emotional 5-hour debate preceding the vote for passage. House Rules Committee Chairman William M. Colmer (D., Miss.) called the riots "an organized conspiracy . . . backed by the Communists." Unless it were checked, he said, we "are going to have a nationwide state of anarchy."

The legislation had not been requested by the Administration. It was opposed by Rep. Emanuel Celler (D., N.Y.), chairman of the House Judiciary Committee, who said he considered the bill "a futile gesture, neither preventive nor curative." "The basic disorder," he said, "is the discontent of the Negro," and the bill "will not allay his anger and frustrations" but "arouse" them "more deeply." Rep. Frank Thompson Jr. (D., N.J.) July 19 called the measure "a bill of attainder aimed at one man—Stokely Carmichael," ex-chairman of the Student Nonviolent Coordinating Committee.

The Senate Judiciary Committee, chaired by Sen. James O. Eastland (D., Miss.), opened hearings on HR421 Aug. 2. Among developments at those hearings:

Aug. 2—The first witnesses heard by the committee were police officials of Cambridge, Md., Cincinnati and Nashville, Tenn., all recently the scenes of racial disorders. All of the witnesses deplored the role of outside agitators in inciting riots in their cities. The Cambridge police chief, Brice Kinnamon, said that the "sole reason" for the Cambridge riot was an inflammatory speech made by H. Rap Brown, chairman of the Student Nonviolent Coordi-

nating Committee (SNCC). Kinnamon produced a tape recording of Brown
urging Cambridge blacks to burn and kill. Brown and ex-SNCC Chairman
Stokely Carmichael were named by Capt. John A. Sarace of the Nashville
police force as organizers of his city's April riots. Cincinnati Police Chief
Jacob W. Schott told the committee that the anti-riot bill "would help in
curbing those people who move around causing these problems."

Some members of the Judiciary Committee spoke out against the proposed anti-riot legislation. Sen. Philip A. Hart (D., Mich.) said that the
bill "and 97 more like it would not have stopped [the riot in] Detroit." Sen.
Sam J. Ervin Jr. (D., N.C.) said it served as "a manifestation of Congress's
outrage" but was impractical because "it defines a crime which can hardly
be proved by evidence." Sen. Edward M. Kennedy (D., Mass.) said that
the bill "may constitute a fraud on the American people" by giving the impression that Congress had taken effective action against the riots.

Aug. 3—Nashville Police Capt. John Sarace testified that Fred Brooks,
20, chairman of SNCC's Nashville unit and a black power advocate, was
operating a "liberation school" where "pure unadulterated hatred for the
white race" was taught. He said that Brooks had access to federal antipoverty funds as director of the OEO-financed North Nashville Student Summer Project. OEO officials denied that Brooks was on the agency's payroll
but conceded that a car leased in Nashville with antipoverty funds could
have been available to Brooks.

2 Plainfield, N.J. police officials told the committee that recent riots in
Plainfield were directed by an outside source, but they could not name the
source.

Aug. 4—The Rev. J. Paschall Davis, 59, chairman of Nashville's Metropolitan Action Commission (MAC), denied Sarace's charges against the "liberation school." He said that MAC, which he described as an arm of the
countywide metropolitan government, had made contracts to pay $7,700
($5,846 from the Office of Economic Opportunity and the remainder from
private funds) for 7 summer projects. One of these was with St. Anselm's
Episcopal Church for the "liberation school." The school was begun June 21
with an enrollment of 75–100 black pupils aged 5–12. The school's purpose
was to teach Negro history, art, English and mathematics. (Brooks had said
the purpose of the school was to "offset 400 years of negative teaching about
black people.") Davis told the committee that payments had been withheld
from the school pending clearance by a 5-member Monitoring & Evaluation
Committee established to enforce federal regulations in the antipoverty program. He said that the only expenses incurred by MAC for the summer
project were for the leasing of a station wagon used by Brooks and for the
purchase of a few supplies.*

---

* In a telegram to Sen. Eastland, chairman of the committee, Davis said
Aug. 8 that his testimony was "not exactly correct." He said that he had
discovered that MAC had agreed July 25 to pay $20 a week to house 4
women—2 teachers and 2 aides in the "liberation school"—and that one was
a SNCC member. The "liberation school" was suspended Aug. 11 on the
recommendation of the Monitoring & Evaluation Committee. The Right
Rev. John W. Vander Horst, Episcopal bishop of Tennessee, ordered the
school removed from St. Anselm's Chapel Episcopal Center. He said: "It
is the judgment of the bishops of the Episcopal Diocese of Tennessee that the

Aug. 11—Washington, D.C. Police Chief John Layton said that "at the moment I have no indication of any violent planned outbreak in the city," but "we've made plans and engaged in training." He named only one local militant group that he considered a possible threat to the peace—the small Black Man's Volunteer Army of Liberation.

Aug. 21—Dr. Nathan Cohen of the University of California opposed the bill, advocated a long-range approach and urged Congress to "face up to what the issue really is rather than to rush in with easy answers." "What is needed on their [Negroes'] part is a sense of integrity on our part," he said. "I don't think integration is the name of the game any more," he declared. "They are more interested in job opportunity, security and housing."

Aug. 22—John A. McCone, ex-director of the Central Intelligence Agency, told the Senators: "I feel very deeply that unless we answer this problem it is going to split our society irretrievably and destroy our country." "The temptation is to say this is hopeless, but I think we have to stay at the job until we find the answer." The anti-riot legislation might be helpful in some circumstances, inasmuch as riots could be suppressed by proper police power. But "what worries me about this is the climate that might prevail in the country for several years. That would be tragic." His study of the Watts area indicated that job and training programs had "partial success" but that a long-range effort was needed, especially in education, with emphasis on "permanent Head Start programs" and smaller classes in the programs.

Aug. 23—Testimony was taken from Norris Morrow, 26, leader of a Tampa, Fla. Negro youth group (the White Hats) that had helped avert a street disorder in June, and Rufus (Catfish) Mayfield, 20, leader of Washing-

---

curriculum of the school apparently deals with and teaches something quite contrary to our Christian heritage of reconciliation and love in the Lord." The school held classes Aug. 16 in Watkins Park in the predominantly black section of Nashville. After the classes park officials told school leaders that a permit was required for public gatherings in the park. When school officials applied for a permit for Mondays, Wednesdays and Fridays through Sept. 1, they were told that the Metropolitan Park Board would not meet until Sept. 6 to consider the request. The Board, however, issued a permit Aug. 24. George Washington Ware, 27, SNCC field worker, was arrested in Nashville Aug. 22 on charges of sedition after he had appeared at an Aug. 21 meeting of the "liberation school." Ware said at the school meeting: "Black people should achieve power by any means necessary, including violence." Ware was arrested on the complaint of 2 Nashville lawyers, State Rep. Charles Galbreath (D.) and Jack Kershaw, a former White Citizens Council member. He was charged with "advocating the overthrow of the government of the U.S. and the State of Tennessee by seizure of political, social and economic power by any means, including violence." Ware was released from jail Aug. 25 on $5,000 bond. The Davidson County (Tenn.) grand jury began an investigation Aug. 28 and cleared Ware of the sedition charges Aug. 29. (Ware had told newsmen in Nashville Aug. 21 that "if they [the white establishment] kill off our leaders, we will kill off their leaders—the Lyndon Johnsons and the Gen. Westmorelands"; if Stokely Carmichael should be killed, Ware warned, Pres. Johnson "had better not stick his head out of doors again ever.")

ton's Pride, Inc., a group of Negro youths working to clean up ghetto neighborhoods. Mayfield opposed the bill.

Aug. 30—Firemen and their representatives urged protection of the law for firemen fighting fires during riots. Secy.-Treasurer Albert E. Albertoni of the AFL-CIO International Association of Fire Fighters reported on a survey showing that 418 firemen had been injured and 4 killed while fighting fires in 8 cities torn by riots. He said the Los Angeles County Fire Department had reported "692 incidents of harassment and attacks [on firemen] since the Watts riot of 1965. In many instances when an incendiary fire is set the building is also booby-trapped" with the intenton of injuring or killing fire-fighters. Similar harassment was reported in other cities.

Dr. John P. Spiegel, director of the Center for the Study of Violence at Brandeis University, named Cleveland, Dayton and Akron, O., Pittsburgh, San Francisco and Boston as cities in which riots might occur.

In an action later denounced as racist, the House refused by 207–176 vote July 20 to consider an Administration bill for a $40 million program to exterminate rats in urban slums. Voting against consideration of the bill were 148 R. & 59 D. Voting for it were 154 D. & 22 R. Instead of enacting the bill, Rep. James A. Haley (D., Fla.) suggested, "let's buy a lot of cats and turn them loose." Rep. H. R. Gross (R., Ia.) joked about "a rat corps" presided over by "a high commissioner of rats." But the laughter provoked by these and similar remarks ended after Rep. Martha W. Griffiths (D., Mich.) pointed out that "rats are a living cargo of death, and you think it's funny." Rats had killed more people "than all the generals in history," she said. A protest was also voiced by Rep. Theodore R. Kupferman (R., N.Y.), who contrasted the bill's defeat with the House's approval July 19 of the anti-riot bill. "Seldom does one find such inconsistency in such a short period," he said. "Yesterday you voted to establish federal supremacy to suppress violence. Today you voted to incite violence. If you . . . came home at night to find one of your children being bitten by a rat, you might very well start a small riot of your own."

The defeat of the rat-control program was denounced by Pres. Johnson later July 20 as a "cruel blow to the poor children of America." He said that only a "small" amount of money was needed for the program, but "the stakes—the health of our children and of every city dweller—are very great." "We're spending federal funds to protect our livestock from rodents and predatory animals," he said. "The least we can do is give our children the same protection that we give our livestock."

Several of the President's proposals formed the basis of an amended Administration bill (HR2516) to defend persons exercising federally protected civil rights. HR2516 was passed by the House

Aug. 16 by 326–93 vote (165 D. & 161 R. vs. 68 D. & 25 R.). The measure then went to the Senate, where a revised version was approved by the Senate Judiciary Committee Oct. 25, but floor consideration was postponed until 1968 under threat of a filibuster.

The bill, which would protect civil rights workers, had been amended in the House to prohibit interference with policemen or firemen performing their duty during a riot. Proposed by Rep. Jim Wright (D., Tex.), the amendment was accepted by voice vote. Another amendment, suggested by Rep. Fletcher Thompson (R., Ga.), to exempt from criminal prosecution under HR2516 law officers lawfully carrying out their duties or enforcing lawful ordinances and laws, was approved by 74–42 vote. A further change, adopted by voice vote, provided that the "speech and peaceful assembly" rights protected under HR2516 did not extend to inciting to riot. This amendment was proposed by Rep. Cramer (R., Fla.) to keep the bill from preventing prosecutions under the anti-riot bill (HR421) passed previously by the House.

One amendment accepted by voice vote was suggested by the Justice Department and proposed by House Judiciary Committee Chairman Celler (D., N.Y.). It would require these 2 elements for prosecution: charges that a defendant acted on account of (1) the victim's race, color, religion, political affiliation or national origin and (2) the victim's participation in one of the activities protected by the bill. But the House rejected by 90–90 vote Rep. Albert W. Watson's (R., S.C.) proposal to protect the civil rights of businessmen under the bill.

Celler Aug. 15 called for passage of HR2516 as a way to alleviate "Negro despair." He said HR2516 and the anti-riot bill "are the reverse and obverse of the same coin."

A bill (HR10805) extending the life of the Commission on Civil Rights through Jan. 31, 1973 was passed by the Senate Nov. 30 and House Dec. 5 and was signed by Pres. Johnson Dec. 14. The annual authorization was limited to $2,650,000, the amount of the fiscal 1968 appropriation.

Republicans Blame Administration

The Republican Coordinating Committee charged July 24 that "widespread rioting and violent civil disorder have grown to a national crisis since the present Administration took office." The committee, in a statement on the growth of urban disorders, warned that "we are rapidly approaching a state of anarchy, and the President has totally failed to recognize the problem. Worse, he has vetoed legislation and opposed other legislation designed to re-establish peace and order within the country."

The statement said that "when city after city across the nation is overwhelmed by riots, looting, arson and murder which mount-ing evidence indicates may be the result of organized planning and execution on a national scale, the federal government must accept its national responsibility" for the situation. It said that "factories for the manufacture of Molotov cocktails have been uncovered by the police," "simultaneous fires have been started in widely sep-arated areas upon the . . . outbreak of rioting" and "public and private meetings of riot organizers from many sections of the coun-try have been repeatedly reported in the press." The committee called on the President to back a GOP proposal for "full-scale in-vestigation of civil disorders" and "Republican legislation designed to prevent rioting."

Making public the statement, the GOP Congressional leaders, Sen. Everett M. Dirksen (Ill.) and Rep. Gerald R. Ford (Mich.), told newsmen that the Republican legislation cited by the document was a D.C. anti-crime bill vetoed in 1966 and the bill, making it a federal crime to cross state lines to incite a riot, recently passed by the House but opposed by U.S. Atty. Gen. Ramsey Clark as ineffective.

Dirksen said there were unproved indications that "there is a timetable" to the rioting. Dirksen said he had information about the existence of a Molotov cocktail factory in New York, but he refused all details when asked whether a factory was needed to make the firebombs. Ford, asked who might be responsible for organization of the rioting, named Stokely Carmichael.

Also present at the meeting of the Coordinating Committee were GOP Chairman Ray C. Bliss and ex-Pres. Dwight D. Eisen-hower. The statement was written by ex-N.Y. Gov. Thomas E. Dewey, Gov. John A. Love (Colo.) and Rep. William C. Cramer (Fla.). Committee members not attending included Gov. George Romney (Mich.), Gov. Nelson Rockefeller (N.Y.), ex-Vice Pres. Richard M. Nixon and ex-Sen. Barry Goldwater (Ariz.).

The committee's statement was denounced as "irresponsible" July 27 by Sen. Thruston B. Morton (Ky.), a former GOP national chairman. Morton deplored the committee's attempt "to fix the blame for a national tragedy" on the President, but he said he equally deplored "the equivocation of the President who sought to derail a potential political opponent at the expense of the people of Detroit." Describing the outbreak of rioting as "the worst domestic crisis since the Civil War," Morton said: "For the love of heaven, let's get this out of the political arena." Morton proposed that a $1 billion "anti-riot chest" be created to make available funds to mayors, without restrictions, for housing, welfare, education and antipoverty programs.

House Speaker John W. McCormack (D., Mass.) said July 24, after conferring with the President, that Pres. Johnson had told party leaders that "public order is the first business of government" but that the riots must not become "an excuse to turn our backs on the evils of poverty and illiteracy, unemployment and despair that are so deeply rooted in our substandard areas across the nation."

Congress Members Urge Probes

Congressional leaders of both parties called July 25 for an investigation of the continued civil disorders. A Republican proposal, introduced in both houses, called for a joint Congressional committee to study (1) the causes of the riots, (2) the ability of police forces to cope with the riots, and (3) evidence of "any [riot] conspiracy" or involvement in the unrest by "any Communist or other subversive organizations."

Senate GOP leader Everett M. Dirksen, sponsor of the proposal, said he wanted the investigation "to see if there is a touch of Red" behind the riots. In the House, GOP leader Gerald R. Ford said: "I can't help but believe that there is in the background some national plan" in the disorders.

Senate Democratic leader Mike Mansfield (Mont.) said July 25 that he did not want an inquiry to become a "political football" and that he preferred that a Presidential commission be formed to look into the unrest.

Mansfield suggested that Congress could make a more meaningful contribution to the situation by acting on Administration proposals for fighting crime and poverty and for gun control. Mansfield Aug. 1 called political remarks about the rioting "demeaning and utterly useless." A major inquiry into the urban riots was scheduled for the Senate Permanent Subcommittee on Investigations, of which Sen. John L. McClellan (D., Ark.) was chairman. The decision to have the subcommittee investigate was made Aug. 1 by the Senate Rules Committee, which had received 5 pro-

posals for investigations.   Sen. John Sherman Cooper (R., Ky.)
urged that the investigation specifically be focused on "economic
and social" factors involved in the riots.   The Rules Committee
rejected Cooper's suggestion by 6–2 vote, but it did direct the Mc-
Clellan panel to search for the "immediate and long-standing
causes" of the riots.

Rep. Edwin E. Willis (D., La.), chairman of the House Committee on Un-American Activities, said July 26 that committee investigators had detected the involvement of "subversive influences"
in some riots.   He announced Aug. 2 that his committee would
search for "evidence of organized subversion precipitating, exploit-
ing and prolonging the riots."   (At a hearing held May 2 by the
Senate Internal Security Subcommittee, Detective Sgt. John Ung-
vary of the Cleveland police force testified that the 1966 Cleveland
riots had been planned and ignited by black nationalist groups and
that there was evidence of "Communist influence" and "exploitation" of the riots.)

Testimony on the background and reasons for the riots was also
heard by other Congressional hearings already in progress:

● Sen. Robert F. Kennedy (D., N.Y.), appearing before the Senate Committee on Banking & Currency July 25 to discuss his proposed slum-housing
program, referred to the "bonus army" of World War I veterans and said:
"Today the army of the dispossessed and disenchanted sits, not just in Washington, but in every major city, in every region and section of the country."
Urban plight "is rapidly becoming the gravest domestic crisis since the War
Between the States."   "Those who break the law and shatter the peace must
know that swift justice will be done and effective punishment meted out for
their deeds.   No grievance, no sense of injustice, however deep, can excuse
the wanton killing of other Americans—whether they are policemen or firemen doing their duty or innocent bystanders in the streets of their city."
● Ex-Asst. Labor Secy. Daniel P. Moynihan, director of the Joint Center of
Urban Affairs at Harvard and the Massachusetts Institute of Technology, told
a Senate Government Research subcommittee July 27 that the current rioting had been foreshadowed by the emergence several years ago of an "urban
lower class," which was a social, not a racial, phenomenon.   Nothing was
done about it, he said, because: (1) "The Negro leadership and organization
did not want to talk about these problems.   It was a painful subject for them.
Also, they probably did not know much about it."   (2) "This country still
has a strong persistent streak of racism in it," and whites who were not racist
"adjust to live with it."   (3) "Washington is a Southern middle class city
with a bureaucracy that is Southern and middle class" and "is uncomfortable
dealing with problems in the North and dealing with Negroes who don't act
like Negroes do in the South."
● OEO Director Sargent Shriver told the House Education & Labor Committee July 31 that "all America is responsible for the riots.   All of us here
in this room.   We are all actors in this American tragedy."   Shriver re-

minded the committee that he had warned in 1966 that Congressional restrictions and reductions in OEO spending would have "great and grave"
effects. "God knows it has been," he declared. "My belief is America is
waiting for something to be done. What we are asking for is the minimum.
I am tired of discussing these things over and over. We ought to get out of
here and go to work," he said.

(Sen. Robert C. Byrd [D., W. Va.] asserted July 25 that "brutal
force" should be used, if necessary, to contain urban riots. He said
adult looters should be "shot on the spot.")

Black Leaders Seek End to Riots

4 black rights leaders appealed in a joint statement July 26 for
an end to the riots in ghettos. The 4 leaders, all of them political
moderates, were the Rev. Dr. Martin Luther King Jr., president of
the Southern Christian Leadership Conference, A. Philip Randolph,
president of the A. Philip Randolph Institute, Roy Wilkins,
NAACP executive director, and Whitney M. Young Jr., executive
director of the National Urban League.

Their statement said: "Riots have proved ineffective, disruptive
and highly damaging to the Negro population, to the civil rights
cause and to the entire nation." "Killing, arson, looting are criminal acts and should be dealt with as such. Equally guilty are those
who incite, provoke and call specifically for such action. There is
no justice which justifies the present destruction of the Negro community and its people. We are confident that the overwhelming majority of the Negro community joins us in opposition to violence in
the streets."

The statement was also critical of the stand taken on the riot
problem by whites and Congress. White Americans, it said, were
"not blameless" because they generally supported restrictions
against Negroes. The 90th Congress, it said, had "exhibited an incredible indifference to the hardships of the ghetto dwellers."

Wilkins June 16 had sent "red alert" messages to the NAACP's
1,500 chapters throughout the country, calling on them to act to
prevent riots and keep the summer cool." The message listed the following general goals: (1) "We want jobs, especially for our youth."
(2) "We want more recreation, more sports, more play areas." (3)
"We want not only antipoverty jobs but activity by people in the
communities on antipoverty projects." (4) "We want the police to
maintain law and order, but with their heads, not their guns." (5)
"We want Congress to pass the 1967 Civil Rights Bill."

A call for an end to the rioting was sounded July 26 by Bayard Rustin, executive secretary of the Randolph Institute. He warned that continued rioting could be "a threat to all civil liberties" and could result in "unconstitutional laws of repression," "a fantastic backlash from white people" and "a fantastic backlash in Congress." "The effect on the [black] leadership could be devastating," he said. "The movement could be destroyed and the leadership passed over to the hands of the destructive elements in the ghettos."

Martin Luther King attacked Congress July 26 as having "created the atmosphere for these riots." He warned Congress July 28 that "the long summer of riots have been caused by the long winters of delay" on social development legislation. In Charleston, S.C. July 30, King called upon the federal government to alleviate black unemployment by programs to expand postal service to 3 deliveries a day, to expand hospital employment and to "give every schoolteacher a teacher's aide."

President Orders Investigation

A Special Advisory Commission on Civil Disorders was appointed by Pres. Johnson July 27 to "investigate the origins of the recent disorders in our cities." The commission was to make recommendations to him, Congress, the state governors and mayors for ways "to prevent or contain such disasters in the future." The President announced the appointment of the commission during a televised address to the nation on the riots.

In his address, the 2d in 3 days on the problem of racial violence, Johnson appealed for "an attack—mounted at every level —upon the conditions that breed despair and . . . violence." He proclaimed Sunday, July 30, a National Day of Prayer for Peace & Reconciliation and announced that he was ordering new training standards for riot-control procedures for National Guard units across the country.

The President said that the nation had "endured a week such as no nation should live through; a time of violence and tragedy." He declared that "the looting and arson and plunder and pillage which have occurred are not part of a civil rights protest." "There is no American right" to loot or burn or "fire rifles from the rooftops," he declared. "That is crime," "and crime must be dealt with forcefully and swiftly and, certainly, under law." "The criminals

L. W. NIXON LIBRARY
BUTLER COUNTY COMMUNITY JUNIOR COLLEGE
Haverhill Road at Towanda Avenue
EL DORADO, KANSAS 67042

79-929

who committed these acts of violence against the people deserve to be punished—and they must be punished," he said.

Those in public responsibility, Johnson said, had "an immediate" job "to end disorder" by using "every means at our command —through local, through police and state officials, and, in extraordinary circumstances, where local authorities have stated that they cannot maintain order with their own resources—then, through federal authority that we have limited authority to use." He said that public officials must help "bring about a peaceful change in America," and he warned officials that "if your response to these tragic events is only business-as-usual, you invite not only disaster but dishonor."

Declaring that "the violence must be stopped—quickly, finally and permanently" and pledging that "we will stop it," Johnson said "it would compound the tragedy, however, if we should settle for order that's imposed by the muzzle of a gun." "We seek peace . . . based on one man's respect for another man, and upon mutual respect for law," he said. He called for "steady progress in meeting the needs of all of our people." "The only genuine, long-range solution" to the problem of racial violence, Johnson said, was in a multi-level attack on the conditions that bred the violence—"ignorance, discrimination, slums, poverty, disease, not enough jobs."

Johnson reviewed the legislation enacted within the past 3½ years in the areas of civil rights, urban aid, health, education and antipoverty action. He urged the enactment of the Administration's "safe streets" and gun-control bills pending in Congress. He deplored the recent defeat in the House of his request for a rat-control program, the reduction of his request for model-cities funds and the reasoning of those who opposed educational and housing aid for poverty areas. "Theirs is a strange system of bookkeeping," he said.

It was a time, Johnson said, not for "angry reaction" but for "action, starting with legislative action to improve the life in our cities. The strength and the promise of the law are the surest remedies for tragedy in the streets." The President warned that "there is a danger that the worst toll of this tragedy will be counted in the hearts of Americans—in hatred, in insecurity, in fear, in heated words which will not end the conflict, but will rather prolong it." He said "most Americans—Negro and white"—were "leading decent, responsible and productive lives" and seeking "safety in their neighborhoods and harmony with their neighbors." "Let us condemn the violent few," he declared, and "remember that it is law-abiding Negro families who have really suffered most at the hands of the rioters." Those "who are tempted by violence" should "think again," he said. "Who is really the loser when violence comes? . . . There are no victors in the aftermath of violence." He stressed that there would be "no bone, or . . . reward, or . . . salute for those who have inflicted . . . suffering."

Johnson named Illinois Gov. Otto Kerner (D.) to head the new commission. New York Mayor John V. Lindsay (R.) was named vice chairman. Other members (all appointments effective July 27): Sen. Fred R. Harris (D., Okla.); Sen. Edward W. Brooke (R., Mass.); Rep. James C. Corman (D., Calif.); Rep. William M. McCulloch (R., O.); Pres. I. W. Abel of the AFL-CIO United Steelworkers; Charles B. Thornton, president and board chairman of Litton Industries; Roy Wilkins, executive director of the NAACP; Katherine Graham Peden, commissioner of commerce of Kentucky; Herbert Jenkins, chief of police of Atlanta, Ga. (Washington attorney David Ginsburg, 55, was named by the President July 31 to serve as executive director of the new commission. Richard M. Scammon, former director of the Census Bureau, was appointed a research consultant to the commission Aug. 2. Theodore A. Jones, a Negro and director of the Illinois Revenue Department, was named by the panel Aug. 1 as staff director.)

Kerner said July 28 that the commission had been asked "to probe into the soul of America." He pledged a thorough study of the problem and a fair hearing for all sides, but he warned that "there is no room in America for any provocateurs who would wish to change the course of our democracy, aimed always at a harmonious society in which all people pursue happiness and freedom without sapping that same strength and purpose from his neighbor."

The President called the commission into session at the White House July 29. He asked members to search for answers, "untrammeled by what has been called the 'conventional wisdom'," to 3 basic questions about the riots: "What happened?" "Why did it happen?" and "What can be done to prevent it from happening again and again?"

Johnson stressed that "one thing should be absolutely clear: This matter is far, far too important for politics. It goes to the health and safety of our citizens—Republicans and Democrats. It goes to the proper responsibilities of officials in both parties."

He urged the commission to examine the question of why riots had occurred in some cities and not in others; of why some persons had broken the law and others had not; of whether any of the disorders had been planned, and of why some had been impossible to contain; of what effect ghetto conditions, federal programs, police-community relationships and mass media had on the riots.

The commission held its first business meeting Aug. 1 in Washington. The session was closed to the press, but Kerner said afterward that FBI Director J. Edgar Hoover, one of the first witnesses heard, had testified that "he had no intelligence on which to base a conclusion of conspiracy" behind the recent racial upheavals. Further comment on Hoover's testimony came Aug. 2 from the commission's executive director, David Ginsburg, who said Hoover had reported that "outside agitators" had played a part in recent black riots but that he had not ascribed much significance to their role. The commission heard testimony Aug. 2 from Sargent Shriver, director of the Office of Economic Opportunity, and from Housing & Urban Development Secy. Robert C. Weaver.

Members of the commission made fact-finding tours of Detroit, Newark, N.J. and New York Aug. 16 and 23 and heard testimony from Detroit Mayor Jerome P. Cavanagh Aug. 15, ex-Central Intelligence Agency Director John A. McCone, Newark Mayor Hugh J. Addonizio Aug. 22 and Michigan Gov. George Romney Sept. 12. The hearings were closed, but the witnesses' prepared testimony was released (a report on Cavanagh's testimony was published Aug. 21). *Among highlights of the testimony:*

Cavanagh—The nation must accept "the principle of reparation for long-standing injustice" and provide many aid programs for Negroes. He recommended: special work-training, educational and community reconstruction programs; direct federal aid to cities for modernizing police forces; reorganization of federal agencies "to make them more responsive to urban needs and to assure a coordinated effort which emphasizes innovation," "block grants to cities" minus restrictions on use to "provide flexibility and fix responsibility where it belongs, right in the community"; tax incentives to induce private capital into rebuilding ghettos and promote new black-owned business; a way to provide "insurance and reinsurance for those willing to invest or live in 'high risk' areas"; an urban development corporation and fund to provide "financial underpinning and the management capabilities needed to create the 'livable' city"; low-cost housing stressing home ownership; neighborhood health and medical emergency centers; a consumer service designed to protect the consumer.

Addonizio—Pres. Johnson was "right" in saying the U.S. "can afford" to finance both the war in Vietnam and urban programs "but it just isn't convinced it must." "Affluent Americans are gripped more by the need to buy a vacation home, a sports car for their college-bound son and a 2d color television set than they are with sharing their affluence with the poor." It was a myth that "the poor, the black or anybody else" could eliminate poverty by attaining political power. "The image of a local so-called power structure with a vested interest in poverty is so absurd but so widely held that it is the greatest despair in the lives of most mayors, particularly in the North."

McCone—Although conditions had been improved and tensions lessened in Watts since the 1965 riots, a dangerous potential to riot still existed in the area.

Romney—"It is later than the nation realizes" and "a magnitude of peaceful effort never previously undertaken by the American people and their private and public institutions" was required to prevent "greater bloodshed and possible destruction of the nation." "The seeds of revolution have been sown in America more by our own failures and shortcomings than by any outside subversive ideology." There must be a "restoration of faith in America and the Constitution," a restoration of "full citizenship" to every American. The primary desire of the Negro was for "human dignity," to be "esteemed by others as others esteem themselves." "Too few whites really know Negroes, and too few Negroes really know whites."

The commission had appointed a special panel, headed by N.J. Gov. Richard J. Hughes, to advise it on the problem of property and liability insurance for residents and businessmen in riot-prone areas. Hughes said Sept. 15 that his group was asking states to formulate "urban area plans" to make fire and extended-coverage insurance available "to all persons whose properties meet reasonable standards of insurability." "Insurance will not be refused simply because property is located in a ghetto area," he said. Speaking at a White House briefing, Hughes said losses on insured property during the summer riots totaled about $100 million, of which $55–$85 million was in Detroit, $10 million in Newark. He said private insurance was "capable of absorbing losses of the magnitude sustained this summer" but that "new approaches" were being considered to provide federal "backing for risks that are not suited to private coverage alone."

(The commission Aug. 10 had urged prompt action to increase the number of Negroes in the National Guard and the Air National Guard. It also recommended improved riot-control training for Guard units and a review of Guard procedures for appointing and promoting officers. The commission reported that only 4,638 [1.15%] of the Guard's total membership of 404,996, were Negroes at the beginning of 1967 and that only 461 [.6%] of the Air National Guard's membership of 77,078 were Negroes. The recommendations were made by the panel in a letter to Pres. Johnson, who immediately forwarded them to Defense Secy. Robert S.

McNamara with a message that the recommendations were "a matter of the highest urgency."*

(Hughes announced Aug. 16 that the Army had approved his state's request to increase its National Guard by 5% "specifically for the purpose of permitting New Jersey to undertake a special recruitment program to bring more Negroes into the National Guard organization." The state's Guard was to return to its original authorized strength after the special recruitment program.)

GOP Governors Propose Anti-Riot Plan

A call for an "action program" against "the tragic epidemic of riots" in U.S. cities was sounded by 8 Republican governors meeting in New York Aug. 10.

Among the state executives' recommendations were: (a) the establishment of a center to provide information to states on urban programs; (b) prompt and firm action by police forces in the early stages of civil disorders; (c) agreements among local law-enforcement groups for pooling of resources to resist rioting; (d) new riot control equipment and procedures for the National Guard; (e) a coordinated public and private attack on the social causes of civil unrest.

The meeting was attended by Govs. Nelson A. Rockefeller (N.Y.) (sponsor of the meeting), George W. Romney (Mich.), Raymond P. Shafer (Pa.), John A. Love (Colo.), Spiro T. Agnew (Md.), John H. Chafee (R.I.), John A. Volpe (Mass.) and Nils A. Boe (S.D.).

The conferees were members of the GOP Governors Association's Policy Committee, of which Rockefeller was chairman. The other committee members, absent from the meeting, were Govs. Ronald Reagan (Calif.), David Cargo (N.M.), Tom McCall (Ore.) and Daniel Evans (Wash.). According to Volpe, all but Reagan,

---

* Maj. Gen. James Cantwell, president of the National Guard Association of the U.S., said in Washington Sept. 18 that efforts to recruit Negroes for the Guard had been ineffective, largely because of Negro unwillingness to join. In his annual report at the 89th annual conference of the association, Cantwell scored the President's Commission on Civil Disorders for criticizing the lack of Negroes in the Guard. The panel's remarks were a "gratuitous slap in the face," he said. "We could have provided a mass of material to show how unproductive our recruiting efforts have been among Negroes. After a lengthy period of intensive effort, they were able to sign up less than 50 qualified persons" in one state, and "other states have reported similar experiences."

who could not be reached for comment, had indorsed the program.
(Reagan had met July 19 with California black leaders to find ways
of preventing summer violence in the state's cities. The group
reportedly said that improved job opportunities would forestall
rioting.)

(In a speech at the Chautauqua [N.Y.] Institution Aug. 4,
Romney declared that "those Americans who preach revolution
and preach the use of guns should be charged with treason."
"There is a criminal element in all races," he said, "and we must
enforce the law without fear or favor among the races." He declared that Stokely Carmichael, black power advocate and ex-chairman of the Student Nonviolent Coordinating Committee, was guilty
of "treason" for a recent speech in Havana, Cuba advocating a revolutionary movement in the U.S.)

Watts Aftermath

Progress in improving the Watts section of Los Angeles since
the 1965 riot was "encouraging but far from satisfying," the
investigating commission headed by ex-CIA Director John A.
McCone said in its final report Aug. 26. "Tensions are still high,"
the report said, but law enforcement agencies appeared to be prepared "to quell any eruption of violence."

The report said that although jobs had been found for 17,900
Watts residents and "a substantial infrastructure of job training has
been developed by federal, state and local agencies, it is quite apparent that the unemployment rate among Negroes has not been
substantially reduced." The report noted that the welfare rolls had
increased to 36,000. (The 2½ square miles at Watts proper had
a population of 40,000. The area of the 1965 rioting covered 40
square miles with 130,000 residents.)

No major educational progress was reported. The commission
cited improvements in auxiliary school services such as libraries,
cafeterias, cut-rate lunches for needy pupils and counseling programs. But the commission said: "These improvements do not go
to the very heart of the problem: a deficiency in environmental experiences which are essential for learning."

The commission found: "The actions taken thus far in Los Angeles, and for that matter elsewhere throughout the United States,
fail to meet the urgent existing need, and unless and until we in
our city and in our state and throughout the United States solve the

fundamental problem of raising the level of scholastic achievement of disadvantaged children, we cannot hope to solve all the problems of our disadvantaged minorities."

The annual Watts Summer Festival, marking the 2d anniversary of the 1965 riot, was held Aug. 7–13. The program, which included art exhibits, films, dance recitals, jazz concerts, basketball and football games, bazaars, handcraft sales and carnival attractions, was sponsored and coordinated by the alumni association of the David Starr Jordan High School. The festivities opened Aug. 7, and Los Angeles Mayor Samuel W. Yorty and Police Chief Thomas Reddin attended the opening ceremony. Muhammad Ali (Cassius Clay), deposed heavyweight champion, served as parade marshall for a 3-hour integrated parade through the heart of Watts Aug. 13. H. Rap Brown, chairman of the Student Nonviolent Coordinating Committee, was kept out of the parade because he had not applied in advance to participate.

OEO (Office of Economic Opportunity) Director Sargent Shriver dedicated the $2.4 million South Central Multipurpose Health Services Center in Watts Sept. 16. The center, financed by an OEO grant to the University of Southern California School of Medicine, would provide all medical, dental and supportive health services on a 24-hour, 7-day-a-week basis to the residents of Watts. It would treat 500 patients a day. Previously Watts had had no hospitals, and the Los Angeles County General Hospital was 11 miles away. (The taxi fare to the county hospital was $7; public transportation cost to the county hospital at least $1.15 and required almost 2 hours travel time.) Watts residents had a share in policy-making in the health center through the Community Health Council—a 25-member council with 19 Watts residents and 6 representatives of local agencies and organizations in the area.

Poverty Aides Defended

Officials and supporters of the antipoverty program defended OEO (Office of Economic Opportunity) workers against charges that they were implicated in riots or other racial clashes:

● OEO Director Sargent Shriver said July 24: "The over-all antipoverty program has turned out to be probably the best anti-riot weapon ever devised. Through all OEO programs we have provided the disadvantaged and previously inarticulate citizens of many communities an opportunity for self-help and for self-expression. We have started to eliminate the basic causes for unrest and impatience. In numerous cases, local antipoverty officials have been particularly helpful in stopping or minimizing violence in situations where tempers had almost reached the breaking point. . . . We have stressed the firm policy of the Office of Economic Opportunity not to permit the use of federal funds for any activities that are contrary to law or are partisan in nature. . . . There will be absolute insistence that every OEO employe and every employe of an OEO grantee scrupulously avoid and resist participation by OEO-founded resources in any activities which threaten public order. . . . I shall insist upon immediate and full penalties for any individuals found guilty of wrong behavior in this connection. Furthermore, I shall insist upon the withholding of OEO funds from any grantee or delegate agency whch is shown to be encouraging or tolerating such behavior."

● Rep. John R. Dellenback (R., Ore.), a member of the House Education & Labor Committee, told Shriver July 31: "I spent 3 or 4 hours last Friday night on the streets of one of our major cities, walking with some of your people, and I was completely favorably impressed by the manner in which these people . . . were making a real effort to stop trouble and not to create it." Another committee member, Rep. Charles E. Goodell (R., N.Y.), said July 31: "Poverty workers generally have helped defuse riots."

● Shriver said on the CBS-TV program "Face the Nation" Aug. 20 that of the 65,000 persons employed in antipoverty programs in 28 cities where disorders occurred during the summer, only 13 were arrested in the disturbances. None of the charges exceeded a misdemeanor, it was reported.

● "Poverty workers are not responsible for riots. It's poverty that is responsible for riots," Shriver told 230 Volunteers in Service to America (VISTA) "summer associates" Aug. 22. Addressing outgoing volunteers who had been working in Washington ghettos, Shriver said that the impact of the recent summer riots had been "harmful" because "lots of people are looking around for a scapegoat and we're a very easy target." He said, however, that even the "model" antipoverty programs in cities such as Detroit and Hartford "are not big enough to get the quantitative results to stop a riot."

● Mayor Harold M. Tollefson of Tacoma, Wash., then president of the National League of Cities, reported July 24 that the antipoverty program had helped minimize and in some cases avert violence. He said: "We are disturbed at recent charges" that the antipoverty program "has been responsible for stirring up [racial] unrest [and violence]. The antipoverty program in city after city has been responsible for just the opposite of that. It has attacked some of the most basic social ills in the community which breed impatience and antagonisms. It has provided the vehicle for the peaceful expression of this impatience. And in city after city, persons associated with the poverty program have actually made important contributions to preventing or minimizing disturbance which has threatened."

● A Labor Department report released July 28 said that young Negroes of the Neighborhood Youth Corps, an antipoverty program, had given invaluable aid during the height of the rioting in Newark and Detroit. According to the report, the youths operated phone switchboards and performed other tasks to relieve regular officers for riot duty.

● Robert Schrank, director of the N.Y. City Neighborhood Youth Corps (NYC) summer program, told 500 delegates at an NYC evaluation conference in New York Sept. 5 that corps members should be credited for easing racial tensions in the slums. "It was a perfect demonstration of what needs to be done in the cities in preventing rioting conditions," he said.

● The OEO announced Sept. 7 that its own investigation of the summer riots showed that antipoverty workers had played a significant rôle in stopping and preventing racial trouble. The investigation included 32 cities that escaped riots and 11 cities that suffered violence. The OEO report said: "Not one police chief or mayor said OEO heightened tensions. On the contrary, most mayors and police officials felt OEO summer programs had helped to prevent violence in their communities."

RIGHTS ORGANIZATIONS & LEADERS

NAACP Activities

The 441,169-member National Association for the Advancement of Colored People (NAACP), the nation's largest civil rights organization, held a tense and acrimonious 58th annual convention in Boston July 10–15. Nearly 2,000 delegates weighed problems ranging from the organization's own internal leadership and its image as a non-militant civil rights group to the recent racial riots and the Vietnam war.

NAACP Executive Director Roy Wilkins, in his keynote address July 10, defended the militants, who, he said, "have shaken up Negroes and whites, both of whom badly needed the treatment. Their service outweighs their disservice." But he went on to warn against racialism that would exclude whites from the civil rights movement. Wilkins had been under fire from militants within the NAACP for his previous criticisms of the ideology of black power.

Sen. Edward W. Brooke (R., Mass.), a Negro, was honored by the convention July 11 with the 1967 Spingarn Award for his "dramatic demonstration that race need be no insurmountable barrier to political advancement." (Brooke had been elected in Nov. 1966 with a plurality of 438,712 votes despite the relatively small Negro population of Massachusetts.) Receiving the award from Sen. Edward Kennedy (D., Mass.), Brooke warned against any effort to exclude whites from the Negro rights movement, but he added that "black power is a response to white irresponsibility." Brooke assailed shortsighted public officials for failing to provide the most elementary service for the Negro communities within their cities." "As a result," he said, "more and more Negroes have come to believe that progress is possible only through militant action. . . ."

NAACP Labor Secy. Herbert Hill told the convention July 12

that the organization planned to file suits in 12 cities to cut off public funds from construction projects where Negroes were denied jobs.   The cities singled out by Hill were Atlanta, Baltimore, Boston, Chicago, Cleveland, Columbus, Los Angeles, New York, Philadelphia, San Francisco and Washington.

Despite Wilkins' apparent retreat on the issue of militancy, his opponents pressed attempts to open the floor to debates on black power and the Vietnam war, to curb Wilkins' power as executive director, and to check his efforts to reassert control over the rebellious Philadelphia branch of the organization.

Cecil B. Moore, president of the NAACP's North Philadelphia branch, arrived at the convention July 13 with a busload of supporters brandishing signs with slogans such as "Roy, Roy, Whitey's Boy."   Moore, who set up a picket line in front of the hotel, came fresh from a legal victory over Wilkins: a New York court July 11 had granted an injunction restraining Wilkins from splitting the Philadelphia chapter into 5 separate units.   Later July 13, however, 5 Philadelphia members requested Moore's suspension for "loose handling" of the branch's funds.   Wilkins suspended Moore July 14 pending a hearing.

The convention took up some of the issues raised by the militants July 14.   A group of West Coast militants calling themselves the "Young Turks" demanded a new distribution of seats on the NAACP Board of Directors to end what they called the organization's "middle-class" image.   They avoided open criticism of Wilkins but rebuked the United Auto Workers union (whose president, Walter P. Reuther, was on the board) for spending union money in attempts to influence votes.   (The union had provided traveling money for some delegates.)   The NAACP Youth Council and the New York State conference of branches also worked to obtain changes in composition of the board.   The Youth Council won convention support July 14 for an increase in its representation from 3 to 17 members on the 60-seat board.   However, despite a sit-in by nearly 500 delegates who refused to leave the ballroom when the July 14 session was suddenly adjourned, no action was taken on the Young Turks' proposals for an overhaul of the board's structure.

(At the annual board meeting held Jan. 3, the NAACP announced that its national membership had re-elected 5 of 6 traditionalists to the national board and elected only one member of the insurgent "Young Turks" faction.   The "Young Turks" had charged in the fall of 1966 that the traditionalist NAACP leadership had failed to adopt new methods as needed in the struggle for civil rights. The insurgents had controlled the nominating committee of the national board and had attempted to depose the older leaders by naming 6 "Young Turk" candidates for the at-large seats. The incumbents, however, contested the election and won 5 of the 6 contests. Those elected were: Walter P. Reuther, president of the United Automobile Workers; Bishop Stephen G. Spottswood, chairman of the board since 1961; Arthur B. Spingarn, former NAACP president; ex-Judge Hubert T. Delaney of N.Y. City; Dr. H. Claude Hudson, a Los Angeles banker; Mrs. Daisy Bates, "Young Turk" candidate and leader during the Little Rock school crisis.)

The convention July 15 adopted a 30-page package of resolutions drawn up by a 50-member resolutions committee under the control of the established leadership. Included in the package was a tersely-worded statement that avoided either indorsing or attacking the Vietnam war while reaffirming the NAACP board's April statement rejecting a merger of the civil rights and peace movements. Another resolution condemned the riots in Newark but added that "much of the blame for this unfortunate eruption must be placed on the city administration for its failure to take corrective action to meet any of the grave social ills of the Negro community." The other resolutions in the package were largely reaffirmations of existing NAACP positions.

Roy Wilkins had reported Jan. 3 that the NAACP's gross income had increased from $1,380,313 in 1965 to $1,408,385 in 1966. He warned that the U.S. faced a prospect of frequent riots unless "we launch a crash program that seriously addresses itself to the gross and disgraceful racial discrimination and inequities in our public school systems in Northern and Western urban centers." (Wilkins, speaking on NBC-TV's "Meet The Press" July 16, backed the use of troops to quell riots wherever and whenever necessary. He restated his view that the riots could be avoided by ending the conditions that caused them.)

Martin Luther King & the SCLC

The 10th annual convention of the Southern Christian Leadership Conference (SCLC), held in Atlanta Aug. 14–17, was highlighted by a call for a campaign of massive civil disobedience in Northern cities. The Rev. Dr. Martin Luther King Jr., SCLC president, called for the civil disobedience drive Aug. 15 to pressure the Johnson Administration and Congress to respond to Negro demands for jobs, housing, better education and more intensive enforcement of existing civil rights legislation. King also urged (a) a repudiation of the Vietnam war and support for a "peace" candidate in the 1968 election and (b) a new emphasis on black consciousness and racial pride.

The delegates held their meetings at the Ebenezer Baptist Church in Atlanta. Large placards in the meeting rooms read: "Black is beautiful and it is so beautiful to be black." Whites comprised approximately 1/5 of the 1,400 persons who attended the opening $10-a-plate banquet. White speakers included Ralph McGill, publisher of the *Atlanta Constitution*; the Right Rev. James A. Pike of the Episcopal Church; Atlanta Mayor Ivan Allen. (This was the first time SCLC convention delegates were welcomed to Atlanta by the mayor.)

Michigan Gov. George Romney sent his respects to the convention Aug. 14 in a telegram in which he "commend[ed]" the SCLC for what it had done in the past and said: "The most important thing now is to look to the future to prevent backlash and to defeat some members of this race [Negro] who want to create separate nations for Negroes and whites."

The keynote speaker, black actor Sidney Poitier, told reporters Aug. 14 that 99% of the nation's Negroes had not been involved in the summer rioting. He said the press should "concentrate on areas of hope, health, strength and things that are constructive." When asked if he supported the Student Nonviolent Coordinating Committee (SNCC), Poitier replied: "Yes, . . . but I have been forced recently to re-examine my relationship with SNCC because of their emphasis on violence. However, . . . SNCC has done remarkable work in helping students get conditions changed."

King told the convention Aug. 15: He would lead massive but nonviolent demonstrations, as an alternative to violence, to disrupt Northern cities in an effort to get federal funds for impoverished Negroes. "To dislocate the functioning of a city without destroying it can be more effective than a riot because it can be longer lasting, costly to the society but not wantonly destructive. Moreover, it is more difficult to quell it by superior force." "Mass civil disobedience can use rage as a constructive and creative force." "It is purposeless to tell Negroes they should not be enraged when they should be. Indeed, they will be mentally healthier if they do not

suppress rage but vent it constructively and use its energy peacefully but forcefully to cripple the operations of an oppressive society.
Civil disobedience can utilize the militance wasted in riots to seize
clothes or groceries many do not even want." Little could be gained
by the President's investigation into the causes of the riots. The
"root causes" of the violence were obvious: unemployment, underemployment, poor housing and discrimination.

King charged that the "policy-makers of the white society"
were responsible for the summer violence. He said: "Our real
problem is that there is no disposition by the Administration nor
Congress to seek fundamental remedies beyond police measures."
"The tragic truth is that Congress, more than the American people,
is now running wild with racism."

King Aug. 16 called on 500 cheering delegates to "drive the
nation to a guaranteed annual income." He said that "the movement must address itself to the restructuring of American society"
and that Negroes lived "in the basement of the Great Society" and
still had a "long way to go." Rejecting violence as the means to
attain the Negro goal, King said riots brought "a few water sprin-
klers and some antipoverty money from scared officials." Reviewing
his "Operation Breadbasket" programs in Cleveland and Chicago,
King said that more than 2,200 new jobs had been won in Chicago
and that jobs with incomes totaling $500,000 had been won by
Negroes in Cleveland.

King predicted Aug. 17 that the SCLC "very, very definitely"
would oppose Pres. Johnson in the 1968 election unless he changed
his handling of the war in Vietnam. He said he thought that the
war was "morally wrong" and that the bombing near China was "a
terribly dangerous development" that could be viewed as "an attempt to taunt the Chinese into making an attack" on U.S. forces
in order to build a consensus support for the war. Dr. Benjamin
Spock, co-chairman of the National Committee for a Sane Nuclear
Policy, told the convention's peace panel Aug. 17 that the peace
movement would support the SCLC in its drive for massive civil
disobedience. The convention Aug. 17 adopted a resolution repu-
diating the war in Vietnam and declaring that the American people
"must have an opportunity to vote into oblivion those who cannot
detach themselves from militarism." The delegates also voted to
initiate a "series of regional Afro-American unity conferences"
with "every sector of the Negro community."

King had been sharply criticized May 20 for lending his "mantle of respectability" to the anti-Vietnam war campaign being conducted by groups alleged to include "well-known Communist allies and luminaries of the hate-America Left." The criticism was made in a position paper issued by Freedom House, a private organization based in New York. Freedom House was directed by a board of trustees headed by ex-Sen. Paul H. Douglas (D., Ill.) and including NAACP Executive Director Roy Wilkins and Sen. Edward W. Brooke (R., Mass.). The paper charged that King had "emerged as the public spear-carrier of a civil disobedience program that is demagogic and irresponsible in its attacks on our government." It said that an anti-war march addressed by King in New York Apr. 15 "had all the earmarks of the old-style 'popular Front' rallies of the 1930s." "The majority of the marchers may have been motivated by their devotion to the cause of peace," the paper alleged, "but the Communists were clearly in evidence among the parade managers." King May 22 denied charges of Communist influence in the anti-war movement. He said Freedom House had "allowed itself to become victimized by the same McCarthy-like tactics that darkened the soul of our nation a few years ago."

King Mar. 30 had announced a reorganization of SCLC's structure. The change, he said, was part of a move to place more emphasis on the problems of Negroes in the North. While the staff of field workers was reduced from 150 to 85, 3 new SCLC departments were added to deal with black economic problems, high school and college recruitment and voter registration. The Rev. Andrew J. Young, 35, SCLC executive director, was named SCLC executive vice president Dec. 13, and William A. Rutherford, 43, a management consultant, was named SCLC executive director.

The U.S. Supreme Court June 12 had upheld, 5–4, the contempt-of-court convictions of Martin Luther King and 7 other black leaders who had led desegregation protest marches in Birmingham, Ala. in 1963 in defiance of a temporary restraining order. The 8 men had been fined $50 and sentenced to 5-day prison terms. The decision adhered to the principle set down by the court in 1922 that laws could be tested by disobedience but that court injunctions first must be obeyed and only later tested. In the majority opinion Justice Potter Stewart said: "No man can be judge in his own case, however exalted his station, however righteous his motives, and irrespective of his race, color, politics or religion." "This court cannot hold that the petitioners were constitutionally free to ignore all the procedures of the law and carry their battle to the streets."

He was joined by Justices Hugo L. Black, Tom C. Clark, John M. Harlan and Byron R. White. In a dissent, Justice William J. Brennan Jr. called the decision a "devastatingly destructive weapon for infringement of freedoms jealously safeguarded. . . ." He was joined by Chief Justice Earl Warren and Justices William O. Douglas and Abe Fortas.

The court Oct. 9 refused to reconsider its decision. King said that it had "turned its back on an appeal to reason and the most fundamental freedom that all Americans cherish" but that he would "willingly and in clear conscience go to jail . . . to make a witness for my basic beliefs."

Those convicted with King were his brother, the Rev. A. D. Williams King of Louisville; the Rev. J. W. Hayes, the Rev. T. L. Fisher and the Rev. J. T. Porter of Birmingham; the Rev. Ralph Abernathy and the Rev. Wyatt Tee Walker of New York, and the Rev. Fred Shuttlesworth of Cincinnati.

Shuttlesworth, Hayes, Fisher and Porter were arrested in Birmingham Oct. 22 and placed in Jefferson County jail. They were released Oct. 27. King, his brother, Abernathy and Walker surrendered to sheriff's deputies Oct. 30 and were placed in the Bessemer, Ala. jail. The 4 men, King suffering from a virus infection, were transferred to a downtown Birmingham jail Nov. 1. They were released Nov. 3, a day early because, Circuit Court Judge William C. Barber said, he didn't want to "work a hardship on anybody."

King in Atlanta Dec. 4 announced plans for a massive civil disobedience campaign to disrupt federal activities in Washington in about Apr. 1968 and to put pressure on Congress and the Administration to act "against poverty" and provide "jobs and income for all." The plan had been proposed publicly by King Aug. 15, and details had been worked out in late November at an SCLC staff meeting in Frogmore, S.C. King said 3,000 demonstrators would be recruited from 10 cities and 5 rural areas and would be trained for 3 months in nonviolent discipline to serve as a nucleus of a "strong, dramatic and attention-getting campaign." King said that the "angry and bitter" moods of many Negroes in the nation's slums could make the campaign "risky" but that Negroes would respond to nonviolence "if it's militant enough, if it's really doing something." "These tactics have done it before," he asserted, "and this is all we have to go on." King said the Washington campaign would be a "last desperate demand" by Negroes, an effort to avoid "the worst chaos, hatred and violence any nation has ever encountered." He said he hoped the non-Negro as well as the Negro poor, black militants and anti-war groups would participate in the protests, but he said all participants must pledge to avoid violence in the campaign. The Rev. Bernard Lafayette Jr., 27, a founder of the Student Nonviolent Coordinating Committee (SNCC) and program administrator of the SCLC, was named by King Dec. 13 to direct the Washington project.

National Urban League

A warning to Negroes to choose "militancy" rather than "extremism" was delivered Aug. 20 by Whitney M. Young Jr., 45, executive director of the National Urban League, in his keynote address at the league's annual conference. The conference was held in Portland, Ore. Aug. 20–24. Young also challenged the "80%" of the white population whose "silence and indifference allows bigots to speak for them and allows the ghetto to exist."

Young condemned the summer race riots as "criminal acts [that] should be put down swiftly and firmly, without the trigger-happy response which killed so many innocent people." "No one is for gradualism," he said, "no one thinks in terms of compromise. So the famous 'moderate vs. militant' is imaginary. What exists is militancy vs. extremism, and that is really a question of responsibility against irresponsibility, . . . building vs. burning. Negro citizens know that responsible militancy is the most effective way in which they can achieve their rights and develop the community strengths which make for power in our society."

Young reiterated his call for a massive domestic "Marshall Plan" and a program of full employment for all willing, able-bodied Americans. He said the Urban League would take the side of "peace and justice here at home" if it became necessary to choose between this and the war in Vietnam.

Mahlon T. Puryear, deputy executive director of the Urban League, announced Aug. 22 the formation of an Office of Veterans Affairs "to insure the returning Negro servicemen and women and their families [from Vietnam] will not face the major problems of readjustment which plagued those who returned after World Wars I and II and the Korean conflict." The initial 2-year demonstration program would cost $170,000; the Rockefeller Brothers Fund agreed to supply $100,000 the first year and $50,000 the 2d year;

the Urban League would pay for the remainder. Puryear said Negroes were serving in Vietnam in "unprecedented and disproportionate numbers due to a high rate of enlistment and re-enlistment generated largely by the superiority of opportunity for training and advancement in the military sector as compared with civilian life."

The league's delegate assembly Aug. 23 directed its resolutions committee to draft a new statement demanding that the government give top priority to financing programs dealing with the domestic problems of poverty and urban blight. The new statement would be a revision of a proposed "statement of concern" called "Vietnam —Guns or Butter," which did not condemn the Vietnam conflict but simply asked for a choice of butter over guns.

Sen. Edward W. Brooke (R., Mass.) told the delegates Aug. 23: "Congress is affected and inhibited by the myths and prejudices of constituents and by the fact that racial prejudice is a working force in this country." "What can the people do when the leaders of a nation refuse to lead? The people must give direction." "I am not an advocate of 'black power' in the sense that term has come to mean violence. But power as the ability to change conditions is the essence of the democratic process. The poor must become full participants in that process." "The slum communities must create political institutions to bargain with and confront the existing political structure." "The civil-rights movement must evolve into a grass-roots political organization or it will be irrelevant to the needs of the people it represents."

Puryear told reporters Aug. 24 that the league would work with black-power and other groups to help ghetto dwellers. Brian G. Banion of Los Angeles, chairman of the resolutions committee, added that "we have been and are working with black-power groups. The adherents of black-power leaders are . . . the people we are trying to reach."

According to an estimate reported by the *N.Y. Times* Jan. 8, the number of jobs the Urban League found for Negroes annually had risen in 5 years from 2,000 jobs to 40,000 jobs in 1966. Whitney M. Young had toured East European countries with 25 major U.S. corporation executives in the fall of 1966 and afterwards reported his conviction that his talks with the executives would open 50,000 jobs for Negroes. The tour had been sponsored by Time, Inc., and Young had joined it to get to know executives who, he said, represented "probably 15% of the gross national product and about 2 million employees." Later, Young said, Henry Ford

2d, one of his companions on the trip, had sent him a $100,000 Christmas check to further his work "any way you wish."

'Snick' & Stokely Carmichael

Stokely Carmichael, 26, was replaced May 12 by H. Rap Brown, 23, SNCC's Alabama director, as chairman of the Student Nonviolent Coordinating Committee. Carmichael said he would remain with "Snick" (SNCC) as a field worker. Stanley Wise, 24, was elected executive secretary and Ralph Featherstone, 27, field secretary in Mississippi and Alabama, was named program director. Carmichael had announced in a TV interview in Chicago Jan. 15 that he would not seek reelection. But Carmichael said that he was "not going to retire." He added in an address in Washington that night that he planned to return to field organizing in the South.

At a news conference in Atlanta May 12, Brown said there would be no change in SNCC's black power policy. He said: "We shall seek to build a strong nationwide black anti-draft program and movement to include high school students, along with college students and other black men of draft age." "We see no reason for black men, who are daily murdered physically and mentally in this country, to go and kill yellow people abroad, who have done nothing to us and are, in fact, victims of the same oppression that our brothers in Vietnam suffer."

In the Aug. 14 issue of its bimonthly *SNCC Newsletter*, SNCC denounced Zionism and charged Israelis with atrocities against Arabs. The article, on the "Palestine problem," also assailed American Jews. The newsletter asked: "Do you know that the Zionists conquered the Arab homes and land through terror, force and massacres; that they wiped out over 30 Arab villages before and after they took control of the area they now call 'Israel'?" A blurred photo entitled "Gaza Massacres, 1956" had this caption: "Zionists lined up Arab victims and shot them in the back in cold blood. This is the Gaza Strip, Palestine, not Dachau, Germany." A cartoon showed a hand, marked with a dollar sign and Star of David, tightening ropes around the necks of Egyptian Pres. Gamal Abdel Nasser and heavyweight boxer Muhammad Ali (Cassius Clay). Another cartoon depicted Israeli Defense Min. Moshe Dayan with dollar signs instead of stars on his shoulders. *The newsletter also charged:*

● "That Israel segregates those few Arabs who remained in their homeland, that more than 90% of these Arabs live in 'security zones,' under martial

law, and are not allowed to travel freely within Israel and are the victims of discrimination in education, jobs, etc."
● "That dark-skinned Jews from the Middle East and North Africa are also 2d-class citizens in Israel, that the color line puts them in an inferior position to the white European Jews."
● "That the United States government has constantly supported Israel and Zionism by sending military and financial aid to this illegal state ever since it was forced upon the Arabs in 1948."
● "That the famous European Jews, the Rothschilds, who have long controlled the wealth of many European nations, were involved in the original conspiracy with the British to create the 'state of Israel' and are still among Israel's chief supporters."
● "That the Rothschilds control much of Africa's wealth."

Some of the views that appeared in the *SNCC Newsletter* echoed those expressed in the August issue of *The Thunderhead, The White Man's Viewpoint,* the publication of the National States Rights Party, a white supremacist organization (headquarters: Savannah, Ga.). *The Thunderhead* defended the Arabs and charged: "Israel napalmed civilians," "Press suppressed atrocity news" and "Huge sums to Israel hurt American taxpayer."

Ralph Featherstone, SNCC program director, said in Atlanta Aug. 14 that the "positions of the 2 organizations may look the same, but I think that you have to probe deeper and look at the philosophical concepts behind the positions." Featherstone conceded that SNCC had solicited help from Arab embassies in preparing the article. He said: SNCC was not anti-Semitic. SNCC was indicting "only Jewish oppressors"—the Israelis and "those Jews in the little Jew shops in the [black] ghettos." SNCC was working toward a "3d world alliance of oppressed people all over the world—Africa, Asia and Latin America." "Actually, there is only one other world in addition to the 3d world, and that's the white world—and Russia is a part of it."

Civil rights leaders Aug. 15 denounced what they described as a SNCC attack on Jews. Whitney M. Young Jr., executive director of the National Urban League, said: "Negro citizens are well aware of the contributions made to the drive for equal rights by Jewish citizens. Negroes have been the victims of racism for too long to indulge in group stereotypes and racial hate themselves." A. Philip Randolph, president of the Bro'hood of Sleeping Car Porters, and Bayard Rustin, executive director of the A. Philip Randolph Institute, issued a joint statement declaring they were "appalled and distressed by the anti-Semitic article." Will Maslow, executive director of the American Jewish Congress, said the SNCC statements were "shocking and vicious anti-Semitism."

At a press conference in New York Aug. 18 Featherstone again defended the *SNCC Newsletter.* He said: "Our position was clearly anti-Zionist, not anti-Semitic. It was a bit disconcerting to us, the reaction from the Jewish community, in that anything that is not pro-Jewish is interpreted as anti-Jewish." "We are not anti-Jewish." "We are not anti-Jewish and we are not anti-Semitic. We just don't think Zionist leaders in Israel have a right to that land."

Theodore Bikel, actor and folk-singer, resigned from SNCC Aug. 16, and Harry Golden, editor and author, resigned Aug. 21. Bikel, a national vice president of the American Jewish Congress, said in a letter released Aug. 16 that he could not belong to "any organization which condones injustice, let alone commits it," and that henceforth he would "fight on the side of those who, like Dr. Martin Luther King, speak with the voice of sane and deliberative determination . . . to unite men as brothers, not divide them by the litmus test of color." Golden said in Charlotte, N.C. that he was resigning "because of the increasing use of anti-Semitism [by SNCC] and their echoing the ideas found in the Ku Klux Klan and the American Nazi Party." He said: "The cartoons in the newsletter are obscene, and this comes in ill grace from an organization from which 2 Jewish boys, [Michael] Schwerner and [Andrew] Goodman, along with Mississippi Negro [James Earl] Chancy, were murdered while doing field work for SNCC in Philadelphia, Miss." *

Carmichael spoke in Detroit Jan. 18 at a conference on "Racism in White America" and denounced the Democratic Party as the "most treacherous enemy the Negro people have." He told white liberals to stay in their own areas and "raise funds and organize whites in the suburbs to support the Negro cause." Carmichael addressed the final session of a 3-day "Conference '67—Survival of Black People" in San Francisco Jan. 29. He urged Negroes to withdraw their support from the Democratic and Republican parties and form a 3d party. But Lincoln Lynch, associate director of

---

* James Baldwin, black novelist and playwright, and Ossie Davis, black author and actor, had resigned as members of the advisory board of *Liberator,* a black nationalist monthly, in protest against the publication of allegedly anti-Semitic articles by Eddie Ellis. The resignations were made public in New York Feb. 27 by the American Jewish Committee. The articles written by Ellis described the alleged exploitation of ghetto Negroes by Jewish merchants and landlords. Ellis also charged that "Zionists" had dominated many Negro colleges and black organizations and had begun to manipulate the civil rights movement.

the Congress of Racial Equality, held that Negroes should play "smart politics" by working through the current parties.

In Puerto Rico Jan. 25 Carmichael had led about 250 demonstrators from the University of Puerto Rico through the suburbs of San Juan to Fort Brooke in Old San Juan in protest against the war in Vietnam and in a demand for Puerto Rican independence. A brief melee erupted when about 50 youths attacked the marchers and hurled stones and eggs. According to Juan Mari Bras, head of the Puerto Rican Pro-Independence Movement, the clash was instigated by the Statehood Republican Party. Carmichael, Mari Bras and 2 other Pro-Independence Movement officials Jan. 26 signed a "protocol of cooperation" on the issues of black power and Puerto Rican independence. The communique said that SNCC and the Pro-Independence group recognized each other as being "in the vanguard of a common struggle against U.S. imperialism."

In a letter to NAACP Executive Director Roy Wilkins Mar. 8, Carmichael had announced SNCC's withdrawal from the Leadership Conference on Civil Rights, a coalition of more than 100 civil rights, labor and religious organizations. Wilkins was chairman of the conference. The conference had asked SNCC and CORE if they wanted to remain in the group. CORE chose to stay in the coalition.

In secret testimony heard by a House Appropriations subcommittee Feb. 16 and released May 16, FBI Director J. Edgar Hoover had charged that Carmichael had been associated with the Revolutionary Action Movement (RAM), which he described as "dedicated to the overthrow of the capitalist system in the U.S., by violence if necessary. . . ." He said: "In espousing . . . black power, Carmichael had been in frequent contact with Max Stanford, field chairman of the RAM, a highly secret all-Negro, Marxist-Leninist, Chinese Communist-oriented organization which advocates guerrilla warfare to obtain its goals." Hoover said that RAM had only about 50 members. Carmichael, at a news conference in Grand Rapids, Mich. May 17, said he would not answer Hoover's "infantile" charges.

Carmichael went to England July 14 for what was reported to be 10 busy days of meetings and speeches. After Carmichael's departure from England, British Home Secy. Roy Jenkins told the British House of Commons July 27 that Carmichael would not be permitted to enter Britain again. Having considered a report prepared by Scotland Yard on Carmichael's activities during his stay in England, Jenkins said, "his presence here is not conducive to the public good." Patrick Wall, a Conservative MP, charged that Carmichael "had been addressing meetings in Britain advocating racial violence." During his stay in England he was reported to have said: "If the British did not accept our principles, I would burn down their homes and factories." Carmichael left London July 24 and arrived in Prague the same day.

Carmichael said Aug. 1 that the Negro was fighting "guerrilla warfare" to attain his rights and that a "revolutionary movement" would be initiated to help him. He made the remarks at a news conference in Havana, Cuba, where he had gone to attend the conference of the Organization for Latin American Solidarity. An "honorary delegate" to the conference, Carmichael addressed it Aug. 2 and said the American Negro was ready to destroy "Yankee imperialism" with urban warfare.

In a broadcast over Havana radio earlier Aug. 2, Carmichael had addressed a message to Maj. Ernesto (Ché) Guevara, Cuban guerrilla leader. He said: "We eagerly await your writings in order to read them, digest them and plan our tactics based on them." (The Cuban news agency *Prensa Latina* had quoted Carmichael July 25 as saying in London that he was going to Havana in response to an April call by Ché Guevara for Latin American revolutionaries to create 2 or 3 more Vietnams. *Prensa Latina* reported that Carmichael had said: "In Newark, we are applying the tactics of guerrilla warfare. We are preparing groups of urban guerrillas for our defense in the cities. This struggle . . . is going to be a struggle to the death." At a press conference in Havana Aug. 1 Carmichael said that "40% of the troops in Vietnam are Negro, and some good may come of it because when they come back they will be trained to kill in the streets." "Guerrilla warfare is the best training for fighting in the cities," he declared, "because they [the whites] will not dare bomb their own cities." He indorsed Guevara's injunction that "you must teach them to hate so you can turn them into an effective fighting machine." Carmichael lauded Cuban-style communism and said that "there are no proletarians in the U.S. Communist Party; it is the party of the rich.")

Closing the solidarity conference Aug. 11, Cuban Premier Fidel Castro urged support for revolution in the U.S. and predicted that such a revolution would come from the "Negro sector." Introducing Carmichael, Castro warned that any punitive action taken by the U.S. against Carmichael would have a "profound repercussion" in Latin America. (The Cuban government magazine *Bohemia* had quoted Carmichael Aug. 4 as saying that his 3 days of talks with Castro were "the most educational . . . and the best apprentice-ship of my public life.")

In an Aug. 17 broadcast over Havana radio Carmichael called on U.S. Negroes to arm for "total revolution." He said: "Comrades of the 3d world of Asia, Africa and Latin America, I want you to know that Afro-North Americans within the United States are fighting for their liberation. It is a struggle of total revolution in which we propose to change the imperialist, capitalist and racialist structure of the United States which oppresses you outside and us within. We have no other alternative but to take up arms and struggle for our total liberation and total revolution in the United States. We were kidnapped and robbed from Africa and therefore we cannot be part of the United States which violates the African continent."

The State Department announced Aug. 24 that it had notified Carmichael and George Washington Ware, 27, SNCC field worker, that their passports had been revoked because they had violated passport regulations by traveling to Cuba. A letter of notification dated Aug. 3, was sent to Carmichael.

The North Vietnamese News Agency reported Aug. 29 that Carmichael had arrived in Hanoi, North Vietnam Aug. 25. He had been invited by the Vietnam Asian-African Solidarity Committee, the agency said. SNCC Chairman Brown had said at a news conference in N.Y. City Aug. 18 that Carmichael "will arrive in Hanoi today" to "investigate and see for himself the savage aggression being carried out" against North Vietnam. Brown said: "Previous investigators of ours who visited the country have reported that the United States is experimenting with weapons there that would be effective in destroying black people in the ghetto without damaging the property." "Mr. Carmichael will see for himself the atrocities being perpetrated against the people of Vietnam, a people who are heroically defending their right to self-determination." (At the news conference Brown called on U.S. Negroes to celebrate Aug. 18 as their "day of independence." He said that Aug. 18, 1965, the day the Watts riots began, was "a day the blacks of Watts picked up their guns to fight for their freedom.")

In a broadcast monitored in Tokyo Aug. 30, Hanoi radio said that in a "recent" meeting in North Vietnam with Ton Quang Phiet, chairman of the Vietnam Afro-Asian Solidarity Committee, Car-michael had pledged the support of American Negroes for Commu-nist North Vietnam in the Vietnamese war.

According to Hanoi Press reports Aug. 31, Carmichael said at a Hanoi meeting: "We [U.S. Negroes] are not reformers, we are not proposing reforms. We do not wish to be a part of the government of the U.S.A. or the American regime." "We are revolutionaries. We want to change the American regime." "We will not be satisfied until we have accomplished this task. In this sense our struggle is a common struggle, and in this sense we are comrades. But we are also [comrades] in a larger sense, since we want to stop cold the greatest destroyers of humanity, the American leadership." Carmichael was reported to have made these remarks at a meeting with Hoang Bac, assistant secretary general of the Solidarity Committee, who was said to have given Carmichael a long lecture on the necessity for perseverance and tenacity in the revolutionary struggle.

Carmichal returned to the U.S. Dec. 11 after a 4-month overseas tour that included visits to Tanzania, Egypt, Algiers, Sweden, Spain, Cuba, England, France, North Vietnam, Guinea and Czechoslovakia. He was met at Kennedy International Airport in New York by U.S. marshals, who confiscated his passport. Carmichael had violated Section 1544, Title 18, of the U.S. Code, which prohibited unauthorized travel to Cuba and North Vietnam. While in Tanzania Carmichael reportedly antagonized African "freedom fighters" by ridiculing their "exaggerated" claims of military victories and of having killed foreign troops. He was quoted Nov. 18 as saying: "Freedom fighters don't fight. Their leaders are too interested in big cars and white women. Half of those leaders don't even know how to use a gun." A spokesman for the African National Congress of South Africa retorted that Carmichael "excelled . . . in meaningless and arrogant demagoguery."

Black Power Conference

The largest and most diverse group of black American leaders ever assembled met in Newark, N.J. July 20–23 for a 4-day National Conference on Black Power. The meeting was convened, against New Jersey Gov. Richard J. Hughes' objection, in the wake of Newark's racial riots.

A militant and separatist mood dominated the delegates—estimated to number 900 to 1,100—representing 197 black organizations in 42 cities throughout the U.S. The delegates included civil rights activists, labor leaders, educators, antipoverty workers, politicians, clergymen, representatives of traditionally moderate Negro groups and avowed revolutionaries. Before the meeting ended, they gave their shouted approval to a series of resolutions setting out a united and independent course for the Negro in America.

The conference, planned since Sept. 1966, was organized by Dr. Nathan Wright Jr., executive director of the Department of Urban Work of the Episcopal Diocese of Newark. The idea for the conference originally had been advanced by Rep.-elect Adam Clayton Powell, who did not attend the meeting but was named honorary co-chairman with Rep. Charles C. Diggs (D., Mich.) and Floyd B. McKissick, national director of the Congress of Racial Equality (CORE).

Whites were barred from all meetings and workshops during the 4-day conference. White newsmen, however, were permitted to attend press briefings, given each day at Cathedral House, headquarters of the Newark diocese. Open hostility was reported July 20 between white newsmen and conference officials, who engaged in several shouting matches. A *N.Y. Times* reporter was pushed out of a ground floor window when he tried to attend a meeting.

In a letter to Gov. Hughes, made public July 16, Wright said that the purpose of the conference was "to concentrate in an introspective way on the means of empowering a largely benighted and hopeless community to stand on its own and to add its unused potential for the enrichment of the lives of all." Wright said July 20 that the meeting had been organized "not to deal with the deficiencies of the white community, but with the empowerment of black people." He said the emphasis would be on "action" not on "talk." In the 14 planned workshop sessions, he said, the delegates would try to find ways in which local black communities could achieve power.

Delegates to the conference included representatives of the National Urban League, Southern Christian Leadership Conference (SCLC), National Association for the Advancement of Colored People (NAACP), Congress of Racial Equality (CORE), Student Nonviolent Coordinating Committee (SNCC), US (a militant black nationalist organization from Watts), the Organization for Afro-American Unity (founded by the late Malcolm X), the militant Mau Maus and the Progressive Labor Party.

Although NAACP Executive Director Roy Wilkins, SCLC Pres. Martin Luther King and Urban League Executive Director Whitney M. Young Jr. did not attend the conference, their representatives were present. Also present were 2 high-ranking officers of the New

York Police Department and William Booth, chairman of New York's Commission on Human Rights.

The conference July 21 adopted resolutions demanding the recall of Newark Mayor Hugh J. Addonizio and "gubernatorial clemency for all those jailed in Newark before this conference ends." Negro comedian Dick Gregory told the delegates: "It would only take 25,000 votes to recall that honky [white] mayor." "In any community," McKissick told the cheering delegates, "where more than 60% of the people are black, we need a black mayor. In fact, the question of a white man's competency becomes irrelevant when a city is more than 60% black. If he is white, he shouldn't be mayor." Alfred Black, chairman of Newark's Human Relations Commission, received a standing ovation when he declared: "The Negro today is either a radical or an Uncle Tom. There is no middle ground."

Earlier in the day, when asked if Negro violence was destined to continue in the U.S., McKissick said: "No sane person could say we are not due for more violence. You will have violence as long as you have black people suppressed." He said that white people who "control the government, the money and the ghettos" were responsible for the violence. "It is the responsibility of the whites to eliminate the conditions that cause violence," McKissick declared. "It is the conditions themselves that make for violence, and only white people have the power to change them."

The delegates July 22 unanimously passed a resolution demanding "full restitution and reparation to all of our black brothers and sisters and their families [in Newark] and that all of our black brothers and sisters be released from jail without bail immediately." The resolution assailed what it called the "massacre of black people" by police, and charged that in the Newark violence "black men and women were indiscriminately murdered, beaten and arrested," and "the wanton destruction of black people's property in the entire black community was maliciously undertaken." The resolution also said the delegates "vigorously affirm the exercise of our unchallengeable right of self-defense."

(The July 22 press briefing was terminated abruptly when a gang of black youths broke into the room shouting "Get the white press out!" They overturned cameras and TV equipment. There were no serious injuries although some newsmen suffered minor cuts. Wright afterward expressed regret for the incident.)

The conference was ended July 23 on a militant note as delegates cheered approval of a series of resolutions aimed at establishing a separate course for American Negroes. The conference also issued a report denouncing the Newark riots as "the inevitable results of the criminal behavior of a society which dehumanizes people and drives men to utter distraction." The report said delegates had taken steps to create a black "3d force" to effect "a balance of power in [the 1968] elections and to remove from critical positions all politicians serving to thwart or subvert black political power." It announced plans for a campaign to triple the number of black Congressmen in 1968.

More than 100 resolutions were adopted. Some called for:

● Condemnation of the war in Vietnam and encouragement of black youths to respond to the military draft with "Hell, no, we won't go!"
● A boycott of all international Olympic competitions and professional boxing matches until the restoration of the heavyweight championship title to Muhummad Ali (Cassius Clay).
● A boycott of Negro churches not committed to the "black revolution."
● The establishment of "black universities" to make "professional black revolutionaries" out of "revolutionary black professionals."
● The creation of "black national holidays" to honor "national heroes" such as the late Malcolm X.
● The establishment of black financial institutions to provide housing and business loans to black neighborhood credit unions.
● A "national dialogue on the desirability of partitioning the U.S. into 2 separate nations, one white and one black."
● A guaranteed annual income for all citizens, "or else black people will be impelled to disrupt the economy of the country."
● Selective buying programs, including a nationwide "buy black" effort to force action for better employment opportunities.
● Paramilitary training for black youths.
● Rejection of birth control programs as a covert attempt to exterminate the Negro.
● Creation of a central black power organization to administer the goals of the conference.
● Censure of all members of Congress who voted to exclude Rep.-elect Adam Clayton Powell.
● The establishment of black housing and building cooperatives.

'New Politics' Convention

A growing schism between black-power leaders and "white liberals" dominated the first convention of the National Conference for a New Politics, which was held in the Palmer House ballroom in Chicago Aug. 31–Sept. 4. The approximately 2,100 delegates represented about 200 groups classifiable as Negro, student, labor, antiwar, antipoverty, dissident Democratic, Communist and otherwise leftist.   Simon Casady, ex-president of the California Democratic Council and co-chairman of the convention, labeled the Communists "the rightwing of this movement" because "they want orderly electoral processes."

Members of the white majority made nearly frantic efforts during the convention to heal the black-white schism, but most conciliatory gestures of the whites were greeted with bitterness and disdain by the black delegates.   The convention Sept. 2 adopted without change a controversial policy statement distasteful to many of the whites but demanded by the Negroes.   And the white majority Sept. 3 yielded to the black minority a full half of the weighted convention votes (ultimately computed at a total of 56,996).

The Negro statement adopted by the convention attacked Israel and pledged unquestioned support to all "liberation wars."   The statement charged that there had been a "systematic exclusion of blacks from the decision-making process . . . in this convention." It said that "this exclusion raised serious doubts that white people are serious about revolutionary change."   The statement charged that the U.S. "system is committed to the practice of genocide, social degradation, to the denial of political and social self-determination of black people, and cannot reform itself."   "There must be revolutionary change," it declared.

Almost all of the black delegates, many of them attired in African-style robes, had boycotted the opening of the convention and had met instead in a "black caucus" with Carlos Russell of Brooklyn presiding.

Floyd B. McKissick, national director of CORE (the Congress of Racial Equality), told the convention Sept. 1: "No longer can the black man be a plank in someone else's platform.   We must be the platform ourselves if we are to survive."   The convention then authorized a peace mission Sept. 1 to offer the black caucus "3 or more" seats on the convention steering committee, but the peace emissaries at first could not find where the black caucus was meeting.   The caucus' meeting room actually was only a few doors away from the whites' meeting place.   When whites finally found the room, Negro guards refused to let them enter, and black leaders refused to come out to talk to them.

The Negroes presented the policy statement to the convention Sept. 2.   They had decided that the convention must accept it as the price of Negro participation.   The convention delegates agreed and, by 17,928-6,834 weighted vote (2,028 abstentions), adopted the statement without change.   One of the statement's requirements was 50% Negro representation on all convention committees although whites out-numbered Negroes at the convention by about 1,500 to 600 and apparently represented an even disproportionately larger number of local members. The delegates, prompted largely by Communist and W. E. B. Du Bois Club members, agreed to the 50% representation and voted 16,359–7,396 Sept. 3 to give the black minority a weighted vote equal to the total weighted vote of the remainder of the convention.

When the Negroes finally took seats, they insisted on—and were granted—a special section roped off from the rest of the convention delegates.

The Negroes' refusal to join in political action with other groups was emphasized in a speech before the convention Sept. 3 by James Forman, director of the national office of SNCC (the Student Nonviolent Coordinating Committee). Forman, dressed in a white, African-style robe and attended by 2 black bodyguards, said: "We [Negroes], and we alone, have the responsibility to wage our own war of liberation as we see fit. . . . We insist on our right to define the manner in which we will fight our aggressors. It is our right, our responsibility, and anyone who does not like it can go to hell. . . . The dispossessed must assume direction and give leadership to the new politics. If you're not going to support us, you go your merry way, and we're going to liberate you whether you want to be liberated or not."

Forman refused to allow a statement on a point of order, and a white delegate then asked, "Is this a dictatorship?" Forman replied, "Yes, and I'm the dictator," but he explained, after several whites stalked out, that he was joking.

McKissick, attended by colorfully costumed bodyguards, had told newsmen Sept. 2: "The black people are not now in a position to coalesce with anybody. Black people are only going to coalesce as equals."

(SNCC Chairman H. Rap Brown, who refused to speak before whites at the convention, reportedly said in a speech at the black caucus that Pres. Johnson was "Hitler's illegitimate child" and that FBI Director J. Edgar Hoover was Hitler's "sister.")

By a narrow vote Sept. 3, the convention decided not to support a 3d-party Presidential candidate in 1968. In the final session Sept. 4, the conference adopted anti-draft and antiwar resolutions. The former resolution advocated "open draft resistance"; the latter, entitled "Which Side We Are On," demanded immediate unconditional withdrawal of U.S. forces from Vietnam.

Among policy statements of the black caucus adopted by the convention Sept. 2, after 4 hours' debate, was the one condemning "the imperialistic Zionist war" between Israel and the Arab states. Another called for the organization of "white civilizing committees in all white communities to humanize the savage and beast-like character that runs rampant through America, exemplified by George Lincoln Rockwell and [Pres.] Lyndon Baines Johnson." The Israel statement was followed by the assertion that this "condemnation does not imply anti-Semitism." (The issue of anti-Semitism, at a convention attended by many Jewish delegates, had come up at the Aug. 31 session, when Negro comedian Dick Gregory said: "Every Jew in America over 30 years old knows another Jew that hates Negroes, and if we hate Jews, that's just even, baby.")

Other adopted policy statements called for: (a) "Total and unquestionable support" for "all national peoples' liberation wars," particularly in Vietnam; (b) immediate reparation for the historic physical, sexual, mental and economic exploitation of black people"; (c) political, economic and social control by blacks in black communities; (d) help to local political groups backing black candidates selected by blacks; (e) the seating of excluded Rep. Adam Clayton Powell as chairman of the House Education & Labor Committee.

Norman Thomas, 82, American Socialist leader, deplored the convention's approval of "black *apartheid*." "In the March on Washington in 1963," he said Sept. 6, "we all went to the capital, white and colored alike, singing, preaching, exemplifying fraternity, equality, integration. Those ideals came out badly in Chicago. In their place we have black *apartheid*."

(At an Aug. 1 news conference in New York, sponsored by the New Politics group, Dr. Benjamin Spock, 64, had attacked Pres. Johnson as "the worst betrayer of the American people" for escalating the war in Vietnam at the expense of domestic programs. The groups' executive director, William F. Pepper, said the war "legitimized" racial violence because wars always had a "pervasive atmosphere which condones violence." Spock said "white America" was guilty of "committing a thousand acts of psychological violence against Negroes for every Negro act of violence.")

Innis Gets Lynch's CORE Job

Roy Innis, 33, chairman of the Harlem (N.Y.) chapter of the Congress of Racial Equality (CORE) and a militant black nationalist, was named Dec. 27 to succeed Lincoln O. Lynch as associate national director of CORE. In announcing the appointment, CORE national director Floyd B. McKissick in New York noted that CORE was establishing economic programs in black communities throughout the U.S.

Defense Fund

A group of 47 black business and professional men and women Mar. 20 announced the creation of a fund-raising organization to be known as the National Negro Business & Professional Committee for the Legal Defense Fund. The group sought to recruit 1,000 men and women to pledge $1,000 annual contributions to the NAACP Legal Defense & Educational Fund, Inc. The new group was organized by Asa T. Spaulding, 65, of Durham, N.C., president of the North Carolina Mutual Life Insurance Co., and Dr. Percy L. Julian, 68, of Oak Park, Ill., director of the Julian Research Institute.

The NAACP Legal Defense & Educational Fund, Inc. Mar. 20 announced the appointment of James M. Nabrit 3d as associate counsel (effective Jan. 1, 1967). Nabrit had been acting associate counsel since 1965. On Mar. 17 he also was named associate counsel of the National Office for the Rights of the Indigent, a new organization established with a $1 million Ford Foundation grant to provide legal aid to indigents. The new group was to be administered by the legal defense fund.

The fund's director-counsel, Jack Greenberg, announced June 6 a new educational project designed to inform Negroes of their rights in housing, health, employment and unemployment benefits. Jean Fairfax was appointed director of the program, called the Division of Legal Information & Community Service. It was financed by a matching $300,000 Rockefeller Foundation grant.

RAM Assassination Plot Charged

15 Negroes (11 men and 4 women), allegedly members of the pro-Peking Revolutionary Action Movement (RAM), were arrested in New York early June 21 on charges of plotting to murder moderate civil rights leaders. The 15 were specifically charged with plotting to assassinate NAACP Executive Director Roy Wilkins, Urban League Executive Director Whitney Young Jr. and at least 3 other moderate rights leaders and of conspiring to advocate

criminal anarchy. A 16th man, Maxwell Stanford, 33, a Negro, alleged leader of RAM, was arrested the same day in Philadelphia.

The arrests followed indictments handed down June 20 against 17 Negroes by a Queens (N.Y. City) grand jury. A warrant was issued for the arrest of the 17th man, John Anderson (also known as John Shabazz), but he was not immediately arrested. Also seized in the pre-dawn raids by 150 policemen in Queens, Brooklyn and Manhattan were 30 weapons, including rifles, shotguns, carbines, 1,000 rounds of ammunition, 150 to 275 packets of heroin, walkie-talkies, subversive literature and radio receivers and transmitters.

Chief Inspector Sanford Garelik of the city Police Department said police had begun their investigation of RAM in July 1965.

The indictments charged that the defendants had organized the Jamaica Rifle Club in Dec. 1966 "to be used as a cover and front for legal possession of weapons." 2 of the men were charged with conspiracy to kill Wilkins and Young. They were Herman B. Ferguson, 47, an assistant principal of N.Y. City Public School 40, and Arthur Harris, 22. 13 defendants were accused of conspiracy to commit arson and 7 were charged with possession of dangerous weapons. According to the police, the defendants had planned to set fires at gasoline stations and a lumber yard.

SCHOOL DESEGREGATION

Integration Spotty in South

The Southern Education Reporting Service (SERS) reported in Nashville, Tenn. Apr. 2 that 16% of the Negro students in the 11 Southern states were attending desegregated schools in 1967. This figure compared to 6% in 1966. Negro student enrollment increased by 74,790 pupils during the current school year, and an additional 305,663 Negroes were placed in desegregated schools. But more Negroes were enrolled in all-black schools than in 1954. Currently 2.6 million Negroes attended all-Negro schools in the 11 Southern states. In 1954 2.2 million Negroes had attended all-Negro schools there.

The SERS also reported increased faculty desegregation in state-supported colleges and universities in the South. In 1966 25 predominantly white and 18 predominantly black colleges had integrated faculties.   In 1967 57 of the 269 predominantly white and 28 of the 38 predominantly black colleges had integrated faculties.

Senate Labor & Education Committee statistics showed in December that 82.7% of black pupils in the South and 54.9% of black pupils in border states attended schools in which 95% or more of the pupils were Negroes.   In the South 75.6% of black pupils went to 100%-Negro schools.   The statistics compiled by the committee:

	Black pupils at schools less than 95% black		Black pupils at schools 95%- 99.9% black		Black pupils at schools 100% black	
	Percent	Number	Percent	Number	Percent	Number
Total, 17 states	17.3	589,620	7.1	239,770	75.6	2,571,540
Southern states	12.5	363,290	4.4	126,160	83.1	2,410,000
Alabama	2.4	6,570	2.3	6,300	95.3	260,900
Arkansas	14.5	17,140	2.1	2,480	83.4	98,650
Florida	14.7	41,120	6.1	17,060	79.2	221,550
Georgia	6.6	22,610	3.3	11,300	90.1	308,450
Louisiana	2.6	6,850	.9	2,370	96.5	254,050
Mississippi	2.6	6,840	.6	1,580	96.8	254,700
North Carolina ..	12.8	44,850	2.8	9,810	84.4	295,650
South Carolina ..	4.9	12,120	1.1	2,720	94.0	232,550
Tennessee	21.9	40,600	9.8	18,170	68.3	126,550
Texas	34.6	117,050	12.7	42,960	52.7	178,250
Virginia	20.0	47,540	4.8	11,410	75.2	178,700
Border states	45.1	226,330	22.7	113,610	32.2	161,540
Delaware	84.8	20,440	15.2	3,660	0	0
Kentucky	88.5	38,230	0	0	11.5	4,980
Maryland	40.5	88,980	23.5	51,630	36.0	79,150
Missouri	26.7	34,710	37.5	48,750	35.8	46,540
Oklahoma	40.5	24,950	15.2	9,360	44.3	27,290
West Virginia ...	83.4	19,020	.9	210	15.7	3,580

Desegregation Guidelines Upheld

The full U.S. Court of Appeals for the 5th Circuit in New Orleans Mar. 29 affirmed an earlier appeals court decision upholding the legality of the revised federal school desegregation guidelines.   The 8-4 ruling called for the desegregation of all students, teachers, school transportation and school-related activities in the 6 Southern states within the court's jurisdiction—Alabama, Florida, Georgia, Louisiana, Mississippi and Texas—at the start of the fall term.

The court said: "School desegregation cases involve more than a dispute between certain Negro children and certain schools. If Negroes are ever to enter the mainstream of American life, as school children they must have equal educational opportunities with white children." Public school boards and officials "have the affirmative duty under the 14th Amendment of the U.S. Constitution to bring about an integrated, unitary school system in which there are no Negro schools and no white schools—just schools." "Expressions in our earlier opinions distinguishing between integration and desegregation must yield to this affirmative duty we now recognize." "In fulfilling this duty it is not enough for school authorities to offer Negro children the opportunity to attend formally all-white schools. The necessity of overcoming the effects of the dual school systems in this circuit requires integration of faculties, facilities and activities, as well as students."

The desegregation guidelines established rough percentage goals to be used in determining Southern school systems' compliance with the Civil Rights Act of 1964. Southern Congress members argued that the Office of Education's use of percentages violated the section of the act that prohibited its use to correct "racial imbalance." "The percentages," the court said, "are not a method for setting quotas or striking a balance" but were "simply a rough rule of thumb for measuring the effectiveness of freedom of choice as a useful tool."

The ruling came on an appeal by 3 Alabama and 4 Louisiana school boards of a 3-judge decision handed down in New Orleans Dec. 29, 1966. The court had agreed to reconsider the earlier 2-1 decision *en banc* (full court) "in view of the importance of these cases." It heard arguments in Jacksonville, Fla. Mar. 10 from the Justice Department, the original Negro plaintiffs and the 7 school boards.

Those in the majority were Judges John Minor Wisdom of New Orleans, Elbert P. Tuttle of Atlanta, John R. Brown of Houston, Homer Thornberry of Austin, Tex., Irving L. Goldberg of Dallas, Robert A. Ainsworth Jr. of New Orleans, David W. Dyer of Miami and Bryan Simpson of Jacksonville, Fla. Dissenting were Judges Walter P. Gewin of Tuscaloosa, Ala., Griffin Bell of Atlanta, John C. Godbold of Montgomery, Ala. and James J. Coleman of Ackerman, Miss.

Atty. Gen. Ramsey Clark announced Apr. 5 that the Justice Department had filed 8 motions seeking new desegregation plans in accordance with the Mar. 29 ruling. The Circuit Court's model school decree was filed in Birmingham, Ala. with motions in cases against Birmingham, Gadsen, Huntsville and Madison County, Ala. and in Shreveport, La. in cases against La Salle, Rapides, Grant and Avoyelles Parishes. The U.S. District Court in Monroe, La. Apr. 5, on its own motion, reopened cases involving the Louisiana parishes of Concordia, Richland, Lincoln, Bienville, East Carroll and DeSoto.

The Supreme Court Oct. 9 refused to review the Mar. 29 decision. A petition for review had been filed by 9 Alabama and Louisiana school boards.

The Leadership Conference on Civil Rights, the nation's largest coalition of civil rights groups, had presented Health, Education & Welfare Secy. John W. Gardner Apr. 27 with a statement condemning the "slow pace" of school desegregation. Roy Wilkins, chairman of the conference, said: "The country had been misled by Southern members of Congress and Southern state and school officials into believing the guidelines are too stringent." They "are not strong enough." The statement called on the department to concentrate on the "urgent problem" of *de facto* segregation.

An Office of Education survey made public Aug. 19 found no racial discrimination in school operations involving federal money in 3,216 of the 4,878 school districts in the 17 Southern and border states that previously had used dual school systems.

(The Office of Education had announced Mar. 24 that it was ordering universities in the Southeastern Conference to desegregate their sports programs or forfeit federal aid.)

Alabama Orders to Desegregate

A 3-judge federal court in Montgomery, Ala. Mar. 22 ordered 11 Alabama officials, including the State Board of Education and Gov. Lurleen B. Wallace (D.), to begin the desegregation of all public schools in the state at the start of the fall term. This was the first time since the 1954 Supreme Court desegregation ruling that an entire state was placed under a single injunction to end racial discrimination.

The court order called for the desegregation of both students and teachers in Alabama's 99 (of a total 118) school districts not yet covered by federal injunction. State vocational schools and most colleges were included in the ruling. The state was ordered to abandon a school construction program that, the court said, would produce "markedly inferior education opportunities" for Negroes. The court also ruled unconstitutional the Alabama law that provided $185 annual tuition grants to students attending private schools. The court held that the program was intended to "promote and finance a private school system for white students not wishing to attend public schools also attended by Negroes."

The court charged that the state school officials had "through their control and influence over local school boards flouted every effort to make the 14th Amendment a meaningful reality to Negro school children in Alabama." "First," the court said, "they have used their authority as a threat and as a means of punishment to prevent local school officials from fulfilling their constitutional obligations to desegregate schools, and, 2d, they have performed their own functions in such a way as to maintain and preserve the racial characteristics of the system."

The court ordered local school boards to "take affirmative action to disestablish all state-enforced or -encouraged public school segregation."

The court order was signed by Judges Frank M. Johnson Jr. and Richard T. Rives, both of Montgomery, Ala., and H. Hobart Grooms of Birmingham, Ala.

Gov. Wallace Mar. 30 denounced the court order as issued "in malice and animosity." She asked a joint session of the Alabama Legislature to issue, "as an exercise of the police power of this state, a cease and desist order, to be delivered and served upon the 3 federal judges who have issued unfounded decree, advising them that their actions are beyond the police power of the state of Alabama."

A federal district court in Montgomery May 3 declared unconstitutional an Alabama statute countering the federal guidelines for school desegregation. The ruling was on a suit filed by the NAACP. The court said: "The reason is that we think that a state may not, except through court action reviewable by the U.S. Supreme Court, undertake to declare null and void any action of a federal department or agency."

The Supreme Court May 22 refused to stay the enforcement of the immediate desegregation of all public schools in Alabama, and the Supreme Court Dec. 4 affirmed the decision declaring unconstitutional the Alabama tuition grant law and ordering the desegregation of all public schools in the state.

A 3-judge federal court in Montgomery Nov. 3 declared Alabama's teacher-choice and tuition-grant laws to be unconstitutional on the ground that they violated the equal-protection clause of the 14th Amendment. Gov. Wallace had signed the 2 laws Sept. 1.

The teacher-choice law would have permitted "all students, acting through their parent or guardian . . . , to exercise a choice . . . of the race of the teacher desired." It said "no child shall be required to have a teacher of a race different from the one preferred." The court ruled that the law violated the equal-protection clause because "race is the only factor upon which . . . [the law] operates." The tuition-grant law allocated $3 million in state funds for students in private, nonsectarian schools. The court said that the act "was copied almost verbatim from the Louisiana Tuition Grant Statute" and that the law (the 3d of its kind in Alabama) "contains all of the malignant coloring which so fatally marked its 2 predecessors."

Injunctions were issued against the enforcement of the 2 laws. The court order was signed by Appeals Court Judge Rives and District Court Judges Johnson and Grooms.

Gov. Wallace had made passage of the tuition-grant and teacher-choice laws the prerequisite for her approval of state appropriations to Tuskegee Institute, a Negro college. The college had received state funds since 1945 on the ground that it supplied courses for Negroes that were not offered in state-supported black colleges. In the fiscal year ended Sept. 30, Tuskegee had received $670,000. Gov. Wallace who originally had omitted Tuskegee from her budget recommendations, asked the state Legislature Aug. 31 to appropriate $470,000 annually for the school for the next 2 years under the condition that Tuskegee would get the money only if the tuition-grant law were constitutional. The Legislature approved the request Sept. 1.

The federal court in Montgomery Sept. 5 had issued a temporary restraining order against the teacher-choice law. Ex-Gov. George C. Wallace, acting in behalf of his wife, Gov. Lurleen Wallace, refused Sept. 5 to accept notice of the order from U.S. Deputy Marshal James W. Burns.

(The 3-judge court July 28 had issued a permanent injunction prohibiting the Health, Education & Welfare [HEW] Department from withholding federal funds from the 118 Alabama school systems already under federal court order to desegregate. A temporary restraining order had been issued July 14. The ruling came after the Lanett [Ala.] city school system protested that despite its compliance with the court's Mar. 22 desegregation order, the HEW Department had cut off its funds.)

De Facto D.C. Segregation Ruled Invalid

U.S. District Judge J. Skelly Wright ruled in Washington, D.C. June 19 that the *de facto* segregation existing in the District of Columbia's public schools was unconstitutional. Wright ordered the elimination of the city's controversial "track system" of assignment of pupils by ability and the complete desegregation of the district's schools by fall. The Wright decision was considered a landmark in that it extended the 1954 Supreme Court ban on school segregation to include *de facto* segregation, intentional or not, resulting from segregated population patterns.

The ruling came on a suit filed early in 1966 by Julius W. Hobson, 45, an economist for the Social Security Administration and chairman of a Washington civil rights group, ACT. Negroes comprised about 63% of Washington's 810,000 population and 93% of the city's school population of 145,000. Judge Wright, a member of the U.S. Court of Appeals, tried the case as a district judge.

Washington's superintendent of education, Dr. Carl F. Hansen, 61, announced his resignation July 3, effective July 31. Hansen acted after the city's new school board (5 Negroes and 4 whites) voted 7–2 July 1 to accept Judge Wright's decision without an appeal and to deny Hansen his right to appeal it. (The school board had voted 5–4 Mar. 15 to renew Hansen's contract for 3 years. The terms of 3 pro-Hansen members of the board expired June 30, and their replacements were appointed June 12 by the 14 judges of the U.S. District Court in Washington. 2 of those chosen were Negroes, and their appointment resulted in the first black majority in the board's history. The old board had postponed a decision on whether or not to appeal Wright's decision until July 1, when the new members assumed office.)

Wright's sweeping 182-page decision was considered to have gone far beyond the Supreme Court's 1954 ruling in *Brown* v. *Board of Education*. It extended the *Brown* doctrine to the *de facto* segregated school system of a large urban center whose white population had shifted to suburban areas. It also invoked a recent 5th Circuit Court of Appeals prohibition on discrimination by economic status in jury selection as a further bar to segregation in the district's schools.

"The basic question," Wright declared, was whether Hansen and the school board (named separately as defendants in the case) "unconstitutionally deprive the district's Negro and poor public school children of their right to equal educational opportunity with the district's white and more affluent public school children. The court concludes that they do." Wright found that the annual median per pupil expenditure in the district's predominantly Negro schools was $292, "a flat $100 below median per pupil expenditure in predominantly white schools, [of] $392." "All the evidence in this case," he said, "tends to show that the Washington school system is a monument to the cynicism of the power structure which governs the voteless capital of the greatest country on earth."

Wright permanently enjoined further use of the 4-level track system, whereby students were assigned to separate "honors," "regular," "general," and "basic" curriculums in each grade. The system had been introduced by Hansen in 1955 in order to achieve "meaningful integration" and to encourage white children to stay in the public school system. Wright called Hansen's plan an "appeasement of white families." He charged that school officials had "intentionally gerrymandered school districts and had consistently assigned Negroes to "basic" and "general" curriculums that were geared to "blue collar" students. Most whites were enrolled in the "honors" and "regular" programs. Wright declared that the system "insulate[d] the more academically developed white student from his less fortunate black schoolmate." He said that "according to track theory, those who remain in a lower curriculum remain because they are achieving at their maximum level of ability. They are not admitted to—or are at least discouraged from seeking admission to—a higher instructional level because the school system has determined that they cannot 'usefully' and 'successfully' rise above their present level." "The court does not, however, rest its decision on a finding of intended racial discrimination," he continued, but rather on a finding of "the primary constitutional violation" of inferior schools. "Apart from such intentional aspects, the effects of the track system must be held to be a violation of plantiffs' Constitutional rights."

Wright ordered the district's school officials to substantially integrate all teaching faculties by the fall, and to "provide transportation for volunteering children" in predominantly black neighborhoods east of Rock Creek Park wishing to attend "under-populated" predominantly white schools west of Rock Creek Park (Chevy Chase, Cleveland Park, Glover Park and Spring Valley). He called for the elimination of optional attendance zones and directed the school board to file a plan with the court by Oct. 2 to bring about greater racial integration.

The ruling, the first to invalidate *de facto* segregation in a large metropolitan school system, did not incorporate the controversial proposal advanced by Hobson and his attorneys, William M. Kunstler of New York and Jerry D. Anker of Washington: to merge the predominantly black city school system with the predominantly white suburban school systems in neighboring Maryland and Virginia. Wright, however, told the school board to "anticipate the possibility that integration may be accomplished through cooperation with school districts in the metropolitan suburbs." "Certainly, if the jurisdictions comprising the Washington metropolitan area can cooperate in the establishment of a metropolitan transit authority, the possibility of such cooperation in the field of education should not be denied—at least not without first sounding the pertinent moral and social responsibilities of the parties concerned," he said.

At a news conference July 3 Hansen charged that Wright had posed a "threat to local management of public schools." He accused the district's school board of depriving him of a "civil right of the most supreme importance" by denying him the possibility of appealing the ruling "except on forfeiture of my employment." He announced July 7 that he would petition the U.S. Court of Appeals for the right to appeal the ruling as a private citizen.

The Board of Education July 8 appointed Benjamin J. Henley Jr., 55, a Negro, as acting superintendent of schools.

Dr. William R. Manning, 47, superintendent of schools in Lansing, Mich., was appointed superintendent Nov. 7 and sworn in the same day. (The Board of Education vote for Manning was 7–2.) Manning had been named to the post Oct. 27 at a meeting of the board while 2 board members were absent. The Oct. 27 meeting was interrupted by 15–20 militant black activists who objected to the Manning appointment as "nothing but a bunch of Aunt Jemimas and Uncle Toms doing the white man's bidding." When the militant group seized control of the meeting, the school board adjourned. The militants then held a "public forum" and nominated Acting Supt. Henley as superintendent. The school board reconvened later Oct. 27 and unanimously elected Dr. Henley deputy superintendent.

2 black militants, Mrs. Euphemia L. Hayes, a former teacher and ex-school board president, and Julius W. Hobson, 45, an economist for the Social Security Administration and chairman of the Washington civil rights group ACT, filed suits in the U.S. District Court in Washington Nov. 1 to prevent the school board from offering and Manning from accepting the superintendent post. Both suits charged that the closed meetings at which Manning was selected violated the District of Columbia Code and the school board's regulations.

Louisiana Grant System Unconstitutional

A 3-judge federal court in New Orleans ruled Aug. 26 that the Louisiana program of tuition grants for students in private schools was designed to maintain a segregated school system and therefore was unconstitutional. The ruling came in a suit filed by a group of black parents in 1964 against the Louisiana Financial Assistance Commission. The commission had granted $4 million annually for tuition to students who had been eligible to attend public schools but enrolled instead in private schools. The program provided $2 a day based on a 180-day school year.

The ruling was handed down by Appeals Court Judges J. M. Wisdom and Robert A. Ainsworth Jr. and District Judge Herbert W. Christenberry. The court said: The grant schools "are the fruits of the state's traditional policy of providing segregated schools for white pupils. . . . Act 147 [the law creating the program] fitted into the long series of statutes the Louisiana Legislature enacted for over a hundred years to maintain segregated schools for white children." "The state is so financially involved in the discrimination practiced by private schools in Louisiana that any financial aid from the state to these schools or newly organized schools in the form of tuition grants or similar benefits violates the equal-protection clause of the 14th Amendment."

The Justice Department Sept. 1 asked the U.S. District Court in New Orleans for permission to file a complaint seeking the invalidation of a new program that, the department contended, had the same purpose and effect as the old one—"to maintain a racially segregated educational system in Louisiana with state support." The new program, the Louisiana Education Commission for Needy Children, had been created by Act 99 in June 1967 to supplant Act 147 if Act 147 were invalidated. It provided $3½ million per year for tuition grants to private school students eligible for public school.

CRC Scores Bias' Effect, Backs Guidelines

The U.S. Civil Rights Commission Feb. 19 urged new legislation to eliminate racial imbalances in public schools and reported on the "dire effects" of racially segregated school systems. In a report issued Aug. 7, the commission called for stricter enforcement of the federal school desegregation guidelines. Among details of the 2 reports:

Segregation's effects—In its Feb. 19 report, entitled "Racial Isolation in the Public Schools," the commission charged that black students received inferior education in racially segregated schools. It said that compensatory programs to improve ghetto schools by providing additional funds and special services were largely ineffective.

The commission's investigation had been started in 1965 at the request of Pres. Johnson. David K. Cohen, a member of the commission's staff, directed the study. He was assisted by a panel of educators, headed by Harvard Prof. Thomas F. Pettigrew, and by local research teams. *The commission reported:*

● "Negro students typically do not achieve as well in school as white students. The longer they are in school the further they fall behind." Few Negroes attend college; those who did were less likely than similarly educated whites to find white-collar jobs.

● The North as well as the South, through subtle methods such as school-site selection and assignment patterns, worked to perpetuate segregation. The problem was especially acute in large cities where 75% of black elementary students were enrolled in nearly all-Negro schools.

● Negroes were less likely to attend schools with well-stocked libraries or advanced courses in sciences and languages but more likely to attend overcrowded schools. Black students were more likely than white students "to have teachers with low verbal achievement, to have substitute teachers and to have teachers who are dissatisfied with their school assignment."

● Communities tended to regard predominantly black schools as inferior institutions. "Negro students in such schools are sensitive to such views and often come to share them."

● Racial isolation was as serious an impediment to education as a student's background, the quality of the school and the social composition of his classmates. "School attendance in racial isolation generates attitudes on the part of both Negroes and whites which tend to alienate them from members of the other race."

● "The effects of racial composition of schools are cumulative. The longer Negro students are in desegregated schools, the better is their academic achievement and their attitudes. Conversely, there is a growing deficit for Negroes who remain in racially isolated schools."

Without offering specific proposals, the commission called on Congress to establish "reasonable and practical standards" to correct the injustices of racial imbalance. The commission recommended the criterion established by the Massachusetts Legislature and the N.Y. State Commissioner of Education, which defined as racially imbalanced any school in which black pupils constituted more than 50% of the total enrollment. The commission said Congress should make the 50 states rather than the individual school districts responsible for meeting the standards. It urged the federal government to initiate programs of "substantial financial assistance" to plan remedies for imbalance, to provide for construction and for new facilities and to improve the quality of education in all schools.

The report asserted that since the goals of equal educational opportunity and equal housing opportunity were inseparable, Congress ought to enact legislation to (1) "prohibit discrimination in the sale or rental of housing" and (2) "expand programs of federal assistance designed to increase the supply of housing throughout the metropolitan areas within the means of low- and moderate-income families."

The commission called on the Department of Housing & Urban Development to tighten requirements of nondiscrimination in the selection of housing-project sites and in federal relocation programs.

Guidelines enforcement—In its Aug. 7 report, a 262-page document entitled "Southern School Desegregation, 1966–1967," the commission asserted that in 17 Southern and border states more black children (2½ million) were attending all-Negro schools then had done so (2.2 million) before the 1954 Supreme Court desegregation decision.

The commission recommended new laws to permit Negro children and their families to bring civil action for injunctive relief and damages against those who intimidated them because of race or enrollment or attendance at any public school. In 6 of the 63 school districts visited by the commission, "shots had been fired into the dwellings of Negro school children," the report said.

The commission said that many private schools had been established in the South to escape desegregation. (Investigators found 67 in Louisiana, 44 in South Carolina, 35 in Mississippi, 29 in Virginia and 13 in Alabama.) The commission urged the Attorney General to determine whether these segregated private schools could be denied their tax exempt status, and it recommended Congressional action if it was found they could not. (The Internal Revenue Service [IRS] Aug. 2 had issued a new ruling granting tax exemption to private segregated schools whose involvement with state and local governments was not of the kind held unconstitutional by the courts: those who did not receive direct financial aid from any state or local government unit or whose tuition assistance to pupils from a government unit did not constitute more than half of the total financial support for the schools. At that time the IRS had announced that it had approved applications for tax exemption of 42 schools in Alabama, Georgia, Louisiana, Mississippi, North Carolina, South Carolina and Virginia.)

The commission recommended that during the 1967–8 school year, school districts operating under a voluntary free choice plan be required to meet percentage requirements set down in the 1966 guidelines for desegregation.

For the 1968–9 school year and thereafter, the commission said: "The HEW [Health, Education & Welfare Department] should require for all districts which have not achieved substantial desegregation throughout the system a significant increase in the percentage of Negro students attending desegregated schools and in the pace under which all-Negro schools are being disestablished. . . . Freedom of choice should be accepted only where the school district shows that it has met the standards of the guidelines and there has been no harassment or intimidation of Negro parents or children in connection with the exercise of choice." "The HEW should require that . . . schools no longer be racially identifiable on the basis of the racial composition of the faculty or staff. For the 1967–8 school year, the department should require substantial progress toward that end. . . . The Attorney General should request the courts to revise existing school desegregation orders to comply with standards previously set forth."

Girard Integration Order Under Attack

The U.S. 3d Circuit Court of Appeals ruled in Philadelphia Feb. 28 that Girard College did not have to integrate under the terms of the Pennsylvania Public Accommodations Act of 1939. The decision reversed a Sept. 2, 1966 ruling of Federal District Judge Joseph S. Lord 3d and vacated his injunction prohibiting the school from barring Negroes. The appeals court said that 2 courts, the Pennsylvania Supreme Court and the Philadelphia Orphans Court, had previously ruled against the applicability of the 1939 law. It held that Lord had erred in overruling these decisions. The court added, however, that the case raised "grave constitutional questions" on whether or not the barring of Negro boys violated the 14th Amendment of the Constitution, and it sent the suit to the district court to consider this point. But Lord July 5 made permanent his injunction prohibiting Girard College from barring the admission of Negroes solely on the basis of race. The ruling, the 2d since Sept. 27, 1966, was made on the grounds that the constitutional rights of 7 black applicants had been violated. Lord stayed execution of his order pending an appeal by Girard to the U.S. 3d Circuit Court of Appeals. The appeal was filed Aug. 22.

Other Legal Actions

Among other court cases involving the issue of education and civil rights:

● The Justice Department filed suits in U.S. District Court in Monroe, La. Jan. 9 to invalidate the Nov. 8, 1966 school board election in Ward 4 of Madison Parish (county) on the ground that local officials had discriminated against Negroes in providing absentee ballots. This was the first time the department sought to nullify a local or state election. The suit charged that absentee ballots provided had the margin of victory for J. T. Fulton, a white write-in candidate who had received 1,891 votes, in his contest with Harrison Brown, a Negro who had received 1,622 votes. Fulton's total included 510 of the 512 absentee ballots cast in the election. The plaintiffs asked the court to order a new election and to enjoin local officials from depriving citizens of their rights under the 1965 Voting Rights Act.

● The Justice Department filed 3 school desegregation suits Jan. 11: in U.S. District Court in Shreveport, La. against the DeSoto Parish (county) school district; in U.S. District Court in Jackson, Miss. against the Hinds County school district on charges of operating separate schools for white and Negro students; and in U.S. District Court in Meridian, Miss. against the Neshoba County school district on charges of taking legally inadequate steps under a desegregation plan begun in 1965.

● U.S. District Judge Bailey Brown in Memphis Jan. 19 ordered the Shelby County (Tenn.) school board to desegregate its facilities and ease its policy for student transfers beginning in the fall of 1967. The ruling was on a Justice Department motion, filed Jan. 16, asking the court to hold the school officials in contempt for allegedly defying an earlier school desegregation order. The Justice Department had charged that only 198 of the district's 14,765 black students attended formerly all-white schools since the court order and that none of the 25,800 white students attended Negro schools. It said that more than 200 faculty vacancies and more than 100 new faculty positions had been filled on a racial basis and that the only staff integration was the assignment of 8 white coordinators and 3 white interns of the National Teacher Corps to all-Negro schools.

● The Justice Department Mar. 1 filed a motion in the U.S. District Court in Tampa, Fla. to intervene in a private school desegregation suit against Polk County, Fla. Under a Mar. 1965 ruling in the suit, the county had been eliminating its dual school system. The Justice Department contended that the desegregation moves were legally inadequate, and it asked the court to end discrimination in assignment of students and teachers.

● The department Mar. 20 filed a civil suit in the U.S. District Court in Montgomery, Ala. against the Dale County (Ala.) Board of Education to enforce an assurance of compliance with Title VI of the 1964 Civil Rights Act. The department charged that (a) the school authorities assigned students and teachers to schools on the basis of race; (b) the schools were completely segregated, and the Negroes were furnished with inferior programs and facilities. The county had submitted a "freedom of choice" plan to the Health, Education & Welfare Department and had then received more than $100,000 in federal aid for the 1965–6 school year. It had signed a pledge of compliance with the revised HEW guidelines May 11, 1966 to qualify for continued assistance. But the Justice Department charged that "the defendants . . . are continuing to subject Negro students in Dale County to discrimination under programs receiving federal financial assistance."

● The Justice Department Apr. 7 filed suit in the U.S. District Court in Columbus, Ga. against the public schools of Ben Hill County, Ga. The suit called for (a) the desegregation in the fall of the faculties, facilities and programs of the county school system; (b) a preliminary injunction to set a time during the spring to allow students to choose the schools they wanted to attend in the fall. It was the Justice Department's first school desegregation suit in Georgia.

● The U.S. 8th Circuit Court of Appeals in St. Louis Apr. 13 ordered the Altheimer (Ark.) School District to desegregate its faculty no later than the beginning of the 1969–70 school year. The court, in reversing an earlier district court ruling, ordered the county to discontinue its present practice of transporting white and Negro students on separate buses. It also ordered that all future school facilities be built so as to eliminate the effects of segregation.

● The Justice Department Apr. 25 filed a motion in the U.S. District Court in Alexandria, Va. to intervene in a private suit against the Loudoun County (Va.) School Board. The department sought to reopen a 1962 suit that had resulted in a court-approved plan of pupil assignment in May 1963; the Justice Department held that subsequent court decisions had imposed greater obligations on the school authorities to integrate. The department asked for a court order requiring non-racial geographic attendance zones and desegregation of faculties and programs. It charged that Loudoun County had been operating a dual school system, assigning students on a racial basis but allowing them to transfer to white schools on application. 4 of the county's 22 schools were attended only by Negroes, 8 only by whites, 10 predominantly by whites.

● The department Apr. 26 filed a suit in the U.S. District Court in Raleigh, N.C. against the Northampton County (N.C.) Board of Education. The suit charged the county with operating a dual school system. The department said that all 1,897 white students in the county attended solely and predominantly white schools and that 5,325 of the county's 5,538 black students attended all-Negro schools.

● The Justice Department filed suits in U.S. District Court in Macon, Ga. May 29 against the Decatur and Webster County school systems. The suits, charging that both counties maintained dual school systems, sought court orders for the desegregation of their students, faculties and programs. The department alleged that 9 black youths attended white schools in Webster County and that one black youth attended a traditionally white school in Decatur County. It said both counties provided inferior educational opportunities for Negroes.

● The department filed a motion in U.S. District Court in Houston, Tex. June 2 to intervene in a private desegregation suit against the Houston Independent School District, the 6th largest in the nation. In its motion for supplemental relief, the department sought a court order to bring Houston's desegregation plan in line with standards established Mar. 29 by the U.S. 5th Circuit Court of Appeals. The department said a "freedom of choice" plan filed by the district 8 days earlier was "inadequate under existing judicial standards." Negroes comprised 32% (about 75,000) of the students enrolled in Houston schools in 1966. The department said that during the 1965-6 school year only about 7% of the city's black elementary school students and 2% of the black secondary school students had attended desegregated schools. Only 8 black teachers had been assigned to integrated schools in 1965-6.

● A school desegregation suit against the Montgomery County, Miss. school district was filed in U.S. District Court in Oxford, Miss. by the Justice Department June 7. The suit charged that the district maintained a dual school system under its 2-year-old "freedom of choice" plan. Only one Negro, the department said, attended a traditionally white school in the county.

● The department June 19 filed suits in the U.S. District Court in Raleigh, N.C. against the public school systems of Jones and Bertie Counties, N.C. The department asked for court orders to end racial segregation in the 2 systems. During the 1966-7 school year, 1,671 of 1,749 black students in Jones County attended all-Negro schools; all 1,407 white students attended solely or predominantly white schools. All 2,115 white students in Bertie County attended solely or predominantly all-white schools, while 4,320 of the county's 4,648 black students attended all-Negro schools.

● The Justice Department July 5 filed a suit in Oxford, Miss. against the Tunica County, Miss. school system. The department said that only 12 of the county's 3,200 black students attended traditionally white schools at the end of the 1966-7 school year and that no white students attended Negro schools. It also charged that teaching faculties were segregated and the county maintained a segregated system of bus transportation.

● A 3-judge federal court in Lynchburg, Va. July 19 permanently enjoined Virginia from enforcing the racial restrictions of the 1899 will of Indiana Fletcher Williams, founder of Sweet Briar College. The U.S. Supreme Court May 28 had ordered the lower court to hear the college's arguments in its efforts to break the will and desegregate the school. The founder had bequeathed her estate "for the education of white girls and young women."

● The Justice Department Sept. 11 filed suit in the U.S. District Court in Biloxi, Miss. on charges that 13 Noxubee County, Miss. law enforcement officials and private individuals had interfered with court-ordered integration of local schools by threats and intimidation. A 2d suit claimed that school officials had failed and refused to comply with a desegregation order issued by the district court June 2.

● The Supreme Court Oct. 9 refused to review a federal court ruling that Cincinnati school officials were not required by the Constitution to take affirmative action to reduce racial imbalance resulting from neighborhood patterns rather than discriminatory action by public officials.

Equal Education Conference

U.S. Education Commissioner Harold Howe 2d in Washington Nov. 17 told delegates to the 3-day (Nov. 16–18) National Conference on Equal Education (sponsored by the U.S. Civil Rights Commission) that urban educators "must pursue both compensatory education [in ghetto schools] and desegregated schools at the same time." He conceded that "in some cities, where nonwhite school populations approach or exceed 50%, it is unlikely that we will have integrated schools for another generation."

(Howe announced the establishment of a new Division of Equal Educational Opportunity in the Office of Education to help speed school desegregation by providing technical assistance under the 1964 Civil Rights Act. Dr. Gregory R. Anrig was named to head the new division.)

About 30 Negroes and Mexican-Americans picketed the conference Nov. 17 in protest against under-representation of Mexican-Americans at the meeting. (It was reported that about 50 of nearly 1,000 delegates were Mexican-Americans.)

Black College Improvement Urged

The Commission on Higher Educational Opportunity Aug. 29 issued a report urging the South's 104 traditionally black colleges and universities—serving a total enrollment of 123,556 students (more than half of the U.S.' approximately 200,000 black undergraduates)—to take immediate and far-reaching steps to overcome "the handicaps of educational disadvantage and cultural depriva- tion." The 48-page report, including a series of recommendations, was presented at a meeting of the Southern Regional Education Board in White Sulphur Springs, Va. (The commission had been established by the board in 1966 with the aid of a Carnegie Corp. grant to study the problems of Negro higher education in the South.)

The report said: "As a group and for many reasons these insti- tutions do not provide equal higher educational opportunity for their students." "They do not match their predominantly white counterparts in admission standards, breadth and depth of curricu- lum, quality of instruction or preparation of students for employ- ment. They are plagued by grave financial, administrative and teaching problems. Obviously, if they are to become equal par- ticipants in Southern higher education, drastic changes will be necessary."

Among the recommendations the commission made: (1) Long- range planning "to complete the evolution of the South's dual sys- tem of higher education into a single system serving all students." (2) The use of all educational resources "in a massive effort to achieve equality of educational opportunity." (3) Statewide plan- ning including both public and private institutions to provide equal higher educational opportunity. (4) A "full range of programs for vocational technical and academic students and opening-door, low- cost institutions which are geographically accessible to all citizens." (5) The establishment of a regional institute for higher educational opportunity for regional planning and development.

According to a study by Harvard sociologist David Riesman and social critic Christopher Jencks, in the winter 1967 issue of the *Harvard Educational Review,* the majority of black colleges "stand near the tail end of the academic procession."

The Ford Foundation July 7 had announced a $1.1 million program to help 52 Southern Negro colleges with a series of reforms to strengthen their academic programs. F. Champion Ward, a foundation vice president, explained: "This effort is problem- centered, emphasizing specific action where conditions are favorable on such matters as faculty development, compensatory education, administration and student services by colleges, both singly and in cooperation with others." Dr. John A. Griffin, executive director of the Southern Education Foundation, which would receive $361,000 of the grant, said: "Most of the white institutions in the

South . . . are now desegregated, . . . but the numbers of Negroes attending the formerly all-white institutions are small by comparison with the Negroes enrolled in the predominantly Negro colleges. . . ." The Ford Foundation July 11 announced a grant of $108,000 to the National Council of Churches to aid 60 predominantly Negro church-related colleges. A Ford Foundation grant of $120,000 was awarded July 11 to the Texas Association of Developing Colleges, a group of 6 privately supported 4-year, predominantly Negro colleges, for the development of a Texas project under the auspices of the council.

John U. Monro resigned as dean of Harvard College, effective in July, to become director of freshman studies at Miles College, a small Negro college in Birmingham, Ala. The United Negro College Fund had announced that under a grant of $35,000 from the Chase Manhattan Bank Foundation these 6 well-known economists would teach and advise at Southern Negro colleges in the fall 1967 term: Walter W. Heller of the University of Minnesota, Raymond J. Saulnier of Columbia University, Yale Brozen of the University of Chicago, Paul W. McCracken of the University of Michigan, Henry C. Wallich of Yale University and Bertrand Fox of Harvard.

EMPLOYMENT & BIAS

Progress & Problems

The Equal Employment Opportunity Commission (EEOC) reported Jan. 3 that Negroes had made substantial gains in employment in Southern textile mills since the passage of the 1964 Civil Rights Act. The commission noted, however, that "the 406 textile establishments which reported [as required by the 1964 law] revealed gross under-utilization of Negroes on the skilled crafts and white-collar occupations."

The report said that of 10,211 textile mill officials or managers, only 11 were black; of 2,338 persons considered professionals, 3 were black; of 2,104 technicians, 13 were black. The 11,784 white-collar workers included only 149 Negroes. Of 2,985 craftsmen, 690 were black. There were 8,475 Negroes among the 114,075 machine operators, 5,725 Negroes among 19,143 laborers and 1,626 Negroes among 4,021 service workers.

In 103 North Carolina establishments, the report said, employ-

ment increased 312% for black women and 54.8% for Negro men.
3/5 of the 3,043 employes added to the payroll were black.   In
South Carolina Negro employment had increased 58.6%—47.6%
for men and 311.3% for women.

Negro females outnumbered black males in white-collar jobs
by almost 100%, according to a report published Oct. 21 by the
EEOC. The survey, based on mandatory reports from industry,
was viewed as one of the most comprehensive in job discrimination
ever undertaken.

The survey showed that in N.Y. City, white-collar jobs were
held by 38,534 females but only 16,173 Negro males, whereas
519,226 white males and 432,583 white females had white-collar
positions. In Chicago white-collar jobs were held by 7,669 black
males, 19,840 Negro females, 325,653 white males and 261,157
white females.

(The Oct. 21 report indicated that women in general held only
a small portion of the higher-echelon managerial or professional
jobs. Women comprised from ¼ to ⅓ of the total work force
and from ⅓ to ½ of the total white-collar work force. When clerical positions were excluded, the report said, "women's share of
white-collar jobs in these standard metropolitan statistical areas is
cut nearly in half." In Los Angeles females comprised 29.4% of
the work force and held 37.8% of the white-collar jobs. When
clerical jobs were excluded they held 18.2% of the Los Angeles
white-collar jobs, and when low-paying retail sales positions were
also excluded they held only 12.7% of the white-collar positions.)

According to the EEOC data, Negro employment in blue-collar
jobs was extremely high. EEOC statistics on Negro employment
in 9 metropolitan areas:

	Atlanta	Chicago	Cleveland	Kansas City	Los Angeles	New Orleans	New York	San Francisco	Washington
Negro % of population ..	23.0	14.0	13.0	11.2	7.6	30.7	11.5	8.5	25.0
Negro % of total employ-ment	15.2	13.5	11.2	8.9	6.9	20.1	10.0	8.0	22.0
Unemployment rate (Negro and white)	2.6	2.8	3.1	4.1	4.4	4.0	4.0	4.3	2.1
Negro ghetto unemploy-ment rate	15.5	**	15.5	**	10.7	10.0	8.0	12.0	8 to 14
Negro % of white collar jobs	2.3	4.7	3.2	2.1	2.8	3.0	5.7	3.0	8.4
Negro % of blue collar jobs*	33.8	24.7	21.5	17.6	14.5	44.8	22.3	17.7	51.9
Negro % of craftsmen's jobs	6.4	7.1	5.0	5.3	4.1	10.2	5.8	4.5	10.7

*Excluding craftsmen   **Not given

A study conducted by Columbia University's Bureau of Applied Social Research revealed that the number of nonwhite men in professional and managerial positions had increased 56% in the period 1950–60 while the number of whites in such positions had increased 27%. The study, based on U.S. census figures of the country's entire male civilian labor population, showed that federal government hiring accounted for more than half of the new professional and managerial jobs opened to Negroes and for 70% of the clerical and sales positions. The study also found that the number of Negroes in craft occupations had increased 46% in the period while the increase for whites was 13%.

A study released July 1 by the Community Advisers on Equal Employment, a Washington, D.C. civic group, indicated that Negroes had not benefited from the growing job opportunities in metropolitan Washington. In spite of the vast increase of jobs in the suburbs, Negroes were still largely restricted to jobs in the central city. (About 63% of Washington's 810,000 population was black.) Significant "underemployment" of Negroes was found in private industry. In a sampling of nearly ⅓ of private jobs in the area, blacks held less than 3% of the professional jobs, less than 4% of the official and managerial positions and less than 10% of the technical jobs. Negroes occupied 54.5% of the 29,104 District of Columbia government jobs but only 27 of the 206 positions in the 4 highest executive categories. Of the 249,404 federal government jobs in the metropolitan area, Negroes held about 25%. However, the study found that Negroes occupied only 2.2% of the jobs in grades 12 through 18, the highest in civil service ranking.

A report published Oct. 16 by the 20th Century Fund warned that by 1975 "unemployment among Negroes in the South may still be more than double that of Southern whites." The 276-page report, entitled "The Advancing South: Manpower Prospects and Problems," was prepared by Dr. James G. Maddox, economics professor at North Carolina State University; Dr. Vivian W. Henderson, president of Clark College; Dr. E. E. Liebhafsky, chairman of the Economics & Finance Department at the University of Houston, and Herbert M. Hamlin, research consultant at the University of California. The study covered Arkansas, Florida, Georgia, Kentucky, Louisiana, Mississippi, North Carolina, Oklahoma, South Carolina, Tennessee, Texas and Virginia.

The report predicted a drop in black migration from the South in the next 10 years because of the increasing income and job status of Negroes and poor whites. It said the South would lead other regions of the country in gains in real per capita income and in an increasing proportion of investment in plants and equipment. But, the report concluded: "A major obstacle to the South's economic development is its inadequate educational system, particularly for Negroes. The employment outlook facing the Southern Negro is a discouraging one so long as he is undereducated, lacks industrial experience and is subjected to racial discrimination."

In an interview in New York a week before the report's publication, Maddox described the South as a "region in transition." He said: "Formerly it [the South] was the poorest and most underdeveloped region of the country because it depended on farming —and particularly tobacco and cotton farming, which required large amounts of hand labor—and on low wage industries." "The labor-saving technological revolution in Southern agriculture has cut the farm labor force . . . between 1940 and 1960 from 4.2 to 1.7 million persons. . . . Crop acreage declined from 111 million to 81 million." The size of farms in 1960 was twice that of 1930; manhours of labor used on them, however, were fewer than half of the 1940 total. The average *per capita* personal income in the South was half the level of the country's average in 1900. It rose to 60% in 1940 and to more than 75% by 1960. "The South's discriminatory policies are a brake on its economic development. Yet the South, more than any other region, is best suited to become a model democratic multiracial society."

State Contracts Barred in Ohio

U.S. District Judge Joseph P. Kinneary in Columbus, O. May 17 permanently enjoined the state of Ohio from signing contracts with 4 companies for the construction of a $12.8 million medical science building at Ohio State University. He issued the ban because of arrangements by the companies to hire workers through 4 building trades unions that discriminated against Negroes. Kinneary ruled that the state must insure equal job opportunities for blacks on all public works contracts.

The unions accused of discrimination were: the International Brotherhood of Electrical Workers; the International Association of Bridge, Structural & Ornamental Iron Workers; the United Association of Journeymen & Apprentices of the Plumbing & Pipe Fitting Industry of the U.S. & Canada; the Sheet Metal Workers' International Association.

Kinneary declared that the state could not contract for public works projects in which (1) building contractors were "bound by any agreement . . . to secure their labor force exclusively or primarily from any organization or source that does not supply or refer laborers and craftsmen without regard to race, color or membership in the labor union" or (2) labor organizations required, as a condition of employment, "that employes hired by such persons become members of a labor organization within a certain number of days after employment, and membership in such labor organizations is not equally available to all persons without regard to race or color."

The ruling came on a suit filed by the NAACP on behalf of William Ethridge, an electrician, and Jerome Welch, a heavy equipment operator. Ethridge and Welch said they had been denied membership in the unions.

NAACP Executive Director Roy Wilkins hailed the ruling June 27 as a "landmark decision." He announced plans for a nationwide program to "take advantage of the opportunities for expanding employment opened up by this decision." Telegrams sent to Labor Secy. Willard Wirtz and 40 states urged compliance with Judge Kinneary's ruling. Robert Carter, head of the NAACP legal staff, sent instructions to the organization's 1,500 chapters to promote the enrollment of black youths in apprentice training programs, to inventory communities for skilled black labor and to work toward delaying building contracts until black workers were included regardless of their union membership.

Ohio Gov. James A. Rhodes June 1 had signed a bill prohibiting racial discrimination in the hiring of workers for public works projects. Under the law, which had been passed by votes of 77–10 in the Ohio House and 31–0 in Senate, public works projects would be void and unenforceable unless the hiring sources could assure state officials that workers were hired without regard to race, color, religion, national origin or ancestry. The law further required trade unions to certify that nonwhites as well as whites were available for job referrals. Bidders for contracts would be required to submit statements of compliance prior to the awarding of the contract.

(The Columbus chapter of the NAACP charged in a suit filed in U.S. District Court in Columbus Oct. 13 that the Ohio Bureau of Unemployment Compensation discriminated against Negroes in referring applicants for jobs.)

Louisiana March

A march was started in Bogalusa, La. Aug. 10 as a protest against the lack of job opportunities for Negroes. The march ended 106 miles away with a rally at the state capitol in Baton Rouge, La. Aug. 20. The marchers, whose numbers varied between 15 and 92, were escorted by 175 state policemen. The police were joined Aug. 18 by 650 National Guardsmen who had been activated by Gov. John J. McKeithen (D.). The march, organized by the Bogalusa Civic & Voters League, was led by League Pres. A. Z. Young and Lincoln Lynch, associate national director of CORE.

While the march was in progress, 5 white men were wounded in Hammond, La. Aug. 13 when 2 carloads of blacks fired shotguns at a crowd of whites standing outside a bar. Police set up a roadblock in the area, and 12 Negroes were arrested during the night. The incident occurred while the marchers from Bogalusa were holding a rally 7 miles away. Although officials said the shooting had no connection with the march, Gov. McKeithen declared Aug. 14 that the marchers had achieved one of their purposes, "to get somebody shot and get a lot of publicity."

15 white men broke through the police escort and attacked 20 black marchers in Holden, La. Aug. 15. Several Negroes and a deputy sheriff were knocked down in the brief scuffle, and 2 white men were arrested. In Satsuma, La. Aug. 16, about 75 white men charged through the police guard and attacked 25 marchers. Police used billy clubs and carbine butts to disperse the attackers. 4 persons, including a policeman, were treated for head wounds. 8 men were arrested on charges of battery and disturbing the peace.

McKeithen called up 650 National Guardsmen Aug. 17 to protect the marchers. At a news conference the governor said that "if we don't let them march their 6 miles tomorrow, they would be back next week to march, and we might have federal troops and everything like that." A. Z. Young said at a news conference Aug. 17 that the marchers were "not going to protect ourselves, we're just going to march." He said the governor would be "absolutely responsible" if a riot occurred.

The marchers were met by crowds of white hecklers as they moved through Denham Springs, La. Aug. 18. 2 Negroes were struck by bottles, others were pelted with eggs. Young praised the authorities for their protection. He said that without it, "there would have been slaughter out here—slaughter." Before the marchers had set out in the morning, authorities had reported finding a dummy bomb under a bridge on the march route. The marchers were forced to stop constantly throughout the day in order to remove large roofing nails and broken glass that whites had thrown on the road.

In a televised news conference late Aug. 18 McKeithen called the marchers "silly, ridiculous and absurd." He said he would not accept the list of grievances they planned to present to him at the Aug. 20 rally. He added, however, that they "have the right to march" and that he would call up "as many as 1,000 more" Guardsmen to maintain peace. McKeithen activated 850 Guardsmen Aug. 19 but held them in reserve.

The marchers completed their march Aug. 19 with an evening rally at a junior high school auditorium in Baton Rouge. About 300 Negroes attended the rally while 300 whites attended a Ku Klux Klan rally about 4 miles away. National Guardsmen were not present at either meeting.

More than 2,200 Guardsmen and police officers stood guard as Negroes held a mass rally at the state capitol Aug. 20. Young read a statement calling for the election of 10 Negroes running for local offices in Bogalusa and asking McKeithen to hire Negroes in the state-run offices there.

A white supremacist meeting presided over by William V. Fowler, who identified himself as a California organizer for the National Knights of the Ku Klux Klan, followed the Negro rally. Fowler told about 300 spectators that Jews and Communists were responsible for civil rights demonstrations. He said that SNCC Chairman H. Rap Brown and Stokely Carmichael were undercover agents of the Senate Appropriations Committee. Their real names, he said, were John Green and Peter Mulligan. During the rallies 2 Negroes were arrested for failing to move on; one white heckler was taken into custody.

(56 Negroes had been arrested in Bogalusa July 4 for trying to stage a rights march without a parade permit. City officials said the permit had been withheld because of a lack of manpower to police the march. But 125 Negroes staged an all-night march July 23–24 from Bogalusa to the Washington Parish Courthouse in Franklinton, La. to dramatize their support of a House bill designed to protect Negroes and civil rights workers against racist attacks and to demonstrate that "Negroes may safely traverse the highways of this state at night, without fear of violence or intimidation." A. Z. Young and other members of the Bogalusa Civic & Voters League acted as marshals for the 25-mile walk. More than 50 policemen, including 11 state troopers escorted the marchers. Police dispersed a crowd of 300 persons who lined the march route in Bogalusa. 3 white teen-agers were arrested when they attempted to disrupt the march. The march ended at 9:30 a.m. July 24 with a rally on the

steps of the courthouse in Franklinton. Lincoln Lynch of CORE told the crowd: "We are through clapping our hands and marching. From now on, we must be ready to kill." Young said blacks would "burn up Louisiana" if they failed to win equal justice. "If Louisiana starts to burn, it's going to burn, burn, burn," Young declared.)

Employers Accused of Bias

The Justice Department Feb. 27 filed suit in the U.S. District Court in Raleigh, N.C. charging the Dillon Supply Co. of Raleigh with racial discrimination in employment. It was the government's first suit against an employer under the equal employment opportunity section of the 1964 Civil Rights Act. The department alleged that the industrial equipment company assigned blacks to menial, low-paying jobs without regard to their qualifications and kept them in these jobs while providing advancement to others no better qualified. The department sought an injunction to prevent further discriminatory practices and to order Dillon to take reasonable steps to desegregate its operations.

24 Negroes filed suit in the U.S. District Court in Columbia, S.C. Mar. 13 against the Campbell Soup Co. They charged racial discrimination in hiring practices in a plant operated by a Campbell subsidiary. The suit contended that the company's educational tests and requirements discriminated against Negroes who passed dexterity tests but did not meet educational standards. The plaintiffs said the majority of jobs were unskilled ones involved in the dressing, cooking and packaging of poultry and other foods. A Campbell spokesman in Camden, N.J. denied the charges.

2 Negroes, Donald H. Quarles and Ephraim E. Briggs, filed suit in U.S. District Court in Richmond, Va. May 2 against their employer, Philip Morris, Inc., on charges of alleged employment discrimination. They charged that Local 209 of the Tobacco Workers International Union had aided the alleged discrimination. Quarles and Briggs said that the "overwhelming majority" of Negroes had been limited to jobs in a department where tobacco was received and processed for cigarette manufacture and that blacks had been refused transfers to higher paying jobs in other departments. Attorneys for the NAACP Legal Defense & Educational Fund said the suit, recommended in 1965 by the Equal Employment Opportunity Commission, was the first to go to court under the Civil Rights Act of 1964.

The Justice Department sued H. K. Porter Co., Inc., in U.S.

District Court in Birmingham, Ala. June 23 on charges of racial discrimination. The department sought an injunction to prevent discrimination by the company's Connors Steel Division, which operated mills and plants in Birmingham. The suit alleged that the classified jobs "in such a manner as to provide higher paying jobs for white persons" and failed to provide advancement opportunities to Negroes on an equal basis with whites. It said that the company limited, segregated and classified employes "in such a manner as to deprive or tend to deprive Negroes of employment opportunities or otherwise adversely affect their status on account of race."

The Justice Department filed suit in U.S. District Court in Buffalo, N.Y. Dec 7 charging the Bethlehem Steel Corp. with racial discrimination in employment at its Lackawanna, N.Y. plant. It alleged that the Bethlehem Steel plant followed a "pattern and practice of discrimination in employment against Negroes on account of their race." It said that the company hired, referred, transferred and assigned white employes "without regard to qualifications" but placed "stringent requirements on Negroes who apply for hiring, referral, transfer or assignment to the same or similar jobs." The suit charged that in the mechanical and electrical department the company administered and graded job-assignment tests "in a manner so as to give preferential treatment to white applicants and to exclude Negro applicants similarly qualified." Negroes were assigned less desirable jobs than whites with similar or lower qualifications, the suit alleged.

(A Federal District Court in St. Louis May 11 had dismissed a suit filed by 23 Negro employes against the Monsanto Co. and the Oil, Chemical & Atomic Workers union on charges of unfair employment practices. The parties involved had reached an agreement under which 10 qualified Negro employes would be transferred to fill anticipated vacancies.)

Unions Accused

The Justice Department filed suit Apr. 14 in U.S. District Court in Columbus, O. against Local 683 of the International Brotherhood of Electrical Workers (IBEW) on charges of violating the equal employment opportunity section of the 1964 act. The department said the IBEW local discriminated against Negroes and failed to recruit and accept Negroes as members on the same basis as whites. All 706 local members and 91 apprentices were white.

The NLRB ruled May 6 that St. Louis AFL-CIO construction

unions had violated the law in refusing to let their members work with black plumbers from an independent union in the federally assisted construction of the Gateway Arch monument. The NLRB ordered the AFL-CIO St. Louis Building & Construction Trade Council and the St. Louis locals of the Electrical Workers, Pipefitters, Plumbers, Sheet Metal Workers and Laborers unions to stop boycotting companies or persons engaged in or affecting interstate commerce.

The California Fair Employment Practices Commission July 22 ordered Local 12 of the Operating Engineers Union in Los Angeles to hire Joe Harris, 49, a Negro, as a business agent and to promote him when appropriate. The commission charged the union had discriminated against Harris solely on the basis of race.

The Justice Department July 24 filed suit in U.S. District Court in St. Louis, Mo. against the St. Louis-San Francisco Railway Co. and the Brotherhood of Railroad Trainmen on charges of employment discrimination against Negroes. The suit alleged that the railway and the union restricted job opportunities for Negroes and maintained artificial job classifications that limited earnings and advancement for Negroes.

The department July 24 filed suit in U.S. District Court in Cincinnati, O. against Local 212 of the International Bro'hood of Electrical Workers. The department charged that the union excluded Negroes from employment opportunities in the Cincinnati area's electrical trade. It alleged that through an agreement with the Cincinnati chapter of the National Electrical Contractors Association, the local virtually controlled employment opportunities for electricians in the area. Only one Negro, an apprentice, was included in the local's 700 journeymen and 120 apprentices, the department said.

The Justice Department filed suit in U.S. District Court in Cleveland, O. Aug. 8 against Local 38 of the International Brotherhood of Electrical Workers and the Electrical Joint Apprenticeship & Training Committee on charges of unlawful discrimination against Negroes. The suit asked for an injunction against racial discrimination. The suit alleged that Local 38 denied membership to Negroes, that its hiring hall refused to refer black job applicants on the same basis as white applicants and that the local refused to enter collective agreements with contractors who were Negroes or who employed Negroes on the same basis as white contractors who employed only white persons. The suit further charged that the Apprenticeship & Training Committee, which represented local 38, and the Greater Cleveland Chapter of the National Electrical Contractors Association, Inc., discriminated against Negro applicants for apprenticeship in the electrical construction industry.

The N.Y. State Commission for Human Rights Nov. 15 found Local 501 of the International Bro'hood of Electrical Workers and Local 38 of the Sheet Metal Workers guilty of preventing Negroes from obtaining construction jobs. Local 86 of the Plumbers Union was cleared of similar charges. The ruling was on a complaint filed by the New Rochelle Human Rights Commission. Protest demonstrations against the alleged bias had been held in New Rochelle in January and February at the Mall, an 11-acre renewal project that included a department store for R. H. Macy & Co. Nearly 90 persons were arrested during efforts to stop construction by blocking contractors' trucks and union workers. The commission noted that Macy's had offered to subsidize training for Negroes but that the unions would not cooperate. The unions were ordered to "cease and desist" from further discrimination.

The Justice Department Dec. 7 filed suit in U.S. District Court in Cincinnati, O. against Locals 44 and 372 of the International Association of Bridge, Structural & Ornamental Ironworkers and their apprenticeship committees. The department alleged that the locals and committees had failed to recruit and accept Negroes as apprentices on the same basis as whites. All of the 420 members and 25 apprentices in Local 44, the suit said, were white; all of the 190 journeymen and 18 of the 19 apprentices in Local 372 were white.

Bias in Drug Industry

The Equal Employment Opportunity Commission (EEOC) reported Oct. 6 that widespread discrimination against Negroes existed in the nation's drug industry. The commission made public the report following a meeting of EEOC chairman Clifford L. Alexander, Food & Drugs Commissioner James L. Goddard and 24 industry executives whose companies represented more than 70% of the drug industry business. Alexander said at the meeting that if the drug industry did not voluntarily recruit and train Negroes, the government would be forced to resort to the "time-consuming complaint process" to end discrimination. *Among the report's findings:*

● Negroes comprised 5.3% of drug industry employes although they represented more than 12.3% of the population in areas where drug plants were located.

● Negroes held 1.8% of the industry's white-collar jobs, .6% of sales positions and 2.1% of clerical jobs, positions that required no advanced education or specialized training.

● A Negro blue-collar worker in the drug industry had a 1-in-10 chance of becoming a foreman or craftsman; a white blue-collar worker had a 1-in-4 chance.

● One Negro white-collar worker in 33 was an official or manager; one white in 7 held official or managerial positions.

● "Apparently some of the smaller drug companies (250–1,000 employes) utilize Negroes at a higher rate than in some of the larger firms."

● Drug companies were concentrated in New York, New Jersey and Indiana, and more than 80% of the industry's work force was in the Northeast and North Central Regions.

● The industry had a high level of economic activity and had benefited from federal restrictions on importing foreign products.

The EEOC had compiled the data from 328 drug companies employing a total of 133,735 persons in 1966. This was the commission's first report dealing with discrimination in an industry on a nationwide basis.)

Program to Create Jobs in Ghettos

Pres. Johnson Oct. 2 announced a pilot program to attract big business to expand or to build in ghetto communities and to invest in job training programs for the hard-core unemployed. The program was aimed at reducing the risks of investing capital in the economically less attractive urban ghettos. Commerce Secy. Alexander B. Trowbridge appointed William E. Zisch, vice chairman of the board of the Aerojet General Corp., to head the program.

Under the new program: (a) The Small Business Administration would guarantee leases on property, plant and equipment for businesses building or providing jobs in or near a ghetto or rural poverty area. (b) The Labor Department would declare certain ghettos and poverty areas to be labor surplus areas and thereby enable businesses to bid on certain government contracts. (c) Transportation for workers to ghetto plants would be provided by federal funds available under the urban mass transit program. (d) Ghetto employes would receive health services from the Health, Education & Welfare Department. (e) The Federal Economic Development Administration would provide grants to enable big companies to give technical advice to small companies. (f) The federal government would pay the cost of bonding employes against theft and other loss.

Other Government Action

Asst. Treasury Secy. Robert A. Wallace warned the country's 14,000 banks in letters sent out Feb. 18 that they would lose federal deposits if they discriminated against Negroes in hiring, training or promotion. Wallace said banks accepting federal deposits would be expected: to establish "positive" equal employment programs and policies; to state that all qualified applicants would be considered for employment without regard to race, creed, color or national origin; to put posters reading "Discrimination Is Prohibited" in a conspicuous place. All complaints would be reviewed by the Treasury.

Illinois Treasurer Adlai E. Stevenson 3d announced a similar plan for Illinois state deposits. He said at a news conference in Chicago May 6: "State funds will not be deposited in banks or other institutions which discriminate on account of race or religion in either their employment or their services, including the making of loans."

Labor Secy. W. Willard Wirtz May 14 ordered the federal government to refuse bids from contractors who failed to certify that there was no racial discrimination in their facilities. He also ordered contractors to require all prospective subcontractors to submit the same certification in making bids. Wirtz said: "Although progress has been made, in recent years, insuring equal employment opportunities to all Americans, it is an unfortunate fact that many persons are still being denied basic equal employment rights, including the right to the use of their employer's facilities free from segregation on the basis of race, creed, color, or national origin." This was the first time the nondiscrimination clause in government contracts was extended to the bidding procedure.

FIGHT Seeks Jobs at Kodak

During much of 1967 a black organization dubbed FIGHT (for Freedom, Integration, God, Honor—Today) campaigned in Rochester, N.Y. and elsewhere to force the Eastman Kodak Co. to employ more Negroes. FIGHT had been organized after Rochester had been shaken by racial rioting in 1964. It was formed by community organizer Saul D. Alinsky of Chicago with the cooperation of the Rochester-area Council of Churches, and its president, a Negro, was the Rev. Franklin D. R. Florence.

After months of negotiating, Kodak Asst. Vice Pres. John G. Mulder had signed an agreement Dec. 20, 1966 to hire and train 600 unskilled Negroes who would be recruited and counseled by FIGHT. 2 days later Kodak officials repudiated the agreement as "unauthorized" and invalid. They said Kodak "cannot discriminate by having an exclusive recruiting agreement with any organization."

At a news conference in Rochester Jan. 6, Kodak Pres. Louis K. Eilers charged that FIGHT's "talk about employment" was "being used as a screen" for "making a power drive in this community." He held that with the arrival of Alinsky in Rochester, FIGHT had been waging "a continuous war against numerous institutions that help build Rochester." He said FIGHT's demands were "arbitrary and unreasonable" and added that, "to the best of our knowledge, FIGHT has not sent anyone to us to apply for work." (According to Eilers, Kodak currently had 1,200 to 1,500 Negroes among its more than 40,000 employes.)

At a news conference, later Jan. 6, the Rev. Florence showed reporters what he described as duplicates of recently completed job applications of 45 Negroes.

Predominantly Negro groups Feb. 14 picketed Kodak plants and stores carrying Kodak products in Atlanta, Chicago, Detroit and San Francisco.

In March FIGHT bought 10 shares of Kodak stock for $1,442.65 in order to have a voice at the meeting of Eastman Kodak stockholders, which was scheduled to be held in Flemington, N.J. Apr. 25. Then FIGHT sent letters to 700 clergymen and civil rights organizations asking them to persuade other shareholders to withhold their proxies. It was announced in St. Louis Apr. 6 that the presiding bishop of the Episcopal Church (the Rt. Rev. John E. Hines) and the Board for Homeland Ministries of the United Church of Christ had withheld from Kodak management their stock proxies, which represented holdings worth $1 million. The YWCA national board voted in Boston Apr. 24 to rescind proxies on its 2,600 shares of Kodak stock.

About 1,200 persons attended the Kodak shareholders meeting Apr. 25. Soon after the meeting started, the Rev. Florence gave Kodak Chrmn. William S. Vaughn until that afternoon to decide whether or not to reinstate the job program. Then he and 7 supporters walked out of the meeting. Florence returned to the meeting at 2:00 p.m., and Vaughn repeated his refusal to honor the

December agreement. The FIGHT members again walked out of the meeting and called for a national campaign against Kodak. Florence charged that "racial war has been declared on American Negroes by Eastman Kodak," and he raised FIGHT's demand to 2,000 more jobs for Negroes at Kodak. He said a national "black power" strategy meeting would discuss tactics against Kodak.

At the meeting, 84% of Kodak's 80,772,718 shares of stock were voted for management. About 40,000 proxies were withheld on FIGHT's plea.

(In the meantime a new group called Rochester Jobs, Inc. was formed in Rochester Apr. 11 and received promises from more than 40 businesses and industries to hire 1,500 "hard-core unemployed" persons and provide on-the-job training, counseling and remedial education. Among the companies were Kodak, Xerox Corp., the Ritter-Pfaudler Corp., Bausche & Lomb, Graflex, General Dynamics and local banks and utilities. And Kodak announced in Rochester Apr. 27 "the appointment of Uptown Associates, a Manhattan-based Negro public relations and marketing concern headed by Reuben J. Patton." Patton and a Kodak spokesman denied any connection between the FIGHT dispute and the appointment of the black public-relations counsel.)

Kodak and FIGHT reached agreement June 23 to work together on job training and job placement for the city's hard-core unemployed Negroes. The agreement came in a telegram from Kodak Pres. Eilers to the Rev. Florence. Dr. Eilers said in the telegram: "Kodak recognizes that FIGHT, as a broad-based community organization, speaks in behalf of the basic needs and aspirations of the Negro poor in the Rochester area." "There now appears to be an opportunity to create better understanding and to work in mutual respect." "As the result of our discussions, it is my understanding that we are both willing to work together to put these ideas into effect."

4 "constructive and workable" cooperative steps were proposed in Eilers' telegram: (1) Kodak would send employment interviewers into black areas, and FIGHT would advise and guide new employes. (2) FIGHT representatives would assist Kodak interviewers "by informing them of the special problems and perspectives of hard-core unemployed persons and others who, because of a lack of opportunity, are at a disadvantage in getting jobs." (3) Kodak and FIGHT would hold periodic meetings to discuss "various areas bearing on the economic needs and the aspirations of the Negro

community." (4) Kodak would make a slide presentation or movie "which would be useful in motivating the hard-core unemployed."

At FIGHT's 3d annual convention in Rochester June 23, De-Leon McEwen, 29, was elected president of FIGHT. (Florence was ineligible to succeed himself.) The convention also voted to change the word "Integration" in its name to "Independence."

(McEwen announced Nov. 17 that Kodak had decided to institute a program to develop small, independent, locally owned businesses in ghetto areas. The first of the businesses, which was to be started with FIGHT's aid, was to be a microfilming plant that would hire and train 400 to 500 unskilled Negroes. Kodak said it would organize and help finance a community development corporation to provide funds and management advice for the businesses. It would train, advise and consult in the areas of production and marketing and would "consider itself a potential customer for products and services of the new businesses." In a Dec. 15 announcement, Kodak said the small microfilming, camera repair, wood-working and plastic manufacturing businesses it envisioned would probably employ 9–15 workers each.)

Port Gibson Boycott Succeeds

Negroes in Port Gibson, Miss. Jan. 27 ended a 10-month boycott of white businesses after winning a list of concessions from the white community. Charles Evers, state NAACP field secretary, said Jan. 26 that Negroes would "go into a selective buying campaign, conditioned on them [whites] holding up their end of the bargain." The concessions included: (1) a promise from white businessmen to hire 15 black clerks in downtown stores; (2) the appointment of a black policeman and a Negro deputy sheriff; (3) the desegregation of hospitals, schools and public accommodations.

HOUSING & SOCIAL CONDITIONS

Progress Seen, Slum Life 'Worse'

Although more Negroes in the U.S. continued to move into middle-income brackets in recent years, living conditions in the hard-core city slums remained "unchanged or deteriorating," according to a statistical report published Nov. 2. The study, entitled "Social and Economic Conditions of Negroes in the U.S.," was compiled by the Census Bureau and Bureau of Labor Statistics at the request of the President after the summer urban riots.

Pres. Johnson, commenting on the report in a written statement, said: "It does not confirm the diagnosis of bleakness and despair: that there has been no recent progress for Negroes in America and that violence is therefore a logical remedy. It does not confirm the opposite view: that 'Negroes have been given too much.' " "Far from showing 'no progress,' the picture revealed is one of substantial progress," the President continued. "As the nation rode a great tide of social and economic prosperity over the past 7 years, Negroes in America not only kept up with the general advance but in important ways moved ahead of it. . . . Today, for the first time, a substantial number of Negroes in America are moving into the middle class." Nevertheless, he added, "The gap between Negro and white levels of living in America is still large despite progress. What is most troubling is that in many of the worst slum areas of America, life isn't getting better for Negroes, it is getting worse."

Among the study' s major findings:

Population—In 1966 the U.S. had 21½ million Negroes, 11% of the 194 million population. (The number of nonwhites, a category often used in the report, was 23.2 million and included Negroes, Orientals, American Indians.) The percentage of Negroes living in the South since 1940 had decreased from 77% to 55%. The percentage of Negroes increased in the Northeast from 11% to 17%, in the North Central states from 11% to 29% and in the West from 1% to 8%. 56% of Negroes and 27% of whites lived in cities; 13% of Negroes and 37% of whites had moved to urban "fringe" areas. Negroes comprised 1/5 of the central-city populations, ¼ of cities with populations exceeding one million and 4% of inhabitants of suburbs.

Income—The black family's median annual income was $4,463—58% of the white family's $7,722. The percentage of U.S. nonwhite families with annual incomes of $7,000 or more (in constant 1965 dollars) was 28%, up from 6% in 1947 and 17% in 1960. The percentage of U.S. white families with incomes of $7,000 or more in 1966 was 55%, up from 21% in 1947 and 41% in 1960. 41% of nonwhites lived below the government-defined poverty level ($3,300 a year for a nonfarm family of 4), compared to 12% of whites; 14% of nonwhite families and 3% of white families received welfare assistance.

Employment—The nonwhite unemployment rate in the first 9 months of 1967 was 7.3%; the white rate was 3.4%. The nonwhite rate of unemployment, however, was down from 10.2% in 1960. Nonwhites comprised only 6% of professional workers, 3% of the managers and proprietors, 6% of craftsmen and foremen, 42% of domestic workers and 25% of laborers.

Education—The number of years of school completed by the median nonwhite male was 10.5 in 1960 and 12.1 in 1966; the median for white youths was 12.4 in 1960 and 12.6 in 1966. The percentage of nonwhite males who completed high school rose from 36% in 1960 to 53% in 1966; for nonwhite females the percentage rose from 41% in 1960 to 49% in 1966. For white men the comparable percentages were 63% and 73%; for white women 65% and 74%. The percentage of Negroes who finished college increased from 4.3% in 1960 to 6.8% in 1965; the figures for whites were 11.7% and 13.7%. 72% of black first graders in the North and 97% of black first graders in the South attended predominantly Negro schools in 1965. 35% of black 12th graders in cities in the North and 95% in the South attended predominantly Negro schools.

Housing—The percentage of nonwhites living in substandard housing decreased from 44% in 1960 to 29% in 1966. 8% of whites were reported in comparable housing.

Social patterns—In 1950 17.6% of nonwhite families were headed by women; in 1966 the figure was 23.7%. White families headed by women remained fairly constant at 9%. 7 of 10 nonwhite children and 9 of 10 white children lived with both parents. The birth rate was 134 per 1,000 women aged 15 to 44 for nonwhites, 91 per 1,000 for whites. Births out of wedlock were estimated at 26% among nonwhites, 4% among whites.

Hard-core slums—The percentage of nonwhite families living in city poverty areas declined from 77% in 1960 to 62% in 1966. In the Hough section of Cleveland during 1960–5 the percentage of families in poverty grew from 31% to 39%, the number headed by women rose from 23% to 32%, the median family income declined from $4,732 to $3,966. In the Watts area of Los Angeles families in poverty remained at 43%, the number headed by women grew from 36% to 39%, median income remained substantially unchanged, deteriorated housing increased from 14% to 21% and rents were higher. Ghetto unemployment rates were put at 9.3%, compared with a national average of 3.5%.

Military service—Black youths were less likely to enter the armed forces than whites. In 1966 7.9% of Negro men and 9.1% of white men aged 18 to 24 entered the service. Negroes accounted for 9% of the men in military service, 11% of those in Vietnam and 15% of the deaths among American servicemen in Vietnam. 43% of drafted Negroes and 8% of drafted whites failed mental tests at induction; 13% of Negroes and 26% of whites failed medical tests; the reenlistment rate was 46% among eligible Negroes, 18%–20% among whites.

Voting—59% of Negroes and 71% of whites of voting age voted in the 1964 Presidential election. Negro officeholders increased during 1962–6 from 4 to 7 in Congress, from 52 to 148 in state legislatures (including an increase from 6 to 37 in the South).

The U.S. Civil Rights Commission Nov. 22 issued a report calling for an attack on slum problems as the nation's "first priority." The commission reported a general deterioration in the conditions of Negroes living in big-city slums. Unlike other commission studies, the 133-page report, "A Time to Listen . . . A Time to Act," contained testimony of ghetto residents to "provide insights into what slum residents think and feel about the conditions in which they live." The 88 pages of direct testimony from slum residents was taken during commission and state advisory board hearings throughout the U.S. during 1967.

The CRC report held that the summer riots and the growing black militancy should be viewed in the context of the "great frustrations, of laws and programs which promise but do not deliver, of continued deprivation, discrimination and prejudice" in an increasingly prosperous society. The report said: "The problems of our cities and the people who live in them will not be resolved by a search for culprits or conspirators or for solutions which do not cost money or effort. Nor can it justly be argued that remedies for the discrimination suffered by millions of Americans who live in slum ghettos should be deferred on the ground that to do otherwise would be to reward violence." The commission held that the Federal Housing Administration and the Office of Federal Contract Compliance of the Department of Labor had failed to help the poor by not enforcing anti-discrimination policies in federal housing and job projects.

California Housing Amendment Invalid

The U.S. Supreme Court May 29 declared unconstitutional a voter-approved amendment to the California constitution that gave property owners "absolute discretion" in resale and rental of housing. The amendment, on the California ballot as Proposition 14 in the 1964 elections, had been the subject of 2 Supreme Court rulings in 1966. The new ruling apparently over-rode contraditions in the earlier decisions by reversing the amendment in its entirety.

The federal high court decision upheld a California Supreme Court ruling in 2 separate cases brought by Mr. and Mrs. Lincoln W. Mulkey and Mr. and Mrs. Wilfred J. Prendergast. Both couples claimed that Los Angeles and Santa Ana apartment house owners had refused to rent to them because of their race. In the majority opinion, Justice Byron R. White said that the amendment did not merely repeal the state's fair housing legislation but also created "a constitutional right to discriminate on racial grounds in the sale and rental of real property." The amendment "was intended to authorize and does authorize racial discrimination in the housing market," White found. "The right to discriminate is now one of the basic policies of the state," he declared. Chief Justice Earl Warren and Justices William J. Brennan Jr., William O. Douglas and Abe Fortas concurred. Justices John M. Harlan, Hugo L. Black, Tom C. Clark and Potter Stewart dissented.

Flint (Mich.) Plan Defeated

Floyd J. McCree, 44, Negro mayor of Flint, Mich., threatened Aug. 14 to resign after a proposed open-housing ordinance was defeated, 5–3, by the City Commission. But he withdrew his proffered resignation Aug. 28 after receiving wide support for his fight for open housing. McCree had been one of Flint's 9 city commissioners since 1958 and had been elected mayor by the commission in Nov. 1966. (About 25% of Flint's 210,000 population was black. Wages were high and unemployment low in Flint, where Chevrolet and Buick had their home plants. According to a University of Chicago study, housing in Flint was the most segregated in the North.)

4 black city officials—3 members of the Flint Human Relations Commission and a member of the Genesee County Flint Board of Supervisors—had said Aug. 15 that they would resign with McCree, and by Aug. 19 a total of 16 officials, both white and black, had threatened to resign.

About 15 Negroes Aug. 18 staged a sleep-in around City Hall in support of open housing. 3 firebombings were reported Aug. 19. About 7,000 Negroes rallied in front of City Hall Aug. 20 in support of McCree and open housing. Gov. George W. Romney told the demonstrators: "I'm here to support open occupancy. I helped lead the fight for provisions in the Michigan Constitution to abolish discrimination. That's what I stand for."

But the City Commission Aug. 21 rejected, 4–4, a proposal to redraft the open housing ordinance. McCree, who was then hospitalized for a stomach disorder, was absent. About 80 persons continued the sleep-in on the City Hall lawn Aug. 22, and 60 persons slept on the lawn Aug. 23.

McCree announced Aug. 28 that he was withdrawing his oral resignation because of a "massive declaration of support" from state legislators, city and county officials and the general public. He said he thought there was a "strong possibility" the ordinance would be reintroduced and passed.

Groppi Leads Milwaukee Drive

Thousands of Negroes and whites led by the Rev. James E. Groppi, 36, and the Milwaukee Youth Council of the NAACP participated in a series of daily open-housing demonstrations in Milwaukee beginning Aug. 28. The drive was frequently marked by violence. By Oct. 22 more than 375 persons had been arrested; the daily cost to the city included $17,000 to $25,000 in overtime pay for police, and city officials agreed that the demonstrations had seriously affected the city's business.

Groppi, the campaign's controversial leader, was a Roman Catholic priest and the 11th son of an Italian immigrant grocer. He had grown up in the Italian neighborhood on the South Side of Milwaukee. As a youth, he said, he had suffered as a member of a minority group, but "there's no comparison with the injustices directed at the Negro." Groppi attended St. Francis Seminary, where, he said, "I saw the social suffering and ostracism, . . . instances of discriminations [against black students] that were really horrible. I suffered with them then, and I have never stopped suffering." During his deacon year at the seminary, Groppi said, he was "ostracised" because he refused to attend a minstrel show that he thought "insulting to the Negro community." In 1959 Groppi became an assistant pastor in an Italian neighborhood, and in 1963 he was transferred to the predominantly black St. Boniface's Roman Catholic Church on the South Side of Milwaukee. After participating in the Mar. 1965 Selma (Ala.) civil rights march, Groppi returned to Milwaukee and led a boycott against de facto school segregation. In Aug. 1966 Groppi led demonstrations against membership by public officials in the Fraternal Order of Eagles, a national fraternity that restricted its members to Caucasians. In describing Groppi as unchallenged leader of the militant civil rights movement in Milwaukee, Sidney Finley, regional director of the NAACP in Chicago, said: "This is rare, even for Negro leaders, these days." Groppi was often heard to say: "I'm a Negro with white skin."

From the start the marches provoked bitter and violent reaction from white residents of Milwaukee's predominantly Polish South Side. At least 6 persons were injured Aug. 28 in a clash between whites and marchers; 16 persons were arrested. After the disturbance, Mayor Henry W. Maier called on South Side residents to observe a "voluntary curfew." (Maier refused an offer from Gov. Warren P. Knowles to call out the Wisconsin National Guard.)

200 open-housing demonstrators, guarded by an armed police escort, marched again Aug. 29 and were met by nearly 2,000 whites who lined the 2-mile march route to Kosciuszko Park. Many of the whites carried signs that read "white power" and "Polish

power," and some chanted "kill, kill, kill!" Eggs, rocks and bottles were thrown at the marchers. Twice during the march police used tear gas to quell disturbances. At least 6 persons were hospitalized; more than 50 persons were arrested. Late Aug. 29 the marchers were escorted by police to Freedom House, the headquarters of the Youth Council. Policemen charged that Negro snipers fired on the police escorts. Several firebombs were thrown, and Freedom House was set ablaze by a firebomb. The Youth Council blamed the police for the fire. (Freedom House had suffered $2,000 in fire damages Aug. 12 when it was one of 11 arson targets. The police later arrested a white house-wrecking contractor as the alleged arsonist.)

Early Aug. 30 Mayor Maier issued an emergency proclamation banning "marches, demonstrations and parades" between 4 p.m. and 9 a.m. for the next 30 days. Groppi denounced the ban and said it did not apply to rallies. More than 100 of his followers gathered for a rally at the charred remains of Freedom House at 7 p.m. Aug. 30. More than 100 policemen soon arrived to disperse them, but they refused to move. Finally the police charged them and arrested 15. The crowd reassembled on the private property of Freedom House, and for 45 minutes members of the crowd stood confronting the police while singing "We Shall Overcome" and "We Shall Not Be Moved." The police finally moved in and arrested more than 50 persons.

Marches took place Aug. 31–Sept. 1 despite the ban. 58 persons, including Groppi, were arrested Aug. 31 for defying the "state-of-emergency" order.

Joseph P. Fagan, chairman of the Wisconsin Department of Industry, Labor & Human Relations and a spokesman for the governor, accused the mayor Sept. 1 of "suspending the Bill of Rights." Mayor Maier Sept. 1 said he would remove the ban the next day. In making the announcement, Maier denounced Fagan and Groppi. He said: "If anyone . . . wants the Guard called, I say this: The governor can call the Guard any time he wants. . . . Talk directly to the governor and spare me the politics." "I personally think that the Guard at this time would be provocative."

Groppi and Negro comedian Dick Gregory led 1,400 predominantly black demonstrators on a peaceful march from St. Boniface's Church to City Hall Sept. 2. The marchers then continued on to the South Side, where they were met by white hecklers; there were several incidents of fistfighting. Before 1,000 demonstrators marched Sept. 3 from the church to downtown Milwaukee, Groppi told reporters that the marches would continue "until we have a fair-housing bill that says a man can live where he wants."

The Milwaukee Common Council met Sept. 5 and voted 18–1 to ratify the mayor's emergency proclamation banning marches. The dissenting vote was that of Mrs. Vel R. Phillips, the only black member of the council. After the vote Groppi marched out of the meeting accompanied by 200 Negroes and whites. They went to St. Boniface's Church, and Groppi said there would be no "cooling off." He called the Council members "pharisees and hypocrites, a nest of vipers." He said at a rally of 800 persons: "I saw in the Common Council a worse form of racism than I saw in the South Side last week. You have on the South Side honest, dumb white bigots. What I saw this afternoon was dishonest, dumb white bigots. I heard a man say that I preach hate. I preach brotherhood and justice. One of the best ways to teach brotherhood is to preach black power."

500 demonstrators marched downtown the evening of Sept. 5, but only 50 marchers demonstrated Sept. 6. Dick Gregory said at a rally of 600 that "we've got to escalate this thing." Despite his militant stance, however, Groppi was reported to be unwilling to accept the support of advocates of black rebellion such as H. Rap Brown. Joseph Fagan said: "He [Groppi] told me he didn't want anything to do with Rap Brown's ilk."

A planned marathon lie-in at the mayor's office turned into a spree of wanton destruction Sept. 7 when about 75 black youths, "commandos" of the Youth Council, vandalized the reception room of Maier's office. Under orders from Maier not to interfere, policemen watched for nearly 4 hours as the youths pushed and taunted them, ripped stuffing from chairs, broke windows, took over the interoffice phone switchboard and the receptionist's desk, made paper airplanes from memo pads and stuck "black power" stickers, lipstick and hand lotion on a photomural of downtown Milwaukee. A clerk was stranded inside the mayor's conference room. Policemen moved in to rescue him and struggled briefly with the youths. The mayor finally told the police to clear the office. The youths, reduced in number to 35, were given 2 minutes to leave or face arrest for disorderly conduct. They conferred and then marched out of City Hall.

The next morning 15 mothers (13 whites and 2 Negroes) marched to the mayor's office. Mrs. Dan Oleson, speaking for the mothers' group, told the mayor's press secretary, "Our immediate concern is what happened yesterday. We feel the mayor is responsible. He refused to see these young people." The women presented a written statement criticizing the mayor and supporting an open-housing ordinance.

NAACP Executive Director Roy Wilkins said in a telegram to Maier Sept. 7 that "the NAACP does not condone the destruction of property or the defacing of walls" but did back the Youth Council's drive for open housing. NAACP regional headquarters in Chicago appealed Sept. 8 for a "gigantic mass rally" for open housing in Milwaukee, and the NAACP national executive board in New York Sept. 11 reaffirmed its support of the Youth Council's open-housing campaign. (Andrew Tyler, a "commando sergeant" in the Youth Council, told an interviewer Sept. 21 that efforts by outside Negro groups to inject violence into the open-housing campaign had been rejected. About 25 Chicago Negroes had distributed photos and buttons of Stokely Carmichael and Malcolm X Sept. 17 and had urged Milwaukee Negroes to riot.)

Groppi and about 1,000 supporters marched through the South Side again Sept. 9. White hecklers held placards that read "Burn, Groppi, burn," and others shouted "White nigger." The police kept the 2 groups separated. But during the homeward journey, after darkness, several brawls broke out; 4 Negroes and one white man were arrested.

During the afternoon of Sept. 9 Maier proposed an open-housing ordinance requiring the approval of a majority of the city's 28 municipal areas. Groppi said Maier was "passing the buck."

Groppi, Dick Gregory and Mrs. Vel Phillips Sept. 10 led more than 2,300 demonstrators, including civil rights workers from 7 Middle Western states, in a 15-mile protest march to the South Side. At a pre-march rally at St. Boniface's Church, the demonstrators unanimously voted to boycott Milwaukee's largest brewery, the Joseph Schlitz Co. Gregory told the marchers: "This is not a brick and bottle throwing march today. If you see anybody throwing a brick or bottle, hold him." During the march policemen fired 30 rounds of tear gas at white hecklers who threw bottles at marchers. 2 whites and 3 marchers were arrested during an outbreak of fist-fighting in the suburb of West Milwaukee, where several marchers threw bottles and smashed windows. A mob of whites waited for marchers to return to West Milwaukee, but Groppi led them back on a different route. Some whites then turned on the police, who fired tear gas at the mob. 20 persons were arrested.

During an evening march of more than 700 demonstrators Sept. 11, whites pelted marchers with bricks and bottles, and the demonstrators returned the fire; 34 persons were arrested.

At a Sept. 12 press conference Maier denounced white violence and hatred, which he called reminiscent of Nazi Germany. He said he was "force-drafting" 9 civic and religious leaders, including the Most Rev. William E. Cousins, archbishop of Milwaukee and Groppi's superior, to seek a solution. Maier urged the group to meet "immediately" because "the city verged on civil war last night and no one knows what lurks ahead." White demonstrators carrying a cardboard coffin lettered "God is White" and "Father Groppi Rest in Hell" paraded outside the archbishop's residence in the evening. (Cousins Oct. 13 refused to serve on Maier's Special Community Relations Commission. 3 appointees had refused previously.)

Negro marchers avoided the white South Side Sept. 12–13 and demonstrated instead in the black North Side. South Side whites meanwhile gathered in their home neighborhood the evenings of Sept. 12 and 13 to heckle black marchers who did not appear. The whites, armed with bottles, clashed instead with policemen. Faced with a crowd of 2,000 whites Sept. 13, the police used tear gas to halt the bottle-throwing and disperse the mobs. 32 persons were arrested; 3 policemen and 2 civilians were injured.

Archbishop Cousins Sept. 13 announced his support of Groppi in his drive for open-housing legislation. In what was reported to be the first time in the 97-year history of the *Catholic Herald Citizen,* the archdiocesan weekly, the archbishop addressed his 700,000 parishioners in an editorial. The archbishop's editorial said: "Do I agree with everything that Father Groppi has said and done? I certainly do not." But "we are being diverted by emotion and mob psychology into fighting a straw figure while the real enemy goes unscathed." "People are so disturbed by his actions that they lose sight of the cause for which he is fighting, that of freedom and human dignity. As Christians we favor the same just cause." (It was reported Sept. 21 that many South Side Catholics had stopped their subscriptions to the archdiocesan newspaper and withheld their weekly church contributions. Many joined the newly formed Milwaukee Citizens Civic Voice in protest against "forced open housing." The group's spiritual adviser, the Rev. Russell Witon, 38, chaplain at St. Alphonsus Hospital in Port Washington, Wis., said Groppi had become "abusive to the archbishop, to brother priests and to civil authorities.")

The priests' Senate of the Milwaukee Archdiocese Sept. 15

voted 21–7 to support Groppi and his open-housing drive. The Senate, a 3-month-old body elected by 729 priests to advise and consult with the archbishop on church problems, met in closed session. "To the extent that Father Groppi's efforts are directed toward a living charity and social justice, the Senate concurs with Archbishop William E. Cousins in retaining Father Groppi in his present assignment," the statement said. The Senate had considered a plea from the Rev. Eldred B. Lesniewski, assistant director of Catholic Social Services for the archdiocese, that Groppi "be removed from active involvement" in civil rights.

Rights demonstrators picketing City Hall Sept. 15 were joined by a delegation of nuns from Chicago. About 80 clergymen and nuns arrived later from other parts of the country to participate in the open-housing marches. Groppi had announced Sept. 11 that the National Council of Churches had called and expressed its support to the open-housing drive; he also said that the Southeastern chapter of the National Association of Social Workers, the Milwaukee Conference on Religion & Race had offered to work for an open-housing ordinance. In advertisements in Milwaukee newspapers Sept. 16 the American Lutheran Church and the Missouri and Wisconsin Synods of the Lutheran Church voiced support for the open-housing demonstrations. The Interdenominational Ministerial Alliance announced its support of the demonstrations Sept. 17. About 650 Negroes and whites, including clergymen, nuns and laymen who had arrived from out of town in response to pleas from Groppi, were greeted with jeers and curses as they marched from the North Side to the South Side Sept. 16.

Groppi, in a sermon at St. Boniface's Church Sept. 16, said the open-housing campaign was an integrated one. "This is not a struggle between black and white but between right and wrong," he declared. He said "interracial justice is not being preached on the South Side of Milwaukee because the clergy feel it is prudent not to offend their parishioners."

A vigil was held Sept. 29–Oct. 7 at the Lincoln Memorial in Washington, D.C. in support of the Milwaukee open-housing demonstrations as an "alternative to violence." Mrs. Vel Phillips, attending the closing ceremonies, said: "This is the last stand for nonviolence." Mrs. Phillips, Milwaukee's only black alderman, met Oct. 6 with officials of the Justice Department and the Office of the Vice President. She said she was "encouraged that the people here in Washington realize the depth and urgency of our problem. TV correspondent Jim Burns had said on the ABC "Issues and Answers" program Sept. 24, however, that Mrs. Phillips had told him Sept. 23 that "Milwaukee might some day become . . . the 'cradle of the real American revolution in the United States,' meaning by that an armed revolt against the white people of that city."

Groppi's drive was defended by Whitney M. Young Jr. on the Sept. 24 "Issues and Answers" program. "I think Milwaukee is a good example of . . . not black versus white but decent people against those who are still living in the dark ages," he said. "Father Groppi, who is a symbol of that struggle in Milwaukee, has indicated that the real issue—and I agree with him—is open occupancy. It is freedom of choice for the Negro citizen."

Mrs. Vel Phillips had introduced an open-housing ordinance in the Milwaukee Common Council Sept. 19. This was her 5th such action since 1962. The proposed ordinance would prohibit discrimination in the sale, lease or rental of all categories of housing. In an effort to break a deadlock on the issue, the council Oct. 18 created a compromise committee of citizens and aldermen weighted 6–5 in favor of open-housing advocates. The committee Oct. 22 reported unanimously that Milwaukee needed some kind of fair-housing ordinance but did not reach agreement on specific provisions.

The council Dec. 12 enacted a compromise open-housing ordinance by 13–6 vote. Mrs. Phillips voted against the ordinance, which she denounced as "mere tokenism." Groppi assailed the ordinance as "an insult to the black community" and promised that the demonstrations "will continue to intensify." The only change in the existing state law, which excluded an estimated 66% of Milwaukee housing, involved a transfer of enforcement powers from a state agency to the city attorney's office. The ordinance exempted owner-occupied homes, duplexes and apartment buildings of 4 units or fewer.

Louisville Housing Campaign

Open-housing demonstrations, started in 1966, were intensified in Louisville, Ky. Apr. 11 after the city's Board of Aldermen had rejected an open-housing ordinance. After continued protests, however, an open-housing ordinance was passed in mid-December.

Following the Apr. 11 defeat of the proposed open-housing ordinance, the Rev. A. D. Williams King (a Louisville minister, leader of the open-housing drive and brother of the Rev. Dr. Martin Luther King Jr.) and Negro comedian Dick Gregory had led about

350 demonstrators through downtown Louisville. They began at City Hall, where earlier in the day the 12 Republican aldermen had voted 9–3 against a weakened open-housing law. The marchers, accompanied by about 200 Louisville and Jefferson County policemen and about 200 jeering whites, alternately walked on sidewalks and sat in the streets. At one point they blocked the intersection of Broadway and 4th St., downtown Louisville's 2 busiest streets. White youths on the sidewalks chanted "We Want Wallace." Several carried a banner that said "We Don't Want Any Niggers."

White reaction to the previous open-housing marches had grown increasingly bitter. 8 whites had been arrested after they hurled eggs and stones and shouted insults at marchers in a white residential area Apr. 10.

White and Negro open-housing marchers were met Apr. 13 by about 75 whites who burned a cross on the lawn on the Southern Junior High School. King and the Rev. Leo Lesser, a Negro minister, fell to the street under a barrage of rocks and tomatoes from whites. King was later treated for an eye injury.

The Negro community Apr. 14 began a boycott of Louisville's white merchants, including Mayor Kenneth A. Schmied who owned a family furniture store.

At the request of the city, Circuit Judge Marvin J. Sternberg Apr. 14 issued a temporary restraining order forbidding night marches, requiring 12 hours' notice in writing for daylight marches, restricting them to non-rush hours and limiting them to 150 persons. Several hundred persons, however, marched that evening through a white residential section. A police cordon separated the marchers from about 1,000 whites, some of whom threw stones, eggs, firecrackers and other objects. 45 persons were reported arrested for disorderly conduct and parading without a permit.

Spokesmen for the Louisville Open Housing Committee said Apr. 16 that 30 demonstration "technicians" were meeting in the city to map out a strategy against the city injunction. (About 15 staff workers had been in Louisville for several weeks.) Attorneys for the demonstrators filed a petition in the U.S. District Court Apr. 17 to dissolve the injunction. About 100 demonstrators marched through the South Side that evening. They were followed by about 500 whites, who jeered and threw stones, bottles and firecrackers. About 140 policemen were present. 19 white hecklers were arrested.

Police used tear gas and smoke bombs Apr. 18–20 to disperse

whites who tried to disrupt marches. 150 demonstrators were pelted Apr. 18 with garbage, cherry bombs and rocks. 50 marchers, including King, were arrested.

150 open-housing demonstrators, both white and Negro, climbed Apr. 19 from rented trucks that carried them to white neighborhoods and tried to march despite the reinstatement earlier Apr. 19 of the injunction against marches. Riot police moved in after whites, mostly teen-agers, hurled stones through police car windows. 20 alleged hecklers were arrested. 119 demonstrators were arrested on charges of violating the court injunction. (The march leaders who had been arrested did not march Apr. 19 although they had been freed on bail.)

Demonstrators attempted to march again Apr. 20, but about 70–80 were arrested as they climbed out of rented trucks that had brought them to all-white neighborhoods. Police used tear gas to disperse nearly 600 whites, some of whom pelted demonstrators and police with rocks and bottles.

King and 6 other demonstration leaders were convicted Apr. 21 of civil contempt for defying the injunction against marches. They were sentenced to 30-hour jail terms, but the terms were stayed until Apr. 24 to allow them to meet with city leaders to find a solution to the housing complaints.

125 demonstrators were arrested the evening of Apr. 21 when they tried to march in the South Side and in the Churchill Downs neighborhoods of Louisville.

About 300 demonstrators marched through downtown Louisville at noon Apr. 22 without incident. Police made several arrests, however, during a night march on City Hall.

The protest marches were extended to Louisville's affluent East Side Apr. 24. About 50 demonstrators in 2 rented trucks arrived at scheduled march sites but remained in their trucks and conducted a motorized protest, followed by police and press cars, for about 31 miles through downtown and suburban areas.

Members of the Jefferson County and Louisville Human Relations Committee met Apr. 24 with city leaders, then announced an agreement to hold "hard bargaining sessions" to resolve the housing problems. Plans to interrupt the Kentucky Derby were canceled, but the demonstrations had prompted city officials to curtail Derby Week activities early in the week to avert any possible violence.

About 225 persons, mainly from religious orders and including fewer than 10 Negroes, held a 2-hour silent "pray-in" in front of City Hall Apr. 25 to demonstrate support of Negro demands for open housing.

The jailing of King, his aide, the Rev. Leo Lesser, and of 5 other civil rights leaders was again delayed Apr. 25 while their attorneys filed a petition in the State Court of Appeals for a writ of prohibition. The appeals court refused Apr. 26 to stay the 30-hour sentences, but U.S. District Judge James S. Gordon Apr. 27 temporarily postponed the sentences. The 7 civil rights leaders were jailed May 1, however, and a scheduled meeting with Mayor Schmied was consequently canceled. The 7 rights leaders were released May 2.

Only 12 cars and drivers participated in a rush-hour "drive-in" through downtown Louisville May 1. They soon became separated by traffic lights and were not recognizable as an organized group.

After 5 blacks were arrested at Churchill Downs on charges of disorderly conduct at the race track, Gov. Edward T. Breathitt announced May 2 that he would call the National Guard to prevent violence at the Derby. (2 Ku Klux Klan officials announced May 3 that Klansmen would be on hand in Louisville "to help the police keep order," at the Derby. At the track the Klansmen's offers to help were rejected and they were led away by private security guards.)

The Rev. Dr. Martin Luther King Jr. arrived in Louisville May 3. He was met at the airport by his brother, A. D. Williams King, and the other civil rights leaders, who had just come from a closed session with Mayor Schmied. (At the meeting the city officials issued a statement declaring that county and state laws already covered fair housing.) At an airport news conference Dr. King called for "massive pressure" against the city government for open housing legislation. He said: "We know from experience that we have made no strides in the civil rights movement without persistent and consistent pressure . . . and this pressure has to stay alive." Addressing 500 persons at the Greater St. James African Methodist Episcopal Church later May 3, Dr. King criticized the "invisible wall" that separated the whites and the Negroes of the community. He said that behind the wall there existed a "triple ghetto of race, poverty and human misery."

Following a rally at the 5th St. Baptist Church May 5, 40 demonstrators marched to Churchill Downs, where they were arrested for demonstrating in front of the main gate. In the evening of May 5 about 85 demonstrators met at Wyandotte Park in the all-white South End section of Louisville to start a march. 150 helmeted policemen were on hand. Before the march started white hecklers threw stones. Police Chief William E. Binder promptly canceled the demonstration. One white heckler was arrested for rock-throwing, and the marchers were driven in police vans to their cars in a parking lot at the track.

The Kentucky Derby was held May 6 without incident. At Churchill Downs, 1,500 helmeted National Guardsmen and 1,000 city, county and state police were stationed at 10-foot intervals along the track in front of the grandstands. At a morning news conference Dr. King had confirmed reports that civil rights leaders had canceled plans to interrupt the Derby. He said the decision was an "act of good faith to the officials and residents of Louisville."

During the racing activities about 150 Negroes and whites marched for about an hour through nearly deserted streets to City Hall. About 75 Negroes and whites marched through the South End May 8. They were met by white hecklers, mostly teen-agers, who shouted insults and threw stones.

The court order banning night marches was changed May 11 to allow open-housing demonstrations between 6:00 p.m. and 8:30 p.m.

A 3-judge federal court in Louisville Oct. 12 held unconstitutional 3 Kentucky state laws and 3 Louisville city ordinances under which civil rights activists had been arrested during the open-housing demonstrations in the spring. Judge Henry F. Brooks dissented in the 2–1 ruling on the 6 laws. The court, however, upheld an injunction against nighttime marches and declared that local officials had acted properly "to separate the adversaries" during the protests. The state laws declared void were those against criminal syndicalism, conspiracy and vagrancy, and the city ordinances invalidated were those covering the issuance of parade permits, disorderly conduct and loitering and related offenses. The court said the state vagrancy statute was "a catch-all, not specific in expression." The disorderly conduct law, it said, "leaves to the executive and judicial branches too wide a discretion in the application of the law," and the loitering ordinance "appears overbroad and vague." The criminal syndicalism law, the court said, "makes unlawful the mere advocacy of an unlawful method to accomplish a political end."

The Louisville Board of Aldermen Dec. 16 adopted an open housing ordinance by 9–3 vote. The law, which became effective Dec. 27 without the signature of Mayor Kenneth A. Schmied, banned discrimination in the sale or rental of housing on the basis of race, creed or national origin. Schmied said that he indorsed open housing but that he did not approve of fines authorized in the measure or the power it invested in the Louisville and Jefferson County Human Relations Commission for investigating complaints.

Pentagon Acts Vs. Housing Bias

Defense Secy. Robert S. McNamara had announced June 22 that all segregated housing within a 3½-mile radius of Andrews Air Force Base, Md. would be off-limits as of July 1 for all incoming military families. The ruling followed the completion of a survey that found that of 22,000 apartment units "within a reasonable commuting distance" of the base, less than 3% were open to black servicemen and their families. The order affected only apartment buildings and trailer courts. It did not apply to military families already living in segregated buildings. McNamara said at a Pentagon news conference that his order was in accordance with the Defense Department policy of ending "humiliating discrimination" against Negro servicemen.

NAACP Executive Director Roy Wilkins called McNamara's order "a welcome beginning toward the correction of a shameful discrimination." He said the "same injustice" existed "at hundreds of bases throughout the country."

McNamara June 30 extended his directive to apartments and trailer courts within a 7-mile radius of Fort George G. Meade, Md., effective July 12. Similar action was taken against segregated rental housing near Aberdeen Proving Grounds and Edgewood Arsenal, Md. July 11 and near Fort Holabird in East Baltimore, Md. July 21 (effective Aug. 1). The U.S. Naval Academy in Annapolis, Md. announced Aug. 4 that 13 of the city's 17 apartment house owners had agreed to accept Negro servicemen as tenants.

The Defense Department took these anti-segregation actions in the Washington-Baltimore area after almost a year of pressure from a local open housing organization—the Action Coordinating Committee to End Segregation in the Suburbs (ACCESS). The bi-racial committee had staged sit-ins at the Pentagon and had picketed segregated housing in Maryland and Virginia. After meeting with

ACCESS representatives in April, Deputy Defense Secy. Cyrus Vance had ordered housing surveys that resulted in the off-limits declarations.

McNamara said at a press conference Sept. 7 that the Pentagon, extending its campaign to end housing discrimination against black servicemen, would declare off-limits all segregated housing located near military installations throughout the U.S. The initial Pentagon open-housing drive had been limited to the Washington metropolitan area and Maryland. At the beginning of the summer of 1967, only 47 off-base housing facilities with 4,580 units were open to all servicemen. By Sept. 1 housing facilities available to Negroes totaled 19,500 units in 195 facilities.

The Pentagon Sept. 7 released the results of a census of discriminatory patterns in housing located near 300 bases in 46 states. The survey included 25,180 apartments, housing developments and motels containing 900,000 units, all within "normal commuting distance" of the bases. It showed that black servicemen had been barred from "at least" ⅓ of the available housing facilities. Discrimination was most pronounced in the South; in Georgia 35% of the off-base housing was "open" to all and in Louisiana 34% of the facilities afforded equal housing opportunities. Open housing policies had been adopted by all facilities only in 5 states: Connecticut, New Hampshire, Oregon, South Dakota and Wisconsin. In New York 99% of the 207 facilities surveyed were open to Negroes.

McNamara said he considered the results of the study a "shameful story of discrimination against thousands of men in uniform and their families." "Prompt remedial action is essential and we propose to take it." The first target, he said, would be California, where 102,000 servicemen lived off base and, according to the survey, discrimination against Negroes was practiced by 32% of 14,429 facilities. McNamara announced the appointment of Brig. Gen. William E. Ekman to run the Pentagon's national open-housing effort. Ekman had been in charge of the campaign in Maryland and Washington, D.C.

McNamara Dec. 26 again cracked down on operators of rental housing who discriminate against Negro servicemen. He announced that all apartments and trailer court facilities near the Pentagon that were not "available to all military personnel on an equal basis" by Jan. 15, 1968 would be off-limits to all servicemen. McNamara said: "It is clear that military personnel assigned to the

Pentagon area do not enjoy freedom of choice in housing." Fewer than 10% of Negro servicemen could find suitable accommodations. Of the 39,000 apartment units within the Pentagon area, 14,000 were open to Negroes, and 25,000 were segregated. Of the 1,200 Negro military families in the Washington area, only 57% could obtain satisfactory housing.

Bias Barred at A-Smasher Site

The trustees of the Village of Weston, Ill. Feb. 14 unanimously passed a fair-housing ordinance prohibiting discriminatory practices by real estate brokers and salesmen. The action followed efforts by civil rights groups to have Congress withhold approval of Weston as the site for the construction of the world's largest atom smasher pending the vallage's adoption of open housing legislation.

The Atomic Energy Commission (AEC) Jan. 20 had released a statement justifying the selection of the Weston site for the planned $240 million atom smasher. It said that it had "sought and obtained assurances of nondiscrimination" from local government, business and labor groups and that "a progressive attitude" toward equality in employment and education existed in the area. It admitted, however, that it had found "differing views" on the presence of discrimination in housing.

The National Committee Against Discrimination in Housing (NCDH), a national civil rights group composed of 46 labor, religious, civic and civil rights organizations, Jan. 31 challenged the AEC's "good intentions" in its choice. The committee charged that the "community doors" in the Weston area (35 miles west of Chicago) had been "locked to Negroes for generations." It demanded "broad, specific action" by Chicago and by the state of Illinois to insure open housing before the site was approved by Congress.

Among the NCDH charges made in the letter to the AEC were: (1) Weston was the only one of the final candidates for selection that was not covered by a state fair housing law, and the Illinois Legislature "has consistently refused to enact" such a law; (2) the city of Chicago had failed to open suburban housing to Negroes; (3) real estate interests in Du Page County (Weston and the surrounding area) had blocked efforts to enforce Gov. Otto Kerner's executive order banning nondiscrimination in housing.

In testimony before the Joint Committee on Atomic Energy in Washington Feb. 7, Clarence Mitchell, head of the NAACP's Washington chapter, said: "If the AEC had set out to find a site where its colored employes, scientists and visitors would be most likely to encounter discrimination in housing, Weston would clearly qualify for that dubious honor."

Rep. John N. Erlenborn (R., Ill.), whose Congressional district included Weston, denied charges of discrimination in testimony Feb. 8. He said that the AEC should not require a fair housing law. Sen. John O. Pastore (D., R.I.), chairman of the joint committee, replied that approval of the site might hinge on the enactment of local fair housing ordinances.

Other Housing Action

The Detroit Common Council Nov. 28 passed an open-housing bill by 4–2 vote. The measure outlawed discrimination by race, religion or national origin in the sale or rental of housing by owners, real estate brokers, salesmen, advertisers or financial institutions. Exempt from the ban were buildings in which rooms were rented to no more than 3 persons and private sales of real estate. Sellers were permitted "preference" in choosing a buyer as long as there was no discrimination because of race, religion or national origin.

The Michigan House of Representatives Dec. 21 defeated an open-housing bill by 55–47 vote. 21 Republicans and 26 Democrats voted in favor of the measure, which would have banned discrimination in the sale or rental of property, and would have imposed severe fines for violations; 32 Republicans and 26 Democrats opposed the measure.

In an unprecedented action the Federal Trade Commission Dec. 8 issued 2 complaints charging the operators of 9 apartment house complexes in Arlington, Va. with advertising in Washington newspapers that was "false, misleading and deceptive" because they did not state that "these apartments are not available for rental to applicants who are Negro." The commission's vote on the action was 3–1. In his dissent, FTC Chairman Paul Rand Dixon questioned the commission's authority to police advertising. He said: "I agree that the housing problem in America must be resolved. I would suggest, however, that it should be resolved by Congress and not by an administrative agency created to deal with the problems associated with interstate trade and commerce." He said that rather than acting against a handful of apartment owners, the commission should act against "all like parties wherever they might be situated who may have advertised deceptively."

Hunger Controversy

Welfare and Agriculture Department officials warned early in 1967 that thousands of Negroes in 7 Southern states faced virtual starvation as some of the nation's poorest counties ended programs of free distribution of government surplus food to the poor and turned to the sale of federal food stamps. Many of those receiving food assistance were unemployed and unable to pay for food stamps.

According to the Agriculture Department, 208,000 persons in 28 counties in Mississippi had been receiving direct food aid in Apr. 1966. With the conversion to the food stamp program, only 128,000 persons received aid. In Washington County (Greenville), Miss., 20,218 persons had received direct food aid in Apr. 1966; in Apr. 1967 the number receiving aid through the food stamp plan was 10,160. In Jones County, Miss. 17,500 persons had received free food in 1967; only 4,700 of them bought food stamps when the county switched programs in 1966.

The free distribution of surplus farm commodities had begun in many Mississippi counties in 1954, and a 3-year, $375 million food stamp program was enacted in 1964. (The House and Senate Sept. 19 approved a 2-year, $425 million extension of the food stamp program, and Pres. Johnson signed the extension bill Sept. 27). The Food Stamp Act of 1964 had authorized a program to increase the food-buying power of low-income persons. For a small amount of money poor families could purchase government-subsidized stamps whose value at local food stores, was more than the poor families paid. The federal government made up the difference between what the poor paid and the face value of the stamps. State food-stamp programs, set up only when states requested them, replaced the state's existing program of free distribution of government-owned surplus foods.

Agriculture Secy. Orville L. Freeman told the House Agriculture Committee Mar. 15 that the food-stamp program had enabled families to buy 50% more food than they previously received. He said: On the average a family paid about 64% of the total value of the coupons it received monthly; the value of coupons averaged about $6 a month per person; 51,900 retail food stores were authorized to accept coupons; in 1964 some 351,000 persons had participated in 43 pilot programs in 22 states; in Jan. 1967 there were 1.4 million participants in 589 programs in 21 states and the District of Columbia; spending rose from $35.1 million in fiscal 1965 to $70.3 million in fiscal 1966 and to $140 million in fiscal 1967.

(The Agriculture Department reported Sept. 8 that more than 1.8 million poor persons in 838 areas in 41 states and the District of Columbia had participated in the food-stamp program in fiscal 1967.)

Negroes in Jackson, Miss. had denounced the stamp plan Feb. 17 at a hearing on welfare programs conducted by the Mississippi State Advisory Committee to the U.S. Commission on Civil Rights. Anzie Moore, a Negro from Cleveland, Miss. and spokesman for a Bolivar County antipoverty group, said: "Now they're going to sell us stamps. . . . That means starve or go to Chicago. We don't want the stamps unless it's a free stamp program." Mrs. Beulah Mae Miller of Itta Bena, the mother of 6 children, told the committee that except for an occasional cheap flavored drink, her family consumed nothing but surplus commodities (rice, flour, cornmeal, powdered milk and canned meat) "ever since they been giving it."

Kenneth Dean, director of the Mississippi Council on Human Relations, told the Senate Labor & Public Welfare Subcommittee on Employment, Manpower & Poverty Apr. 25: "In 7 Mississippi counties his agency had found "poverty that could, at any given moment, turn into acute hunger or a slow starvation if federal programs are not upgraded." His agency's report mentioned a family "too poor to participate in a poverty program" and said that adults in such families fluctuated between the "human and subhuman level." "It is not accurate to describe these victims of poverty as starving. A large number of people do not have a balanced diet or adequate food for normal development." His spot checks in Hinds, Bolivar, Washington, Yalobusha, Grenada, Lafayette and Madison Counties showed "poverty situations that are of such extreme nature that the people involved do not have adequate food, housing, clothing or health care."

The Senate Feb. 20 had approved by voice vote a resolution authorizing $165,000 for a year-long study by the subcommittee of the antipoverty programs of the Office of Economic Opportunity. Subcommittee Chairman Joseph S. Clark Jr. (D., Pa.) and subcommittee member Sen. Robert F. Kennedy (D., N.Y.) toured half a dozen Mississippi communities Apr. 11. During a visit to Freedom City, a 400-acre project sponsored by the Delta Ministry of the National Council of Churches, the project director, John Bradford, said there was no money for food stamps, "milk, or eggs or juice." Families subsisted on grits, rice, soybeans and "whatever is donated," he reported.

The subcommittee, in a letter delivered to the White House Apr.

28 (made public Apr. 29), asked Pres. Johnson to invoke emergency measures to fight hunger in Mississippi and wherever else it existed. The letter said: The food-stamp program was inadequate; many families had no cash income and therefore could not buy stamps. Subcommittee members had "heard testimony and observed . . . conditions of malnutrition and widespread hunger in the delta counties of Mississippi that can only be described as shocking and which we believe constitute an emergency." A family with 13 children "told us that they had had grits and molasses for breakfast, no lunch, and would have beans for supper. Some of the children could not go to school because they had no shoes, and had distended stomachs, chronic sores of the upper lip, and were extremely lethargic—all of which are the tragic evidence of serious malnutrition."

The Office of Economic Opportunity (OEO), at the President's request, issued a news release expressing its "hearty concurrence" with the subcommittee letter. It said, however, that similar "crises" existed in the states of the Senators who signed the letter. The OEO release said: "We should at this point in the fiscal year realize that every additional dollar devoted to Mississippi would divert money from other areas desperately in need"; 18 months previously Administration officials had described the critical nature of the situation and had "literally begged that the minimum requests submitted to Congress to finance these programs be granted"; the Agriculture Department could not lawfully issue free food stamps, and it could not authorize emergency action under the Food Stamp Act.

OEO Director Sargent Shriver May 3 announced a $1 million emergency grant for a 4-month Food Stamp Loan Program in 20 poor counties in Alabama, Arkansas, Georgia, Louisiana, Mississippi, South Carolina and Tennessee. Theodore M. Berry, director of Community Action Programs (CAP), said that CAP would make small cash loans ($2 to $12 a month depending on the size of the family) to "a head of family or individual who had been certified as eligible [by the local welfare department] to purchase federal food stamps and has shown that he is unable to purchase the food stamps without . . . such a loan." Berry also said poor people would be hired as county loan aides to find all eligible households and inform them of the program.

A team of doctors studied the situation under a Field Foundation subsidy and told the Senate subcommittee June 16 that nutritional and medical conditions in Mississippi were "shocking." The doctors urged the government to permit the rural poor to obtain food stamps free. " 'Malnutrition' is not quite what we found," the doctors said. "The boys and girls we saw were hungry—weak, in pain, sick; their lives are being shortened. . . . They are suffering from hunger and disease and directly or indirectly they are dying from them—which is exactly what 'starvation' means." The doctors gave their testimony after a 4-day inspection of conditions in Humphreys, Leflore, Clarke, Wayne, Neshoba and Greene Counties, Miss.

The doctors composing the team were: Dr. Robert Coles, a child psychiatrist with the Harvard University Health Service; Dr. Raymond Wheeler, an internist from Charlotte, N.C. and executive committee chairman of the Southern Regional Council; Dr. Alan Mermann, a pediatrician and assistant clinical professor at Yale Medical School; Dr. Joseph Brenner of the MIT medical department. Brenner, who had spent a year in East Africa, said that health conditions in the South were as bad or worse than those among the primitive tribal Africans in Kenya or Aden. The doctors said the families they saw were totally isolated and outside the "American money economy."

Gov. Paul B. Johnson Jr. of Mississippi announced Aug. 4 that a team of prominent Mississippi doctors had found no evidence of starvation in the state. The 5 doctors, selected by the governor from a list of specialists at the University of Mississippi Medical Center and the Mississippi State Medical Association, had inspected Washington, Bolivar, Humphreys and Leflore counties. Johnson said the physicians reported that "in none of the counties could any condition approaching starvation be found to support the charges of death by starvation." He asserted that the recent allegations were "unfair and exaggerated," although it was true that "in many localities sanitary conditions are below the acceptable minimum and there are varying degrees of undernutrition, malnutrition and anemia as there are in other parts of the nation." The Mississippi doctors attributed the inadequate housing, clothing, medical and dental care and diet to low income, ignorance of budgeting, meal planning and personal hygiene and overloaded health and welfare staffs.

These changes in the food-stamp program went into effect July 1: (1) a reduction of more than ½ in the cost of food stamps; (2) a reduction in the minimum monthly purchase by families from $2 a person to 50¢ a person (for $12 a family of 6 had received food stamps worth $70); (3) a proposal to get county boards of supervisors to underwrite the cost of minimum stamp purchases for families without income; (4) an increase in trained federal workers to recruit, hire and train new "program aides" to work with the poor on nutrition, food buying and food preparation. (5 new federal commodity marketing and service offices were set up in Mississippi, effective Sept. 1.) The changes also allowed for a longer conversion period for the change from direct distribution of federal food to the food-stamp program.

Welfare Recipients Demonstrate

More than 1,000 welfare recipients—most of them black—picketed the Health, Education & Welfare Department building in Washington, D.C. Aug. 28 in protest against the welfare restrictions in the House-passed Social Security bill. The mass protest came at the end of the first convention of the National Organization for Welfare Rights, a coalition of 250 local Welfare Rights organizations in 70 cities.

The demonstrators distributed a resolution denouncing the Social Security bill as "a betrayal of the poor, a declaration of war upon our families, and a fraud on the future of our nation." Dr. George A. Wiley, who had organized the Welfare Rights Movement in 1966 in a drive to improve welfare benefits and extend them to persons not yet covered, said at the convention Aug. 26 that the long-term objectives of the movement were to build a national organization of poor people based on the model of organized labor.

None of the 16 Senators the convention delegates invited to meet with them in the caucus room in the old Senate Office Building were present. N.Y. Sens. Jacob K. Javits (R.) and Robert F. Kennedy (D.) sent staff aids who spoke to the convention.

Thousands of welfare recipients had demonstrated in cities and towns across the country June 30 in protest against inadequacies of the welfare system. Most demonstrators carried "basic need forms" prepared by the National Welfare Rights Movement. The forms, which included blank space for listing minimum requirements for food, clothing, rent and furniture, said, in part: "Federal and state laws require that families be provided with welfare benefits adequate to insure a minimum standard of health and decency. Contrary to these laws, I do not get enough money in my welfare grant to meet my family's needs."

Some 45 members of Mothers for Adequate Welfare in Boston marched to Boston Common for a noon rally. They asked that policemen be removed from welfare offices and that welfare recipients be included on boards making decisions about welfare problems.

About 200 persons rallied in front of the County Board of Public Assistance in Philadelphia and demanded "rights and respect" for welfare recipients. They carried signs that read: "Millions for the moon—pennies for us." "Our kids go hungry while you make us wait." "Welfare is a right, not a privilege."

150 persons staged a 5-mile march to Cuyahoga County Welfare Department in protest against inadequate welfare payments. About 40 welfare recipients picketed branch offices of the Cook County Public Aid Department on the North and West Sides of Chicago. More than 100 welfare recipients staged a one-mile march from Pershing Square to the County Board of Supervisors' hall in the Civic Center in Los Angeles. They carried signs that read: "Stop welfare brutality." "General relief O.K. for dogs, not for us." "Aid to the dead is like putting sugar on the ocean." "More money now."

Nearly 800 Negroes staged a "poor people's march" from the Negro Masonic Temple in Jackson, Miss. to the state capitol Aug. 14. The marchers were stopped at the doors to the statehouse by state troopers. Charles Evers, NAACP state field director for Mississippi, said the Agriculture Department had "food stores by the millions being eaten by worms, and my people are going hungry." Dr. Aaron Henry, NAACP state president, said the march was a response to an alleged statement of Gov. Paul Johnson's that the only Negroes he had seen were "big, fat, black and greasy."

More than 600 poor people from N.Y. City—most of them Puerto Ricans and Negroes—rallied in Washington, D.C. Oct. 16 in a campaign for massive increases in federal antipoverty spending. after hearing speeches on the Mall near the Capitol, they marched to the Mount Carmel Baptist Church for a "poor people's Congressional hearing." None of the Congress members invited to the hearing attended. The demonstration was sponsored by the Citywide Community Action Groups, headed by Major R. Owens.

Alabama Aid Threatened

Alabama was threatened Jan. 12 with the loss of federal aid to its welfare and mental health programs because of its refusal to comply with Title VI of the Civil Rights Act of 1964. Health, Education & Welfare Secy. John W. Gardner announced in Washington that federal support for Alabama welfare programs (estimated at $95.8 million for the fiscal year ending June 30) would be ended Feb. 28 unless the state complied with Title VI and administered programs without racial discrimination.   This was the first time welfare funds had been threatened because of racial discrimination.

The U.S. Public Health Service announced in Washington Jan. 13 that the Alabama Department of Mental Health was ineligible for federal funds (estimated at from $750,000 to $800,000) because of noncompliance with the 1964 Civil Rights Act.

Federal welfare aid to Alabama represented about ¾ of its general public assistance and more than ½ of its child welfare programs.   HEW (Health, Education & Welfare) Department efforts to achieve compliance by Alabama had begun Aug. 17, 1965 when U.S. Welfare Commissioner Ellen Winston notified the state that it was not in compliance.   After a hearing, a hearing examiner recommended Apr. 6, 1966 that federal aid be terminated.   Miss Winston accepted the examiner's recommendation after further hearings, and she referred the case to Gardner Nov. 16, 1966.

Alabama, the only state that did not comply with the civil rights regulations, filed suit in U.S. District Court in Birmingham, Ala. Jan. 13 to enjoin the HEW Department from withholding federal aid because of the alleged racial discrimination.   The suit charged Gardner's action violated his powers under Title VI.   Gardner assured the Senate Finance Committee Feb. 23 that Alabama would continue to get federal welfare aid until any legal questions were settled.

(Gardner announced at a news conference May 10 that civil rights enforcement powers in HEW programs would be transferred to his office from the 5 agencies currently charged with them.   The action, he said, came in response to a Congressional mandate issued in 1966 by the House Appropriations Subcommittee on Health, Education & Welfare.   The 5 bureau chiefs included U.S. Commissioner of Education Harold Howe 2d who had established the controversial school desegregation guidelines in 1966.   His office had been responsible for initiating non-compliance actions against southern school district.   At the news conference, Gardner said his action "implies no change in the department's compliance policies.")

POLITICS & PUBLIC SERVICE

6 Negroes in Congress

The 90th Congress convened Jan. 10 with 6 black members, including one Senator—Edward W. Brooke (R., Mass.), 48, the 3d Negro to serve in the Senate and the first to enter that body since the 1870s (during the Reconstruction era).

7 Negroes had actually been elected to Congress in Nov. 1966, but the House Jan. 10 barred Adam Clayton Powell Jr. (D., N.Y.) from taking his seat pending an investigation of his qualifications.

(Julian Bond, 26, a Negro, was finally sworn in as a Georgia House member Jan. 9. Bond had twice been barred from the seat by previous legislatures for supporting statements opposing the draft and U.S. policy in Vietnam.)

House Excludes Powell

Adam Clayton Powell Jr., 58, a member of the House of Representatives since 1946, was excluded from Congress Mar. 1 by House vote on the ground that he had misused public funds and was in contempt of court.

The Congressional action against the controversial black Representative began Jan. 9, the day before Congress convened. He was ousted as chairman of the House Education & Labor Committee Jan. 9 and then was barred Jan. 10 from taking his House seat pending an investigation of his qualifications. Powell publicly attributed the moves against him to anti-Negro prejudice. Commenting on the 122 Democrats who had voted against him, Powell told backers from Harlem Jan. 10: "Jesus had one Judas; I had about 120."

Although not sworn in as a Congress member, Powell was entitled to his salary and staff. This was the first time in 46 years that a House member had been refused his seat for reasons other than a contested election. It was the first time since 1925 that a House chairman had been deposed and the first time in 160 years that one had been ousted for a reason other than party disloyalty.

Powell was stripped of his chairmanship Jan. 9 by the House Democratic caucus by a voice vote that Powell estimated as 75% against him. The vote was on a motion, presented by Rep. Morris K. Udall(Ariz.), to elect Rep. Carl D. Perkins (Ky.), next to

Powell in seniority on the committee, as chairman. Udall reportedly based his appeal for support of his motion on a Jan. 3 House Administration Committee report indicating that Powell had misused his committee's travel money. The Administration Committee report, based on an investigation by a subcommittee headed by Rep. Wayne L. Hays (D., O.), did not recommend penalties against Powell, but it also ordered Powell's estranged wife, Yvette Marjorie Flores Powell, dropped from Powell's office payroll. It said there was a "strong presumption" that Mrs. Powell, who was being paid $20,578 a year, was not complying with statutory requirements that she work for it in the District of Columbia or the state or district represented by Powell.

Powell reportedly did not mention race in defending himself at the caucus and did not deny using committee funds for his personal travels. Later, however, he called himself a "black Dreyfus" and told newsmen "it was a lynching—Northern style." In a statement released by his office Jan. 5, Powell had charged that "a political conspiracy of enormous dimensions . . . has not only been mounted against Adam Clayton Powell, but against black political leadership, black people and black progress." (Rep. Hays said Dec. 5: "I suspect if Powell were white he would have been investigated earlier.")

House Republican (minority) leader Gerald R. Ford (Mich.) Jan. 10 presented the exclusion resolution, which was adopted by 364–64 vote. The resolution gave subpoena power to a special House committee to investigate and present recommendations on Powell's "right" to be sworn in "as well as his final right to a seat." The Ford resolution was similar to a resolution previously prepared by Rep. Lionel Van Deerlin (D., Calif.). Van Deerlin, who had announced in 1966 that he would propose the exclusion of Powell, had led the current move to discipline Powell. In a statement released the night of Jan. 10 Powell blamed his discomfiture on "the Northern liberal bigots who are now in control of the Democratic Party." He called on "black people everywhere along with our white friends to begin to consider the feasibility of a new independent course of action in which they are the balance of power in all elections."

Negro groups and leaders were almost unanimous in their opposition to the action against Powell. Almost without exception they denounced the moves against Powell as attacks on American Negroes in general.

Support for Powell had been expressed Jan. 2 by the Baptist Ministers Conference of Greater New York (400 black clergymen) Jan. 2; by the NAACP in a resolution presented by NAACP Executive Secy. Roy Wilkins Jan. 3; by the Council of Elected Negro Democrats (51 members in New York) Jan. 7; by Floyd McKissick, national chairman of CORE; by the National Urban League and by Bayard Rustin Jan. 9. McKissick and other black leaders echoed Powell's charge that the disciplining of Powell was the "political castration" of a Negro because he had achieved power. Wilkins told newsmen Jan. 13 that there had been no organized civil rights effort behind Powell's fight for his seat because "Powell never called on the civil rights movement. . . . He never thought they had the power to help him." He said the movement had not known how serious Powell's trouble was and had not considered it likely he would lose his chairmanship. "Only Adam's office knew of the tremendous volume of mail received by Congressmen against Powell," Wilkins said. "If we had known this—we could have done something."

Rallies in Powell's behalf were held in Washington by about 5,000 persons, most of them Negroes, who gathered at the Metropolitan Baptist Church Jan. 8 and then by about 1,000 supporters who held a 6-hour vigil on the steps of the Capitol Jan. 10. The demonstrators came not only from Powell's Harlem (N.Y. City) district but from the Bedford-Stuyvesant section of Brooklyn (N.Y. City) and from Philadelphia Baltimore, Chicago and other cities. Powell appeared at the Jan. 10 rally and urged his constituents to "put a moratorium on" payment of taxes until he was seated. "You no longer have a Congressman," he said. Stokely Carmichael told the demonstrators that "the main cat to focus on is [Pres.] Lyndon Baines Johnson" for Powell's problems.

Powell's exclusion from his seat was deplored Jan. 10 by both U.S. Senators from New York—Robert F. Kennedy (D.) and Jacob K. Javits (R.). Kennedy said he was "disturbed" at this deprivation of representation "for at least 5 weeks and . . . even before the committee investigating this matter has made any findings or rulings on the charges."

The House's action against Powell was denounced Jan. 13 by the Rev. Dr. Gayraud S. Wilmore Jr., executive director of the United Presbyterian Commission on Religion & Race. "While liberals sell their brothers down the river for the sake of principles which are more honored in the breach than in observance," he said, "the racists and crypto-racists use every gimmick in the courts and legislatures to take care of their own."

A "Negro summit conference" on the Powell case, scheduled for Jan. 25 in Washington, was called off Jan. 22 "because demand for attendance and participation was too great for meaningful and creative discussion." Plans for the conference had been announced Jan. 12 by A. Philip Randolph, president of the AFL-CIO Bro'hood of Sleeping Car Porters, who said Powell's loss of his committee chairmanship and temporary loss of his seat "reflected the greatest crisis in Negro-white relations." Randolph and other prominent black leaders Jan. 22 issued a statement charging that Powell had been "denied due process" and his constituents "deprived of representation." The signers included the Rev. Dr. Martin Luther King Jr., Roy Wilkins and Whitney M. Young Jr.

Powell supporters failed to persuade large numbers of Negroes to strike for one day Feb. 13 in protest against the application of an ethical "double standard" by the House against Powell. The strike movement, led by the Rev. Albert Cleage Jr. of Detroit with the support of Negro comedian Dick Gregory, was opposed by most national black leaders.

A select committee to investigate Powell's right to his seat had been named by House Speaker John W. McCormack (D., Mass.) Jan. 19. The members were Emanuel Celler (D., N.Y.), chairman; James C. Corman (D., Calif.); Claude D. Pepper (D., Fla.); John Conyers Jr. (D., Mich.); Andrew Jacobs Jr. (D., Ind.); Arch A. Moore Jr. (R., W.Va.); Charles M. Teague (R., Calif.); Clark MacGregor (R., Minn.); Vernon W. Thomson (R., Wis.). All 5 Democrats named to the panel had voted in the Democratic caucus Jan. 10 for a defeated resolution to seat Powell pending his investigation.

The committee opened its public hearings Feb. 8. Powell, accompanied by 7 lawyers, appeared Feb. 8 but refused to respond to questions other than those regarding his age, citizenship and residency, which involved the constitutional requirements for membership in the House. His lawyers contended that Powell met these requirements and, therefore, should be seated. They said the committee lacked authority to investigate other matters. They presented motions on the committee to limit the inquiry, call it off, seat Powell or grant him the "attributes of an adversary proceeding" and "all rights and protection" of the constitution. Ruling that "this is not an adversary proceeding," Chairman Celler denied the motions. In a brief filed with the committee Feb. 20, Powell's lawyers contended that Congress was not a continuing body and could not expel or punish a member for acts committed in a previous Congress.

Testimony Feb. 14 disclosed that Powell had paid for some Miami-to-Bimini flights (Powell had a vacation home in Bimini) by checks drawn on Huff Enterprises, Ltd. The committee uncovered little information about Huff Enterprises other that that its address was Powell's Congressional office and that its incorporators included Corinne Huff (president), Bahamas Prime Min. Lynden O. Pindling, C. Sumner Stone (Powell's chief assistant), Powell staff member Emma T. Swann and ex-chief Powell investigator Odell Clark.

Powell's estranged wife, Mrs. Yvette Marjorie Flores Diago Powell, 35, testified before the committee Feb. 16. She said she had received not more than 4 salary checks in 6 years, had not received nor endorsed 19 salary checks made out to her and cashed, had not authorized Powell to receive her checks and endorse them, had not signed any income tax form in the past 2 years and had not performed any official duties in Washington or New York for at least 1½ years. She said the "support" she had received from Powell amounted to less than half of the $20,578 annual salary she was supposed to be receiving as Powell's employe.

The committee recommended Feb. 23 that Powell be seated but publicly censured in the House by the House Speaker. The committee also recommended that Powell be required to pay the House $40,000, that he be dropped to last in House seniority and that beauty-contest winner Corinne Huff, a secretary who frequently traveled with Powell at Congress' expense, be dropped from the House payroll. If Powell did not appear by Mar. 13 to be sworn into office, the committee concluded, his seat should be considered vacant.

The committee found that Powell had "permitted and participated in improper expenditures of government funds for private purposes" and that he had "improperly maintained" his wife on his payroll although she either performed no official duties or her duties wer not performed as required by law, in Washington or in Powell's state.

The payment was assessed against Powell "as punishment," and the recommendation for censure was based on the committee's finding of "gross misconduct." The panel held that Powell' conduct "has reflected adversely on the integrity and reputation of the House and its members." In addition to citing payroll and travel abuses the panel called Powell's conduct towards the New York courts "contumacious" and his refusal to cooperate with the select committee and a previous House panel probing his activities "contemptuous." The report specifically charged that Powell had "wrongfully and willfully appropriated" public funds totalling $46,226.48 to "his own use" and to the use of others. In addition, it charged that Powell, as chairman of the Education & Labor Committee, had "made false reports on expenditures of foreign exchange currency."

The report was signed by all 9 members of the select committee. 2 appended additional comments: Pepper said he "feels strongly that Mr. Powell should not be a member of the House"; Conyers stated his belief "that punishment of Mr. Powell beyond severe censure is improper." At the news conference at which the committee's report was released, Conyers, 37, the only Negro on the committee, said he felt that "racial considerations" had brought Powell to this point but that "on this committee the racial aspects of this case were never used." He said he was "proud to have been a member" of the committee and intended to support its conclusions.

The House voted Mar. 1 to exclude Powell from the 90th Congress. This was the 3d time in history, and the first time in 46 years, that the House had excluded a duly-elected candidate. The vote was on an amendment, offered by Rep. Thomas B. Curtis (R., Mo.), deleting the Select Committee's recommendations and stating that Powell "is excluded from membership in the 90th Congress and the Speaker shall notify the governor of New York of the existing vacancy." His substitute proposal was accepted by 248–176 vote (125 R. & 123 D. vs. 117 D. & 59 R.). The House, by 307–116 vote (173 R. & 134 D. vs. 105 D. & 11R.), then adopted H.Res. 278 as amended by the Curtis substitute. On a final roll call, the House voted by 309–9 to include the Select Committee report preamble, embodying its findings, in the resolution. The exclusion action prevailed despite the strong support expressed by majority leader Carl Albert (Okla.) and minority leader Ford for the select committee's recommendation to seat Powell and punish him.

Powell was at his vacation home in Bimini at the time of the House action.

Powell's exclusion was denounced by many Negro and civil rights leaders as stemming from anti-Negro prejudice. CORE national director McKissick said Mar. 1 that the action against Powell was "a slap in the face of every black man in the country." Dr. Martin Luther King Jr. said that "even the infamy of a McCarthy . . . was treated with only a mild reprimand compared to the brutal silencing of a people's Congressman." A. Philip Randolph called Powell's ouster "a mockery of democracy without precedent" and warned that it "could generate a racial reaction with overtones of violence and disorder and misguided revenge." Whitney Young Jr. said the "shocking" House action "denies the basic right of his constituents to representation of their own choosing." UN Undersecy. Ralph J. Bunche asserted that "there can be no reasonable doubt that if Adam Powell had been white he would have his seat today." "Emotion, prejudice and hypocrisy too obviously ran deeply in the action of the House," Bunche declared.

A letter notifying N.Y. Gov. Nelson A. Rockefeller of the vacancy in the Powell district was sent by House Speaker John W. McCormack Mar. 2. Rep. Morris Udall (D., Ariz.) said Mar. 2 that Powell had escaped punishment by the House for "a long time" solely because he was a Negro. "If he'd been a white man," Udall said, "we'd have gotten to him a long time ago. But this racism thing held a lot of people off."

Rep. Carl D. Perkins (D., Ky.), who succeeded Powell as chairman of the House Education & Labor Committee, had confirmed Feb. 11 that 12 former Powell aides, 6 of them Negroes, had been dropped from the committee staff. Among them was C. Sumner Stone, Powell's $25,890-a-year chief assistant. The dropping of the black employes was protested by Clarence Mitchell of the NAACP.

(New York State Supreme Court Justice Emilio Nunez Feb. 17 had refused to find Powell guilty for the 5th and 6th times of contempt of court. Calling Powell a "lawless lawmaker," Nunez said that convicting Powell would provide a basis for "delaying tactics." U.S. District Judge Sylvester J. Ryan in New York Feb. 20 dismissed a suit brought by 92 constituents seeking to void an order for Powell's arrest for criminal contempt of court. The State Court of Appeals in Albany Mar. 2 canceled $100,000 of a $155,785 damage award against Powell. The court held 6–1 that Powell would not have to pay the $100,000, representing punitive damages, because "his conduct was not so gross and wanton as to bring it within the class of malfeasances for which punitive damages . . . should be awarded." The other $55,785 represented compensatory damages and included $46,500 of an original judgment against Powell for defaming Mrs. Esther James.)

Powell filed suit in U.S. district court in Washington Mar. 8 to regain his Congressional seat. The action was brought by Powell and 13 voters from his Congressional district against House Speaker McCormack and other House leaders and officers. But the suit was dismissed Apr. 7 by U.S. Judge George L. Hart Jr. on the ground that the court lacked jurisdiction. Powell had charged in his suit that the House had exceeded its authority in excluding him since he met the only constitutional qualifications for House membership—age, citizenship and residency. He also charged that the exclusion subjected non-white citizens of Powell's district "to the pains and penalties of discrimination" and deprived them of due process of law because of the costs of the special election necessitated by the alleged unconstitutional exclusion.

A special election to fill Powell's seat was scheduled Mar. 6 for Apr. 11, and James H. Meredith announced Mar. 7 that he would run against Powell in the special election. But Meredith withdrew as a candidate Mar. 13. Meredith, 33 a law student at Columbia University and a prominent civil rights activist, had said in announcing his candidacy that the election was "one of the most important in the history of this country and certainly in this century. . . . The future of the Negro will be affected." But his candidacy was met with almost solid opposition from local black leaders. Meredith's withdrawal was announced Mar. 13 after a private meeting with CORE leader McKissick and Charles Evers, NAACP leader in Mississippi. Evers told a newsman later he had begged Meredith "not to destroy the faith we have in you."

Powell won by almost a 7–1 margin the special 18th Congressional District election in New York Apr. 11 for the seat left vacant when the House had excluded him. Although he did not appear in the district during the campaign—he was subject to arrest on contempt citations if he appeared in New York—Powell won 27,900 votes to 4,091 for Mrs. Lucille Pickett Williams (R.) and 427 for the Rev. Erwin F. Yearling, a Conservative Party candidate. In the Nov. 1966 election, Powell had received 74% of 61,287 ballots cast; in 1964, 84% of 111,012 votes cast.

Despite his election victory, Powell made no further attempt to claim his House seat during 1967. He spent the rest of the year in Bimini, coming only on Sundays (to avoid arrest) to New York, where he served as pastor of Harlem's Abyssinian Baptist Church.

(In Bimini July 26 Powell called the riots in Detroit and other U.S. cities "a necessary phase of the black revolution.")

More Negroes in Federal Jobs

A report released by the Civil Service Commission Jan. 9 showed that Negroes had constituted 13.9% of the federal payroll June 30, 1966. This compared with 13% in 1962 and 13½% in 1965. The 1966 Negro total was 320,000, of whom 109,658 (9.7% of the total employes) were listed as general schedule employes (white collar workers). One salary category, the entrance grades of GS–1 through 4, showed an absolute increase but percentage drop from 64,727 Negroes (19.3% of the total employes) in 1965 to 65,548 (18.6% of the total) in 1966. In the other salary categories: 31,205 Negroes (10.1% of the total) were in grades GS–5 through 8 ($5,331 to $9,183 a year) in 1966, compared with 30,039 Negroes (9.6%) in 1965; 9,642 Negroes (3.8% of the total) were in grades GS–9 through 11 ($7,696 to $12,056) in 1966, compared with 9,125 Negroes (3.4%) in 1965; 3,363 Negroes (1.6% of the total) were in grades GS–12 through 18 ($10,270 to $25,890) in 1966, compared with 2,815 Negroes (1.3%) in 1965.

The NAACP, the National Urban League and the National Alliance of Postal & Federal Employes announced in Washington Oct. 17 the creation of a National Equal Employment Opportunity Committee to fight discrimination in the postal service. Thomas C. Hall, a New York Lawyer, was named head of the committee. Ashby G. Smith, president of the postal union, said that Negroes comprised 15% of the postal force but held only 2% of the jobs above Grade 4 (letter carriers and clerks). In Washington's main post office, he said, the work force was 93% black but the supervisory staff was 11% black.

Marshall Joins Supreme Court

Pres. Johnson June 13 appointed Solicitor Gen. Thurgood Marshall, 59, as an associate justice of the Supreme Court. He succeeded Justice Tom C. Clark who retired June 12. Marshall, the son of a Pullman car steward and great-grandson of a slave, was the first Negro appointed to the Supreme Court.

In announcing the nomination, Johnson noted Marshall's "distinguished record" and said: "He is best qualified by training and by very valuable service to the country. I believe it is the right thing to do, the right time to do it, the right man and the right place." Atty. Gen. Ramsey Clark said he had made a "strong recommendation" that Marshall be appointed to the high court.

Marshall's legal reputation had been won as a specialist in civil rights cases. As special counsel for the National Association for the Advancement of Colored People and counsel for the NAACP Legal Defense & Educational Fund, Inc., he had argued 32 lawsuits before the Supreme Court. One of these cases had led to the 1954 high court ruling declaring racial segregation in public schools unconstitutional.

Candidate Qualification Change Valid

A 3-judge Federal court ruled in Jackson, Miss. Oct. 27 that Mississippi could change its qualifications for political candidates without violating the 1965 Voting Rights Act. Such changes had been challenged as designed to make it harder for black candidates to get their names on ballots.
The court ruled on a suit filed against Gov. Paul B. Johnson and other state officials by the Rev. Clifton Whitley and other black candidates in the 1966 Congressional elections. The suit had challenged a 1966 Mississippi legislative act (a) increasing the number of petition signees necessary to qualify an independent to run for office; (b) prohibiting persons who voted in primaries from running as independents; (c) requiring independents to qualify by the date specified for party candidates.

Negroes Win Election Victories

Negroes were elected mayor in 2 major cities during state and municipal elections Nov. 7. Among election developments:
● In Cleveland, O. Nov. 7, State Rep. Carl B. Stokes, 40, a black Democrat, defeated Seth B. Taft (R.), 44, grandson of Pres. William Howard Taft and a nephew of the late Sen. Robert A. Taft, by a vote of 129,318 to 127,674. Stokes received about 94½% of the black votes, Taft about 80% of the white votes. (Black registration was estimated at 125,000. Republican registration totaled only about 39,000. The city's population of 811,000 included about 285,000 Negroes.) 78% of the electorate voted.

In winning the Democratic primary Oct. 3, Stokes, a lawyer, had defeated incumbent Mayor Ralph S. Locher, 110,769 votes to 92,033; Stokes got 95% of the black vote and about 14% of the white vote. Stokes was aided in the primary by a large black turnout of at least 74% of 127,000 registered black voters. About 60% of the more than 200,000 registered whites voted. Both candidates had pledged to work against racial violence and had urged voters not to vote on a racial basis. Stokes' victory was hailed Oct. 4 by Vice Pres. Hubert H. Humphrey, and Democratic National Chairman John M. Bailey Oct 4 pledged aid for his election campaign.

Stokes, who had been opposed in the primary by the regular Democratic organization, was considered a moderate; he had declared against "black-power" advocates, opposed a police review board and supported Administration policy on Vietnam. He was indorsed by the *Plain Dealer*. Before he was sworn in Nov. 13 as the first Negro elected mayor of a major U.S. city, Stokes appointed whites to the posts of public safety director, chief police prosecutor and police chief.

● In Gary, Ind Nov. 7, Richard G. Hatcher, 34, a Democrat, became the city's and Indiana's first black mayor by defeating Joseph B. Radigan (R.), 45, a white, by a vote of 39,330 to 37,941. Hatcher received about 95% of the black vote and about 14% of the white vote. Although about 55% of the city's population of 180,000 were Negroes, there were several thousand more whites than Negroes registered. Democratic registration heavily outnumbered Republican registration.

Hatcher was indorsed by national and state Democrats—notably Sen. Birch Bayh (Ind.), Sen. Robert F. Kennedy (N.Y.) and Vice Pres. Humphrey—but opposed by the local Democratic organization, led by John Krupa, Lake County Democratic chairman and circuit court clerk. Just prior to the election, a special 3-judge U.S. district court panel Nov. 6 enjoined Lake County election officials from attempting to "dilute" the black vote and ordered a "fair and nondiscriminatory" election. The court acted after consolidating separate suits brought by Hatcher and the U.S. Justice Department. The plaintiffs presented evidence of registration rolls padded with names of non-existent white voters and of the removal of black registrants from the rolls. The National Guard was called out by Gov. Roger D. Branigin for duty in the city during the election, but no disorder was reported.

• In Memphis, Tenn. Oct. 5, State Rep. A. W. Willis Jr., 42, a wealthy black lawyer and businessman, ran a poor 4th in a nonpartisan election for mayor. Returns indicated that much of the black vote—78,655 registration compared to 152,562 white registration—went to the white incumbent, Mayor William B. Ingram Jr., who had campaigned on the theme that Willis could not win and that a vote for him would be "throwing your vote away." Ingram was the 2d-highest vote-getter. In the run-off Nov. 7, Ingram was defeated by the top vote-getter, ex-mayor Henry Loeb, 46, a conservative. Willis was the first Negro in modern times to try to win election as mayor of a major Southern city.

• In Mississippi Nov. 7, Robert G. Clark, 37, became the first Negro elected to the state Legislature since Reconstruction; he defeated state Rep. J. P. Love (D.), a 12-year veteran. Clark was backed by the Mississippi Freedom Democratic Party. Mississippi Negroes were also elected to 6 county posts; another 15, primary victors, were unopposed for local posts.

• In Virginia Nov. 7, Dr. William Ferguson Reid (D.), 42, a physician, became the first Negro to be elected to the General Assembly since 1891; he ran 4th among 11 candidates for 8 House seats.

• In Louisiana Nov. 4, Negroes were assured of representation in the state House of Representatives for the first time in 88 years as the result of a primary victory by Stephen K. Morial, who was unopposed in the general election. 2 other black candidates for the Legislature won their primaries but faced white oppostiion in the Feb. 6, 1968 general election. 23 other Negro legislative candidates lost.

(The Justice Department had reported July 6 that more than half of the eligible Negro voters in Alabama, Georgia, Louisiana, Mississippi and South Carolina had registered to vote. Registration in the 5 Southern states was estimated at 1¼ million. This was an increase of 78% [700,000] since the 1965 Voting Rights Act was passed. According to the 1960 census, 2,402,000 Negroes were eligible to register in the 5 states.)

Elected Negroes Meet

300 elected black public officials attended the first National Conference of Negro Elected Officials at the University of Chicago Sept. 29–Oct. 1.

In the opening address Sept. 29 Manhattan (N.Y. City) Borough Pres. Percy E. Sutton, co-chairman of the conference, called on Negroes to use "the power that is inherent in our office" to deal with urban problems.   He said: "The loudest and most clearly heard voices on power today are not those of elected leaders of our communities but of those who speak without the restraining weight of any responsibility."   Frequently, they "unleash upon the communities of our country forces of violence and destruction without a countering force of construction.   These are the voices of people who by their language pretend to possess and to wield the thunderbolts of an entire people's hurts, angers, resentments and frustrations."

Dr. Kenneth B. Clark, sociologist and president of the Metropolitan Applied Research Center in New York, told the conferees Sept. 30 that although "black power" might be the "sour-grapes phenomenon" of civil rights, in the ghettos it was "a powerful political reality which cannot be ignored."   "Black power," Clark said, "does have tremendous psychological appeal for the masses of Negroes, who have nothing to lose, and some middle-class Negroes who are revolted by the empty promises and the moral dry rot of affluent America."   He said some advocates of black power were "racial racketeers," but others were "sincere" and "reasonable men with whom rational communication is not only possible but could be fruitful."   Clark urged elected Negro officials to find "some formula whereby there can be a reasonable working relationship with some elements of Negro nationalism."   He warned that they might become the targets of black extremism because many Negroes reject such "tokens of racial progress" as the achievement of high positions by individual Negroes.

Pentagon to Train Black Police

The Defense Department pressed forward with a program to train Negro servicemen to become policemen in civilian life, and the Lawyers' Committee for Civil Rights Under Law formed in 1963 on the suggestion of Pres. John F. Kennedy, announced in Washington Oct. 4 that it would help the Pentagon program.   The committee agreed to furnish lawyers in various cities to persuade local officials to hire black police recruits.   The program would be directed by ex-Asst. Atty. Gen. John Douglas.

The committee released statistics showing that the greatest percentages of black police officers in the nation's major cities were in Baltimore, with 1,260 Negroes on a force of 3,502 officers; Philadelphia, with 1,260 Negroes out of 6,300 officers, and Chicago, with 2,940 out of 11,761. New York had only 1,355 Negro officers on its 27,112-man force. Among other cities included in the survey: Los Angeles, 320 Negroes on a force of 6,392; Detroit, 170 Negroes out of 4,876; Houston, 45 of 1,509; Dallas, 140 of 1,405; Boston, 44 of 2,779; Buffalo, 24 of 1,720; Birmingham, 1 of 524.

Defense Secy. Robert S. McNamara, acting Nov. 21 on Pres. Johnson's request, issued a memo directing the Army, Navy and Air Force Secretaries to give early discharges to military personnel to enter civilian police forces. The memo said that discharges should be given up to 90 days early to military personnel "who have a written offer of specific law enforcement employment or recruit training from a civilian governmental police agency and who request early release in order to take up such employment." McNamara said he hoped the early discharges would make it "possible within the next several months to fill a sizable number of the 15,000 nationwide police vacancies."

OTHER DEVELOPMENTS

7 Convicted of Rights Workers' Murder Conspiracy

An all-white federal jury of 5 men and 7 women in Meridian, Miss. Oct. 20 convicted 7 white men of conspiracy in the 1964 murder of 3 civil rights workers near Philadelphia, Miss. 8 men were acquitted, and mistrials were declared in the cases of 3 men on whom the jury could not reach a verdict. The 3 years of litigation by the Justice Department and investigation by the FBI had cost about $1 million.

Those found guilty were: Cecil R. Price, 29, chief deputy sheriff of Neshoba County; Sam Holloway Bowers Jr., 43, imperial wizard of the White Knights of the Ku Klux Klan; Horace Doyle Barnette, 29, former Meridian automotive parts salesman; Jimmy Arledge, 30, a Meridian truck driver; Billy Wayne Posey, 30, Williamsville (Miss.) service station operator; Jimmie Snowden, 34, Meridian laundry truck driver; Alton Wayne Roberts, 29, Meridian mobile home salesman. All were freed on $5,000 bond each by Oct. 23.

The men were convicted of conspiring to deny "life or liberty without due process." The government charged that: (a) Price had arrested Michael H. Schwerner, 24, of New York, a white field worker for the Congress of Racial Equality (CORE); Andrew Goodman, 20, of New York, a white college student, and James E. Chaney, 21, of Meridian, a Negro plasterer; (b) Price held the 3 youths while a lynching party assembled; (c) then Price released them and allowed them to be captured by the mob, which turned them over to gunmen to be murdered.

Those who were acquitted had not been accused of participating in the slayings. They were: Lawrence A. Rainey, 43, sheriff of Neshoba County; Bernard Lee Akin, 52, Meridian house-trailer dealer; Travis Maryn Barnette, 38, a Meridian auto mechanic; James Thomas Harris, 32, a Meridian truck driver; Frank J. Herndon, 48, Meridian drive-in restaurant operator; Olen L. Burrage, 37, Philadelphia (Miss.) trucking company operator and owner of the farm on which the bodies were buried; Herman Tucker, 38, Philadelphia contractor and builder of the dam in which the bodies were found; Richard Andrew Willis, former Philadelphia policeman.

There were no verdicts reached on Edgar Ray (Preacher) Killen, 42, fundamentalist minister and sawmill operator; Ethel Glen (Hop) Barnett, Democratic nominee for Neshoba County sheriff, and Jerry McGrew Sharpe, 28, Meridian pulpwood hauler.

The defendants were tried under conspiracy indictments returned against 19 men Feb. 27 by a federal grand jury that included 5 blacks and 6 women. Earlier indictments had been dismissed after a July 20, 1966 guideline decision of the U.S. 5th Circuit Court of Appeals invalidated the traditional federal jury selection system of the South for excluding Negroes and women. The 19 men indicted were charged under the felony provision of an 1870 federal civil-rights statute. Earlier indictments had been dismissed by U.S. District Judge W. Harold Cox Feb. 25–26, 1965 and reinstated by the Supreme Court Mar. 28, 1966. Cox had dismissed the charges again Oct. 6, 1966 at the request of the Justice Department because of the July 20, 1966 Appeals Court ruling that juries had to be selected from lists representing both sexes and all races.

The Feb. 27 indictments charged that Rainey, Price and Willis had acted under color of state law to carry out a "Klan assassination plot." Neither Barnett nor Bowers had been named in the earlier indictments. The new indictments omitted Jimmy Lee Townsend, 19, one of those previously indicted. After their indictment, 18 of the men surrendered to federal marshals in Meridian Feb. 28. They were released the same day by U.S. Commissioner Richard E. Wilbourn 2d under $5,000 signature bonds as authorized by the Federal Bond Reform Act of 1965. The 19th man indicted was James Edward Jordan, 41, a former Meridian construction worker currently living in northern Florida and reportedly the FBI's key witness.

Judge Cox Sept. 1 had scheduled the trial for Oct. 9 and had issued instructions for the selection of a 250-member jury venire from all of southern Mississippi. The 12-member jury was chosen Oct. 9; at least 17 of the prospective jurors had been Negroes and were included in the panel from which the final 12 were chosen. Defense attorneys, however, peremptorily rejected all of the Negroes. Prospective jurors of both races who had participated in civil rights activities were asked to step aside.

During the trial Police Sgt. Carlton Wallace Miller testified Oct. 11 that he had joined the local klavern of the White Knights of the Ku Klux Klan in late March or April 1964 and had become a paid informer for the FBI the following September. Miller, who had been a member of the Meridian police force for 20 years, identified 11 of the 18 defendants as either members of the Klan or as having been present at Klan meetings. Miller said that most Klan discussions centered on opposition to integration. He said that at one meeting Edgar Ray Killen, who had recruited him for the Klan, explained the various kinds of "pressure" to be used against civil rights workers: "To begin with, we were to call them up or go see them, threaten them on the job, things of that nature," but the pressure would include "whippings, beatings. . . . After the pressure was applied and they didn't respond, then we were to apply physical pressure." Finally, he said, "there was elimination"; "that's a term for murdering them, killing them." Miller said Killen had once discussed a plan to "whip" Schwerner but later called it off. "Mr. Killen told us to leave him alone, that another unit was going to take care of him," Miller testified. "His elimination had been approved of by the imperial wizard." Miller said that about a week after the 3 rights workers disappeared, "Mr. Killen told me they had been shot and were dead and were buried 15 feet in a dam." Miller testified that Killen said he had come to Meridian after receiving word by phone that the rights workers were in custody. According to Miller, Killen then contacted Frank J. Herndon, also a Klan member, and "got some boys together—and went to Philadelphia." Miller quoted Killen as saying that the rights workers had been run down after a 90–100 mph highway chase.

James E. Jordan, the government's key witness and a former Klan member, named 7 defendants as actual participants in the slayings. (Jordan, indicted on the same conspiracy charges, was not a defendant.) Jordan described how Deputy Price had jailed the 3 youths, had held them until the mob assembled, then had released them only to recapture them after a highway chase. The youths, he said, were driven to the site of the slayings in the deputy's car. Jordan told the court that he was posted as lookout a short distance down the road. "I heard car doors slam, some loud talk that I could not distinguish, and then I heard several shots," he said. Then he walked down the road and found the youths on the ground, apparently dead. The Klansmen were "milling around," Jordan declared, but they removed the signs of the shootings. The bodies were put in the back of the station wagon, he testified, and were hauled to the dam in Neshoba County, where a bulldozer buried them. Jordan said that Sam Bowers, identified as imperial wizard of the White Knights, had approved the slayings. He reported that Bowers had said Schwerner was "a thorn in the side of everyone living, especially the white people, and should be taken care of."

Jordan said he had decided to tell the FBI the story because "they said they would help me out of town, which they did." Jordan received $3,000 from the FBI to buy a car and rent a trailer to move his family. During the next year they gave him $100 a week. After he became employed at $55 a week, the FBI reduced his weekly payment to $25. Jordan admitted under cross-examination that he had been convicted of 4 crimes involving "using a car without the owner's consent," "checks," "petty larceny" and "grand larceny."

The court Oct. 13 heard a statement signed by Horace D. Barnette, a defendant identified as a member of the lynching party. The statement charged Jordan with killing one of the rights workers. Henry Rask, an FBI agent, told the court that he had obtained the 10-page statement from Barnette during a 5-hour session Nov. 20, 1964 at a motel near Springhill, La. Rask said that he and James A. Wooten, another FBI agent, had talked with Barnette Nov. 19, 20 and 21 and that Barnette had said the slayings "had been bothering him and he wanted to tell us about it." Rask said that a few months later it was "common knowledge" that Barnette had given a statement to the FBI and that he "began to fear for his life." Wooten testified that he had given Barnette 2 checks for $200 and $100, respectively, " for services rendered and wages lost" during 27 interviews. Cox then admitted Barnette's statement but said that references to any defendant except Barnette must be blocked out.

Barnette's statement, read to the court by Assistant Atty. Gen. John Doar, said: The rights workers had been driven to the shooting site with Jordan. Schwerner was hauled from the back of the car and asked: "Are you that nigger lover?" Schwerner answered: "Sir, I know just how you feel." Then a mob member "took a pistol in his hand and shot Schwerner." "Schwerner fell to the left so that he was lying alongside the road, and Goodman spun around and fell back toward the bank in back." At that point Jordan stepped forward and said: "Save one for me." Jordan pulled Chaney out onto the road with him. "I remember Chaney backing up, facing the road and standing on the bank on the other side of the ditch, and Jordan stood in the middle of the road and shot him. Jordan then said: "You didn't leave me anything but a nigger, but at least I killed me a nigger."

The defense called on Mrs. Beverly Rawlings to testify Oct. 17 in an effort to discredit Jordan. Mrs. Rawlings said that some time around Sept. 1, 1964 Jordan had indicated to her that he had shot Chaney.

The 7 convicted men were sentenced by Judge Cox Dec. 20 to prison terms ranging from 3 to 10 years, then released on bond pending their appeals. Bowers and Roberts received the maximum terms of 10 years. Price and Posey each received 6-year sentences. 3-year sentences were imposed on Arledge, Snowden and Barnette. In announcing the sentences Cox said the terms were "indeterminate"; he thus made the defendants eligible for immediate consideration for parole.

(District Atty. William H. Johnson Jr. in Decatur, Miss. declared Oct. 20 that the Justice Department was responsible for the fact that no state charges had been filed in 1964 against suspects in the slayings. Johnson charged that the FBI had sent in 200 agents who "swept up most of the evidence before the state investigators could secure enough." "In 2 or 3 terms of court, we subpoenaed FBI agents and others supposed to have evidence. Mr. [Nicholas] Katzenbach [then Attorney General] refused to let them come. They refused to allow me to see statements in the case or talk to the witnesses." At the time the Justice Department reportedly promised full disclosure after completion of the case.

(Roy K. Moore, an FBI agent in charge of the bureau's office in Jackson, Miss., said Oct. 21 that the FBI had offered to "turn over everything to aid a local prosecution of the case." Moore said that the FBI had met with Miss. Gov. Paul B. Johnson Jr. and other state officials Dec. 2, 1964, 2 days before the FBI had made arrests in the case. Although Gov. Johnson reportedly seemed interested in filing state charges, Moore said, the state officials decided to let the federal government proceed alone. "We offered the whole package" Dec. 2, Moore declared, and "there was nothing that kept them from making an investigation on their own.")

Other Homicide Cases

An all-white Elmore County grand jury had failed Jan. 16 to return an indictment in the case of ex-Deputy Sheriff Harvey King Conner of Elmore County, Ala., who was accused of beating a black prisoner who later died. The victim, James Earl Motley, 27, had died from severe head injuries in the Wetumpka, Ala. jail Nov. 20, 1966. Conner had been deputy sheriff until Jan. 16, when a new sheriff assumed office and did not reappoint him.

Dr. Joseph R. Benson, the coroner, said Jan. 13 that he had issued a formal opinion that Motley's death was "accidental." He said Motley had fallen twice and had struck his head on entering the jail. Benson cited this injury as the probable cause of death. He maintained that the beating was not severe enough to kill Motley. The Justice Department Jan. 17 then filed a misdemeanor charge against Conner in U.S. District Court in Montgomery, Ala., but Conner was acquitted of this charge Apr. 12. The criminal information filed by the government Jan. 17 charged that Conner "did wilfully assault, strike, beat and injure James Earl Motley . . . with the intent and purpose of imposing summary punishment on him and did thereby wilfully deprive" Motley of his civil rights. The Justice Department instituted its misdemeanor prosecution under a Reconstruction statute barring the deprivation of rights under "color of law."

William Haywood James, 42, a white carpenter, was convicted in Atlanta Feb. 8 of the fatal shooting of Hulet M. Varner Jr., 16, a Negro. The Sept. 10, 1966 shooting had touched off the 2d night of rioting in the predominantly black section of Atlanta. In unsworn testimony Feb. 7, James had said that black youths standing in front of an apartment building had shouted "Hey baby" at his wife as he drove through the area. He said that when he stopped for a traffic light they attacked him, and he fired his pistol "a couple of times" in self-defense. The all-white jury of 10 men and 2 women returned a verdict of guilty with a recommendation of mercy. James, who was also serving a 6-year prison sentence for assault with intent to murder in an unrelated case, was sentenced to life in prison.

12 men charged in the death of Hattiesburg (Miss.) black leader Vernon Dahmer, all allegedly members of the White Knights of the Klan, were indicted by a federal grand jury in Jackson, Miss. Feb. 28 on conspiracy charges under the Federal Voting Rights Act of 1965. They were charged with conspiring to "intimidate, threaten and coerce" Dahmer because of his work in voter registration drives. 11 of the men were charged on a 2d count of carrying out the actual act of intimidating Dahmer by firing into his home and setting both his home and his grocery store on fire. Those indicted on the conspiracy charge were: Sam H. Bowers Jr.; Henry Edward De Boxtel, 30, Laurel restaurant worker; Howard Travis Giles, 37; Mordaunt Hamilton Sr., 58, of Petal, owner of a hardware store in Hattiesburg; Charles Lamar Lowe, 23, of Laurel; Clifton Eudell Lowe, 50, a Laurel painter and carpenter; Melvin Sennett Martin, 33, Laurel wood-processing worker; Emanuel Benjamin Moss, 52, Laurel carpenter; Deavours Nix, 42, Laurel cafe owner; Charles Richard Noble, 23, Laurel wood-processing worker; Billy Roy Pitts, 23; Cecil Victor Sessum, 30, Ellisville welding shop worker. Lawrence Byrd Sr., 44, was named as "co-conspirator" but not as a defendant.

The U.S. Court of Appeals for the 5th Circuit in New Orleans Apr. 27 upheld the civil rights conspiracy convictions of Alabama Ku Klux Klansmen Eugene Thomas and Collie Leroy Wilkins Jr. in connection with the 1965 slaying of Mrs. Viola Gregg Liuzzo. The Klansmen had been sentenced to 10 years in prison. William O. Eaton, a 3d Klansman convicted on the charge, had died Mar. 10, 1966.

Meredith Completes March

James H. Meredith, the first Negro to be admitted knowingly by the University of Mississippi (in 1962) and currently a Columbia University law student, resumed his "march against fear" in Mississippi June 24. He completed the hike July 4 in Canton, Miss.

Meredith started on U.S. Highway 51 from the point (2 miles south of Hernando, Miss.) where he had been shot June 6, 1966, the 2d day of his voting-rights walk from Memphis, Tenn. to Jackson, Miss. He had told reporters June 17 that the purpose of the renewed march would be "to challenge, expose and extinguish that all-pervasive fear that permeates the existence of the Negro" and to "encourage political preparation for political participation by Negroes in the U.S., especially in the 2 states where participation is lowest—New York and Mississippi."

Meredith was accompanied by James Catel, 24, a black student at City College of New York; Edward Rickman, 18, a Negro from Detroit; Guy Smythe, 19, a student at Stanford University, and Alfred Ross, 19, a student at the University of Pennsylvania. Others joined him later. The Mississippi Highway Patrol and FBI agents followed the marchers, and no harrassment was reported although white spectators appeared at various points along the march route. Meredith's greatest difficulty came from a sore heel tendon and blisters on his feet.

Meredith celebrated his 34th birthday June 25, the 2d day of his 11-day trek. He was greeted by fewer than 50 blacks and a few curious but peaceful whites as he concluded his 162-mile march at 11:02 a.m. July 4 at the steps of the county courthouse in Canton, Miss. He told reporters that it was important to finish the march because "the Negro has a whole history of failures and incompletions." He said "the last 11 days have shown that the state and the local police officers, if they choose to, can afford protection for Negroes."

Mixed-Marriage Bans Invalidated

The U.S. Supreme Court June 12 unanimously invalidated Virginia's 1924 "racial integrity law," which banned marriage between whites and nonwhites. (The law had been upheld by the Virginia Supreme Court of Appeals.) The court's ruling on interracial marriages dealt specifically with the case of Richard P. Loving, 33, a white, and his part-Negro, part-Indian wife, Mildred, 27, who had been married in Washington, D.C. in 1958. The Lovings, natives of Caroline County, Va., were prosecuted on their return to the state after their marriage. The court's opinion, written by Chief Justice Earl Warren, stated: "We have consistently denied the constitutionality of measures which restrict the rights of citizens on account of race." "There can be no doubt that restricting the freedom to marry solely because of racial classifications violates the central meaning of the [Constitution's] equal protection clause." The ruling was considered sufficiently broad to void the antimiscegenation laws of 15 other states.

The Oklahoma Supreme Court ruled in Oklahoma City July 10 that the state's antimiscegenation law was unconstitutional.

The Maryland House of Delegates had voted 97–25 Mar. 3 to approve a Senate-passed bill repealing the state law banning interracial marriages.

Other Supreme Court Action

The U.S. Supreme Court refused Feb. 13 to hear the suit of 2 whites and 2 Negroes who challenged the 1871 Congressional act abolishing home rule in Washington, D.C. The plaintiffs said the law had been enacted for the purpose of preventing Negroes from voting. Federal district and appeals courts had refused to hear the complaints on the ground that they were "insubstantial."

The high court Feb. 13 let stand the 1963 contempt-of-court convictions of 8 civil rights demonstrators who had violated an injunction against job bias protests on the premises of a St. Louis, Mo. bank.

The court ruled unanimously Feb. 13 that the 6th Amendment's guarantee of a speedy trial was binding on state courts. The court ruled on the appeal of Peter H. Klopfer, a Duke University zoology professor, who had been indicted for criminal trespass after taking part in a Feb. 1964 sit-in at a Chapel Hill, N.C. restaurant. The jury had failed to reach a verdict in the Mar. 1964 trial, and a mistrial had been declared. A year later Klopfer had demanded a new trial or a dismissal of the case. The judge granted the prosecutor's motion for a *nolle prosequi,* a procedure that permitted the prosecutor to retain the indictment without bringing the ·case to trial

The Supreme Court confirmed Mar. 13, in a 7–2 decision, a 3-judge federal panel's ruling that the state of Louisiana was subject to the key provisions of the Voting Rights Act of 1965. The state had sought exemption from the act's provisions for the suspension of literacy tests and the use of federal registrars in areas where fewer than 50% of the adult population had voted in the 1964 elections.

An Aug. 15, 1966 ruling of the U.S. 5th Circuit Court of Appeals reversing the convictions and death sentences of Edgar Labat and Clifton A. Poret, both Negroes, for the 1950 rape of a white woman was upheld by the Supreme Court Apr. 10. The appeals court had ruled that the men were denied a fair trial because Negroes had been systematically and unconstitutionally excluded from the Louisiana jury system.   The court ordered the men retried or released.   (A New Orleans grand jury reindicted Labat and Poret Apr. 12.)

The Supreme Court ruled 8–1 Apr. 11 that the Civil Rights Act of 1871 (which declared that "every person" violating another's civil rights was liable for his action) did not affect the common-law immunity of judges.   The court also upheld the common-law immunity of police officers who violated a person's civil rights while acting with probable cause and in good faith.   The ruling came on suits filed by 4 clergymen arrested and convicted in 1961 when they tried to integrate the Jackson, Miss. bus terminal.

Public Accommodations Cases

The U.S. Justice Department filed 4 suits Jan. 6 in a campaign to end illegal racial discrimination in public accommodations.   The suits were filed: (1) in U.S. District Court in Hattiesburg, Miss. against Jackie D. Jefcoat of Laurel, Miss., who was accused of "intimidating, threatening and coercing Negroes seeking service at a restaurant in Laurel" (Jefcoat was not connected with the restaurant); (2 and 3) in U.S. District Court in Raleigh, N.C. against Elliot's Cafe of Hertford, N.C. and its operator for allegedly refusing to sell food to blacks for consumption on the premises, and against the Skylight Inn of Ayden, N.C. and its operator, for allegedly refusing to serve Negroes except in a reserved portion of the restaurant; (4) in U.S. District Court in Roanoke, Va. against the Blue Ridge Grill of Galax, Va. and its operators for allegedly refusing to serve Negroes except in the restaurant's kitchen.

The first public accommodations suit in Maryland was filed by the Justice Department Jan. 9 in U.S. District Court in Baltimore against Bernie Lee's The Pub, a restaurant, and its operator for allegedly refusing to serve Negroes on the same basis as whites.

Roy Elder McKoy, 43, owner of the Belvoir Restaurant in Marshall, Va. was convicted of contempt of court in Alexandria, Va. Apr. 28 after he refused to comply with a court order to desegregate his restaurant.   The Justice Department had asked the federal court Feb. 23 to hold McKoy in contempt for allegedly violating an Oct. 17, 1966 desegregation order by refusing to serve a group of white and Negro persons because of race.   U.S. District Judge Oren R. Lewis had refused the contempt citation Mar. 7 on the ground that the complainants were "a bunch of busybodies going around and organizing trouble and then coming in and wanting me to put people in jail." In response to a 2d application by the Justice Department, Lewis Apr. 28 found McKoy guilty of contempt for refusing to serve a small mixed group. McKoy was released from prison May 1 after he swore that he would not discriminate if he reopened his restaurant. McKoy's contempt citation was the 2d filed under the public accommodations section of the 1964 Civil Rights Act. McKoy was the first jailed under that section of the act.

The U.S. 5th Circuit Court of Appeals in New Orleans ruled 2–1 Sept. 6 that the 1964 Civil Rights Act did not extend to amusement parks that did not offer "exhibitions for the entertainment of spectators." The 3-judge federal court ruled on the case of a black mother who contended that she and her 2 children had been denied access to Fun Fair Park, operated by Amusement Enterprises Inc. on the airline Highway at Baton Rouge, La.

The Justice Department Sept. 21 filed 4 civil suits in Raleigh, N.C. and Baltimore, Md. on charges of racial discrimination by places of public accommodation. The suits brought to 100 the number of actions alleging such violations under the 1964 Civil Rights Act. In 2 suits the government charged that a lodging place in Mayo, Md. owned by Elgar S. Kalb and a group of cottages in Nags Head, N.C. owned by Alvah E. and Lida Holland Sadler discriminated against Negroes; the suits asked the court to prohibit discrimination and to enjoin racial segregation at Beverley Beach in Anne Arundel County, managed by Kalb, and at the Bay Carry-Out Shops at the beach. In the other 2 suits the government charged that Negroes were denied equal service at the Tip Top Drive-In at Henderson, N.C. and the Triple H. Restaurant at Cherryville, N.C.

Texas Passes Rights Bill

The Texas Legislature Apr. 5 cleared its first major civil rights bill since Reconstruction. (In 1957 laws were enacted to maintain segregation in the state's public schools.) The new legislation provided penalties of up to $1,000 fine and one year imprisonment for state officials who discriminated on the basis of race, religion, color or national origin in carrying out official duties, including employment licensing, use of public facilities, contract letting and participation in state programs.

1968

Martin Luther King Jr., foremost leader of the nonviolent civil rights movement in the U.S., was assassinated in Memphis. The nation's ghettos reacted with violent rioting in more than 100 urban areas. But another reaction was Congress' passage of a major civil rights bill. Many black militants said King's murder marked the death of the nonviolent movement and, presumably, an acceleration of violence. Numerous racial riots unconnected with King's death took place across the country. Examining the recent history of U.S. violence, the President's Commission on Civil Disorders had concluded that the nation was moving toward 2 "separate and unequal" societies based on race. The largely black Poor People's Campaign brought 9 caravans of poor people to Washington to agitate for legislation to reduce poverty. School integration made less progress than anticipated, and black students agitated for black-studies programs and more black students and teachers at U.S. colleges.

ASSASSINATION OF MARTIN LUTHER KING

The Rev. Dr. Martin Luther King Jr., 39, Nobel Peace Prize winner and acknowledged leader of the nonviolent civil rights movement, was shot to death by a sniper in Memphis, Tenn. Apr. 4.

The news of King's assassination evoked expressions of dismay and shock across the U.S. and throughout the world. The killing precipitated rioting and violence in Washington, Chicago and other U.S. cities. 34 persons were killed and thousands injured and arrested in the disorders by Apr. 10. More than 20,000 regular federal troops and 34,000 National Guardsmen were sent to the troubled cities during the week after King's death as local authorities called for help to end the disorders.

Pres. Lyndon B. Johnson, reflecting the nation's grief, delivered a nationwide TV address in which he lauded the slain black leader and appealed to "every citizen to reject the blind violence that has struck Dr. King, who lived by nonviolence."

Pre-Assassination Protests in Memphis

King had come to Memphis to lead and participate in demonstrations in support of a strike by the city's predominantly black sanitation workers.

The sanitation workers' strike had begun Feb. 12 over demands for a 33% pay raise, recognition of the American Federation of State, County & Municipal Employes as bargaining agent, a dues checkoff system, seniority rights, health and hospitalzation insurance and other fringe benefits. But it had developed into a general civil rights protest by the city's black community.

(Negroes comprised 40% of the city's 550,000 population and about 90% of the Sanitation Department workers.)

Mayor Henry Loeb had broken off negotiations with union representatives Feb. 14. He contended that the strike was illegal under the terms of a 1966 state Supreme Court decision banning public employes' strikes. The garbage collectors Feb. 15 defied the mayor's ultimatum to return to work or be replaced, and the city began hiring new workers. By Feb. 16 88 new workers had been added to a force of 40 nonstrikers and 30 supervisors operating the city's garbage trucks.

The NAACP (National Association for the Advancement of Colored People) Feb. 16 and the Shelby County Democratic Club (a black political and social organization) Feb. 17 urged massive civil disobedience to demonstrate support for the strikers.

Violence erupted during a march Feb. 23 by 1,000 strikers after the City Council rejected the union's demand for a dues check-off. Police said the disturbance began when the protesters tried to overturn a patrol car; witnesses said polcemen knocked marchers to the pavement. Police moved in with nightsticks and cartridges of Mace, an antiriot gas, to quell the disturbances.

About 100 black ministers Feb. 25 called for a boycott of all downtown businesses owned by city councilmen and of the city's 2 daily newspapers, *The Commercial Appeal* and the *Press-Scimitar*. Black ministers and civil rights leaders led 300 persons on a march through downtown Memphis Feb. 26.

121 strike leaders were arrested after a sit-in at the City Hall Mar. 5. 7 union officials, including Jerry Wurf, of Washington, president of the American Federation of State, County & Municipal Employes, were sentenced to 10 days in jail and fined $50 each Mar. 6 on their conviction of contempt in disobeying a Feb. 24 injunction restraining them from encouraging or engaging in the strike. 9 persons marching in sympathy with striking garbage collectors were arrested Mar. 13. Bayard Rustin, executive director of the A. Philip Randolph Institute, and Roy Wilkins, executive secretary of the NAACP, expressed their support of the strike at a mass rally in Memphis Mar. 14.

The Southern Regional Council (a foundation-supported research and information organization) Mar. 23 issued a report describing the strike as "merely a symptom of Memphis' larger problem." The report said the white community had failed to respond to black grievances, and it charged the police with "injudicious" acts. In Memphis, the report said, the record of police behavior "has not been a notably bad one," but "the police spark was present" in the recent disturbance. In fact, the report concluded, the Memphis disorder revealed that police departments "have become themselves direct and dangerous influences toward disorder."

A 16-year-old Negro boy, Larry Payne, was slain in Memphis Mar. 28 shortly after violence and looting broke up a protest march led by King. Gov. Buford Ellington (D., Tenn.) called up 4,000 National Guardsmen and ordered a curfew.

The Mar. 28 disturbances had begun when Negro students at

the Hamilton High School, who were prevented from leaving school to join King's protest march, began pelting policemen with bricks. The march from the Claiborne American Methodist Episcopal Temple to City Hall had barely begun when 30-70 black youths darted alongside the procession and began smashing store windows along Beale Street and looting the stores. 250 city and county police moved in with riot clubs and tear gas and sealed off one end of the street. Almost immediately 4,000 National Guardsmen armed with rifles and bayonets entered the area in armored personnel carriers. Another 8,000 were placed on alert. The Memphis Transit Authority stopped all bus service, and Mayor Loeb ordered a 7 p.m.-5 a.m. curfew. Estimates of the number of protesters ranged from a low of 6,000 to King's figure of 20,000 marchers.

At the outbreak of the rioting King was removed from the scene and taken to a nearby motel. Most of the marchers returned to the church. After King left, police began firing tear gas at the Negroes, looters and bystanders alike. Several persons were reported beaten by police. Larry Payne was shot and killed when, according to police, he turned on a policeman with a butcher knife. About 60 persons were reported injured. More than 150 persons were arrested, about 40 of them on looting charges. It was said that of 155 stores with their windows smashed, only 35% had window displays damaged and only 5% had been entered.

Pres. Johnson declared in Washington Mar. 29 that federal assistance to Memphis, should it be necessary, would be available. But, he cautioned, "our system of government and our society depend on capable local law enforcement." The President said: "The tragic events in Memphis yesterday remind us of the grave peril rioting poses. This nation must seek change within the rule of law in an environment of social order. Rioting, violence and repression can only divide our people. Every one loses when a riot occurs. I call upon all Americans of every race and creed, the rich and the poor, the young and old, our governments, businesses, unions and churches to obey the law and to preserve conditions of social stability which are essential to progress. I urge local law enforcement to deal firmly, but always fairly and without fear, with every infraction of law—to work unceasingly to prevent riots, and to train diligently to control them should they occur. I urge state law enforcement to prepare full support for local law enforcement whenever aid is needed to maintain order. Order must be preserved."

Earlier Mar. 29, in a speech to the Committee on Political Education (COPE) of the AFL-CIO, Johnson had asserted that "mindless violence—destroying what we have all worked so hard to build —will never be tolerated in America."

Several hundred persons escorted by police and National Guardsmen marched through downtown Memphis Mar. 29 in support of the striking sanitation workers. Many of the demonstrators wore placards that said: "I am a man."

At a news conference in Memphis Mar. 29, King said he would lead another "massive" civil rights demonstration in Memphis. He conceded that he had been "caught with a miscalculation" in the Mar. 28 protest. "If I had known there was a possibility of violence yesterday, I would not have had that particular march," he declared. King, however, reaffirmed his determination to conduct a "Poor People's Campaign" he had scheduled for Washington beginning Apr. 22. "We are fully determined to go to Washington. We feel it is an absolute necessity," he said. At a news conference in Washington Mar. 31, however, King conceded that either the President or Congress might be able to persuade him to call off the campaign by making "a positive commitment that they would do something this summer" to help the country's slums. But, he said, "I don't see that forthcoming."

King Shot to Death

King was shot at 6:01 CST Apr. 4 as he leaned over the 2d-floor railing outside his room at the Lorraine Motel in the black section of Memphis. The bullet hit him in the right side of the neck. He was pronounced dead at St. Joseph's Hospital at 7:05 p.m. after emergency surgery.

King, who had returned to Memphis to lead a 2d march in support of the city's striking sanitation workers, had been discussing plans for the proposed march with 2 of his aides, the Rev. Jesse Jackson and the Rev. Ralph David Abernathy, before going out to dinner. The assassin fired the single shot from a rooming house less than 100 yards away and then fled.

Atty. Gen. Ramsey Clark flew to Memphis Apr. 5 with Justice Departmet officials on Pres. Johnson's orders. Clark said at a news conference that the FBI was looking for the assassin in several states. He reported that "all the evidence indicates that this was the act of a single individual." FBI agents and Memphis police collected a small suitcase, a caliber 30.06 Remington pump rifle with a telescopic sight that had been discarded in a nearby doorway, and a number of fingerprints. Memphis Police Director Frank Hollomon said that the evidence indicated that the shot had been fired from a bathroom of the rooming house at 420 South Main Street. Witnesses saw a white man run from the house immediately after the shooting.

The Rev. Abernathy, 42, was named Apr. 5 to succeed King as president of the Southern Christian Leadership Conference (SCLC). The SCLC's first activity under his lealership, Abernathy said, would be to carry out the march in Memphis that King had planned to lead. This massive demonstration was held Apr. 8 with King's widow, Mrs. Coretta Scott King, taking her husband's place in the front rank ahead of an estimated 42,000 silent marchers, including thousands (estimated at 30% of the total) of whites. The march ended with a rally in front of City Hall, where Mrs. King urged the crowd to "carry on because this is the way he would have wanted it." But, she cried, "how many men must die before we can really have a free and true and peaceful society? How long will it take?"

King's body was put on public view at the Ebenezer Baptist Church in Atlanta Apr. 6. Mrs. King, in a statement made at the church, asked all who "loved and admired" her husband to "join us in fulfilling his dream" of finding a "creative rather than a destructive way" of solving the racial crisis of the nation. "He knew that this was a sick society, totally infested with racism and violence that questioned his integrity, maligned his motives, and distorted his views," she said, "and he struggled with every ounce of his energy to save that society from itself." Mrs. King had gone Apr. 5 from Atlanta to Memphis and had returned with her husband's body on a plane chartered by Sen. Robert F. Kennedy (D., N.Y.).

King was buried at South View Cemetery in Atlanta Apr. 9 after funeral services at the Ebenezer Baptist Church, of which he had been pastor, and after a general memorial service at Morehouse College. King's coffin was carried through the streets to the college on a faded green farm wagon pulled by 2 Georgia mules. It was carried later to the cemetery in a hearse. Dozens of national leaders were among the 50,000 to 100,000 marchers who followed the wagon on its 3½-mile course. Vice Pres. Hubert H. Humphrey attended as the President's representative.

In accordance with Mrs. King's request, the funeral service included a tape recording of King's last sermon, preached at the church Feb. 4: ". . . If any of you are around when I have to meet my day, I don't want a long funeral. And if you get somebody to deliver the eulogy, tell him not to talk too long. . . . Tell him not to mention that I have a Nobel Peace Prize—that isn't important. . . . I'd like somebody to mention that day that Martin Luther King Jr. tried to give his life serving others. I'd like for somebody to say that day that Martin Luther King Jr. tried to love somebody. . . . I want you to be able to say that day that I did try to feed the hungry . . . that I did try in my life to clothe the naked . . . that I did try in my life to visit those who were in prison . . . that I tried to love and serve humanity. Yes, if you want to, say that I was a drum major. Say that I was a drum major for peace . . . for righteousness. . . ."

President Urges Unity

Pres. Johnson, in a televised address Apr. 4, expressed shock and sorrow at "the brutal slaying" of King but hope "that all Americans tonight will search their hearts as they ponder this most tragic incident." The President spoke from the White House. Mrs. Johnson and he had conveyed their sympathy to Mrs. King, he said, and he knew that "every American of goodwill joins me in mourning the death of this outstanding leader and in praying for peace and understanding throughout this land."

"We can achieve nothing by lawlessness and divisiveness among the American people," Johnson said. "It's only by joining together, and only by working together, can we continue to move toward equality and fulfillment for all of our people."

The President, in his address, announced the postponement of a conference he had scheduled in Hawaii on Vietnam. The Hawaii conference was canceled Apr. 5 so that Johnson could remain in Washington to deal with the repercussions of King's slaying—violence, arson and looting in Washington, Chicago and other American cities. The President spent most of Apr. 5 meeting with moderate black leaders, Congress members and officials of the District of Columbia. Federal troops were brought to Washington later that evening to restore order there. Johnson also led his guests in a 12-car motorcade to the National Cathedral to attend a memorial service for King.

Back at the White House Apr. 5, the President again went before the nation on TV to proclaim Sunday, Apr. 6, a national day of mourning for King and to announce that he had asked Congress, in adjournment over the weekend, to convene in joint session "at the earliest possible moment" to hear his proposals "for action—constructive action instead of destructive action—in this hour of national need." "The spirit of America weeps for a tragedy that denies the very meaning of our land," the President said. "It is the fiber and the fabric of the Republic that's being tested. If we are to have the America that we mean to have, all men of all races, all regions, all religions must stand their ground to deny violence its victory in this sorrowful time and in all times to come."

He believed "deeply," Johnson asserted, that "the dream* of Dr. Martin Luther King Jr. has not died with him. Men who are white, men who are black, must and will now join together as never in the past to let all the forces of divisiveness know that America shall not be ruled by the bullet but only by the ballot of free and of just men." The work to remove "some of the stones of inaction and of indifference and of injustice" had begun, he said, "and we must move with urgency and with resolve and with new energy in the Congress and in the courts and in the White House and the statehouse and the city halls of the nation, wherever there is leadership—political leadership, leadership in the churches, in the homes, in the schools, in the institutions of higher learning—until we do overcome."

Johnson said he had not "understate[d] the case" when he spoke Mar. 31 "of the divisiveness that was tearing this nation apart."

---

* King had spoken of his "dream" Aug. 28, 1963 in a speech before the Lincoln Memorial during a massive "March on Washington" in a demand for equal rights for Negroes. Excerpts from the address: "So even though we face the difficulties of today and tomorrow, I still have a dream. I have a dream that one day this nation will rise up and live out the true meaning of its creed: 'We hold these truths to be self-evident, that all men are created equal.' I have a dream that one day on the red hills of Georgia the sons of former slaves and the sons of former slave owners will be able to sit down together at the table of brotherhood. I have a dream that one day even the state of Mississippi, a state sweltering with the people's injustice, sweltering with the heat of oppression, will be transformed into an oasis of freedom and justice. I have a dream that my 4 little children will one day live in a nation where they will not be judged by the color of their skin, but by the content of their character. I have a dream that one day every valley shall be exalted, every hill and mountain shall be made low, the rough places will be made plain, and the crooked places will be made straight, and the glory of the Lord shall be revealed and all flesh shall see it together."

"But together," he declared, "a nation united and a nation caring and a nation concerned and a nation that thinks more of the nation's interest than we do of any individual self-interest or political interest—that nation can and shall and will overcome." In his proclamation Apr. 5, the President referred to King as "a leader of his people" and "a teacher of all people." "The quest for freedom, to which he gave eloquent expression, continues," Johnson asserted. He urged Americans to "resolve before God to stand against divisiveness in our country and all its consequences."

The American flag was flown at half-staff at all federal facilities in the U.S. and abroad and in all U.S. territories and possessions until King's interment.

Among the black and other leaders who conferred with the President Apr. 5 were: Housing & Urban Development Secy. Robert C. Weaver; Supreme Court Justice Thurgood Marshall; Mrs. Dorothy I. Height, president of the National Council of Negro Women; Whitney M. Young Jr. of the National Urban League; Bayard Rustin of the A. Philip Randolph Institute; Gary (Ind.) Major Richard G. Hatcher; Washington Commissioner Walter E. Washington; the Rev. Leon Sullivan of the Opportunities Industrialization Center in Philadelphia; U.S. District Judge A. Leon Higginbotham Jr.; Roy Wilkins and Clarence Mitchell Jr. of the NAACP; Bishop George W. Baber of the American Methodist Episcopal Church; the Rev. Walter E. Fauntroy of the District of Columbia Council.

Among Administration and Congressional leaders attending the conferences were: Vice Pres. Humphrey; Defense Secy. Clark M. Clifford; Senate Democratic leader Mike Mansfield (Mont.); House Speaker John W. McCormack (D., Mass.); Sen. Thomas H. Kuchel (R., Calif.); Reps. Carl Albert (D., Okla.) and William M. McCulloch (R., O.).

Nation Pauses in Tribute

King's death preempted the nation's attention: There were memorial marches and rallies throughout the U.S., many public school systems closed, public libraries and museums were shut, many businesses and the stock exchanges were closed, seaports from Maine to Texas shut down as longshoremen and seamen stopped work, the UN flag flew at half-mast, the opening of the baseball season (scheduled for Apr. 8) was postponed, the Stanley Cup hockey playoffs were postponed, the playoffs in the American and National Basketball Associations were postponed, Hollywood's Oscar-award presentation ceremony was postponed, the Presidential nomination campaign abruptly halted.

Most major Negro organizations and leaders paid high tribute to King and urged a continuance of his fight against discrimination in the nonviolent spirit. But militant black leaders said King's death marked the death of the nonviolent movement and urged retaliation in kind.

Julius Hobson of Washington said Apr. 4 that "the Martin Luther King concept of nonviolence died with him. It was a foreign ideology anyway—as foreign to this violent country as speaking Russian." United Black Front Chrmn. Lincoln O. Lynch called on black people Apr. 4 "to abandon the unconditional nonviolent concept expounded by Dr. King and adopt a position that for every Martin Luther King who falls, 10 white racists will go down with him. There is no other way. White America understands no other language."

But Sen. Edward W. Brooke (R., Mass.), a Negro, said Apr. 4 that "the sorrow which all Americans of good will feel at this terrible loss must bind us together, not rend us apart."

James Farmer, ex-national director of the Congress of Racial Equality (CORE), said Apr. 4 that "the only fitting memorial to this martyred leader is a monumental commitment—now, not a day later—to eliminate racism." CORE itself Apr. 6 called on "all black people to stop their normal activities . . . [Apr. 9] in honor and memory of Dr. King, his principles, his contribution to all mankind, the supreme sacrifice that he made and the legacy that he gave the world." CORE National Director Floyd McKissick, however, asserted Apr. 4 that King's philosophy of nonviolence had died with him. "White people are going to suffer as much as black people," McKissick said.

Sen. Robert F. Kennedy (Mass.), who later in 1968 was also cut down by an assassin's bullet, was campaigning for the Democratic Presidential nomination when King was slain. Kennedy said at a streetcorner rally of Negroes in Indianapolis Apr. 4: "Those of you who are black can be filled with hatred, with bitterness and a desire for revenge. We can move toward further polarization. Or we can make an effort, as Martin Luther King did, to understand, to reconcile ourselves and to love." "Dr. King dedicated himself to justice and love between his fellow human beings. . . .

It's up to those of us who are here . . . to carry out that dream, to try and end the divisions that exist so deeply within our country and to remove the stain of bloodshed from our land." "I ask you now to return home to say a prayer for the family of Martin Luther King, that's true, but more important to say a prayer for our country . . . and to say a prayer for understanding and . . . compassion. . . ."

Kennedy added in Fort Wayne, Ind. Apr. 10: "Laws and programs are only part of any answer. It is necessary to find ways to reopen and deepen the channels of communication between white and black America and to halt the dangerous drift toward isolated enmity which may soon find us looking at each other across impassable barriers of suspicion and anger and hatred. This is a job for every American." In Lansing, Mich. Apr. 11, he proposed a "national impact project" in which unemployed Negroes would be employed in rebuilding their ghettos. He said: The project should "match our great unfulfilled needs—for housing and schools, roads and recreational facilities, public facilities and public services—with the hundred of thousands of men and women, without jobs and in menial jobs, whose fury and frustration has wracked our cities these last 4 years. We can return hope while meeting the most urgent needs of the nation. We can build new cities—and a new community among men." The program could be a better answer than "welfare handouts" and could be a means for injecting into the often "rigid [and] inefficient" governmental process "the force with the skills, the talent and the energy to undertake this awesome task—the private enterprise system."

Sen. Eugene J. McCarthy (Minn.), also campaigning for the Democratic Presidential nomination, said in Compton, Calif. that King's assassination "does not in any way weaken or lessen the importance of his [King's] goals." King "felt all Americans had an equal right to health care without regard for race," McCarthy declared. "He felt they should have the equality which is the basis of the American way of life. He saw the need for equal opportunity in education and the right to a decent home."

NAACP Executive Director Roy Wilkins warned Apr. 8 against retaliation. Despite the "talk about 'get whitey,' 'kill 10 whites for every Negro killed,'" he said, "the people who lose their lives are Negroes." He announced that the NAACP was mounting a nationwide drive against racial violence and stressing jobs for the unemployed and better community relations. King, he said, would have been "outraged" by the disorders following his assassination, and "millions of Negroes in this country" were opposed to violence. Wilkins criticized black-power leader Stokely Carmichael. It was reported, he said, that Carmichael had responded in a reasonable manner on first hearing of King's death, but, "the next day, miraculously, as if somebody had come to see him and talked to him, comes that talk about 'get your guns.' " "I am sorry, I don't know Mr. Carmichael and his connections well enough to guess whether he is his own man. . . . Of course, I am concerned." (Wilkins Apr. 4 had expressed concern about "a racial collision." He had warned that "too many officials in key states and local positions are interpreting 'riot control' and 'law and order' to mean a crackdown racially on Negro Americans.")

National Urban League Executive Director Whitney M. Young Jr. said in a TV talk Apr. 7 that "the only thing more tragic" than King's death "would be that the only response would be black anger and white sympathy." "What we need today is black determination and white action," he said. "We must have concrete, tangible action that will remove the iniquities in our society."

Services of "penitence and dedication" in memory of King had been called for in a joint statement issued Apr. 5 by Dr. Arthur S. Fleming, president of the National Council of Churches, Rabbi Jacob Philip Rudin, president of the Synagogue Council of America, and the Most Rev. John F. Dearden, president of the National Conference of Catholic Bishops.

Several Southern leaders Apr. 6 praised King and his cause of nonviolence. Atlanta Mayor Ivan Allen Jr. said King's death "takes from Atlanta one of its greatest citizens of all time." The Fulton County (Atlanta) commissioners, in a joint statement, called King "the incomparable leader of a large segment of American citizenry." Louisiana Gov. John J. McKeithen called for "a rededication to the cause which he espoused during his lifetime—nonviolence with peace and good will to all men."

Memphis Strike Settled

The sanitation workers' strike, the cause for which King had gone to Memphis and to his death, was settled 2 weeks after the assassination.

Pres. Johnson had sent Labor Undersecy. James Reynolds to Memphis Apr. 5 to meet with representatives of the city and the strikers' union, the American Federation of State, County & Municipal Employes, in hopes of breaking the deadlock.

The U.S. District Court in Memphis Apr. 3 had enjoined King

from leading his 2d protest march in Memphis Apr. 8, but after King's death, Bayard Rustin, executive director of the A. Philip Randolph Institute, the Rev. James Bevel and the Rev. James Lawson, chairman of the Congress on the March for Equality (COME), announced plans Apr. 5 to hold the march as a memorial tribute as well as a demonstration of support for the strike.

During the night of Apr. 4–5 more than 30 persons were injured in rioting in Memphis. At least 3 major fires were reported and dozens of stores looted. There were several reports of sniper fire. The first death resulting from violence was reported Apr. 6. Gov. Buford Ellington immediately ordered 4,000 National Guardsmen into the city, and Mayor Henry Loeb reinstated a 7 p.m.–5 a.m. curfew.

Loeb said Apr. 5 that "in view of the tragic circumstances" the city would withdraw its objection to the march. He said that in response to the demands of Gov. Ellington, he would meet with the strike mediator to "get this thing behind us and find a solution to our differences." He made little headway that day, however, in 2 meetings, one with 144 Negro and white clergymen and the other with 9 black schoolteachers. The clergymen led a memorial march Apr. 5 down 7 city blocks past the National Guardsmen. At a memorial service later they adopted a resolution asking the mayor to end "racial prejudice and arrogant paternalism" in Memphis.

The march King had planned took place Apr. 8 with some 42,000 silent marchers participating.

A settlement of the 65-day strike was reached Apr. 16 by negotiators for the city and the American Federation of State, County & Municipal Employes (AFSCME) under the direction of Labor Undersecy. Reynolds. It was ratified unanimously by the union's members and approved by the City Council with one dissenting vote. The agreement included a 2-step 15¢-an-hour salary increase (increases of 10¢ an hour May 1 and 5¢ Sept. 1); city recognition of the union as the "designated representative" of the city's public works employes; a dues checkoff; promotions on the basis of seniority; a "no-strike" clause. (The workers had been paid $1.60 and $2.25 an hour.) AFSCME Pres. Jerry Wurf said the agreement was "a good settlement that couldn't have been achieved without the coalescence of the union and the Negro community."

Suspected Assassin Captured

James Earl Ray, 40, King's alleged assassin, was arrested by Scotland Yard detectives at Heathrow Airport in London June 8.

Ray had been the subject of an intensive manhunt. The news of his arrest was announced in the U.S. by Atty. Gen. Clark. Ray was apprehended when he went to the airport to board a plane for Brussels. Arrested on charges of possessing a fraudulent Canadian passport and of carrying a revolver without a permit, Ray was taken to London's Cannon Row police station and detained under conditions of maximum security.

Ray was arraigned on the London charges June 10 under the name Ramon George Sneyd (the name on his passport). The same day, at the request of the U.S. embassy, the Bow Street Magistrate's Court issued a provisional warrant for his extradition to the U.S. to stand trial for murder. The U.S. formally applied for Ray's extradition June 12. He was extradited July 2 and returned to the U.S. July 19 for trial. On arraignment in Memphis July 22, he entered a plea of not guilty; he was charged with murder and carrying a dangerous weapon.

The search for Ray was said to have been the most extensive in police history. The FBI issued a federal fugitive warrant in Birmingham, Ala. Apr. 17 charging Eric Starvo Galt, 36, with conspiracy in the assassination of King. The warrant charged that Galt —later revealel to be Ray—had conspired with a man "whom he alleged to be his brother" to "injure, oppress, threaten or intimidate" King. A Tennessee warrant charging Galt with first-degree murder was issued in Memphis the same day. The FBI also released 2 photographs of Galt.

The FBI then announced Apr. 19 that Eric Starvo Galt was an alias of James Earl Ray of Illinois, who had escaped from the Missouri State Penitentiary Apr. 23, 1967 after serving 7 years of a 20-year sentence for armed robbery and auto theft. His identity was announced after an extensive investigation of fingerprint records. Ray was reported also to have used the aliases of James McBride, James Walton, W. C. Herron and James O'Connor. Earlier aliases cited by the FBI had included John Willard and Harvey Lowmyer. Later reports included the name Paul Bridgman.

Ray was indicted under the name of Eric Starvo Galt in Memphis Apr. 23 on charges of murder and conspiring to violate the civil rights of King. He was reindicted May 7 under his real name. When Ray was apprehended in London June 8 he was traveling under the name of Ramon George Sneyd, a Toronto police constable.

After his arrest, the FBI and Justice Department released the following information on Ray's travels following his 1967 escape from prison: Ray had arrived in Birmingham in the summer of 1967 and had established his new identity as Eric Starvo Galt. He bought a white 1966 Mustang auto and obtained a driver's license in that name. During the fall and winter he made several trips to the West Coast. He left Los Angeles for New Orleans Dec. 15, 1967 and returned Dec. 21.

The FBI said that Ray, using the name John Willard, had checked into a rooming house facing the Lorraine Motel in Memphis, where King was staying, on the afternoon of Apr. 4. He refused a room on the north side of the house, but took one near the back with a view of the balcony outside King's room. One roomer reported that he saw Willard emerge from the bathroom with something wrapped in newspaper after the murder shot was fired. A Remington 30-06 pump rifle with a telescopic sight and a case containing binoculars were found lying on the sidewalk a few feet from the entrance of the rooming house. The gun, traced through its serial number by the FBI, had been purchased in Birmingham, Ala. by Ray.

Shortly after the assassination Ray went to Canada, the FBI said. By Apr. 16 he had taken up residence in a Toronto rooming house. A Canadian passport in the name of Sneyd was issued to Ray Apr. 24 in Ottawa and was sent to him in Toronto. Ray reportedly flew from Toronto to London May 6 and on to Lisbon May 7. He obtained a 2d passport May 16 from the Canadian embassy in Lisbon, claiming that the original had been spoiled. He returned to London May 17 and apparently remained there until his arrest.

Conspiracy Called Unlikely

The likelihood that King's murder was the work of a conspiracy had been discounted by Atty. Gen. Clark in Memphis Apr. 5 immediately after the slaying. At an impromptu news conference, Clark said that there was no evidence of a "widespread plot—this appears to have been the act of a single individual." He reiterated Apr. 7: "We have evidence of one man on the run. There is no evidence that more were involved."

But as evidence accumulated a widespread feeling grew that more than one person had been involved in the slaying and that Ray might have been a hired killer. Among the indications of a conspiracy: a broadcast on the police radio band shortly after the slaying reporting that a white Mustang auto was being pursued in a direction opposite to that apparently taken by Ray; the evidence of heavy spending by Ray under the alias of Galt in various parts of the country; the 3 other aliases used by Ray in the U.S. and Canada and his extensive travels in the U.S., Canada and Europe.

The day after Ray's capture, however, Atty. Gen. Clark, interviewed on the ABC-TV program "Issues and Answers," again asserted that Ray had acted alone. "We have no evidence of any other involvement by any other person or people," he said. Asked whether he thought that someone had "bankrolled" Ray's travels to Europe and Canada, Clark said: "He is a person . . . who lived a life of crime, who obtained funds, money, through crime, and I think we can reason that there is a very plausible possibility as to the source of his funds."

VIOLENCE FOLLOWING KING'S DEATH

Riots in 125 Cities

At least 125 cities in 28 states and the District of Columbia were hit by the racial disturbances that followed Martin Luther King's assassination. With the exception of the Southwest, Northwest and Northern Plains, no area of the country was exempt from the disorders. Among the cities affected:

Alabama—Birmingham, Mobile, Tuscaloosa, Tuskeegee.

Arkansas—El Dorado, Fayetteville, Hot Springs, Malvern, North Little Rock, Paris, Pine Bluff.

California—Berkeley, East Palo Alto, Oakland, Pittsburg, Vallejo.

Colorado—Denver.

Connecticut—Hartford, New Haven.

Delaware—Wilmington.

Florida—Fort Pierce, Gainesville, Miami, Pensacola, Tallahassee, Tampa.

Georgia—Albany, Atlanta, Fort Valley, Macon, Savannah.

Illinois—Carbondale, Chicago, Joliet, Peoria, Rockford.

Iowa—Des Moines, Knoxville, Marshalltown.

Kansas—Topeka, Wichita.

Kentucky—Frankfurt.

Louisiana—New Orleans.

Maryland—Baltimore, Frederick, Hagerstown.

Massachusetts—Boston.

Michigan—Albion, Battle Creek, Detroit, Grand Rapids, Jackson, Kalamazoo, Lansing, Roseville, Royal Oak.

Minnesota—Minneapolis.

Mississippi—Clarksdale, Cleveland, Crystal Springs, Greenville, Greenwood, Holly Springs, Itta Bena, Jackson, Lorman, Meridian, Oxford.

Missouri—Jefferson City, Kansas City, St. Louis.

New Jersey—Bridgeton, Newark, Trenton.

New York—Buffalo, Greenburgh, Hamilton, Ithaca, Monticello, N.Y. City, Port Chester, Syracuse.

North Carolina—Charlotte, Durham, Goldsboro, Greensboro, High Point, Lexington, New Bern, Raleigh, Weldon, Wilmington, Wilson, Winston-Salem.

Ohio—Cincinnati, Dayton, Toledo, Youngstown.

Pennsylvania—Aliquippa, Braddock, Johnstown, Lancaster, Pittsburgh, Philadelphia, West Chester.

South Carolina—Hampton, Orangeburg.

Tennessee—Memphis, Nashville.

Virginia—Richmond, Suffolk.

West Virginia—Wheeling.

Washington, D.C.

Baltimore, Chicago, Kansas City, Mo. and Washington, D.C. were the hardest hit of the cities rocked by the racial violence that swept the country in the wake of the assassination. These nationwide figures were reported by the *N.Y. Times* Apr. 14:

Deaths—46 (a total confirmed by the Justice Department Apr. 23). All but 5 of those killed were Negroes, and 32 of the deaths occurred in the hardest hit cities mentioned above. (*Time* magazine reported in its Apr. 19 issue that the death toll stood at 43. *Time* gave these statistics: 36 were black. 14, all but one of whom were black, were under 21 years of age. 25 died from bullet wounds. 8 were killed by unknown assailants, 9 by private citizens and 13 by police; 10 died in fires and 3 from other causes. In contrast to the rioting in the summer of 1967, the National Guardsmen and federal troops were not charged with any of the killings.)

Injured—at least 2,600 persons, almost half of them in Washington. Most of the injured were black.

Arrests—21,270. Most of the arrests were for looting.

Property damage—$45 million (a rough estimate provided by insurance companies). Most of the damage resulted from fires.

Troops involved—55,000, of which 21,000 were federal troops and 34,000 were National Guardsmen. The federal troops were sent to Baltimore, Chicago and Washington. 22,000 additional federal troops were on ready-alert for possible deployment.

The Defense Department reported May 18 that the cost of using federal troops in the riots following the assassination totaled $5,375,400. The expenses covered deployment of 35,890 regular soldiers and Marines and federalized National Guardsmen in

Washington, Baltimore and Chicago, the moving and maintainance of 22,074 regular soldiers in stand-by position, the flying of troops thousands of miles, pay and allowances for National Guardsmen and upkeep. The American Insurance Association estimated May 15 that insurance companies would pay $67 million for losses incurred in the rioting. Washington was reported to have suffered the heaviest damage, $24 million; Chicago's damage was reported to total $13 million and Baltimore's $12 million. New York damage was estimated at $4.2 million.

Betty Furness, the President's adviser on consumer affairs, told a Senate Banking subcommittee Apr. 19 that she believed there had been "selective looting and burning of stores" in the violence that erupted following King's assassination. She said ghetto merchants whose stores suffered were those believed guilty of fraudulent practices, overpricing, high interest rates and selling inferior quality goods, "whether it was true or not." Miss Furness said ghetto residents made 93% of their purchases on an installment basis and generally paid 40%–60% more than middle-income Americans. (She had asked at the convention of the American Society of Newspaper Editors in Washington Apr. 18: "Is it so startling that stores were burned in Watts where the mark-up on television sets ranged as high as 160% above prices for the exact model in other parts of Los Angeles?")

Among developments in cities where disorders took place after King was slain:

Baltimore—6 persons died in the racial violence that erupted in Baltimore Apr. 6, and the National Guard and federal troops were called in to quell the rioting. More than 700 persons were reported injured Apr. 6–9, more than 5,000 arrests were made, and the number of fires reported exceeded 1,000. (378,000, or 41%, of Baltimore's 930,000 inhabitants were black.)

Gov. Spiro T. Agnew declared a "state of emergency and crisis" in Baltimore Apr. 6 after black youths set at least 20 fires, smashed windows and looted stores in the predominantly black section of East Baltimore. Police temporarily gained control of the area when they sealed off a 5-block section of the commercial Gay Street section. But violence was renewed, and the governor called in 6,000 National Guardsmen and the state police at 10 p.m. to aid the city's 1,100-man police force. Guardsmen were armed with bayonets and tear gas and were instructed to carry their guns unloaded. Agnew banned the sale of liquor, firearms and gasoline in containers. Mayor Thomas D'Alesandro 3d, 38, imposed an 11 p.m.–6 a.m. curfew.

4 persons were killed the night of Apr. 6: one Negro and one white were victims of a fire caused by a fire bomb; 2 blacks were shot to death in 2 separate tavern incidents. More than 300 persons were reported injured. The level of violence rose during the night, fell by morning and then increased steadily throughout Apr. 7. The curfew was reimposed at 4 p.m. Maj. Gen. George M. Gelston, Maryland adjutant general, kept the National Guardsmen under strict orders not to shoot unless fired on and to return fire only when given orders by an officer or when the source of attack could be definitely identified.

At nightfall Apr. 7 Agnew declared that he had "determined that federal reinforcements are necessary in the city." 2,995 federal troops were immediately dispatched to Baltimore, and Lt. Gen. Robert H. York, a paratroop officer, assumed over-all command from Gelston.

Despite the curfew, bands of youths roamed the city streets, looting and setting fires. Fires were reported scattered over a wide area of the city and not concentrated in particular areas, as in other cities. By morning violence subsided.

Pres. Johnson sent an additional 1,900 federal troops to Baltimore Apr. 8 to reinforce the 2,995 federal troops sent earlier, the 5,953 mobilized National Guardsmen and 1,500 state and local police on duty.

In sections east and west of Baltimore's downtown business district, troops used tear gas Apr. 8 to dispell mobs who were reportedly bombarding police and firemen with rocks and bottles and interfering with efforts to control fires. Food and drug shortages were reported. As looting and arson spread late Apr. 8 the first sniper fire was reported.

The rioting's 6th fatality was reported early Apr. 9 when a Negro was found burned to death in an apartment over a grocery store that had been firebombed. Scattered incidents of looting and arson were reported Apr. 9. At the urging of civil rights leaders, military and police officials agreed Apr. 9 to permit blacks to patrol ghetto neighborhoods as "peacemakers" to try to bring an end to the vandalism. State Sen. Clarence Mitchell 3d, a Negro, had met with 150 slum residents that afternoon for a "peace rally" and to have them "pass the word" that the patrols would be out at night to ease the tension. After the 7 p.m. curfew took effect, 16 black "block leaders" under police and military escort toured the riot-torn areas, where they urged residents to obey the curfew and clear the streets.

Curfew restrictions were eased Apr. 10 while federal troops continued patrols. City workers were sent to East Baltimore to begin removing debris and cleaning the area. Agnew urged Pres. Johnson and Maryland Congressmen to act to bring civil disorders under provisions of disaster relief laws.

About 80 elected and appointed black officials walked out of a meeting with Agnew Apr. 11 after he charged them with failing to help enough in preventing the riots. He also accused militant young Negroes of inciting the black community to violence. Before the governor finished his remarks someone yelled: "Let's have a black caucus . . . it's an insult." They then walked out and held a meeting at a black parish church in west Baltimore. Agnew had also told the group: "It's no mere coincidence that a national disciple of violence, Mr. Stokely Carmichael, was observed meeting with local black power advocates and known criminals in Baltimore Apr. 3, 1968—three days before the Baltimore riots began."

The governor Apr. 12 asked Washington to withdraw the federal troops and defederalize the National Guard as soon as possible. 2,000 troops were removed immediately, and the remaining troops were removed Apr. 13. The National Guard was relieved of active duty Apr. 14 when Agnew lifted the state of emergency and lifted bans on gun and gasoline sales.

Boston—Massachusetts National Guardsmen were placed on stand-by alert in Boston Apr. 5–6 after sporadic rock throwing and looting in the Roxbury and Dorchester districts Apr. 4–6. 15,000 persons, mostly whites, staged a 3-mile memorial march for King. They were joined by Negroes from Roxbury.

The United Front, a coalition of civil rights groups, presented a list of 21 demands to the city Apr. 8 at a rally attended by 10,000 blacks in White Stadium in Roxbury. The demands included black control of ghetto police stations, black ownership of all ghetto businesses, the payment of $100 million by the city to the Roxbury section, where about half of the city's 85,000 Negroes lived, the employment of blacks only in Roxbury schools and black control of social welfare and antipoverty programs. Boston Mayor Kevin H. White Apr. 9 rejected the demands.

Chicago—11 Negroes died in racial violence that swept Chicago Apr. 5–7. Federal troops and National Guardsmen were called to the city to quell the disorders, in which more than 500 persons were injured and nearly 3,000 arrested. 162 buildings were reported entirely destroyed by fire, and a score more were partially destroyed. Total property damage was estimated at $9 million. (1.3 million, or 16%, of Chicago's 8,282,000 inhabitants were black.)

The disturbances began Apr. 5 when black youths, released from school early in honor of King, began roving downtown streets and smashing windows. They swept through the downtown Loop seciton and by nightfall had caused severe damage in the 2300 and 2400 blocks of West Madison Street. 4 deaths were reported: 2 looters were shot, one person died in a fire, and another person was shot to death. One fireman was wounded by a sniper.

6,000 National Guardsmen were mobilized the afternoon of Apr. 6 by Lt. Gov. Samuel H. Shapiro after he consulted with Gov. Otto Kerner, who was in Florida. Under the command of Brig. Gen. Richard T. Dunn, the Guardsmen joined the city's 10,500 policeman. They were instructed to shoot only in self-defense and then to shoot only at definite targets.

Early Apr. 6 Mayor Richard J. Daley and Gen. Dunn made a tour of the riot area and declared the situation "under control." Later in the day, however, violence was renewed with increased vigor and spread from the West Side to the South Side and the Near North Side. 800 arrests and 125 major fires were reported during the day. By evening the major ordered a 7 p.m.-to-6 a.m. curfew for everyone under 21 years of age; he barred the sale of firearms and liquor. 1,500 additional Guardsmen were called into the city. The Guardsmen and the police were ordered to take more "aggressive action" against lawbreakers.

In the evening of Apr. 6, after 9 blacks had been killed in the disorders, Shapiro asked Pres. Johnson for federal aid to quell the "serious domestic violence in or near the city of Chicago." The first of some 5,000 federal troops ordered to the city began arriving at 9:30 p.m. The President also sent Deputy Atty. Gen. Warren Christopher to Chicago as his special representative.

While troops took control in the North and West Sides of the city Apr. 6, the situation on the South Side deteriorated. Firemen trying to put out fires were under constant attack by snipers. By nightfall thousands of Negroes were reported homeless. The Chicago Conference on Religion & Race set up "Operation Home" to find temporary quarters for the displaced. The Chicago Commission on Human Relations established a "rumor control center." 3 emergency bond courts were set up to speed the processing of arrest cases.

Sporadic incidents of sniper fire, looting and arson were reported Apr. 7 as federal troops continued to patrol the city. Police reported 11 black deaths, 7 of them directly and 4 indirectly related to the rioting. Of the 7 directly-related deaths, all were of men, 6 shot, one stabbed. Of the 4 others, one was shot, one died of a skull fracture and 2 died in fires.

Shapiro said at a news conference Apr. 8 that the emergency had ended. Troops, National Guardsmen and police, however, continued to patrol the city. Members of 2 major black South Side gangs, the Blackstone Rangers and the East Side Disciples, agreed to suspend hostilities and aid patrols to prevent further outbreaks of violence and destruction. Although no violence was reported Apr. 8, the 7 p.m.-to-6 a.m. curfew remained in effect. 5 black militants were arrested Apr. 8 on charges of conspiracy to commit arson; they were held on $120,000 bond. Those arrested were Frederick (Doug) Andrews, 29, founder of the Garfield Organization (announced purpose: the improvement of economic conditions on the West Side); Edward Crawford, 46, president of the National Negro Rifle Association; Andrew Brown, 24, of the Garfield Organization; Curlee Reed, 19, and Anthony Williams, 17.

Daley ended the curfew Apr. 10. The 5,000 federal troops left the city Apr. 12. Daley and Gov. Kerner had asked Pres. Johnson to withdraw the troops and return the National Guardsmen to state control.

18 Negroes who had been jailed for a week filed suit Apr. 12 on charges that the chief justice of the Cook County Circuit Court and other county officials were "suspending due process of law" by failing to act on their cases. The prisoners charged that they had been denied preliminary hearings and were unable to post the "excessive" bonds that had been "set without proper bond hearings." Following charges by the predominantly black Cook County Bar Association that there was a "deplorable breakdown in judicial processes" in the handling of the arrests, the county magistrates held an extraordinary court session Apr. 14 and reduced bond for 207 prisoners. Bond had been set at from up to $1,000 for disorderly conduct to $120,000 for arson and conspiracy charges.

Daley announced at a news conference Apr. 15 that he was instructing policemen "to shoot to kill" arsonists and to "shoot to maim or cripple" looters in any future rioting. His orders, transmitted to police through Police Supt. James B. Conlisk, said: "Such force as is necessary including deadly force shall be used" to prevent the commission of such forcible felonies as arson, attempted arson, burglary and attempted burglary and " to prevent the escape of the perpetrators." Daley said that he had thought those orders were in effect during the Apr. 5–7 violence but that he had discovered that morning that policemen had been instructed to use their own discretion as to whether to shoot. Daley said he thought that arson was "the most hideous crime." He declared: "If anyone doesn't think this was a conspiracy, I don't understand."

Cincinnati—Ohio Gov. James A. Rhodes ordered 1,200 National Guardsmen to Cincinnati Apr. 8 to quell rioting that erupted following a memorial service for King in the predominantly black suburb of Avondale. 2 people were killed in the disorders. Mayor Eugene Ruehlman imposed a 7 p.m.-to-6 a.m. curfew and ordered all liquor stores and gasoline stations to close.

The disorders spread after James Smith, a black guard, accidently shot and killed his wife while trying to ward off youthful looters from the English Jewelry Store. Rumors spread, however, that Mrs. Smith had been killed by a frightened policeman. Firebombing, looting and window smashing followed.

In suburban Mount Auburn, black teen-agers dragged Noel Wright, 30, a white graduate student and art instructor at the University of Cincinnati, and his wife from their car Apr. 8. They stabbed Wright to death, and 3 black girls beat Mrs. Wright.

A white youth was attacked by black youths in downtown Cincinnati and stabbed repeatedly.

About 200 persons were reported arrested, including 40 juveniles. Damage resulting from some 55 fires was estimated at about $150,000. The Avondale business association said damage from theft and vandalism was approximately $200,000.

400 National Guardsmen patrolled the city Apr. 9, and no disturbances were reported. The curfew restrictions were removed Apr. 10 and the Guard withdrawn Apr. 12.

Detroit—4,000 National Guardsmen and 400 state policemen were sent to Detroit Apr. 5 to help 4,200 city police quell racial violence. Mayor Jerome P. Cavanagh proclaimed a state of emergency Apr. 5 and ordered an 8 p.m.-to-5 a.m. curfew. 2 Negroes were killed by policemen in looting incidents Apr. 5. Gov. George Romney said one looter was killed "accidentally."

1,483 persons were arrested Apr. 5–9; 802 of the arrests were for curfew violations. 12 persons were injured. 378 fires were reported.

Romney Apr. 10 reduced the curfew to 1 a.m.-to-5 a.m. He announced the end of the state of emergency Apr. 12 and said that the National Guard would be withdrawn gradually.

(Scattered incidents of violence were reported Apr. 8–9 in Grand Rapids, Kalamazoo, Benton Harbor, Niles and Lansing, Mich.)

(The New Detroit Committee, appointed Aug. 3, 1967 to plan rebuilding of the city following the racial violence there in July 1967, issued a 160-page report Apr. 18 describing the city's progress as "woefully inadequate." The report said: "In no respect has a single basis for alienation and bitterness been completely overcome. In no respect has a single opportunity for future improvement been fully exploited." The report was critical of the failure of building trades unions to find qualified black members. It criticized city health care programs for the poor and said that Detroit public schools were "on the brink of financial chaos.")

Kansas City—6 Negroes were shot and killed in racial violence that erupted in Kansas City, Mo. Apr. 9–11. 3,000 National Guardsmen were called to the city, and order was restored by Apr. 14.

The violence began Apr. 9 after police fired tear gas into a crowd of about 1,000 blacks who had gathered at city hall to hear an address by Mayor Ilus W. Davis. The Negroes, mostly teenagers, had marched to the building to protest the city's decision to keep the schools open that day—the day of the funeral of Martin Luther King—in contrast to the decision of neighboring Kansas City, Kan. to close its schools. The police said they had fired the tear gas after a Negro threw a bottle at them. The crown then dispersed but began a rampage in the black East Side area; they smashed windows, set fires and looted stores. By the end of the night one Negro had been shot and killed by police while he was looting a liquor store; 57 persons were injured (7 by gunfire) and about 270 were arrested. About 75 fires were set, and windows were broken in some 200 business establishments. The city imposed a 9 a.m.-to-6 a.m. curfew, and 300 to 400 National Guardsmen were called in.

The most serious Kansas City violence broke out Apr. 10. The first incident occurred in the morning outside predominantly black Lincoln High School, where students were milling around waiting for classes to begin. Police urged the students to go inside the building, but, when they apparently felt that the students were putting up resistance, they fired tear gas into the crowd. The students ran into the school, and the police followed and fired tear gas again inside the building. The school was evacuated, and most of the students went home. Despite the incident, the city remained relatively calm most of Apr. 10, and Mayor Davis announced in the afternoon that the curfew would be lifted that night.

About an hour later, however, crowds of blacks began roaming through the East Side, and the situation quickly got out of hand. Rioters threw Molotov cocktails at police and National Guardsmen, set about 70 fires, looted stores and harassed police and firemen with sniper fire. 4 Negroes were shot and killed by unknown persons in a 4-block area of sniper fire along Prospect Street. 22 persons were injured, about half of them by gunfire, and about 150 persons were arrested, most of them for destruction of property and curfew violations. Police reported that their command post was under sporadic fire, and the police academy was severly damaged by fire. Davis ordered all police to duty, reinstated the curfew, closed all taverns and liquor stores and banned the sale of guns, ammunition and gasoline in closed containers. The National Guard force was increased during the day to 3,000 men.

Although the violence fell off considerably Apr. 11, Davis declared a state of emergency and imposed a dusk-to-dawn curfew. One Negro was shot and killed by police in a gunfight; his death raised the 3-day toll to 6. Only 5 confirmed sniping incidents and minor arson were reported Apr. 12, and nobody was injured. Scattered sniping and firebombing continued Apr. 13, but the city moved the curfew back to 11 p.m.

Officials announced Apr. 14 that order had been restored and that about 2,500 of the National Guardsmen were being sent home. One battalion of military police and about 100 state troopers remained on duty in the city. Davis lifted the ban on gasoline sales but not on the sale of firearms and ammunition.

Nashville—Sporadic incidents of looting, firebombing and vandalism were reported in Nashville's black neighborhoods Apr. 5-9. About 4,000 National Guardsmen were sent into the city Apr. 5-6. 2,000 Guardsmen sealed off the campus of the predominantly black Tennessee A & I State University Apr. 6 after 2 students were wounded in violence Apr. 5 and 50 Guardsmen dispersed a crowd of about 200 students with tear gas. The city was placed under curfew and liquor sales were banned. After calm was restored, the curfew and liquor ban were removed Apr. 14.

•

New York—The disorders in New York City Apr. 4-5 were considered relatively minor. The police followed a policy of using large numbers of policemen rather than firearms to restore and maintain order, and many black leaders, including militants, urged Negroes to "cool it" and forego rioting.

Bands of black youths roved the streets of Harlem and Brooklyn's Bedford-Stuyvesant areas Apr. 4 after the announcement of King's death. Mayor John V. Lindsay made a walking tour of Harlem at 10:40 p.m. and urged crowds to go home. Several fires were reported, and store windows were smashed and their contents looted.

Scattered incidents of looting were reported throughout Apr. 5. Police Commissioner Howard R. Leary put the city's 28,788-man police force on an emergency basis, and Fire Commissioner Robert O. Lowery declared "a fire emergency" and held all units on an overtime basis. Police were instructed: "There will be no indiscriminate use of the gun. In these situations, a firecracker can get everybody to draw his weapon. You will not use your revolvers to pick off snipers. In case you see snipers, take cover, notify the command and a special sniper team will be sent. We want looters arrested, but . . . we don't want to hurt anyone." Police Apr. 5 reported 94 arrests, 30 persons injured, including 10 policemen, and 158 incidents of looting, arson and rock throwing.

Volunteer peace-keepers who fanned out through black ghetto neighborhoods in Harlem and Bedford-Stuyvesant Apr. 5 were credited with keeping violence to a minimum. Members of Harlem's CORE, Harlem Youth Unlimited, the Harlem Cadet Corps and the Manhattan NAACP walked through ghetto areas, talked to the people and urged restraint. One peace-keeping group was led by Charles Kenyatta, leader of the para-military Harlem Mau Maus. Manhattan Borough Pres. Percy Sutton made a radio appeal for peace, and Mayor Lindsay appealed on TV, and walked through Harlem and Bedford-Stuyvesant.

In the early evening Apr. 5 police arrested 28 black youths in the Times Square area after 50 to 100 youths smashed windows and looted stores there.

Lindsay walked through Harlem and Bedford-Stuyvesant again Apr. 6 and reported that the area "seemed calm." 5,000 suburban residents—most of them white—met at the Kingsbridge Armory in the Bronx Apr. 6 and signed up for a campaign to clean up 50 blocks in Harlem, Bedford-Stuyvesant and other slum areas Apr. 20.

10,000 persons marched through Harlem Apr. 7 and then met in Central Park to pay tribute to King. Among the leaders of the march were Gov. Nelson A. Rockefeller and Charles Kenyatta, who walked arm-in-arm.

Lindsay Apr. 8 issued a proclamation declaring Apr. 9 a day of mourning throughout the city.

Newark, N.J.—Sporadic looting broke out in Newark Apr. 9 after dozens of fires were set in the city's predominantly black Central Ward. 15 persons were arrested; 6 persons were reported injured in the fires, and 600 persons were left homeless. 500 black youths patrolled the streets in the evening urging the community to "cool it." Mayor Hugh J. Addonizio Apr. 10 praised the Negroes and whites for cooperating in trying to keep the peace.

A fire described as the worst in Newark's history raged through the Central Ward Apr. 20. 35 buildings were destroyed and 500 persons were left homeless, but there were no deaths or major injuries.

Oakland, Calif.—Bobby James Hutton, 17, an officer of the militant Black Panther Party, was killed and 4 other persons were wounded during a 90-minute gun battle between Negroes and police in predominantly black West Oakland Apr. 6. 2 policemen and Eldridge Cleaver, 32, Black Panther "education minister" and author of the recently published *Soul on Ice,* were among those injured; 8 persons were arrested.

According to the police, firing erupted when policemen stopped to question occupants of 3 parked cars. As the patrolmen stepped from their car, they reportedly were shot at without warning. Then the civilian occupants of the cars fled to a nearby building. Police reinforcements arrived, traded gunfire with the men in the house and then used tear gas. The men in the house finally agreed to surrender. Hutton emerged first. One report indicated that someone had shouted that Hutton had a gun; Police Chief Charles Gain said Hutton bent over and began to run. "The officers could not see his hands clearly and, assuming he was still armed, then ordered him to halt," Gain said. "Upon failure to do so, they fired at him." Black Panther Chairman Bobby George Seale, 31, asserted Apr. 7 that witnesses had "said that Hutton was shot when his hands were in the air." He added Apr. 12 that the police had ordered Hutton to run and then had shot him.

Pittsburgh—Violence swept black areas of Pittsburgh Apr. 4-8. 5,200 National Guardsmen and 375 state police were called in to assist the 1,500-man city police force. More than 1,100 persons were arrested, but hospitals reported treating fewer than 40 persons. The police and Guardsmen were ordered not to shoot looters.

Scattered incidents of vandalism and firebombings were reported Apr. 5, but the disorders spread Apr. 6 from the predominantly black Hill district to the North Side, where black gangs set fires, smashed windows and stoned cars. Mayor Joseph M. Barr Apr. 6 ordered bars and liquor stores in the city closed, and Gov. Raymond P. Shafer ordered all liquor stores in the state closed. More than 90 persons were reported injured.

Shafer Apr. 7 declared a state of emergency, imposed a 7 p.m. to 5 a.m. curfew and called in the state police and National Guardsmen. 2,200 Guardsmen and 300 state police moved into the city immediately. Among the 24 persons reported injured Apr. 7 were 2 Guardsmen, 3 firemen and 4 policemen. About 1,000 persons marched from the Hill to downtown Pittsburgh Apr. 7 in a tribute to the late King that was delayed while the marchers waited for sufficient police protection.

New violence was reported in the Homewood-Rushton district Apr. 8. The number of fires reported since Apr. 4 rose to 190.

1,000 additional National Guardsmen were moved into the city Apr. 9, although the city was generally reported calm. Barr lifted the curfew restrictions Apr. 10, and the National Guardsmen were withdrawn from the city Apr. 11-12.

Trenton—Harlan M. Joseph, 19, a black member of the Mayor's Council and divinity student at Lincoln University (Oxford, Pa.), was shot to death in Trenton Apr. 9 by Michael A. Castiello, a white policeman. The shooting took place during the 2d night of sporadic outbreaks of racial violence. State police were called in to aid city policemen, and Gov. Richards J. Hughes Apr. 10 placed National Guardsmen on standby alert. More than 235 persons were arrested Apr. 9-12, in most cases for violating a 9 p.m. to 6 a.m. curfew imposed by Mayor Carmen J. Armenti Apr. 9. 30 persons were injured; dozens of stores were looted and/or damaged by fire.

According to police, Joseph was one of 5 black youths who smashed the display windows of a haberdashery store across the street from City Hall and stole apparel. Police said Joseph was "a looter, and loot was recovered from his person." Detective Capt. Leon Foley said that Patrolman Castiello had fired a warning shot in the air and then had tried to wound one of the fleeing youths in the leg. "But his gun was jostled by the crowd just as he fired,"

Foley said "and the bullet struck the Joseph kid in the back." Other witnesses said the Joseph youth was trying to stop the looters and was not looting.

Hughes withdrew the Guard Apr. 12.

Washington—The nation's capital Apr. 4-7 experienced its worst outbreak of racial violence. 9 persons died. 1,202 persons were reported injured, including some policemen, firemen and military personnel. 6,306 persons were arrested. 1,130 fires were reported. And 13,600 federal troops were moved into the city before the disorders were quelled. (63% of Washington's 810,000 inhabitants were black.)

Looting and vandalism had erupted in Washington late Apr. 4 after ex-Chairman Stokely Carmichael of the Student Nonviolent Coordinating Committee had led about 50 youths down 14th Street to urge stores to close as a sign of respect for King. The group, shouting "Close the stores—Martin Luther King is dead," swelled to more than 400 persons about a mile north of the White House.

Within an hour blacks began smashing store windows and looting, despite a plea by the Rev. Walter E. Fauntroy, vice chairman of the City Council, to Carmichael to disband his group and go home. But Carmichael reportedly refused to stop his march.

According to the *N.Y. Times,* Carmichael urged members of the crowd: "If you don't have a gun, go home." "When the white man comes he is coming to kill you. I don't want any black blood in the street. Go home and get you a gun and then come back because I got me a gun." But the *Washington Post* reported that Carmichael simply urged rioters to stop looting and "go home." "Not now, not now," he was quoted as shouting to looters.

Carmichael declared at a news conference the morning of Apr. 5: "When white America killed Dr. King last night she declared war" on black America. There was "no alternative to retribution." "Black people have to survive, and the only way they will survive is by getting guns."

Rioting in Washington Apr. 5 was generally held to 3 predominantly low-income black sections of the city—a 10-block strip along 14th Street N.W., a 10-block strip along 7th Street N.W. and a 12-block strip along H Street N.E. The downtown area near the Capitol and the White House suffered minor damage.

At 4:02 p.m. Apr. 5 Pres. Johnson signed a proclamation declaring that "a condition of domestic violence and disorder" existed. He issued an executive order mobilizing 4,000 regular

Army and National Guard troops to supplement the city's 2,800-man police force. Police and troops were ordered to avoid excessive force. The troops were dispatched with the following orders: "I will, if possible, let civilian police make arrests, but I can, if necessary, take into temporary custody rioters, looters and others committing crimes. I will not load or fire my weapon except when authorized in advance by an officer under certain specific conditions, or when required to save my life." The President named ex-Deputy Defense Secy. Cyrus R. Vance as his special representative in the crisis.

Washington Commissioner (Mayor) Walter E. Washington issued an emergency order setting a 5:30 p.m.-to-6:30 a.m. curfew and halting the sale of firearms and liquor. By 11 p.m. the death toll had climbed to 6, of whom 3 persons had been shot as looters.

A new wave of looting and arson broke out Apr. 6, and the curfew was extended to 4 p.m. An additional 8,000 federal troops were moved into the city; more than 9,500 troops were put on street patrol, and 3,000 were held in reserve. Serious food shortages began to be reported Apr. 6. Hundreds of persons were homeless.

Pres. Johnson made a helicopter tour of the city Apr. 6. Sen. Robert F. Kennedy (D., N.Y.) and his wife, Ethel, toured 22 riot-torn blocks Apr. 7 with the Rev. Walter Fauntroy.

A return to normality was reported Apr. 8 after the death toll had reached 8, including 7 blacks. The District of Columbia Redevelopment Land Agency made a preliminary estimate that damage to buildings totaled $13 million. City agencies, church groups and the Agriculture Department began distributing tons of food Apr. 8. Mayor Washington said that 35 distribution centers had been established to supply food to nearly 185,000 riot victims. Emergency housing and jobs were being provided at special centers established throughout the city. The curfew was set back one hour.

Troops remained on duty Apr. 9, but the number of daytime patrols was decreased. Mayor Washington Apr. 11 reduced the curfew hours to midnight to 4 a.m. and eased the liquor sale restrictions. A gradual withdrawal of troops from the city was begun Apr. 12, when 3,726 troops were ordered out by midnight. Mayor Washington ended the curfew Apr. 12.

'Shoot-to-Kill' Controversy

There was widespread reaction to Chicago Mayor Richard J. Daley's instructions to Chicago police Apr. 15 to "shoot to kill" arsonists and to "shoot to maim or cripple" looters in future rioting.

Justice Department officials acknowledged Apr. 13 that methods of riot control in the violence that followed Martin Luther King's death had been based on a "humanitarian" plan of restraint and a minimum use of gunfire, the *N.Y. Times* reported Apr. 14. The policy, largely the work of Atty. Gen. Ramsey Clark and ex-Deputy Defense Secy. Cyrus R. Vance, called for the use of "overwhelming law enforcement manpower" coupled with military and police restraint. The heavy use of tear gas was substituted for gunfire. A department official said: "That old stuff about 'looters will be shot on sight' is for the history books and maybe the movies. It's for people who don't know how it is to be in a riot where, if you shoot, they shoot back and you've got a lot of dead cops and troops along with the dead citizens." "We have drawn back from all that the law allows because it is our duty to stop riots, not to kill rioters."

In New York, Mayor John V. Lindsay said at a news conference Apr. 16: "We happen to think that protection of life . . . is more important than protecting property or anything else. . . . We are not going to turn disorder into chaos through the unprincipled use of armed force. In short, we are not going to shoot children in New York City." The FBI had "cautioned against overresponding to disturbances," Lindsay said. "There were incidents last summer when persons thought to be looters were killed but it turned out upon later investigation that they were not looters."

At a news conference in Trenton Apr. 16, N.J. Gov. Richard J. Hughes scored the shooting of looters and arsonists. "My own judgment is that the sanctity of human life is such that an intelligent response by the police will result in arrests rather than shootings," Hughes declared.

Following an address to the American Society of Newspaper Editors in Washington Apr. 17, in response to a question from the audience, Atty. Gen. Clark repudiated Daley's instructions as "a very dangerous escalation of the problems we are so intent on solving." "I think that to resort to deadly force is contrary to the total experience of law enforcement in this coutry," Clark said. "I do not believe it [the use of deadly force] is permissible except in self-defense or when it is necessary to protect the lives of others." Earlier in his speech, Clark had sharply critized the indiscriminate use of force since it could provoke counter-attack by rioters and encourage "terrorist and guerilla tactics" and risk "permanent alienation among minorities." He said that the FBI manual prohibited the use of "deadly force" except for self-defense or to "protect the lives of others."

Daley, in a statement Apr. 17 to the City Council, revised his comment. He said: Arsonists and looters "should be restrained if possible by minimum force" but could not be given "permissive rights" for their criminal behavior. Residents of the West Side, where most of the violence occurred, "had one universal demand—protect us from the arsonists, from the looter, from the mob and its leaders." "We cannot resign ourselves to the proposition that civil protest must lead to death or devastation, to abandonment of the law that is fundamental for the preservation of the rights of the people and their freedom."

Pres. Johnson, in a letter to Defense Secy. Clark M. Clifford, praised the "wise and restrained use of force" by federal troops and National Guardsmen in the rioting following King's death. The President noted that not one death had been caused by military forces. He said that the more than 26,500 Army troops and 47,000 National Guardsmen had "fulfilled with distinction an assignment that was regrettable but unavoidable."

(Atty. Gen. Clark warned in a speech in Chapel Hill, N.C. Aug. 15 that current "loose talk of shooting looters" was likely to "cause guerrilla warfare in our cities and division and hatred among our people." Observers assumed that his remarks were intended to answer a statement made July 30 by Spiro T. Agnew. Agnew, in a New York speech, had called "the agonizing of a police officer who couldn't bring himself to kill a looter over a pair of shoes" an example of "the insidious relativism" that had entered American thinking. He had said that the guilt of a looter could not be measured by the value of property stolen. Agnew had critized the Kerner commission report for blaming white racism and excusing individual responsibility in the cause of riots.)

OTHER UNREST & RIOTS

Police Slay 3 Students in Orangeburg

3 black youths were shot to death and at least 34 persons were wounded in a confrontation between police and students at South Carolina State College in Orangeburg, S.C. Feb. 8. The deaths were the culmination of racial violence that had begun there Feb. 5 with student protests against the segregation of a local bowling alley.

The violence resulted in the mobilization of the National Guard and the 2-week closing of the college.

The series of incidents began when students from the predominantly black adjoining campuses of South Carolina State College and Claflin College demonstrated Feb. 5 in front of the All Star Bowling Lanes. They resumed the demonstrations Feb. 6, and 15 of them were arrested on trespassing charges. One policeman and 7 students were injured and hospitalized Feb. 6 as the disorders grew more violent.

Gov. Robert E. McNair Jr. mobilized a unit of the National Guard Feb. 6 and placed another on alert Feb. 7. 200 National Guardsmen were brought to Orangeburg Feb. 7, and 2 more Guard units were sent to Orangeburg Feb. 8.

Students at State College began throwing rocks and bottles at passing cars Feb. 7, and about 100 helmeted highway patrolmen were then sent to seal off the campus. Classes at State College were suspended Feb. 7, and M. Maceo Nance Jr., acting president of the college, protested against alleged police brutality. Nance proposed an economic boycott of downtown Orangeburg instead of demonstrations.

The 3 deaths took place late Feb. 8 in what was at first reported as an exchange of gunfire between policemen and students. According to an original report, Negroes opened fire on police and firemen who were trying to put out a grass fire. It was reported later, however, that the students did not shoot. Instead, a trooper was merely knocked down by a piece of lumber thrown by a student; the state troopers thought he was shot and opened fire, killing 3 black students.

Gov. McNair proclaimed a state of emergency Feb. 9 and ordered a 5 p.m. curfew. 600 National Guardsmen were ordered to help seal off the college campuses, which were nearly deserted by early Feb. 9. McNair blamed the violence on "black power advocates who represented only a small minority of the total student bodies" at the 2 schools. He said that Cleveland Sellers, 23, state coordinator for the Student Nonviolent Coordinating Committee (SNCC), was responsible for the trouble. Sellers, wounded in the shooting Feb. 8, had been arrested and held under $50,000 bond.

(The Justice Department announced Feb. 10 that it was investigating the slaying of the 3 black youths. In a suit filed in Federal District Court in Columbia, S.C., the department Feb. 10 charged Harry K. Floyd and Carolyn R. Floyd, owners of the bowling alley, and E. C. Floyd and Hanna Floyd, operators of the snack bar at the alley, with violating the 1964 Civil Rights Act by refusing to permit Negroes to use the facilities on an equal basis with whites. A federal district judge issued a nondiscrimination order against Floyd Feb. 23, and 2 black patrons were admitted to the bowling alley Feb. 26. The Justice Department Feb. 13 filed a motion in support of a private suit that sought an injunction to end alleged discrimination in patient facilities and medical care at the publicly-owned Orangeburg Hospital. The department also asked the court to affirm a Jan. 8 Health, Education & Welfare Department order to end federal support for the hospital for noncompliance with desegregation requirements.)

800 local Negroes met in Orangeburg Feb. 11 and called for the immediate removal of the National Guard and the suspension of law enforcement officers responsible for alleged police brutality. They announced plans for a boycott of white businesses to enforce a series of demands. Dr. C. H. Thomas Jr., local NAACP president, said that 62.9% of the total county population of 17,000 was black. The Negroes also demanded that the city make restitution to the families of the 3 dead youths. Their demands included: placing blacks in appointive city and county jobs; the addition of "an equitable number of Negroes" to local and state police forces; elimination of the county dual school system; busing of pupils for racial balance.

It had been announced Feb. 10 that Mayor E. O. Pendarvis and the City Council had established a biracial Human Relations Commission to find the cause of the violence and avert further outbreaks. State NAACP officials Feb. 13 critized the commission on the grounds that its black members had been appointed without NAACP recommendation. (The South Carolina Task Force for Community Uplift, a biracial organization formed in the fall of 1967 and endorsed by McNair, urged all South Carolina municipalities Feb. 22 to form biracial groups immediately to deal with the causes of "possible racial upheaval in their midst.")

The Southern Regional Council said Feb. 24, in a 42-page report entitled "Events at Orangeburg," that the shootings showed the dangers of "get tough" police tactics. The report said: "The events also would at least suggest the implications of forces in motion not just in Orangeburg but across America in 1967-68, including 'black power' and white overreaction to its emotional mood, the tendency to violence by Negroes dismayed by the failure of nonviolent and other peaceful protest against social injustice and inequity still enduring, the national tendency nearing public policy to a fear of riots amounting to phobia and a response to Negro unrest with massive police and military force." Although the governor had said that the police shot only after they thought they had been fired on, "no one has been able to find any weapons that the students might have used. No one . . . saw any students with guns."

In its report, the council asked why police had not used "less lethal methods of riot control, such as tear gas or Mace," and why students had not been warned before the shooting. It said that SNCC coordinator Sellers apparently "had little influence on the campus" and had little effect in trying to encourage the organization of a Black Awareness Coordinating Committee.

Students returned to the State College campus Feb. 26. McNair announced Mar. 5 that he had rescinded his state-of-emergency order and that the National Guard had been withdrawn.

About 2,500 Negro students throughout North and South Carolina and Virginia had demonstrated Feb. 15 in protest against the Orangeburg slayings. Violence erupted in Durham, N.C. as students threw bricks and broke windows. 2 policemen were injured; 2 students were arrested.

200 State College students burst in on the General Assembly at the State Capitol in Columbia, S.C. Mar. 7 to present an 8-point list of grievances. 6 students were arrested. The grievances included demands for: suspension of the heads of the State Law Enforcement Division, State Highway Patrol, National Guard and Orangeburg City Police; a $12 million appropriation for operations of the college; and $10,000 awards from the state to the families of the slain students.

A federal grand jury in Columbia, S.C. Nov. 8 refused to indict 9 state highway policemen in the shooting of the 3 Negro students in Orangeburg. Gov. McNair Nov. 8 called the jury's decision "a conclusive and fair judgment of the incident." (The jury of 18 men and 5 women included 2 Negroes.) But the U.S. Justice Department Dec. 20 insisted that the 9 patrolmen be brought to trial, and it filed charges in Federal District Court in Columbia. The Justice Department accused the policemen of violating the constitutional rights of the Negroes.

Student Unrest Elsewhere

Racially motivated demonstrations, boycotts and disorders took place among students in almost every part of the U.S. during 1968. The disturbances involved high-school as well as college students.

School decentralization disputes and black high-school students' demands led to demonstrations and disorders in schools across the nation during the fall. In Boston a school dispute overflowed into the streets as students clashed with police in Boston's South Side. Elsewhere black students boycotted classes to press for educational reforms. In the South demonstrations centered around desegregation disputes. Violence between black and white students caused officials to close high schools temporarily in several cities.

Results of studies of high school racial disorders following the assassination of Martin Luther King in April were reported in the *N.Y. Times* Dec. 16. The Riot Data Clearinghouse of the Lemberg Center for the Study of Violence at Brandeis University in Waltham, Mass. said that 91 such incidents were reported in April, compared with 42 incidents for all of 1967. Among the disorders reported were black student demonstrations and boycotts in demands for educational reforms (including more emphasis on black culture studies) in high schools in White Plains, N.Y. (April and May), Camden, N.J. (May 9), Newark, N.J. (May 13-20), Yonkers, N.Y. (May 17), and Pittsburgh, Pa. (May 31-June 8). Fighting between white and black students was reported in Westbury, N.Y. and Newark, N.J. 1,200 Negro high school students in Cincinnati, O. demonstrated Apr. 30 in protest against the transfer of 4 black seniors to a center for problem youth.

2 pupils required hospital treatment after scuffles between white and black students Sept. 20 and 23 at Bladensburg High School in Washington, D.C. Continued racial tension led to 40% absenteeism at the school Sept. 25. Clashes between white and black students also disrupted high schools in Linden, N.J. (Sept. 20), Denver (Sept. 25), Waterbury, Conn. (Sept. 26) and Grand Rapids, Mich. (Dec. 16-17). Officials temporarily closed high schools after interracial incidents in Summit, Ill. (Sept. 10), Teaneck, N.J. (Sept. 18), Trenton, N.J. (Sept. 26), Lancaster, Pa. (Oct. 30), Syracuse, N.Y. (Oct. 28 and Dec. 2) and Hillsborough, N.C. (Nov. 1).

Among developments in various areas:

Alcorn A & M—At predominantly black Alcorn Agricultural & Mechanical College in Lorman, Miss., state troopers fired tear gas late Feb. 20 into a group of 200 student demonstrators. The demonstrators were protesting the dismissal of 3 students who had passed out campaign literature for Congressional candidate Charles Evers. Alcorn Pres. J. D. Boyd said the students had been dismissed after they cursed him when he accused them of being drunk.

The troopers said they had fired when snipers opened fire and students refused to return to their quarters. The students said there was no reason for calling the state troopers.

The state patrol said sniper fire was heard from 2 dormitories, but students denied hearing shots. A 2d flare-up occurred shortly before dawn Feb. 21 when students threw bottles and bricks at the state troopers, who claimed to be pinned down by sniper fire. 6 persons were injured; 3 were hospitalized. There were no arrests.

Berkeley—Disputes over a course given by Black Panther Information Min. Eldridge Cleaver led to rock-throwing demonstrations and 2 sit-ins on the Berkeley campus of the University of California Oct. 23; about 200 students were arrested Oct. 23–24. Plans for a 3d sit-in failed Oct. 25 due to lack of support. Protesting students demanded full academic credit for Cleaver's course, Social Analysis 139X, which had been limited to a noncredit status by the California Board of Regents. (The board voted Sept. 20 that guest appearances were limited to one per quarter in a course given for credit; Cleaver's course was to include 10 lectures.) The university had provided classroom facilities for the noncredit course. The board Oct. 18 rejected a resolution, submitted by Gov. Ronald Reagan, that "no university facilities shall be used for a program of instruction following the substance of Social Analysis whether for credit or not in which Mr. Cleaver appears more than once as a lecturer."

Bluefield—In the wake of racial disturbances at Bluefield State College, the West Virginia State Board of Education voted Nov. 26 to close the dormitories and reopen the school Dec. 2 as a commuter college. Policemen had patrolled the campus Nov. 16 following rock-throwing attacks on the student union building and the president's home; the school had been closed indefinitely Nov. 22 after a bomb had damaged the physical education building. Black students had submitted demands that included: more cultural events on campus; resignation of the president, academic dean and other administrators; longer library hours; black history and culture courses; additional financial aid for black students. (About 450 of the school's 1,400 students were black.)

Boston—A school decentralization dispute led to a boycott of the Christopher Gibson School in a predominantly black neighborhood in Boston's Dorchester area. Police Sept. 5 had refused entry to Benjamin F. Scott, a principal selected by a neighborhood action group, and community members then led some 150 primary grade students out of the school to attend "liberation" classes at the nearby Robert Gould Shaw Neighborhood House. Only 30 pupils out of an enrollment of 550 showed up at the Gibson school for classes Sept. 6. Some 100 others went again to the Shaw House, where classes were held under the auspices of the Committee of Concerned Citizens for the Gibson School.

Helmeted policemen and black youths scuffled Sept. 25–28 in the streets of Boston's Roxbury section. The violence followed a "black power" rally that grew out of demonstrations by high school students who demanded the right to wear African dress to classes and to organize black student unions. Negroes looted several stores after the rally Dec. 25 and pelted policemen from rooftops with rocks, cans and pieces of asphalt. City Council member Thomas I. Atkins, a Negro, said Sept. 28 that the dispute "went into the streets because the school system was too rigid to respond" to student unrest. Mayor Kevin H. White Sept. 26 announced the formation of a biracial committee to study tensions in the school system and school decentralization proposals.

Roxbury's Martin Luther King Jr. middle school was closed indefinitely Dec. 5 after student rioting in which a black teacher, Emery Miller, was attacked by black pupils. This was the 3d time since September that the school had been closed because of student disorders. The school had been the center of a conflict between the black community and the predominantly white school department. The Dec. 5 outbreak bollowed the appointment of a white principal, John J. Bradley, to replace John A. Joyce, a Negro, who had resigned because he could not control disorders at the school.

Boston University—About 300 black students barricaded themselves inside Boston University's Administration Building for more than 12 hours Apr. 24. The students, members of an Afro-American group, demanded the admission of more black students, financial aid for black students, the employment of more black faculty members and courses in black history. They also demanded that the university name the building housing the School of Theology in memory of the Rev. Dr. Martin Luther King Jr.

Bowie—About 300 of the 500 students at predominantly black Bowie State College in Bowie, Md. boycotted classes Mar. 27–29 in a demand for better housing, educational facilities and teachers and for courses in black history. Students seized the administration building late Mar. 29 and closed off the campus. But after Gov. Spiro T. Agnew Mar. 30 refused the student demand for a meeting with him until they relinquished control of the campus, they vacated the building. About 225 Bowie students were arrested in Annapolis Apr. 4 when they refused to leave the State House after a sit-in there in a demand for a meeting with Agnew.

Brown & Pembroke—Almost all of the Negroes at Brown University and its women's affiliate, Pembroke College, in Providence, R.I. boycotted classes Dec. 6–9 in a dispute with the school over black enrollment and recruitment. The Negroes demanded 11% black enrollment as a "minimum goal." (Current black enrollment: about 2%.) The boycott ended after the university announced a plan for a 3-year $1.1 million "intensive program for development of the black students" and a programmed increase in the number of Negroes admitted in each school.

Cheyney—400 of the 1,800 students at predominantly black Cheyney State College in Cheyney, Pa. occupied the campus administration building May 6–8 in a demand for improved curriculum, better teaching and investigation of administration handling of student money. The vice president of the board of directors announced May 10 that Dr. Leroy Banks Allen, president of the college, had submitted his resignation. Cheyney had been closed Mar. 22–24 after 100 state troopers were called in to quell 300 students who were protesting the expulsion of an undergraduate for disciplinary reasons.

Chicago—Harrison High School in Chicago was closed Oct. 9 after scattered fires were reported and black students walked out of classes for the 3d day. Students in several Chicago high schools had been demonstrating for 3 days in a demand over the teaching of Afro-American history courses and the hiring of black teachers and administrators.

Colgate—400 to 500 Colgate University students and faculty members staged a sit-in in the university's administration building in Hamilton, N.Y. Apr. 10–14 in protest against discriminatory fraternity housing practices. The demonstrators, led by the Association of Black Collegians, demanded the revocation of the charter of the Phi Delta Theta fraternity, which they contended had never admitted a Negro and had blackballed a Jewish student earlier in the year. Dr. Vincent M. Barnett Jr., Colgate president, revoked the fraternity's charter Apr. 12, and the sit-in ended Apr. 14 after the university pledged to end the discriminatory housing practices.

The faculty had voted 69–18 Apr. 8 to end selective fraternity housing on the campus, to censure Phi Delta Theta and to remove the charter of Sigma Nu. Sigma Nu, one of 15 fraternities on the 1,800-student campus, had been closed by Barnett Apr. 7 after a white student inside the fraternity house had fired blank cartridges at Robert Bony, secretary of the Association of Black Collegians. The faculty also asked that "residential facilities authorized by the university be opened to all students on an equal basis so as to abolish the practice by which current members of living units select new members."

Columbia—Normal operations at Columbia University (New York City) were virtually ended for the academic year after a group of left-wing students and a group of black students and non-students seized and occupied 5 university buildings Apr. 23–24. The seizures were in protest against the university's construction of a gymnasium in city-owned Morningside Heights Park, and in protest against the university's ties with the Institute for Defense Analyses (IDA). The demonstrators held the buildings until Apr. 30, when the university administration asked the city police to clear the buildings. The police were called in after efforts to negotiate an end to the take-over had failed. About 700 persons were arrested and 148 injured as the police ended the occupation.

The use of police on the campus provoked additional protests at the university. A general student-faculty strike was called. The focus of the new protests, uniting diverse groups, extended to questions of the structure of the university and the role of faculty and students in determining university policy.

The initial protest had involved members of the leftwing Students for a Democratic Society (SDS), members of the Students' Afro-American Society and a number of residents of Harlem, the black community adjacent to the university. At noon Apr. 23 Mark Rudd, 20, president of SDS' campus chapter, led about 150 persons to Low Memorial Library in protest against the gymnasium project and against Columbia's ties with the IDA, a 12-university research consortium. The demonstrators protested that IDA aided in the war effort in Vietnam. The gym project was denounced as racist and a symbol of Columbia's usurpation of neighborhood land without regard for neighborhood residents. (Columbia had planned 2 gyms on 2.1 acres of the 30-acre park—a $10 million gym for Columbia College undergraduates and a $1.6 million gym for the Harlem [black and Puerto Rican] community. The university had agreed to finance services and heat for the community building at a cost of $75,000 annually. The university had acquired the land from the city in Aug. 1961.)

Barred from Low Library by guards, the demonstrators marched to the site of the new gym and tore down a section of fence. They then marched to Hamilton Hall, headquarters of Columbia College, the men's undergraduate school. There they held Acting Dean Henry S. Coleman and 2 other officials as prisoners for more than 24 hours. On the orders of the black students, the white students, led by Mark Rudd, left Hamilton Hall at 5 a.m. Apr. 24 and marched to Low Library, where they occupied and ransacked the office of Dr. Grayson Kirk, president of the university.

The Negroes in Hamilton Hall released Coleman Apr. 24, but the demonstrators refused to meet with officials without a guarantee of amnesty for themselves.

An emergency faculty committee met the evening of Apr. 24 and recommended that the university halt the construction of the gym but continue its affiliation with IDA. The committee voted against amnesty and recommended that a tripartite committee (students, faculty members and administrators) be set up to determine discipline for the demonstrators.

At a news conference Apr. 25 Dr. Kirk rejected the student demand for amnesty.

2 more buildings were seized Apr. 25, when about 100 white students took Fayerweather Hall, a social science building, and about 100 white students seized Avery Hall, the architecture building.

Early Apr. 26 students seized a 5th building, the mathematics building. This brought the number of people in 5 seized buildings to about 700.

All classes were canceled Apr. 26, and the campus was sealed off after about 250 black high school students, shouting "black power" invaded the campus in support of the black demonstrators.

The university administration announced Apr. 26 that it had suspended work on the gym (in response to a request from the mayor).

H. Rap Brown, chairman of the Student Nonviolent Coordinating Committee (SNCC), and ex-SNCC Chrmn. Stokely Carmichael met with students in Hamilton Hall at 1 p.m. Apr. 26. Brown then said that the demonstrators were "fighting against the racist policies" of Columbia. As for the gym, he said: "If they build it up, people in Harlem should blow it up."

The university's board of trustees, in a statement issued Apr.

27 by board chairman William E. Peterson, denounced the "small minority" of students who had seized the buildings and praised the "overwhelming majority" of students for their restraint. The statement said the trustees had advised Kirk "that they wholeheartedly support the administration position that there shall be no amnesty accorded to those who have engaged in this illegal conduct." Peterson declared: The trustees "not only support the president's stand, but affirmatively direct that he shall maintain the ultimate disciplinary power over the conduct of students of the university." He said the trustees would support the administration's temporary suspension of work on the gym.

University faculty members of professorial rank voted 466–40 Apr. 28 to condemn the violence and student occupation of buildings. They called for the establishment of a tripartite committee to work out a "fair disposition of the disciplinary problems arising from the current disruption." An *ad hoc* faculty group Apr. 28 issued a statement urging Mayor John V. Lindsay to meet with representatives of the trustees, the community and the faculty to "adopt an alternative" to the gym. The statement also urged (a) the creation of a tripartite commission with "ultimate judicial review on all matters affecting university discipline," (b) the revision of university statutes dealing with disciplinary matters, (c) the adoption of a "new approach of collective responsibility," (d) the application of "uniform penalties to all violators of university rules" and (e) suspension of work at the gym site and the evacuation of the occupied buildings.

Kirk Apr. 29 proposed a peace plan that, he said, embodied the "essential spirit" of the *ad hoc* faculty group proposals.

The university administration finally requested the night of Apr. 29–30 that the police end the seizure of the buildings. In response to this request, 1,000 city policemen, armed with nightsticks, moved onto the campus at 2:20 a.m. Apr. 30 and cleared the occupied buildings. 132 students, 4 faculty members and 12 policemen were reported injured in the forcible removal of the white students, but the 85 black students in Hamilton Hall were removed without incident. Dr. Kenneth Clark, City College psychology professor, later praised police control at Hamilton Hall as "an extraordinary professional job."

According to a report prepared by the university and released May 8 by Dr. George W. Fraenkel, dean of the graduate faculties, 707 persons had been arrested in the police raid. The report said that 524 of the persons arrested were registered university students, 181 were "not identified as Columbia students," and 2 were faculty members. 239 of those arrested were students at Columbia College and represented 8.79% of the college's total enrollment. 111 Barnard College students were arrested; they represented 6.01% of the undergraduate girls' college total enrollment.

A student strike was announced at 7:15 a.m. Apr. 30 by J. Michael Nichols, vice president of the Student Council. Nichols said the strike had been indorsed by the presidents of the undergraduate Student Council, the Graduate Student Council and the General Studies Student Council. He called for the resignation of Kirk and demanded "the names of those who approved of this [police] brutality and violence."

Kirk announced May 8 that "important actions" had been taken to meet the strikers' demands and to "provide a basis for assurance about Columbia's immediate and long-run future." He cited a general consensus on the need to reexamine the structure of the university. He said the trustees had agreed to withhold a decision on the gym pending "full consultation and negotiation with community and city representatives."

Kirk announced his retirement Aug. 23. He was succeeded by Andrew W. Cordier, 67, dean of the university's School of International Affairs, who was to serve as acting president.

Cordier Nov. 7 announced the appointment of I. M. Pei to head the university's planning and expansion programs. Cordier asserted at a news conference: "There will be consultation—a great deal of consultation—with the people of the neighborhood."

The City Board of Estimate Aug. 16 had unanimously approved a $25 million apartment project in the Columbia University area. The project, involving 7 sites in the Morningside Heights section, was backed by the city's Housing & Development Administration. Local black and Puerto Rican tenant associations had opposed the project.

The university's Teachers College Nov. 26 announced a $60 million plan for campus expansion. The proposed project would include housing for poorer residents of the community as well as for graduate students and faculty members. In announcing the project, Teachers College Pres. John H. Fischer said: "So far as we know . . . we are the first academic institution to provide housing for the public on its own campus."

Cornell—About 60 of the 150 black students at Cornell University seized the Economics Department office Apr. 4 and held the department chairman captive for 6 hours in protest against alleged racist remarks of another professor, the Rev. Michael McPhelin, a Jesuit priest. An investigation commission reported May 1 that "if individual 'blame' is to be assigned, many must bear its burdens, including faculty and administration as well as students." It recommended against severe punishment for the demonstrators.

Howard University—Several thousand Howard University students in Washington participated in a sit-in demonstration in the campus' administration building Mar. 19–23 and forced the halting of all school operations. The demonstration was triggered by threatened disciplinary action against 39 students, but it extended also to such issues as student control over school affairs and curriculum and criticism of the alleged "Uncle Tom" attitude of the administration. The demonstration was ended by agreement on a compromise plan offered by "liberals" among the university's trustees. (Howard, a private, predominantly black university, had 8,600 students and received more than half of its funds from the federal government.)

The sit-in started late Mar. 19 when 500 to 1,000 students took control of the administration building after the administration refused to drop charges against 39 students who had disrupted the Charter Day ceremony Mar. 1. The students had swarmed onto the stage at the end of the program when the school's president, Dr. James M. Nabrit Jr., failed to announce promised changes in the university's disciplinary and academic procedures. After the 39 students received disciplinary summonses under the terms of the old rules Mar. 18–19, a list of demands was issued to administration officials. The demands included: the dismissal of charges; the resignation of Nabrit; "faculty control over academic affairs and student control over student affairs"; establishment of a "black awareness institute"; creation of a new disciplinary code; amnesty for protesters. Student Council Pres. Ewart Brown explained Mar. 21: "We want Howard University to relate to the black community the way Harvard and MIT relate to the white community."

University officials warned the students Mar. 22 to evacuate the building by Mar. 25 or face possible arrest.

After holding a series of meetings with representatives of the board of trustees, including Dr. Kenneth C. Clark, black psychology professor at City College in New York, the students Mar. 23 accepted a compromise settlement and ended the demonstration.

Under the agreement: the university would resume normal operations and the administration promised to "enter into immediate meetings with students and faculty in order to establish a judicial tribunal, in which students would have the major responsibility to hear and determine the charges lodged against the 39 students recently charged with misconduct"; demonstrators would be granted amnesty.

Anthony Gittens, a demonstration leader, said after the compromise was accepted: "If we didn't believe Howard University was on its way to becoming a black university, we wouldn't have come out of those doors."

Illinois—About 250 black students were arrested in Urbana Sept. 10 following a 2-day sit-in in the University of Illinois Student Union. The youths, most of them students in the university's Project 500 for the educationally disadvantaged, were protesting "discrimination" in campus housing and "bad faith" by the university in providing financial aid. Approximately $5,000 in damage was done to the Student Union during the demonstration. 213 black freshmen involved in the sit-in were given "reprimands of record" Dec. 12 by the university's Committee on Student Discipline; the reprimands were not to be included in the students' official transcripts. None of the 213 students were dismissed from the university.

Joliet—A 10-day-old boycott of classes by black students in Joliet, Ill. was supported Oct. 27 by black community leaders, who called for a one-day general strike of all Negroes living in the area. The Action Committee urged Negroes to stay home from work in protest against "school discrimination and police brutality."

New Haven—Black and white students clashed for more than 30 minutes at Hillhouse High School in New Haven, Conn. Feb. 5 and about 20 minutes at Lee High School Feb. 6. 5 students at Lee High were arrested, and several others suffered minor injuries. New Haven Mayor Richard C. Lee Feb. 6 ordered "police patrols on a saturation basis" at the schools to prevent further outbreaks. About ½ of Lee High's 1,500 students (⅓ black) and ⅓ of the 1,800 students (50% black) at Hillhouse stayed home Feb. 7, and about 150 black students staged a walk-out from classes at Hillhouse at noon.

Northwestern—More than 100 black students seized the Finance Building at Northwestern University (total enrollment: 8,875) in Evanston, Ill. May 3. They surrendered the building May 4 after the administration granted many of their demands.

The demonstration was sponsored by the Afro-American Student Union and a black student group called For Members Only (FMO). Demonstrators issued a list of demands that included a university policy statement "deploring the viciousness of white racism"; more scholarships for Negroes and an increase in the number of black students; separate living quarters for black students by the fall; courses in black history, literature and art; black counselors provided by the university "to help us cope properly with the psychological, mental, and academic tensions resulting from dualism of our existence as black college students." About 15 white students seized the office of the dean of students in another building May 3 in sympathy with the black students. The Negroes ended their 36-hour sit-in May 4 after the administration agreed to most of their demands. The university said: It "recognizes that throughout its history it has been a university of white establishment—not to gainsay that many members of its administration, faculty or student body have engaged themselves in activities directed to the righting of racial wrongs. . . . This university with other institutions must share responsibility for the continuance over many years of these racist attitudes."

Ohio State—About 150 students—half of them black—seized the administration building at Ohio State University in Columbus Apr. 26 and held 2 vice presidents and 4 staff members for several hours. The demonstration was ended after the university president, Novice G. Fawcetts, announced that the school would establish an office of black student affairs.

Oshkosh—The Wisconsin State University board of regents Dec. 20 expelled 90 black students for their part in ransacking the administration building and occupying the president's office at Oshkosh State University Nov. 21. (The expelled students were among 94 suspended after the Nov. 21 outbreak.) About 100 students, almost the entire black enrollment, had been arrested following the melee, which followed university Pres. Roger Guiles' refusal to meet black demands for a black student union and more Afro-American courses. During a meeting of the regents in Madison Dec. 6, about 200 students had forced their way into the meeting room and demanded the reinstatement of the suspended students.

Philadelphia—After 9 days of clashes between white and black students in 7 Philadelphia high schools, Mayor James H. Tate denounced the Board of Education Oct. 16 as "inept" and promised to end the confrontations, which had temporarily closed several of

the schools.   An emergency "hot line" phone system was established so that Philadelphia high school principals could communi-
cate with one another in case of trouble.

San Fernando Valley—In a 3-hour demonstration Nov. 4, 300
students at San Fernando Valley State College occupied 2 floors of
the administration building and held captive Acting Pres. Paul
Blomgren and about 35 other persons.   The seizure ended after
Blomgren agreed to "amnesty" for the demonstrators.   The students, members and supporters of the Black Student Union and
Students for a Democratic Society, were protesting alleged racial
discrimination in campus athletics and pending reductions in the
Federal Educational Opportunities Program.   Dr. Blomgren Nov. 5
canceled the amnesty, which he called "null and void" because it
had been signed "under duress" and to insure the safety of personnel
being "held hostage."   "I cannot permit 100 or even 200 to dictate
to 18,400 students what will be done and how," he said.   A Los
Angeles County grand jury Dec. 20 indicted 28 students on charges
ranging from kidnap to assault in connection with the Nov 4
demonstration.

(Blomgren's office was destroyed Dec. 8 in a fire that caused
damage estimated at $100,000.   Officials reported evidence of
arson.)

San Francisco State—Acting Pres. S. I. Hayakawa closed San
Francisco State College for the Christmas holidays Dec. 13, one
week earlier than scheduled, after 2 weeks of violent campus disturbances involving up to 3,000 students and 600 policemen.

Hayakawa, 62, who had become acting president Nov. 26, had
taken a hard line towards student agitators and had brought police
on campus to quell the uprisings and keep classes open.   The college had been in constant turmoil since Nov. 6, when dissident students, led by the Black Student Union (BSU) and supported by
the 3d-World Liberation Front (non-black minority groups) and
Students for a Democratic Society (SDS), called for a student
strike.   The students had announced 15 demands, among them the
reinstatement of a suspended black instructor, George Mason Murray, the establishment of a virtually autonomous department of
black studies and the admission of any black student who applied,
regardless of his qualifications.

In advancing the Christmas recess, Hayakawa noted his concern
for the "safety and welfare of the young people who might be attracted to our campus. . . ."   (High schools in the area officially

began their holidays Dec. 13, and the college Student Strike Committee had announced plans to involve high-school students in its demonstrations the next week.) Hayakawa also cited the need for time to plan a new black studies program scheduled to begin in the spring semester. In addition, Local 1352 of the American Federation of Teachers had planned to start a strike Dec. 16. The union had predicted that its 200 faculty members at the college would be joined by an additional 100–150 of the college's 1,100 faculty members.

At a news conference Dec. 13 Hayakawa reiterated his conviction that campus order should receive primary attention. He said he refused to allow student government a role in college disciplinary courts because of the "utterly irresponsible and rebellious body of student officers who now claim to represent the student body." He added: "I will not try to come to terms with anarchists, hooligans or yahoos."

Hayakawa announced Dec. 26 that the college had received $300,000 in surplus state college funds for the spring semester; the money would be used to prevent the layoff of 120 faculty members and the cancellation of several courses. In addition, Hayakawa announced that the proposed 4-year course of studies leading to a degree in black studies would begin in Jan. 1969. (Dr. Nathan Hare, named to head the new program, had already assailed it as a "paper department" probably created in "an effort to whitewash the black demands.")

The disturbances on the 18,700-student campus had begun more than a year previously. A racially-inspired violent outbreak Dec. 6, 1967 had resulted in intense criticism of Pres. John Summerskill by trustees of the state college system for his refusal to call the police. Summerskill Feb. 22 announced his resignation (effective Sept. 1) and condemned the state administration of Gov. Ronald Reagan for failure to "give higher education the constructive leadership it requires and deserves from that quarter." In the wake of continued demonstrations, Glenn Dumke, chancellor of the California state college system, announced May 24 that Summerskill's resignation would become effective immediately. He was succeeded May 30 by Robert Smith, 52.

Smith also met the opposition of the state trustees when he refused to assign English instructor Murray to a non-teaching position. Murray, a Black Panther member and BSU leader, had allegedly urged black students to bring arms to campus; his supporters argued that he had merely urged Negroes to defend themselves. (The *Los Angeles Times* had quoted Murray as saying in an address to about 1,000 students in the college amphitheater Oct. 24: "If students want to run the college—if the administration won't go for it—then you control it with a gun." "We are all slaves. The only way to become free is to kill all slave masters." Asked whom the slave masters were, Murray replied: members of the boards of education and "the people in the Statehouse, the White House, the Pentagon, the Supreme Court and the Chase Manhattan Bank.") When Chancellor Dumke ordered Murray's suspension Oct. 31, Smith complied but suspended him with pay. The strike called Nov. 6 was in response to his suspension.

Continued disorder and violence led Smith to officially close the college Nov. 13 "until we can rationally open it"; the faculty had voted that day to suspend classes. The state trustees Nov. 18 ordered the immediate reopening of the college and stipulated that there was to be "no negotiation, arbitration or concession" to the students involved in the disturbances; the board was headed by Gov. Reagan, an ex-officio trustee of the state college system.

Citing inability to resolve the conflicts between the students, the faculty, the administration and the state trustees, Smith submitted his resignation Nov. 26 and requested reassignment to "job duties other than college administration." Hayakawa, an internationally known semanticist, was immediately named acting president.

With the support of San Francisco police, Hayakawa opened classes Dec. 2. But clashes built up during the week and climaxed Dec. 5 when police used Mace and drew guns to keep 400 demonstrators away from the administration building. 25 persons were reported arrested, one for carrying an automatic pistol. More than 85 persons were arrested in demonstrations throughout the week; about a dozen were injured.

Hayakawa fulfilled some of the students' demands in announcing Dec. 6 that: (a) a black-studies program, including 11 teaching positions, would be started immediately; (b) the 128 unused places in a newly instituted special admissions program for 426 educationally deprived students were to be filled in the spring; (c) a nonwhite director of student financial aid would be appointed to deal with nonwhite student problems. Hayakawa did not yield to the strikers' demand for amnesty for suspended students. He added that the police would remain on campus to keep order. Militant student leaders labeled his proposals unacceptable and vowed new resistance.

Clashes with police took place Dec. 9 as a rally turned into an attempt to break into a classroom building. That night, on the recommendation of faculty members, Hayakawa temporarily lifted the suspension of 44 students. Conflict continued, however, and another week of demonstrations brought on the announcement of the early Christmas recess.

Gov. Reagan Dec. 17 commended Hayakawa's strong action in handling the crisis at San Francisco State. Asserting that police would ring the campuses in California "if that's what they must do," he said that "there is no longer any room for appeasement or give." Reagan suggested the formation of "concerted plans to get rid of those professors who've made it apparent that they are far more interested in closing the school than in fulfilling their contracts to teach, and likewise, ridding the campus of those part-time students or those non-students who are the militant leaders there."

San Mateo—Violence erupted at the College of San Mateo Dec. 13 as about 150 minority-group students smashed windows, doors and TV cameras in a 20-minute rampage through the campus. More than a dozen white students were beaten by the rioters with metal pipes and tire irons. The clashes followed a rally sponsored by the 3d World Liberation Front and the New Black Generation to support their demand for an autonomous ethnic-studies division. Pres. Robert L. Ewigleben, 40, ordered the school opened for classes Dec. 16 "as an armed camp with riot police on campus to maintain order." More than 300 policemen guarded all buildings and admitted only authorized faculty members, students and employes to the campus.

(The College of San Mateo, in a 2-year-old program to provide college education for nonwhites, had already increased its enrollment of such students from less than 100 to about 1,000. Almost 7,000 of its students were white.)

Santa Barbara—Protesting against alleged racial discrimination, 20 members of the Black Student Union at the University of California at Santa Barbara seized a classroom building and held it for 9½ hours Oct. 14. They left after 7 of their 8 demands had been approved by Chancellor Vernon Cheadle. The demands included the hiring of more black coaches, professors and administrators; the establishment of a college of black studies and a graduate program in Afro-American studies, and establishment of a racial grievance commission.

Social Circle, Ga.—Black students held lie-in demonstrations Feb. 14–16 at the Social Circle Training School, an all-black elementary school in Social Circle, Ga. about 30 miles southeast of Atlanta. But about half of the black pupils ignored the demonstrations and continued to attend classes. (The demonstrations grew out of a January protest against "deplorable conditions" at the school. At that time 2 black teachers and one white teacher had called parents to tour the school; the county school superintendent ordered the teachers to return to their classes, they refused, and he dismissed them.)

50 of the demonstrating Negroes were dragged from the path of the school buses Feb. 14. 2 state troopers were injured and hospitalized; 2 persons were arrested. 44 demonstrators who sprawled on the ground in the path of the school buses Feb. 15 were arrested. Buses bypassed the demonstrators Feb. 16 by an alternative route. The Southern Christian Leadership Conference (SCLC) Feb. 19 announced a moratorium on the lie-in demonstrations. The SCLC said, however, that it still demanded the reinstatement of the 3 dismissed teachers, the dismissal of school principal Clyde Carr, relief of overcrowding in buses, the hiring of more substitute teachers and improvement of sanitation and food in the school.

72 Negroes, more than half of them juveniles, were arrested in Social Circle, Ga. Mar. 26 during a demonstration against "deplorable" conditions at the school.

Swanquarter—In Swanquarter, N.C., a town of 400 residents in Hyde County, black high school students demonstrated daily beginning Nov. 8 in protest against a county school integration plan that had been reluctantly approved by the U.S. Health, Education & Welfare Department. Some 800 of the 850 black students in the county had boycotted classes since Sept. 10, when school opened. Led by Golden Fricks, a coordinator for the Southern Christian Leadership Conference, the protesters objected to a plan for the eventual closing of the county's 2 all-black schools, Peay and Davis, and the busing of the children to Matamuskeet, the previously all-white county school. They demanded that all 3 schools be integrated. The children protested by carrying squawking white chickens (to symbolize the white school board) and blocking traffic in demonstrations that resulted in almost 80 arrests in 4 days. National interest was attracted by an incident Nov. 11 when Mamie Harris, 17, was injured when she leaped from a 2d-story window to escape smoke grenades that police had hurled into the Hyde County courthouse to clear a room of demonstrators. The demonstrations had begun after county officials announced that families whose children were boycotting classes would not receive welfare payments beginning Dec. 1. All 3 schools in the county were closed Dec. 5 after black youths tore up the principal's office at one of the all-black schools and bomb threats were received at the 2 other county schools.

Trinity—200 Trinity College students in Hartford, Conn. occupied the school's administration building Apr. 22–24 in a demand that the trustees approve a $150,000 scholarship program for Negroes. The demonstration was led by the new Trinity Association of Negroes, which included nearly all of the school's 20 nonwhite students. (The total enrollment was 1,160 students.) The demonstrators also called for courses in black history, "the psychology of the ghetto" and community development. At the start of the demonstration Apr. 22 the students held Trinity Pres. Albert C. Jacobs and 6 other trustees captive in the building for more than 3 hours. The demonstration ended Apr. 24 when the trustees pledged $15,000, to be matched by student fund raising, and promised to "go as far beyond that as the budget of the college will allow" for new scholarships. Dr. Jacobs also promised that "Trinity will admit as many qualified Negro students as are available and will provide adequate financial aid for them."

Tuskegee—About 250 black students at Tuskegee Institute in Tuskegee, Ala. held 12 of the school's trustees captive in the college guest house for 12–13 hours Apr. 7 in protest against the trustees' refusal to grant student demands for reform. After a confrontation with Sheriff Lucius Amerson, a Negro, who threatened to bring in the National Guard, the students released their captives. The trustees included retired Gen. Lucius Clay, Rep. Frances Bolton (R., O.), Tuskegee Institute Pres. Luther H. Foster and National Foundation Pres. Basil O'Connor. Students had boycotted classes Mar. 25–26 to demonstrate grievances against the administration. They called for the abolition of the compulsory Reserve Officers Training Corps program, the awarding of athletic scholarship grants, changes in the campus curfew regulations and improvements in housing and dining-hall conditions.

Tuskegee Pres. Foster announced Apr. 12 that the school was abolishing the compulsory military training program and would offer athletic scholarships.   Students would be charged a special fee of $10 to help meet the costs of the financial aid program.

After a 2-week shut-down ordered by the trustees as a result of the student demonstrations, classes were resumed at Tuskegee Apr. 22.

Worth County, Ga.—All 5 black schools in Worth County, Ga. were closed Dec. 12 following boycotts that were, in part, a response by the black community to the week-long detention of 2 black school children.   The sisters Yvonne Denice Young, 11, and Dorothy Bell Young, 14, had been among a handful of black children who had voluntarily entered the county's all-white schools.   On a formal charge of "delinquency," the sisters had been removed from their school Dec. 4 and placed in a juvenile detention center 20 miles away.   For 24 hours Leroy and Ida Mae Young could not learn where their daughters were, and for 4 days they were prevented from seeing them.   The girls were finally released Dec. 10. (The Youngs had been active in a local desegregation drive.)

The sisters had been arrested on charges of using obscene and profane language, refusing to obey the orders of a school bus driver and attacking a child in the bus.   Yvonne told newsmen Dec. 13 that she had fought with a white boy after he had kicked her younger brother.   Dorothy acknowledged using obscene language in response to a white youth who had called her a "nigger."

11 Killed in Cleveland Riots

A small band of armed black nationalists fought Cleveland police with rifles in the city's Glenville ghetto district the night of July 23–24.   This was the first reported case in which black extremists had carried out threats to mount an attack in a major city.

7 persons were killed in the first wave of shooting between the group of nationalists and police.   3 of them were nationalists, 3 were white policemen, and one was a Negro who had attempted to aid the police.   3 more black victims were killed in other Cleveland shooting incidents the same night; an 11th person, also a black, was slain by a sniper in suburban Cleveland Heights July 26.   23 persons were wounded, more than 15 of them in the initial gunfight.

The shooting led to an explosion of racial tension in which burning and lootings caused an estimated $1½ million of property damage.   Although 3,100 National Guardsmen were sent to Cleveland, the relatively rapid restoration of order was widely credited to the efforts of the city's Negro mayor, Carl B. Stokes.

The initial attack was attributed to a small militant group called the Black Nationalists of New Libya, led by Ahmed (Fred) Evans, 37, an astrologer and currently the head of an antipoverty project in the Glenville area. Evans surrendered to police late July 23, reportedly after his carbine had jammed during the fight. (He was arraigned July 26 on 3 charges of first-degree murder in the deaths of 3 policemen slain in the Glenville gunfight.) Although police said they had received prior warnings that coordinated extremist attacks would occur in Cleveland, Detroit, Chicago and Pittsburgh July 24, the 3 other cities remained calm. It was reported July 28 that Evans had instigated the attack after being informed that he was being evicted from his home and that his antipoverty project would not be permitted to move into premises promised to it.

Although reports conflicted as to exactly how the shooting began, press and news magazine accounts specified that the first shots were fired by a group of Evans' followers. According to a police summary of the events, issued July 31, a group of armed nationalists fired on police in a squad car outside Evans' headquarters. The police, who had been keeping the headquarters under surveillance, radioed for reinforcements and fled. A municipal tow truck attempting to remove an abandoned car from the section was then fired on, and the driver was wounded.

The police reinforcements, armed with semi-automatic weapons, arrived in the area and began returning the fire of the extremists. The black group, said to number 7 men, occupied several Glenville buildings. The 3 policemen, the Negro aiding them and one nationalist were killed in the early part of the gunfight. The bodies of 2 more extremists were found later in the ruins of one of the buildings; they had been killed by police bullets before the building was set afire and burned to the ground.

Acting while the Glenville gunfight was still underway and as rioting was beginning to spread to other nearby black communities, Mayor Stokes asked Ohio Gov. James A. Rhodes to send National Guardsmen to the city. Rhodes complied late July 23, and by the early morning hours of July 24 the first Guard units had entered Glenville. The gunfire and rioting had already halted, at least partially because of heavy rain that swept the city that night. 48 persons were arrested July 23–24 in connection with the violence.

Stokes conferred July 24 with Cleveland black leaders, primarily from the Hough and Glenville ghetto areas, and announced late in the day that he had accepted their requests for withdrawal of the National Guardsmen and white police from the ghetto districts. The sections were cordoned off, and responsibility for the maintenance of order was entrusted to the city's 125-odd black policemen and to hastily-organized black citizens' patrols. The Rev. de Forest Brown, president of the Hough Development Corp. and spokesman for the black leaders, said July 24 that "we . . . have accepted the responsibility to restore law and order out of a chaotic situation."

National Guardsmen were sent back into the black sections July 25 after scattered violence and looting had begun again late in the day. Announcing the measure in a televised message to the city, Stokes said that the 24-hour withdrawal of the troops had helped to restore calm, that the black volunteers had done their work "admirably" but that the renewed violence required the return of the troops. Stokes, who previously had closed all bars and liquor stores in the area, ordered a 9 p.m.-to-6 a.m. curfew in the section and appealed to all residents to obey police and Guardsmen.

Few incidents and only a very few arrests were reported to have occurred July 26–27, and the 400 National Guardsmen actually sent to the black districts were withdrawn and returned to their armories July 27. With the restoration of calm, Stokes lifted the curfew and ordered the resumption of routine police protection in the area.

Commenting on the Cleveland violence July 27, Stokes was reported by *Time* magazine to have said: The Glenville outbreak was "uniquely different from any other city in the country. The others were a spontaneous reaction to an unresponsive environment. But this was a small group of determined men who planned an attack on the police." (Phil Hutchings, a newly-named program director of the Student Nonviolent Coordinating Committee, said at a New York press conference July 27 that the Cleveland eruption was "the first stage of a revolutionary armed struggle.")

A report released by Stokes Aug. 9 said there was no "tangible" proof that the policemen murdered by snipers July 23 had been lured into a trap. Stokes said that the trouble had started as the result of a "spontaneous action" and that there was no evidence to connect the shootings with recent sniping incidents in other cities.

5 black nationalists were indicted by a Cuyahoga (county) grand jury Aug. 26 on charges of first degree murder in the July 23 shooting of 3 policemen and a civilian. Those indicted were Fred

Evans, Lathan Donald, 20, Alfred Thomas, 18, Leslie Jackson, 16, and John Hardrick Jr., 17.

3 Die in Miami Violence

While speakers at the Republican National Convention in Miami Beach, Fla. were decrying violence and lawlessness in the nation's cities, racial tensions exploded in Liberty City, a Negro section of northwest Miami several miles from Convention Hall. The disorders grew into 2 days of looting, fire bombing and shooting in which 3 persons were killed and scores injured. Gov. Claude Kirk called in the National Guard Aug. 8.

The violence erupted at a black "vote power" rally the evening of Aug. 7 when a white newsman refused to show his credentials. 52 persons were arrested that night, and an 8-square-block area of Liberty City was cordoned off by police. Mayor Steve Clark of Miami toured the area appealing for calm, as did Kirk and the Rev. Ralph D. Abernathy, who had brought the late Martin Luther King's "Poor People's Campaign" to Miami Beach Aug. 6 to make its protest visible at the Presidential-nomination convention. Kirk and Abernathy left the convention to go to the scene of the unrest. Abernathy broadcast a TV appeal to Miami's citizens to stay off the streets and help restore order. "Let us move now in constructive channels to put an end to this violence," Abernathy said. The acting Miami police chief, Lt. Col. Paul Denham, reported that calm had returned to the troubled area by 10 p.m., 4 hours after the rioting began.

More serious violence broke out the afternoon of Aug. 8 when Negro crowds battled police at the site of a meeting that both Kirk and Abernathy had promised to address. Neither appeared. As the rioting continued, 1,000 armed National Guard troops were sent to the area, and the Florida Highway Patrol riot wagon, an armored truck that spewed tear gas, went into action. Motorists driving home from work were dragged from their cars and beaten. Several liquor and grocery stores were looted, and fires were set. A curfew was imposed over a 250-block area. Kirk warned that "whatever force is needed" would be used to quell the violence. But by 4 p.m., Sheriff E. Wilson Purdy reported that the situation was "under firm control," although Guardsmen and police continued to patrol the streets.

During the course of the Aug. 8 rioting, 3 Negroes were killed in gun battles with the police. The dead were J. J. Austin, 28, thought by police to have been a sniper, Moses Cannon, 27, and Ejester B. Cleveland, 45, a passerby who had been caught in the cross-fire.

At one point the disorders spread to within a mile of the Miami Beach convention area. Dade County Mayor Chuck Hall accused "people from out of town" of instigating the trouble. "It is no accident," he said, "that the first race riot in recent Miami history broke out during the Republican National Convention, when the city was swarming with newspaper, wire-service and television reporters."

City and county officials agreed Aug. 10 to release without bond about 250 of those arrested during the riots; the officials also sent medical teams into black areas to treat persons suffering from the effects of tear gas. In return, black leaders in Miami promised to work to cool the tempers of Negroes angered at the police force's alleged brutality in quelling the violence. The 8 p.m.-to-6 a.m. curfew remained in effect through Aug. 11, but National Guard patrols were reduced.

(Miami had an estimated 200,000 black residents in a population of 1.2 million. The unemployment rate in the city's black areas was about 10%, and 4 out of 5 of the unemployed were aged 16–22. More than 50% of the employed ghetto residents were in low-skill, low-salaried jobs. Miami business leaders had pledged 2,000 summer jobs for black youths but had provided only 500. Several junior high and high schools in the area were reported to be integrated, but the majority of black students attended all-black or predominantly-black ghetto schools. An Urban League housing specialist, Clifford A. Strauss, called Miami "the most racially segregated city in the country no matter how much money you have to spend.")

Violence in Other Communities

Among racial developments that took place throughout the U.S. during 1968:

Akron—More than 100 persons were arrested by police and National Guardsmen during 2 days of rioting in Akron, O. July 17–18. Mayor John Ballard declared a state of emergency and imposed a dusk-to-dawn curfew July 18 after fire bombs and looting disrupted the city's major black section in Southwest Akron. At one point a crowd of up to 100 Negroes charged a group of National Guardsmen and threw chairs and bottles before they were repelled by tear gas. After a stricter curfew had been imposed and more National Guard patrols had been added, relative calm was reported in the city July 22.

Berea—A Negro, George Boggs, 32, and a white man, Elza Rucker, 30, were killed in a clash originating at an outdoor meeting of the National States' Rights Party in Berea, Ky. Sept. 1. Authorities said that 3 carloads of blacks had fired shots into the rightist gathering and that the whites then chased them and fired back from their cars. 5 other persons were reported injured as some 40 shots were exchanged. 8 whites and 6 Negroes were arraigned on charges Sept. 2 as a result of the gun fight.

Boston—3 Negroes were shot to death and 2 others wounded Nov. 13 when 5 other blacks invaded the headquarters of the New England Grass Roots Organization (NEGRO), a ghetto self-help association, and opened fire in the Roxbury District of Boston. The *Boston Globe* reported Dec. 8 that 3 arrested suspects and 2 of the victims were involved in a consortium of black organizations that had received a $1,969,425 Labor Department contract for job training.

Those slain were: Guido St. Laurent, 38, the blind founder of NEGRO; Carnell S. Eaton, 33, salaried director of the Roxbury-Dorchester-South End-Greater Boston Consortium (NEGRO was a member of the consortium), which had received the $1,969,425 contract in July (2 weeks before his death Eaton had been promoted to national sales director for Woolman Systems, Inc. of New York —Woolman Systems had contracted under the federal program to employ the consortium's training staff); and Harold King, 50, chairman of a Cleveland job training consortium advised by Woolman Systems.

A Suffolk County Grand Jury Dec. 3 indicted Alvin Campbell, 35, his brother Arnold, 33, and Dennis Chandler, 29, for the murders. All were consortium employes hired by Eaton, and Alvin Campbell had become director when Eaton was promoted by Woolman Systems.

(The *Boston Globe* reported Dec. 29 that the Labor Department had canceled the $1,969,425 contract. The FBI had been investigating the program for possible fraud. The *Globe* reported that only 12 trainees had been hired by the consortium and that no federal funds had been spent through the program. All salary and other expenses had been borne by Woolman Systems.)

Brooklyn—4 policemen were wounded in 2 sniping incidents near the same street corner in the Crown Heights section of Brooklyn (New York City) in August and September. Patrolmen Thomas Dockery, 31, and Leonard Fleck, 28, were wounded by shotgun blasts Aug. 2 as they left their car to answer a false call for help. Sgt. Peter Kunik and Patrolman James C. Rigney were injured Sept. 12 by shots fired from the top of a 4-story apartment building when their car stopped for a red light.

Chicago suburbs—A curfew was imposed in 2 adjacent suburbs of Chicago—Harvey and Dixmoor—following a disorder Aug. 6 in which 6 policemen were injured by shotgun pellets. Cook County Undersheriff C. Bernard Carey Aug. 7 blamed the disturbance on a group of young Negroes, the Black Elephants, said to be an affiliate of the city's Blackstone Rangers. The shots were fired as about 150 policemen were restoring order after some 200 young blacks had begun stoning cars along a street dividing the 2 suburbs. The area had been tense following the fatal shooting of a black youth by a policeman several weeks earlier.

Detroit area—A state policeman and a black youth were killed and 2 policemen were wounded in the Detroit suburb of Inkster Aug. 7-8. In the opening incident, a passing motorist and 2 policemen in a patrol car, one black and one white, were shot and slightly wounded by snipers Aug. 7. Detective Robert R. Gonser, 34, investigating in the area in an unmarked car early Aug. 8, was killed by a shot fired by an occupant of another car. James E. Matthers, 16, was killed, reportedly by police, when he ran during questioning after Gonser's death.

Louisville—2 Negroes were killed May 30 in violence that swept Louisville, Ky. May 27-39. Gov. Louie B. Nunn activated the National Guard to quell the disorders. More than 400 persons were arrested and at least 50 injured.

The violence began May 27 when policemen tried to disperse a street-corner rally in protest against the reinstatement of a policeman accused of using excessive force in the arrest of a Negro. According to an eyewitness, youths started throwing rocks and bottles at police. Sporadic sniper fire was also reported; police denied returning the shots. Gangs of black youths then roved the business district, smashing windows and looting stores and restaurants. About 800 people were reported involved.

375 National Guardsmen were ordered to the scene May 27 in response to a request by Mayor Kenneth Schmied, who imposed an

8 p.m. to 5 a.m. curfew. 104 people were arrested, and 20 persons were reported injured, 4 of them by gunshots.

The violence continued May 28. National Guardsmen clashed with brick-throwers in a 20-block section of the West End, and there were several reports of sniper fire. Disturbances were also reported in a 10-block black community in the East End, where police moved in on youths making firebombs. An additional 550 troops were mobilized. Guardsmen sealed off a 6-block West End area. More than 150 persons were arrested and 15 injured.

Schmied met with some 30 black youths May 29 and agreed to remove the Guardsmen and end the curfew. At dusk however, when a crowd of more than 300 persons gathered, the police asked for aid and the National Guard returned.

2 black youths were shot to death May 30 in looting incidents as gangs roamed streets and engaged in rock-throwing battles with the police.

Los Angeles—3 Negroes were killed and about 44 persons, including 6 policemen, were injured Aug. 11-12 when a 3-hour clash between police and blacks brought to a violent close the 3d annual Watts Summer Festival in Los Angeles. A week previously 2 incidents at the beginning of the festival had left 3 Negroes killed and 6 other persons injured. The Watts festival was held to commemorate the Watts riot of Aug. 1965.

The Aug. 11-12 clash took place after an angry crowd began throwing rocks and bottles at several policemen who were arresting a black woman on a drunken driving charge late Aug. 11. Soon after police reinforcements arrived, gunfire came from the crowd of several thousand people who were leaving the festival. A police officer said that he had seen people in the crowd being hit by shots. Police Chief Thomas Reddin said Aug. 12 that "there were indications" that one of the 3 Negroes killed had been shot by police but that the other 2 were not shot by police. During the violence that followed, shops were broken into, guns were stolen and fire-bombs were thrown. 35 people were arrested.

In one of the earlier incidents, Stephen K. Bartholomew, 21, Robert Lawrence, 22, and Thomas Melvin Lewis, 18, had been killed Aug. 5 and 2 white policemen, Norman J. Roberge, 29, and Ruby Limas, 25, had been injured in a gunfight at a gas station about 8 miles northwest of Watts after the police had stopped the men for questioning. Reddin told newsmen Aug. 6 that 2 of the 3 men killed had been Black Panthers members.

The festival had been closed temporarily Aug. 6 after 4 persons in the crowd were wounded by men firing from moving cars. Police said that some shots had been returned from the crowd.

Newport News—The fatal shooting Sept. 1 of Floyd D. Price, 55, a Negro, by a white policeman, James F. Sims, sparked a riot that caused an estimated $2 million worth of damages in a predominantly black business district in Newport News, Va. According to Police Chief W. F. Peach, Price had been shot after he had fired on Sims with a gun he had taken from a patrolman who had been beaten unconscious by 15 blacks who were preventing the arrest of a woman on a drunkenness charge. About 20 minutes after the shooting, small bands of Negroes began to swarm through the streets setting off firebombs, smashing windows and looting. 200 local and state police sealed off the neighborhood at sundown Sept. 2 to prevent new violence.

Paterson—A federal grand jury in Newark Dec. 18 indicted 8 members of the Paterson, N.J. police force on charges that they had violated and conspired to violate the civil rights of Negroes. The indictment, under the 1872 Civil Rights Act, stemmed from alleged police brutality July 1-6 in suppressing racial disturbances that had followed the arrest and alleged mistreatment of a Puerto Rican man. 5 nights of rioting and fire-bombing had ended in the arrest of 88 adults and scores of juveniles.

The indictment grew out of charges that policemen had thrown tear gas into the Southern Christian Leadership Conference office while a meeting was in progress, assaulted individual Negroes and willfully damaged the property of black-owned businesses. Sgts. Peter E. LeConte, George Gsell and Abraham Hemsey and Patrolmen Angelo DeChellis, Philip Bevacqua, Joseph David Grossi, Emil Scarmazzo and Carl Gorman were named in various counts of the indictment.

A Passaic County grand jury had attributed the alleged police brutality and vandalism to "a relative handful of misguided police officers" and had returned no indictment.

Peoria—10 policemen and a reporter were wounded by gunfire in a predominantly black neighborhood in Peoria, Ill. July 30. They were shot after a rock-throwing incident involving about 50 youths escalated into an exchange of shotgun fire with police.

St. Paul—2 nights of violence began in St. Paul, Minn. Aug. 30 at a teenage dance. It resulted in 12 arrests and injuries to 52 persons, including 4 policemen wounded by gunshots. The violence started after 2 off-duty policemen had taken a gun away from a youth at the dance. They were quickly surrounded by a number of other youths who began throwing rocks, bottles and chairs at them. About 10 shots were fired, and police reinforcements dispersed the crowd with tear gas. Stores were firebombed Aug. 31, and vandalism was reported in the Summit-University section, where most of the city's 10,000 Negroes lived.

Washington—Violence flared in Washington, D.C. following incidents in which Negroes were shot by white policemen. In the wake of rising criticism of police action, city authorities took steps to remove officers involved in slayings from active duty pending investigation and to limit police use of firearms.

Following the fatal shooting of a black pedestrian by a motorcycle policeman Oct. 8, some 250 young blacks protesting the incident blocked traffic and set fires until they were dispersed by police using tear gas. Elijah Bennett, 22, the victim, had been fatally shot earlier in the day by Pvt. David Allen Roberts as the 2 men struggled after Roberts had stopped Bennett for an alleged jaywalking violation.

A willful homicide verdict was delivered against Roberts by a coroner's jury Oct. 16, but a federal grand jury cleared Roberts of the charge Nov. 13 by deciding that there were no grounds for criminal prosecution in the shooting. A grand jury Oct. 14 had also refused to indict 5 policemen involved in the fatal shooting July 14 of Theodore R. Lawson, a Negro, and 2 policemen involved in the shooting and wounding of another black, Marvin D. Vincent.

A disorder was set off Nov. 2 by the wounding of 2 black women by a white policeman, Pvt. Thomas Snow, 24. Snow had shot Mamie B. Haskins, 53, after she reportedly threatened him with a knife. Eva Loretta Walker, 18, was wounded by a stray bullet. Rumors that the women had been killed sparked a disturbance in which 3 cars were burned, several persons beaten and 13 persons arrested. At a ghetto intersection, black youths threw bricks at cars driven by whites, and 3 white men were pulled from their cars and beaten.

The Black United Front had voted July 18 to seek community control over policemen in ghetto areas. The front had said earlier, citing 7 incidents in the past year of citizens killed by police bullets in Washington, that the shooting of a district policeman would be "justifiable homicide." The National Capital Area Civil Liberties

Union Aug. 1 also called for more citizen control over police policy, and it demanded stricter discipline in police misconduct cases.

(After conferring with members of the City Council on ways to respond to ghetto unrest after shooting incidents involving police, Mayor Walter E. Washington Oct. 9 announced a new policy whereby a policeman involved in a slaying would be removed from duty pending preliminary investigation of the incident.

(After 2 shootings, one when a white policeman mistakenly shot and killed undercover black policeman Willie C. Ivery, 25, Mayor Washington Nov. 30 pleaded with the city to end "these senseless shootings." He called on the City Council to take action to curb the use of firearms. The council Nov. 21 had adopted guidelines to limit police use of guns.)

Wilmington—Gov. Charles L. Terry Jr. Sept. 4 defended his greatly-criticized decision to retain National Guard forces that had been patrolling the streets of Wilmington, Del. since they were called in Apr. 9 to quell riots following the murder of Martin Luther King. Commenting on the arrest Sept. 1 of 6 black militants and the recovery of guns and ammunition stored in their homes, Terry asserted that National Guard patrols had "stopped at least 2 riots" in the city that summer. (Terry also demanded that federal funds be withdrawn from the Wilmington Youth Emergency Action Council. Police had said that 4 of the 6 militants arrested were council workers.)

(Terry, 68, was defeated in November for a 2d term as governor. The Republican victor, Russel W. Peterson, 51, had pledged to reduce the Guard in Wilmington. But in an interview reported in the *N.Y. Times* Nov. 17, Peterson said that to pull the Guard out entirely in Jan. 1969 might risk renewed violence.)

CIVIL DISORDERS INVESTIGATED

The President's National Advisory Commission on Civil Disorders warned Feb. 29 that America "is moving toward 2 societies, one black, one white—separate and unequal." Reporting after a 7-month study of the racial disorders of the summer of 1967, the commission asserted that "this deepening racial division is not inevitable." With adequate action, it said, "the movement apart can be reversed."

The 11-member advisory commission, headed by Illinois Gov. Otto Kerner, had been appointed by Pres. Johnson July 27, 1967 to answer 3 basic questions about the summer riots: "What happened?" "Why did it happen?" and "What can be done to prevent it from happening again?" In addition to Kerner, the members of the commission were: New York Mayor John V. Lindsay (R.), vice chairman of the commission; Sen. Fred Harris (D., Okla.); Roy Wilkins, executive director of the NAACP; Sen. Edward W. Brooke (R., Mass.); Herbert Jenkins, Atlanta police chief; Rep. James C. Corman (D., Calif.); Rep William M. McCulloch (R., O.); I. W. Abel, president of the United Steelworkers of America; Charles B. Thornton, president of Litton Industries; Mrs. Katherine G. Peden, ex-commerce commissioner of Kentucky.

"White racism," the commission charged, was chiefly responsible for the "explosive mixture" of discrimination, poverty and frustrations in the black ghetto that was vented in violence. The report said: "What white Americans have never fully understood—what the Negro can never forget—is that white society is deeply implicated in the ghetto. White institutions created it, white institutions maintain it, and white society condones it."

The commission called for a "massive and sustained" national commitment to action. It recommended sweeping reforms in federal and local law enforcement, welfare, employment, housing, education and the news media. While the programs would require "unprecedented levels of funding and performance," the commission said, "there can be no higher priority for national action and no higher claim on the nation's conscience."

In response to the question "What happened?" the commission said: There were no "typical" riots. "The disorders of 1967 were unusual, irregular, complex and unpredictable social processes." The commission cited allegedly discriminatory police practices, unemployment and underemployment and inadequate housing as the most pervasive and intense of the specific grievances. The commission held that the 1967 disorders "were not caused by, nor were they the consequence of, any organized plan or 'conspiracy.' "

In answer to the question "Why did it happen?" the commission declared that while the factors were "complex and interacting," "the most fundamental is the racial attitude and behavior of white Americans toward black Americans." The results of these white racial attitudes were: "Pervasive discrimination and segregation in employment,education and housing"; "black in-migration and white exodus," which "produced the massive and growing concentrations of impoverished Negroes in our major cities"; the converging of segregation and poverty on youth of the black ghettos "to destroy opportunity and enforce failure."

The commission presented nearly 160 recommendations to answer the question "What can be done?" They included:

● The decentralization of city governments to make them more responsive to people's needs.

● "The creation of 2 million new jobs in the next 3 years"—550,000 in the first year.

● "On-the-job training by both public and private employers with reimbursement to private employers for the extra costs of training the hard-core unemployed."

● "Sharply increased efforts to eliminate *de facto* desegregation in our schools through substantial federal aid."

● "Substantial federal funding of year-round quality compensatory education programs."

● Establishment of "uniform national standards of welfare assistance at least as high as the annual 'poverty level,'" with the federal government paying "at least 90% of total payments."

● A "national system of income supplements based strictly on need."

● A "comprehensive and enforceable federal open housing law to cover the sale or rental of all housing, including single family homes."

● Efforts to "bring within the reach of low and moderate income families, within the next 5 years, 6 million new and existing units of decent housing, beginning with 600,000 units in the next year."

● A privately organized and funded institute of urban communications to train and educate journalists in urban affairs, to recruit more Negros as journalists, to improve police-press relations and to review the press coverage of riots and racial problems.

The commission warned against trying to control urban disorders by equipping police with "mass destruction weapons," which were "designed to destroy, not to control."

The commission said that "despite instances of sensationalism, inaccuracy and distortion, newpapers, radio and television tried on the whole to give a balanced, factual account of the 1967 disorders." The report charged, however, that "important segments of the news media failed to report adequately on the causes and consequences of civil disorders and on the underlying problems of race relations."

The commission released a summary of its report Feb. 29; the full 1,400-page (250,000-word) report was released Mar. 2. An abridgment of the official summary follows:

INTRODUCTION

The summer of 1967 again brought racial disorders to American cities, and with them shock, fear and bewilderment to the nation. The worst came during a 2-week period in July in Newark and then in Detroit, each set off a chain reaction in neighboring communities. . . .

. . . [The commission undertook] a broad range of studies and investigations. We have visited the riot cities; we have heard many witnesses; we have sought the counsel of experts across the country.

This is our basic conclusion: Our nation is moving toward 2 societies, one black, one white—separate and unequal.

Reaction to last summer's disorders has quickened the movement and deepened the division. Discrimination and segregation have long permeated much of American life; they now threaten the future of every American.

This deepening racial division is not inevitable. The movement apart can be reversed. Choice is still possible. Our principal task is to define that choice and press for a national resolution. To pursue our present course will involve the continuing polarization of the American community and, ultimately, the destruction of basic democratic values . . . .

This alternative will require a commitment to national action—compassionate, massive and sustained, backed by the resources of the most powerful and the richest nation on this earth. From every American it will require new attitudes, new understanding, and, above all, new will. . . .

Violence and destruction must be ended—in the streets of the ghetto and in the lives of people.

Segregation and poverty have created in the racial ghetto a destructive environment totally unknown to most white Americans. . . .

It is time now to turn with all the purpose at our command to the major unfinished business of this nation. . . .

It is time to make good the promises of American democracy to all citizens—urban and rural, white and black, Spanish surname, American Indian and every minority group.

Our recommendations embrace 3 basic principles: To mount programs on a scale equal to the problems; to aim these programs for high impact in the immediate future in order to close the gap between promise and performance; to undertake new initiatives and experiments that can change the system of failure and frustration that now dominates the ghetto and weakens our society.

These programs will requires unprecedented levels of funding and performance, but they neither probe deeper nor demand more than the problems which called them forth. There can be no higher priority for national action and no higher claim on the nation's conscience. . . .

WHAT HAPPENED?

Chapter 1: Profiles of Disorder

The report contains profiles of a selection of the disorders that took place during the summer of 1967. These profiles are designed to indicate how the disorders happened, who participated in them, and how local officials, police forces and the National Guard responded. Illustrative excerpts follow:

Newark—. . . It was decided to attempt to channel the energies of the people into a nonviolent protest. . . . Negro leaders began urging those on the scene to form a line of march toward the city hall. Some persons joined the line of march. Others milled about in the narrow street. From the dark grounds of the housing project came a barrage of rocks. Some of them fell among the crowd. Others hit persons in the line of march. Many smashed the windows of the police station. The rock throwing, it was believed, was the work of youngsters. . . .

Almost at the same time, an old car was set afire in a parking lot. The line of march began to disintegrate. The police . . . sallied forth to dispose the crowd. A fire engine, arriving on the scene, was pelted with rocks. As police drove people away from the station, they scattered in all directions.

A few minutes later a nearby liquor store was broken into. . . . However, only a few stores were looted. Within a short period of time, the disorder appeared to have run its course.

On Saturday, July 15, [Director of Police Dominick] Spina received a report of snipers in a housing project. When he arrived he saw approximately 100 National Guardsmen and police officers crouching behind vehicles, hiding in corners and lying on the ground around the edge of the courtyard. Since everything appeared quiet and it was broad daylight, Spina walked directly down the middle of the street. Nothing happened. As he came to the last building of the complex, he heard a shot. All around him the troopers jumped, believing themselves to be under sniper fire. A moment later a young Guardsman ran from behind a building. The Director of Police went over and asked him if he had fired the shot. The soldier said yes, he had fired to scare a man away from a window; that his orders were to keep everyone away from windows. Spina said he told the soldier: "Do you know what you just did? You have now created a state of hysteria. Every Guardsman up and down this street and every state policeman and every city policeman that is present thinks that somebody just fired a shot and that it is probably a sniper."

A short time later more "gunshots" were heard. Investigating, Spina came upon a Puerto Rican sitting on a wall. In reply to a question as to whether he knew "where the firing is coming from?" the man said: "That's no firing. That's fireworks. If you look up to the 4th floor, you will see the people who are throwing down these cherry bombs."

By this time 4 truckloads of National Guardsmen had arrived and troopers and policemen were again crouched everywhere looking for a sniper. The Director of Police remained at the scene for 3 hours, and the only shot fired was the one by the Guardsman. Nevertheless, at 6 o'clock that evening 2 columns of National Guardsmen and state troopers were directing mass fire at the Hayes Housing Project in response to what they believed were snipers.

Detroit—. . . A spirit of carefree nihilism was taking hold. To riot and destroy appeared more and more to become ends in themselves. Late Sunday afternoon it appeared to one observer that the young people were "dancing amidst the flames."

A Negro plainclothes officer was standing at an intersection when a man threw a Molotov cocktail into a business establishment at the corner. In the heat of the afternoon, fanned by the 20- to 25-mph. winds of both Sunday and Monday, the fire reached the home next door within minutes. As residents uselessly sprayed the flames with garden hoses, the fire jumped from roof to roof of adjacent 2- and 3-story buildings. Within the hour the entire block was in flames. The 9th house in the burning row belonged to the arsonist who had thrown the Molotov cocktail.

Employed as a private guard, 55-year-old Julius L. Dorsey, a Negro, was standing in front of a market when accosted by 2 Negro men and a woman. They demanded he permit them to loot the market. He ignored their demands. They began to berate him. He asked a neighbor to call the police. As the argument grew more heated, Dorsey fired 3 shots from his pistol into the air. The police radio reported: "Looters, they have rifles." A patrol car driven by a police officer and carrying 3 National Guardsmen arrived. As the looters fled, the law enforcement personnel opened fire. When the firing ceased, one person lay dead. He was Julius L. Dorsey.

As the riot alternately waxed and waned, one area of the ghetto remained insulated. On the northeast side the residents of some 150 square blocks inhabited by 21,000 persons had, in 1966, banded together in the Positive Neighborhood Action Committee (PNAC). With professional help from the Institute of Urban Dynamics, they had organized block clubs and made plans for the improvement of the neighborhood. When the riot broke out, the residents, through the block clubs, were able to organize quickly. Youngsters, agreeing to stay in the neighborhood, participated in detouring traffic. While many persons reportedly sympathized with the idea of a rebellion against the "system," only 2 small fires were set—one in an empty building.

According to Lt. Gen. [John L.] Throckmorton and Col. Bolling, the city, at this time, was saturated with fear. The National Guardsmen were afraid, and the police were afraid. Numerous persons, the majority of them Negroes, were being injured by gunshots of undetermined origin. The general and the staff felt that the major task of the troops was to reduce the fear and restore an air of normalcy. In order to accomplish this, every effort was made to establish contact and rapport between the troops and the residents. The soldiers—20% of whom were Negro—began helping to clean up the streets, collect garbage, and trace persons who had disappeared in the confusion. Residents in the neighborhoods responded with soup and sandwiches for the troops. . . .

New Brunswick—. . . A short time later, elements of the crowd—an older and rougher one than the night before—appeared in front of the police station. The participants wanted to see the mayor. Mayor [Patricia] Sheehan went out onto the steps of the station. Using a bullhorn, she talked to the people and asked that she be given an opportunity to correct conditions. The crowd was boisterous. Some persons challenged the mayor. But, finally, the opinion, "She's new! Give her a chance!" prevailed.

A demand was issued by people in the crowd that all persons arrested the previous night be released. Told that this already had been done, the people were suspicious. They asked to be allowed to inspect the jail cells. It was agreed to permit representatives of the people to look in the cells to satisfy themselves that everyone had been released.

The crowd dispersed. The New Brunswick riot had failed to materialize.

Chapter 2: Patterns of Disorder

The "typical" riot did not take place. The disorders of 1967 were unusual, irregular, complex and unpredictable social processes. Like most human events, they did not unfold in an orderly sequence. However, an analysis of our survey information leads to some conclusions about the riot process.

In general:

● The civil disorders of 1967 involved Negroes acting against local symbols of white American society—authority and property in Negro neighborhoods —rather than against white persons.

● Of 164 disorders reported during the first 9 months of 1967, 8 (5%) were major in terms of violence and damage; 33 (20%) were serious but not major; 123 (75%) were minor and undoubtedly would not have received national attention as "riots" had the nation not been sensitized by the more serious outbreaks.

● In the 75 disorders studied by a Senate subcommittee, there were 83 deaths. 82% of the deaths and more than half of the injuries occurred in Newark and Detroit. About 10% of the dead and 36% of the injured were public employes, primarily law officers and firemen. The overwhelming majority of the persons killed or injured in all the disorders were Negro civilians.

● Initial damage estimates were greatly exaggerated. In Detroit, newspaper damage estimates at first ranged from $200 million to $500 million; the highest recent estimate is $45 million. In Newark, early estimates ranged from $15 million to $25 million. A month later damage was estimated at $10.2 million, 80% in inventory losses.

In the 24 disorders in 23 cities which we surveyed:

● The final incident before the outbreak of disorder, and the initial violence itself, generally took place in the evening or at night at a place in which it was normal for many people to be on the streets.

● Violence usually occurred immediately following the occurrence of the final precipitating incident and then escalated rapidly. With but few exceptions, violence subsided during the day, and flared rapidly again at night. The night-day cycles continued through the early period of the major disorders.

● Disorder generally began with rock and bottle throwing and window breaking. Once store windows were broken, looting usually followed.

● Disorder did not erupt as a result of a single "triggering" or "precipitating" incident. Instead, it was generated out of an increasingly disturbed social atmosphere, in which typically a series of tension-heightening incidents over a period of weeks or months became linked in the minds of many in the Negro community with a shared network of underlying grievances. At some point in the mounting tension, a further incident—in itself often routine or trivial—became the breaking point and the tension spilled over into violence.

● "Prior" incidents, which increased tensions and ultimately led to violence, were police actions in almost half the cases; police actions were "final" incidents before the outbreak of violence in 12 of the 24 surveyed disorders.

● No particular control tactic wes successful in every situation. The varied effectiveness of control techniques emphasizes the need for advance training, planning, adequate intelligence systems, and knowledge of the ghetto community.

● Negotiations between Negroes—including young militants as well as older Negro leaders—and white officials concerning "terms of peace" occurred during virtually all the disorders surveyed. In many cases, these negotiations involved discussion of underlying grievances as well as the handling of the disorder by control authorities.

● The typical rioter was a teenager or young adult, a lifelong resident of the city in which he rioted, a high school dropout; he was, nevertheless, somewhat better educated than his nonrioting Negro neighbor and was usually underemployed or employed in a menial job. He was proud of his race, extremely hostile to both whites and middle-class Negroes and, although informed about politics, highly distrustful of the political system.

● In a survey of Negro males between the ages of 15 and 35 residing in the disturbance area in Newark, about 45% identified themselves as rioters, and about 55% as "noninvolved." But a Detroit survey revealed that only approximately 11% of the total residents of 2 riot areas participated in the rioting, over 16% identified themselves as "counter-rioters," who urged rioters to "cool it," and about 73% identified themselves as "noninvolved."

● Most rioters were young Negro males. Nearly 53% of arrestees were between 15 and 24 years of age; nearly 81% between 15 and 35.

● In Detroit and Newark about 74% of the rioters were brought up in the North. In contrast, of the noninvolved, 36% in Detroit and 52% in Newark were brought up in the North.

● Numerous Negro counter-rioters walked the streets urging rioters to "cool it." The typical counter-rioter was better educated and had higher income than either the rioter or the noninvolved.

● The proportion of Negroes in local government was substantially smaller than the Negro proporton of population. Only 3 of the 20 cities studied had more than one Negro legislator; none had ever had a Negro mayor or city manager. In only 4 cities did Negroes hold other important policy-making positions or serve as heads of municipal departments.

● Although almost all cities had some sort of formal grievance mechanism for handling citizen complaints, this typically was regarded by Negroes as ineffective and was generally ignored.

● Although specific grievances varied from city to city, at least 12 deeply held grievances can be identified and ranked into 3 levels of relative intensity:

    First level of intensity: (1) Police practices; (2) unemployment and underemployment; (3) inadequate housing.

    2d level of intensity: (4) Inadequate education; (5) poor recreation facilities and programs; (6) ineffectiveness of the political structure and grievance mechanisms.

    3d level of intensity: (7) Disrespectful white attitude; (8) discriminatory administration of justice; (9) inadequacy of federal programs; (10) inadequacy of municipal services; (11) discriminatory consumer and credit practices; (12) inadequate welfare programs.

● The results of a 3-city survey of various federal programs—manpower, education, housing, welfare and community action—indicate that, despite substantial expenditures, the number of persons assisted constitute only a fraction of those in need.

● The background of disorder is often as complex and difficult to analyze as the disorder itself. But we find that certain general conclusions can be drawn: Social and economic conditions in the riot cities constituted a clear pattern of severe disadvantage for Negroes compared with whites, whether the Negroes lived in the area where the riot took place or outside it. Negroes had completed fewer years of education and fewer had attended high school. Negroes were twice as likely to be unemployed and 3 times as likely to be in unskilled and service jobs. Negroes averaged 70% of the income earned by whites and were more than twice as likely to be living in poverty. Although housing cost Negroes relatively more, they had worse housing—3 times as likely to be overcrowded and substandard. When compared to white suburbs, the relative disadvantage is even more pronounced.

A study of the aftermath of disorder leads to disturbing conclusions. We find that, despite the institution of some post-riot programs:

● Little basic change in the conditions underlying the outbreak of disorder has taken place. Actions to ameliorate Negro grievances have been limited and sporadic; with but few exceptions, they have not significantly reduced tensions.

● In several cities, the principal official response has been to train and equip the police with more sophisticated weapons.

● In several cities, increasing polarization is evident, with continuing breakdown of interracial communication and growth of white segregationist or black separatist groups.

Chapter 3: Organized Activity

The President directed the commission to investigate "to what extent, if any, there has been planning or organization in any of the riots." To carry out this part of the President's charge, the commission established a special investigative staff supplementing the field teams that made the general examination of the riots in 23 cities. The unit examined data collected by federal agencies and congressional committees, including thousands of documents supplied by the Federal Bureau of Investigation, gathered and evaluated information from local and state law enforcement agencies and officials, and conducted its own field investigation in selected cities.

On the basis of all the information collected, the commission concludes that: The urban disorders of the summer of 1967 were not caused by nor were they the consequence of, any organized plan or "conspiracy."

Specifically, the commission has found no evidence that all or any of the disorders or the incidents that led to them were planned or directed by any organization or group, international, national or local.

Militant organizations, local and national, and individual agitators, who repeatedly forecast and called for violence, were active in the spring and summer of 1967. We believe that they sought to encourage violence and that they helped to create an atmosphere that contributed to the outbreak of disorder. . . .

WHY DID IT HAPPEN?

Chapter 4: The Basic Causes

In addressing the question "Why did it happen?" we shift our focus from the local to the national scene, from the particular events of the summer of 1967 to the factors within the society at large that created a mood of violence among many urban Negroes.

These factors are complex and interacting: they vary significantly in their effect from city to city and from year to year; and the consequences of one disorder, generating new grievances and new demands, become the causes of the next. It is this which creates the "thicket of tension, conflicting evidence and extreme opinions" cited by the President.

Despite these complexities, certain fundamental matters are clear. Of these the most fundamental is the racial attitude and behavior of white Americans toward black Americans. . . .

White racism is essentially responsible for the explosive mixture which has been accumulating in our cities since the end of World War II. At the base of this mixture are 3 of the most bitter fruits of white racial attitudes:

● Pervasive discrimination and segregation in employment, education and housing have resulted in the continuing exclusion of great numbers of Negroes from the benefits of economic progress.

● Black in-migration and white exodus have produced the massive and growing concentrations of impoverished Negroes in our major cities, creating a growing crisis of deteriorating facilities and services and unmet human needs.

● In the black ghettos segregation and poverty converge on the young to destroy opportunity and enforce failure. Crime, drug addiction, dependency on welfare, and bitterness and resentment against society in general and white society in particular are the result.

These 3 forces have converged on the inner city in recent years and on the people who inhabit it. At the same time, most whites and many Negroes outside the ghetto have prospered to a degree unparalleled in the history of civilization. Through television and other media, this affluence has been endlessly flaunted before the eyes of the Negro poor and the jobless ghetto youth.

Yet these facts alone cannot be said to have caused the disorders. Recently, other powerful ingredients have begun to catalyze the mixture:

● Frustrated hopes are the residue of the unfulfilled expectations aroused by the great judicial and legislative victories of the civil rights movement and the dramatic struggle for equal rights in the South.

● A climate that tends toward approval and encouragement of violence as a form of protest has been created by white terrorism directed against non-violent protest; by the open defiance of law and federal authority by state and local officials resisting desegregation; and by some protest groups engaging in civil disobedience who turn their backs on nonviolence, go beyond the constitutionally protected rights of petition and free assembly and resort to violence to attempt to compel alteration of laws and policies with which they disagree.

● The frustrations of powerlessness have led some Negroes to the conviction that there is no effective alternative to violence as a means of achieving redress of grievances and of "moving the system." These frustrations are reflected in alienation and hostility toward the institutions of law and government and the white society which controls them and in the reach toward racial consciousness and solidarity reflected in the slogan "black power."

● A new mood has sprung up among Negroes, particularly among the young, in which self-esteem and enhanced racial pride are replacing apathy and submission to "the system."

● The police are not merely a "spark" factor. To some Negroes, police have come to symbolize white power, white racism and white repression. And the fact is that many police do reflect and express these white attitudes. The atmosphere of hostility and cynicism is reinforced by a widespread belief among Negroes in the existence of police brutality and in a "double standard" of justice and protection—one for Negroes and one for whites. . . .

In the summer of 1967, we have seen in our cities a chain reaction of racial violence. If we are heedless none of us shall escape the consequences.

Chapter 5: Rejection & Protest: An Historical Sketch

The causes of recent racial disorders are embedded in a tangle of issues and circumstances—social, economic, political and psychological—which arise out of the historical pattern of Negro-white relations in America. In this chapter . . . we describe the Negro's experience in America and the development of slavery as an institution. We show his persistent striving for equality in the face of rigidly maintained social, economic and educational barriers, and repeated mob violence. We portray the ebb and flow of the doctrinal tides—accommodation, separatism, and self-help—and their relationship to the current theme of black power. We conclude: The black power advocates of today consciously feel that they are the most militant group in the Negro protest movement. Yet they have retreated from a direct confrontation with American society on the issue of integration and, by preaching separatism, unconsciously function as an accommodation to white racism. Much of their economic program, as well as their interest in Negro history, self-help, racial solidarity and separation, is reminiscent of Booker T. Washington. The rhetoric is different, but the programs are remarkably similar.

Chapter 6: The Formation of Racial Ghettos

Throughout the 20th century the Negro population of the United States has been moving steadily from rural areas to urban and from South to North and West. In 1910, 91% of the nation's 9.8 million Negroes lived in the South and only 27% of American Negroes lived in cities of 2,500 persons or more. Between 1910 and 1966 the total Negro population more than doubled, reached 21.5 million, and the number living in metropolitan areas rose more than 5-fold (from 2.6 million to 14.8 million). The number outside the South rose 11-fold (from 880,000 to 9.7 million).

Negro migration from the South has resulted from the expectation of thousands of new and highly paid jobs for unskilled workers in the North and the shift to mechanized farming in the South. . . .

As a result of the growing number of Negroes in urban areas, natural increase has replaced migration as the primary source of Negro population increase in the citites. . . .

Basic data concerning Negro urbanization trends indicate that:

● Almost all Negro population growth (98% from 1950 to 1966) is occurring within metropolitan areas, primarily within central cities. (Note—A "central city" is the largest city of a standard metropolitan statistical area, that is, a metropolitan area containing at least one city of at least 50,000 inhabitants.)

● The vast majority of white population growth (78% from 1960 to 1966) is occurring in suburban portions of metropolitan areas. Since 1960, white central-city population has declined by 1.3 million.

● As a result, central cities are becoming more heavily Negro while the suburban fringes around them remain almost entirely white. The 12 largest cities now contain over ⅔ of the Negro population outside the South and ⅓ of the Negro total in the United States.

● Within the cities, Negroes have been excluded from white residential areas through discriminatory practices. Just as significant is the withdrawal of white families from, or their refusal to enter, neighborhoods where Negroes are moving or already residing. . . . The refusal of whites to move into "changing" areas . . . means that most vacancies eventually are occupied by Negroes.

● The result . . . is that in 1960 the average segregation index for 207 of the largest United States cities was 86.2. In other words, to create an unsegregated population distribution, an average of over 86% of all Negroes would have to change their place of residence within the city.

Chapter 7: Unemployment, Family Structure & Social Disorganization

Although there have been gains in Negro income nationally and a decline in the number of Negroes below the "poverty level," the condition of Negroes in the central city remains in a state of crisis. Between 2 and 2.5 million Negroes—16% to 20% of the total Negro population of all central cities—live in squalor and deprivation in ghetto neghborhoods.

Employment is a key problem. It not only controls the present for the Negro American but, in a most profound way, it is creating the future as well. Yet, despite continuing economic growth and declining national unemployment rates, the unemployment rate for Negroes in 1967 was more than double that for whites.

Equally important is the undesirable nature of many jobs open to Negroes. Negro men are more than 3 times as likely as white men to be in low-paying, unskilled or service jobs. This concentration of male Negro employment at the lowest end of the occupational scale is the single most important source of poverty among Negroes.

In one study of low-income neighborhoods, the "subemployment rate," including both unemployment and underemployment, was about 33%, or 8.8 times greater than the overall unemployment rate for all United States workers.

Employment problems, aggravated by the constant arrival of new unemployed migrants, many of them from depressed rural areas, create persistent poverty in the ghetto. In 1966, about 11.9% of the nation's whites and 40.6% of its nonwhites were below the "poverty level" defined by the Social Security Administration (currently $3,335 per year for an urban family of four). Over 40% of the nonwhites below the poverty level live in the central cities.

Employment problems have drastic social impact in the ghetto. Men who are chronically unemployed or employed in the lowest status jobs are often unable or unwilling to remain with their families. The handicap imposed on children growing up without fathers in an atmosphere of poverty and deprivation is increased as mothers are forced to work to provide support.

The culture of poverty that results from unemployment and family breakup generates a system of ruthless, exploitative relationships within the ghetto. Prostitution, dope addiction and crime create an environmental "jungle" characterized by personal insecurity and tension. Children growing up under such conditions are likely participants in civil disorder.

Chapter 8: Conditions of Life in the Racial Ghetto

A striking difference in environment from that of white, middle-class Americans profoundly influences the lives of residents of the ghetto.

Crime rates, consistently higher than in other areas, create a pronounced sense of insecurity. For example, in one city one low-income Negro district had 35 times as many serious crimes against persons as did a high-income white district.

Poor health and sanitation conditions in the ghetto result in higher mortality rates, a higher incidence of major diseases and lower availability and utilization of medical services. The infant mortality rate for nonwhite babies under the age of one month is 58% higher than for whites; for one to 12 months it is almost 3 times as high. The level of sanitation in the ghetto is far below that in high income areas. Garbage collection is often inadequate. Of an estimated 14,000 cases of rat bite in the United States in 1965, most were in ghetto neighborhoods.

Ghetto residents believe they are "exploited" by local merchants; and evidence substantiates some of these beliefs. A study conducted in one city by the Federal Trade Commission showed that distinctly higher prices were charged for goods sold in ghetto stores than in other areas. . . .

Chapter 9: Comparing the Immigrant & Negro Experience

In this chapter, we address ourselves to a fundamental question that many white Americans are asking: why have so many Negroes, unlike the European immigrants, been unable to escape from the ghetto and from poverty. We believe the following factors play a part:

The maturing economy—When the European immigrants arrived, they gained an economic foothold by providing the unskilled labor needed by industry. Unlike the immigrant, the Negro migrant found little opportunity in the city. The economy, by then matured, had little use for the unskilled labor he had to offer.

The disability of race—The structure of discrimination has stringently narrowed opportunities for the Negro and restricted his prospects. European immigrants suffered from discrimination, but never so pervasively.

Entry into the politcal system—The immigrants usually settled in rapidly growing cities with powerful and expanding political machines, which traded economic advantages for political support. Ward-level grievance machinery, as well as personal representation, enabled the immigrant to make his voice heard and his power felt. By the time the Negro arrived, these political machines were no longer so powerful or so well equipped to provide jobs or other favors and were unwilling to share their remaining influence with Negroes.

Cultural factors—Coming from societies with a low standard of living and at a time when job aspirations were low, the immigrants sensed little deprivation in being forced to take less desirable and poorly paid jobs. Their large and cohesive families contributed to total income. Their vision of the future—one that led to a life outside of the ghetto—provided the incentive necessary to endure the present. Although Negro men worked as hard as the immigrants, they were unable to support their families. The entrepreneurial opportunities had vanished. As a result of slavery and long periods of unemployment, the Negro family structure had become matriarchal; the males played a secondary and marginal family role—one which offered little compensation for their hard and unrewarding labor. Above all, segregation denied Negroes access to good jobs and the opportunity to leave the ghetto. For them, the future seemed to lead only to a dead end.

Today, whites tend to exaggerate how well and quickly they escaped from poverty. The fact is that immigrants who came from rural backgrounds, as many Negroes do, are only now, after 3 generations, finally beginning to move into the middle class. By contrast, Negroes began concentrating in the city less than 2 generations ago and under much less favorable conditions. . . .

WHAT CAN BE DONE?

Chapter 10: The Community Response

Our investigation of the 1967 riot cities establishes that virtually every major episode of violence was foreshadowed by an accumulation of unresolved grievances and by widespread dissatisfaction among Negroes with the unwillingness and inability of local government to respond.

Overcoming these conditions is essential for community support of law enforcement and civil order. City governments need new and more vital channels of communication to the residents of the ghetto; they need to improve their capacity to respond effectively to community needs before they become community grievances; and they need to provide opportunity for meaningful involvement of ghetto residents in shaping policies and programs which affect the community.

The commisson recommends that local governments:

● Develop Neighborhood Action Task Forces as joint community-government efforts through which more effective communication can be achieved and the delivery of city services to ghetto residents improved.

● Establish comprehensive grievance-response mechanisms in order to bring all public agencies under public scrutiny.

● Bring the institutions of local government closer to the people they serve by establishing neighborhood outlets for local, state and federal administrative and public service agencies.

● Expand opportunities for ghetto residents to participate in the formulation of public policy and the implementation of programs affecting them by improved political representation, creation of institutional channels for community action, expansion of legal services, and legislative hearings on ghetto problems.

In this effort, city government will require state and federal support. The commission recommends:

● State and federal financial assistance for mayors and city councils to support the research, consultants, staff and other resources needed to respond effectively to federal program initiatives.

● State cooperation in providing municipalities with the jurisdictional tools needed to deal with their problems; a fuller measure of financial aid to urban areas; and the focusing of the interests of suburban communities on the physical, social and cultural environment of the central city.

Chapter 11: Police & the Community

The abrasive relationship between the police and the ghetto community has been a major—and explosive—source of grievance, tension and disorder. The blame must be shared by the total society.

The police are faced with demands for increased protection and service in the ghetto. Yet the aggressive patrol practices thought necessary to meet these demands themselves create tension and hostility. The resulting grievances have been further aggravated by the lack of effective mechanisms for handling complaints against the police. Special programs for bettering police-community relations have been instituted but these alone are not enough. Police administrators, with the guidance of public officials and the support of the entire community, must take vigorous action to improve law enforcement and to decrease the potential for disorder.

The commission recommends that city government and police authorities:

● Review police operations in the ghetto to ensure proper conduct by police officers and eliminate abrasive practices.
● Provide more adequate police protection to ghetto residents to eliminate their high sense of insecurity, and the belief of many Negro citizens in the existence of a dual standard of law enforcement.
● Establish fair and effective mechanisms for the redress of grievances against the police, and other municipal employes.
● Develop and adopt policy guidelines to assist officers in making critical decisions in areas where police conduct can create tension.
● Develop and use innovative programs to ensure widespread community support for law enforcement.
● Recruit more Negroes into the regular police force and review promotion policies to ensure Negro officers full opportunity for fair promotion.
● Establish a Community Service Officer [CSO] program to attract ghetto youths between the ages of 17 and 21 to police work. These junior officers would perform duties in ghetto neighborhoods but would not have full police authority. The federal government should provide support equal to 90% of the cost of employing CSOs on the basis of one for every 10 regular officers.

Chapter 12: Control of Disorder

Preserving civil peace is the first responsibility of government. Unless the rule of law prevails, our society will lack not only order but also the environment essential to social and economic progress.

The maintenance of civil order cannot be left to the police alone. The police need guidance, as well as support, from mayors and other public officials. It is the responsibility of public officials to determine proper police policies, support adequate police standards for personnel and performance and participate in planning for the control of disorders.

To maintain control of incidents which could lead to disorders, the commission recommends that local officials:

● Assign seasoned, well-trained policemen and supervisory officers to patrol ghetto areas and to respond to disturbances.
● Develop plans which will quickly muster maximum police manpower and highly qualified senior commanders at the outbreak of disorders.
● Provide special training in the prevention of disorders and prepare police for riot control and for operation in units, with adequate command and control and field communication for proper discipline and effectiveness.
● Develop guidelines governing the use of control equipment and provide alternatives to the use of lethal weapons. . . .
● Establish an intelligence system to provide police and other public officials with reliable information that may help to prevent the outbreak of a disorder and to institute effective control measures in the event a riot erupts.
● Develop continuing contacts with ghetto residents to make use of the forces for order which exist within the community.
● Provide the machinery for neutralizing rumors, including creation of special rumor details to collect and evaluate rumors that may lead to a civil

disorder, and to disseminate effectively the true facts to the ghetto residents and leaders.

The commission believes there is a grave danger that some communities may resort to the indiscriminate and excessive use of force. The harmful effects of overreaction are incalculable. The commission condemns moves to equip police departments with mass destruction weapons, such as automatic rifles, machine guns and tanks. Weapons which are designed to destroy, not to control, have no place in densely populated urban communities.

The commission recognizes the sound principle of local authority and responsibility in law enforcement but recommends that the federal government share in the financing of programs for improvement of police forces both in their normal law enforcement activities as well as in their response to civil disorders.

To assist government authorities in planning their response to civil disorder, this report contains a Supplement on Control of Disorder. It deals with specific problems encountered during riot control operatons, and includes:

● Assessment of the present capabilities of police, National Guard and Army forces to control major riots, and recommendations for improvement;

● Recommended means by which the control operations of those forces may be coordinated with the response of other agencies, such as fire departments, and with the community at large;

● Recommendations for review and revision of federal, state and local laws needed to provide the framework for control efforts and for the call-up and interrelated action of public safety forces.

Chapter 13: The Administration of Justice Under Emergency Conditions

In many of the cities which experienced disorders last summer there were recurring breakdowns in the mechanisms for processing, prosecuting and protecting arrested persons. These resulted mainly from long-standing structural deficiencies in criminal court systems and from the failure of communities to anticipate and plan for the emergency demands of civil disorders. In part, because of this, there were few successful prosecutions for serious crimes committed during the riots. In those cities where mass arrests occurred many arrestees were deprived of basic legal rights.

The commission recommends that the cities and states:

● Undertake reform of the lower courts so as to improve the quality of justice rendered under normal conditions.

● Plan comprehensive measures by which the criminal justice system may be supplemented during civil disorders so that its deliberate functions are protected and the quality of justice is maintained.

Such emergency plans require broad community participation and dedicated leadership by the bench and bar. They should include:

● Laws sufficient to deter and punish riot conduct.

● Additional judges, bail and probation officers and clerical staff.

● Arrangements for volunteer lawyers to help prosecutors and to represent riot defendants at every stage of proceedings.

● Policies to ensure proper and individual bail, arraignment, pre-trial, trial and sentencing proceedings.

● Procedures for processing arrested persons, such as summons and release, and release on personal recognizance, which permit separation of minor of-

fenders from those dangerous to the community, in order that serious offenders may be detained and prosecuted effectively.
● Adequate emergency processing and detention facilities.

Chapter 14: Damages: Repair & Compensation

The commission recommends that the federal government:
● Amend the Federal Disaster Act—which now applies only to natural disasters—to permit federal emergency food and medical assistance to cities during major civil disorders, and provide long-term economc assistance afterwards.
● With the cooperation of the states, create incentives for the private insurance industry to provide more adequate property-insurance coverage in inner-city areas. . . .

Chapter 15: The News Media & the Riots

. . . The President asked: "What effect do the mass media have on the riots?"

The commission determined that the answer to the President's question did not lie solely in the performance of the press and broadcasters in reporting the riots. Our analysis had to consider also the over-all treatment by the media of the Negro ghettos, community relations, racial attitudes and poverty —day by day and month by month, year in and year out.

A wide range of interviews with government officials, law enforcement authorities, media personnel and other citizens, including ghetto residents, as well as a quantitative analysis of riot coverage and a special conference with industry representatives lead us to conclude that:
● Despite instances of sensationalism, inaccuracy and distortion, newspapers, radio and television tried on the whole to give a balanced, factual account of the 1967 disorders.
● Elements of the news media failed to portray accurately the scale and character of the violence that occurred last summer. The over-all effect was, we believe, an exaggeration of both mood and event.
● Important segments of the media failed to report adequately on the causes and consequences of civil disorders and on the underlying problems of race relations. They have not communicated to the majority of their audience— which is white—a sense of the degradation, misery and hopelessness of life in the ghetto.

These failings must be corrected, and the improvement must come from within the industry. Freedom of the press is not the issue. Any effort to impose governmental restrictions would be inconsistent with fundamental constitutional precepts.

We have seen evidence that the news media are becoming aware of and concerned about their performance in this field. . . . But much more must be done, and it must be done soon. The commission recommends that the media:
● Expand coverage of the Negro community and of race problems through permanent assignment of reporters familiar with urban and racial affairs and through establishment of more and better links with the Negro community.
● Integrate Negroes and Negro activities into all aspects of coverage and content, including newspaper articles and television programming. The news media must publish newspapers and produce programs that recognize the existence and activities of Negroes as a group within the community and as a part of the larger community.

● Recruit more Negroes into journalism and broadcasting and promote those who are qualified to positions of significant responsibility. Recruitment should begin in high schools and continue through college; where necessary, aid for training should be provided.

● Improve coordination with police in reporting riot news through advance planning, and cooperate with the police in the designation of police information officers, establishment of information centers and development of mutually acceptable guidelines for riot reporting and the conduct of media personnel.

● Accelerate efforts to ensure accurate and responsible reporting of riot and racial news through adoption by all news gathering organizations of stringent internal staff guidelines.

● Cooperate in the establishment of a privately organized and funded Institute of Urban Communications to train and educate journalists in urban affairs, recruit and train more Negro journalists, develop methods for improving police-press relations, review coverage of riots and racial issues and support continuing research in the urban field.

Chapter 16: The Future of Cities

By 1985, the Negro population in central cities is expected to increase by 72% to approximately 20.8 million. Coupled with the continued exodus of white families to the suburbs, this growth will produce majority Negro populations in many of the Nation's largest cities. The future of these cities, and of their burgeoning Negro populations, is grim. Most new employment opportunities are being created in suburbs and outlying areas. The trend will continue unless important changes in public policy are made.

In prospect, therefore, is further deterioration of already inadequate municipal tax bases in the face of increasing demands for public services, and continuing unemployment and poverty among the urban Negro population.

3 choices are open to the nation:

● We can maintain present policies, continuing both the proportion of the nation's resources now allocated to programs for the unemployed and the disadvantaged, and the inadequate and failing effort to achieve an integrated society.

● We can adopt a policy of "enrichment" aimed at improving dramatically the quality of ghetto life while abandoning integration as a goal.

● We can pursue integration by combining ghetto "enrichment" with policies which will encourage Negro movement out of central city areas.

The first choice, continuance of present policies, has ominous consequences for our society. The share of the nation's resources now allocated to programs for the disadvantaged is insufficient to arrest the deterioration of life in central city ghettos. Under such conditions, a rising proportion of Negroes may come to see in the deprivation and segregation they experience, a justification for violent protest or for extending support to now isolated extremists who advocate civil disruption. Large-scale and continuing violence could result, followed by white retaliation and, ultimately, the separation of the 2 communities in a garrison state.

Even if violence does not occur, the consequences are unacceptable. Development of a racially integrated society, extraordinarily difficult today, will be virtually impossible when the present black ghetto population of 12.5 million has grown to almost 21 million.

To continue present policies is to make permanent the division of our country into 2 societies; one, largely Negro and poor, located in the central cities; the other, predominantly white and affluent, located in the suburbs and in outlying areas.

The 2d choice, ghetto enrichment coupled with abandonment of integration, is also unacceptable. It is another way of choosing a permanently divided country. Moreover, equality cannot be achieved under conditions of nearly complete separation. In a country where the economy, and particularly the resources of employment, are predominantly white, a policy of separation can only relegate Negroes to a permanently inferior economic status.

We believe that the only possible choice for America is the 3d—a policy which combines ghetto enrichment with programs designed to encourage integration of substantial numbers of Negroes into the society outside the ghetto.

Enrichment must be an important adjunct to integration, for no matter how ambitious or energetic the program, few Negroes now living in central cities can be quickly integrated. In the meantime, large-scale improvement in the quality of ghetto life is essential.

But this can be no more than an interim strategy. Programs must be developed which will permit substantial Negro movement out of the ghettos. The primary goal must be a single society, in which every citizen will be free to live and work according to his capabilities and desires, not his color.

Chapter 17: Recommendations for National Action

Introduction. No American—white or black—can escape the consequences of the continuing social and economic decay of our major cities. Only a commitment to national action on an unprecedented scale can shape a future compatible with the historic ideals of American society.

The great productivity of our economy, and a federal revenue system which is highly responsive to economic growth, can provide the resources. The major need is to generate new will—the will to tax ourselves to the extent necessary to meet the vital needs of the nation. . . .

The major goal is the creation of a true union—a single society and a single American identity. Toward that goal, we propose the following objectives for national action:

● Opening up opportunities to those who are restricted by racial segregation and discrimination and eliminating all barriers to their choice of jobs, education and housing.

● Removing the frustration of powerlessness among the disadvantaged by providing the means for them to deal with the problems that affect their own lives and by increasing the capacity of our public and private institutions to respond to these problems.

● Increasing communication across racial lines to destroy stereotypes, to halt polarizaton, end distrust and hostility and create common ground for efforts toward public order and social justice. . . .

Employment. Pervasive unemployment and underemployment are the most persistent and serious grievances in the Negro ghetto. They are inextricably linked to the problem of civil disorder. . . .

The 500,000 "hard-core" unemployed in the central cities who lack a basic education and are unable to hold a steady job are made up in large part of Negro males between the ages of 18 and 25. In the riot cities which we surveyed, Negroes were 3 times as likely as whites to hold unskilled jobs, which are often part time, seasonal, low-paying and "dead end."

Negro males between the ages of 15 and 25 predominated among the rioters. More than 20% of the rioters were unemployed, and many who were employed held intermittent, low status, unskilled jobs which they regarded as below their education and ability.

The commission recommends that the federal government:

• Undertake joint efforts with cities and states to consolidate existing manpower programs to avoid fragmentation and duplication.

• Take immediate action to create 2 million new jobs over the next 3 years —one million in the private sector—to absorb the hard-core unemployed and materially reduce the level of underemployment for all workers, black and white. We propose 250,000 public sector and 300,000 private sector jobs in the first year.

• Provide on-the-job training by both public and private employers with reimbursement to private employers for the extra costs of training the hard-core unemployed, by contract or by tax credits.

• Provide tax and other incentives to investment in rural as well as urban poverty areas in order to offer to the rural poor an alternative to migration to urban centers.

• Take new and vigorous action to remove artificial barriers to employment and promotion, including not only racial discrimination but, in certain cases, arrest records or lack of a high school diploma. Strengthen those agencies such as the Equal Employment Opportunity Commission, charged with eliminating discriminatory practices, and provide full support for Title VI of the 1964 Civil Rights Act allowing federal grant-in-aid funds to be withheld from activities which discriminate on grounds of color or race.

The commission commends the recent public commitment of the National Council of the Building & Construction Trades Unions, AFL-CIO, to encourage and recruit Negro membership in apprenticeship programs. This commitment should be intensified and implemented.

Education. Education in a democratic society must equip children to develop their potential and to participate fully in American life. For the community at large, the schools have discharged this responsibility well. But for many minorities, and particularly for the children of the ghetto, the schools have failed to provide the educational experience which could overcome the effects of discrimination and deprivation. This failure is one of the persistent sources of grievance and resentment within the Negro community. The hostility of Negro parents and students toward the school system is generating increasing conflict and causing disruption within many city school districts. But the most dramatic evidence of the relationship between educational practices and civil disorders lies in the high incidence of riot participation by ghetto youth who have not completed high school.

The bleak record of public education for ghetto children is growing worse. In the critical skills—verbal and reading ability—Negro students are falling farther behind whites with each year of school completed. The high unemployment and underemployment rate for Negro youth is evidence, in part, of the growing educational crisis.

We support integration as the priority education strategy; it is essential to the future of American society. In this last summer's disorders we have seen the consequences of racial isolation at all levels, and of attitudes toward race, on both sides, produced by 3 centuries of myth, ignorance and bias. It is indispensable that opportunities for interaction between the races be expanded. We recognize that the growing dominance of city school district populations by disadvantaged minorities will not soon be arrested. No matter how great the effort toward desegregation, many children of the ghetto will not, within their school careers, attend integrated schools.

If existing disadvantages are not to be perpetuated, we must drastically improve the quality of ghetto education. Equality of results with all-white schools must be the goal.

To implement these strategies, the commission recommends:

● Sharply increased efforts to eliminate *de facto* segregation in our schools through substantial federal aid to school systems seeking to desegregate either within the system or in cooperation with neighboring school systems.
● Elimination of racial discrimination in Northern as well as Southern schools by vigorous application of Title VI of the Civil Rights Act of 1964.
● Extension of quality early childhood education to every disadvantaged child in the country.
● Efforts to improve dramatically schools serving disadvantaged children through substantial federal funding of year-round quality compensatory education programs, improved teaching and experimentation and research.
● Elimination of illiteracy through greater federal support for adult basic education.
● Enlarged opportunities for parent and community participation in the public schools.
● Reoriented vocational education emphasizing work-experience training and the involvement of business and industry.
● Expanded opportunities for higher education through increased federal assistance to disadvantaged students.
● Revision of state aid formulas to assure more per student aid to districts having a high proportion of disadvantaged school-age children.

The welfare system. Our present system of public welfare is designed to save money instead of people and tragically ends up doing neither. This system has 2 critical deficiencies:

First, it excludes large numbers of persons who are in great need and who, if provided a decent level of support, might be able to become more productive and self-sufficient. . . .

2d, for those who are included, the system provides assistance well below the minimum necessary for a decent level of existence and imposes restrictions that encourage continued dependency on welfare and undermine self-respect.

A welter of statutory requirements and administrative practices and regulations operate to remind recipients that they are considered untrustworthy, promiscuous and lazy. Residence requirements prevent assistance to people in need who are newly arrived in the state. Regular searches of recipients' homes violate privacy. Inadequate social services compound the problems.

The commission recommends that the federal government, acting with state and local governments where necessary, reform the existing welfare system to:

● Establish unform national standards of assistance at least as high as the annual "poverty level" of income, now set by the Social Security Administration at $3,335 for an urban family of 4.

● Require that all states receiving federal welfare contributions participate in the Aid to Families with Dependent Children-Unemployed Parents Program (AFDC-UP) that permits assistance to families with both father and mother in the home, thus aiding the family while it is still intact.

● Bear a substantially greater portion of all welfare costs—at least 90% of total payments.

● Increase incentives for seeking employment and job training, but remove restrictions recently enacted by the Congress that would compel mothers of young children to work.

● Provide more adequate social services through neighborhood centers and through family-planning programs.

● Remove the freeze placed by the 1967 welfare amendments on the percentage of children in a state that can be covered by federal assistance.

● Eliminate residence requirements.

As a long-range goal, the commission recommends that the federal government seek to develop a national system of income supplementation based strictly on need with 2 broad and basic purposes:

● To provide, for those who can work or who do work, any necessary supplements in such a way as to develop incentives for fuller employment;

● To provide, for those who cannot work and for mothers who decide to remain with their children, a minimum standard of decent living, and aid in saving children from the prison of poverty that has held their parents.

A broad system of supplementation would involve substantially greater federal expenditures than anything now contemplated. . . . Yet if the deepening cycle of poverty and dependence on welfare can be broken, if the children of the poor can be given the opportunity to scale the wall that now separates them from the rest of society, the return on this investment will be great indeed.

Housing. After more than 3 decades of fragmented and grossly underfunded federal housing programs, nearly 6 million substandard housing units remain occupied in the United States.

The housing problem is particularly acute in the Negro ghettos. Nearly ⅔ of all nonwhite families living in the central cities today live in neighborhoods marked with substandard housing and general urban blight. 2 major factors are responsible:

First: Many ghetto residents simply cannot pay the rent necessary to support decent housing. In Detroit, for example, over 40% of the nonwhite occupied units in 1960 required rent of over 35% of the tenants' income.

2d: Discrimination prevents access to many nonslum areas, particularly the suburbs, where good housing exists. In addition, by creating a "back pressure" in the racial ghettos, it makes it possible for landlords to break up apartments for denser occupancy and keeps prices and rents of deteriorated ghetto housing higher than they would be in a truly free market.

To date, federal programs have been able to do comparatively little to provide housing for the disadvantaged. In the 31-year history of subsidized federal housing, only about 800,000 units have been constructed, with recent production averaging about 50,000 units a year. By comparison, over a period only 3 years longer, FHA insurance guarantees have made possible the construction of over 10 million middle and upper-income units.

2 points are fundamental to the commission's recommendations:

First: Federal housing programs must be given a new thrust aimed at overcoming the prevailing patterns of racial segregation. If this is not done, those programs will continue to concentrate the most impoverished and dependent segments of the population into the central-city ghettos where there is already a critical gap between the needs of the population and the public resources to deal with them.

2d: The private sector must be brought into the production and financing of low and moderate rental housing to supply the capabilities and capital necessary to meet the housing needs of the nation.

The commisson recommends that the federal government:

● Enact a comprehensive and enforceable federal open housing law to cover the sale or rental of all housing, including single family homes.
● Reorient federal housing programs to place more low and moderate income housing outside of ghetto areas.
● Bring within the reach of low- and moderate-income families within the next 5 years, 6 million new and existing units of decent housing, beginning with 600,000 units in the next year.

To reach this goal we recommend:

● Expansion and modification of the rent supplement program to permit use of supplements for existing housing, thus greatly increasing the reach of the program.
● Expansion and modification of the below-market interest rate program to enlarge the interest subsidy to all sponsors and provide interest-free loans to nonprofit sponsors to cover pre-construction costs and permit sale of projects to non-profit corporations, cooperatives and condominiums.
● Creation of an ownership supplement program similar to present rent supplements, to make home ownership possible for low-income families.
● Federal writedown of interest rates on loans to private builders constructing moderate-rent housing.
● Expansion of the public housing program, with emphasis on small units on scattered sites, and leasing and "turnkey" programs.
● Expansion of the Model Cities program.
● Expansion and reorientation of the urban renewal program to give priority to projects directly assisting low-income households to obtain adequate housing.

CONCLUSION

One of the first witnesses to be invited to appear before this commission was Dr. Kenneth B. Clark, a distinguished and perceptive scholar. Referring to the reports of earlier riot commissions, he said: "I read that report . . . of the 1919 riot in Chicago, and it is as if I were reading the report of the investigating committee on the Harlem riot of '35, the report of the investigating committee on the Harlem riot of '43, the report of the McCone Commission on the Watts riot. I must again in candor say to you members of this commission—it is a kind of Alice in Wonderland—with the same moving picture re-shown over and over again, the same analysis, the same recommendations . . . and the same inaction."

We have provided an honest beginning. We have learned much. But we have uncovered no startling truths, no unique insights, no simple solutions.

The destruction and the bitterness of racial disorder, the harsh polemics of black revolt and white repression have been seen and heard before in this country. It is time now to end the destruction and the violence, not only in the streets of the ghetto but in the lives of people.

Pres. Johnson said Mar. 6 that the report was "one of the most thorough and exhaustive studies ever made." Meeting at the White House with members of the Joint Savings Bank-Savings & Loan Committee on Urban Problems, the President lauded the commission members as "about the ablest persons I ever knew." He then cited his own message to Congress on city problems and said he "undertook everything we could conceive of that we had the resources to undertake." "We may have undertaken more than Congress will give us the resources to do," he added. His civil rights message showed that "we are not unaware of the problems," he said, but "they always print that we don't do enough. They don't print what we do." He asserted that "you cannot correct the errors of centuries in 4 years or 40 years." Johnson asked the businessmen to "do what you can."

Johnson, at his news conference Mar. 22, reiterated his views on the report. "We thought the report was a very thorough one, very comprehensive and made many good recommendations," he said in response to a question about the criticism of "some people in public life who expressed disappointment" because he did "not react the way they felt you should to the report." Johnson stated, however, that he "did not agree with all of the recommendations." He cited the report's housing proposals and asserted that his own proposals in that area were more realistically obtainable. The President also said: "We felt that over all the commission wanted to be and was constructive and helpful." A good many of the things they recommended we had already made decisions on." "We think it was a good report made by men of good will that will have a good influence. We hope that every person in the country can read it and try to take action as they can to implement it."

(But Johnson spoke out May 20 against "the diagnosis of fatal sickness in our society." Speaking at an Arthritis Foundation dinner in New York, the President said he refused to accept the charges of indifference and of "deep racism." "To me," he said, "the fact that we recognize a gap—a gap between achievement and expectation— represents a symptom of health, a sign of self-renewal, a sign that our prosperous nation has not succumbed to complacency and self-indulgence. I suppose there will be many who call me a Pollyanna for saying that. . . . [But] I simply refuse to accept the diagnosis of fatal sickness in our society." "We are on the move," Johnson maintained. "The age-old ills which agitate our communities can be solved. They will not be solved if we give way to crippling despair. They will not be solved if we delude ourselves with labels and slogans which are substitutes for ideas—not ideas. They will be solved by realism, by determination, by commitment, by hope and by self-discipline. They will be solved by the impatience of the American people—but not by pessimism." He denounced those who were "bad-mouthing our country all day long, all week long." "I refuse to accept a diagnosis of deep racism," Johnson said, "because I see a people struggling as never before to overcome injustice. I cannot ignore the progress we have made in the decade to write equality in our books of law."

(At a meeting with leaders of the American Bar Association at the White House May 21, the President said that "a degree of intolerance and almost totalitarian vehemence" existed in U.S. society. He urged emphasizing the relationship between law and freedom in order to give Americans the "strength and elasticity and the will to endure, and the sense to change." These were "very extraordinary times," Johnson said, ". . . full of danger and . . . promise. . . . Our old institutions today are under serious challenge. There is tension beween the generations, between the 'haves' and the 'have nots,' between the schooled and the unschooled. . . . The line between freedom and license has become unclear to many people. Threats and counterthreats fill the air every day. There is a degree of intolerance and almost totalitarian vehemence that says, 'Either see it my way or you will be sorry.'")

Vice Pres. Hubert H. Humphrey had told the National Housing Conference in Washington Mar. 4 that the commission's warning that the nation was moving toward 2 "separate and unequal" societies was "open to some challenge." If it did happen, he said, "it will not be so much because any specific government failed. It will be because our free society failed." Humphrey said in reply to commission criticism: "We have known about those needs for some time. Why haven't we done something? The answer is that we have been doing something." "Our progress has been dramatic" in view of the fact that the country "tripled its investment in health and education in the last 4 years, increased the number of people in job-training programs 10-fold, established a new ministry of urban affairs and passed sweeping legislation to provide equal rights to all its citizens." (Pres. Johnson's press secretary, George Christian, said Mar. 5 that Humphrey's challenge to the conclusions of the commission were his alone and not those of the Administration.)

Humphrey conceded that the government action so far meant little to "the Negro father who is unable to buy decent shelter for his growing family." Because of the very progress he cited, he said, "the sufferings that remain are going to continue to become all the more intolerable." "That need not and must not mean violence," he said, "but it does mean that it may be some years before the intensity of the urban crisis will subside." (In Tallahassee, Fla. Mar. 1 Humphrey had told a Florida State University audience that the commission's report had revealed the need for "a tremendous, co-ordinated, massive program of rehabilitation and social action.")

Humphrey Mar. 24 again urged caution in accepting the conclusions of the report. Addressing a triennial convention of B'nai B'rith Women in Washington, Humphrey said: "Let us not fall into the error of condemning whole societies—white or black or German or Arab or Chinese. Let us not look for scapegoats." "Separatism in America today is a minority movement, led by white and black extremists who can take advantage of current frustrations but do not speak for the bulk of Americans, black and white." It was necessary to "maintain some historical perspective," for "we are not just starting out." In the 1960s the country had "experienced the greatest breakthroughs in race relations in the past 100 years. The commission's conclusion that "white society condones" black ghettos "comes dangerously close to a doctrine of group guilt."

Humphrey said in a Mar. 28 speech, however, that "I believe the most important and principal conclusions of the report are right." The *Washington Post* reported Mar. 28 that Sen. Fred R. Harris (D., Okla.), a member of the civil disorders commission, had released a Mar. 8 letter in which Humphrey had praised the report as a "document of immense value and importance." The letter continued: "The results of the commission report have surely achieved the President's mandate that you 'find the truth and express it.' Due to your diligence and energy but especially due to your sensitivity and understanding of America's racial crisis, we now possess a document of immense value and importance. All of us now face the task of eradicating the injustices and inequalities you have documented so dramatically. The commission's eloquence and honesty will be a crucial factor" in the effort's success.

Republican Presidential candidate Richard M. Nixon had said in a radio interview in Keene, N.H. Mar. 6: "One of the major weaknesses of the President's commission is that it, in effect, blames everybody for the riots except the perpetrators of the riots." "And I think that that deficiency has to be dealt with first. Until we have order we can have no progress." "I believe that we've got to make it very clear to potential rioters that in the event something starts next summer that the law will move in with adequate force to put down rioting and looting at the first indications of it." The commission had "put undue emphasis on the idea that we are in effect a racist society, white racists versus black racists." "There is a great deal of prejudice in the U.S., and there will continue to be a great deal of prejudice, and I think this talk that tends to divide people, to build a wall in between people, doesn't help in breaking down this prejudice. What we need is more talk about reconciliation, more talk about how we're going to work together."

Civil rights leaders had generally applauded the report. The Rev. Dr. Martin Luther King Jr., exactly one month before his assassination, had said in Atlanta Mar. 4 that the commission members "deserved the gratitude of the nation because they had both the wisdom to perceive the truth and the courage to state it." The report, he said, "is a physician's warning of approaching death [of American society], with a prescription to life. The duty of every American is to administer the remedy without regard for the cost and without delay."

Floyd B. McKissick, national director of the Congress of Racial Equality, had said at a news conference in New York Mar. 1: "We're on our way to reaching the moment of truth. It's the first time whites have said: 'We're racists.' Now's the time to seek common truths."

National Urban League Executive Director Whitney M. Young Jr. said Mar. 1 that the report proved that the country "stands on the brink of disaster." He praised the commission for "pointing out that the real problem is racism, the bigotry of white people." "This will be the last study of Negroes," he said. "What is needed now is the remedial education of white people."

Dr. Arthur S. Fleming, president of the National Council of Churches, and Dore Schary, national chairman of the Anti-Defamation League of B'nai B'rith, pledged Mar. 1 that their organizations would provide support in the implementation of the commission's recommendations.

Some Congressional reaction was critical of the commission. Chairman George H. Mahon (D., Tex.) of the House Appropriations Committee said Mar. 1 that he was disappointed by the commission's call for billions of dollars in federal expenditures. "If you can't pass a surtax of 10%, how can you expect to pass a surtax of 50% to 100% to cover the cost of massive new programs?" Mahon said that by raising expectations among the poor, "you may stir up trouble, rather than pour oil on troubled waters."

The ranking Republican on the House Banking Committee,

Rep. William B. Widnall, said the proposals were "very ambitious" and "won't work." Rep. Albert Watson (R., S.C.) said that charges of white racism were an "incredible rationalization." Rep. F. Edward Hébert (D., La.) called the report "propaganda ad nauseam."

The mayors of 6 cities that had suffered racial disorders in 1967 indorsed the report Mar. 3 on the NBC-TV program "Meet the Press." Atlanta Mayor Ivan Allen Jr. said: "We are responsible for the condition the Negro is in today. It is a matter of first priority that we do what this commission reports and that it be accomplished within a reasonable length of time." His views were supported on the program by Mayors Carl Stokes of Cleveland, Jerome Cavanagh of Detroit, Hugh Addonizio of Newark, Henry Maier of Milwaukee and Samuel W. Yorty of Los Angeles. Stokes "reject[ed] the idea that in order to meet these problems you have to solve the Vietnam question." He said: "Congress has consistently used the excuse of Vietnam to cut down on domestic problems. And yet anytime we need an appropriation for something that is sexy and dramatic, they are able to come up with this money."

Housing & Urban Development Secy. Robert C. Weaver told the Senate Banking Subcommittee on Housing Mar. 6 that the commission's housing proposals were unrealistic. He said: "It's not physically impossible" to do in the next 5 years what the Administration proposed for 10 years—construction of 4 million new housing units and rehabilitation of 2 million existing units—"but it is highly improbable. Our best judgment, based on the analysis of labor and the construction industry, is that we've gone about as far as we can go." Sen. Edward Brooke (R., Mass.), a commission member, told Weaver: "We consider our recommendations very real. These goals are not only possible but they are needed."

Labor Secy. W. Willard Wirtz, speaking in Washington Mar. 21 at the 20th annual meeting of the National Civil Liberties Clearing House, an association of nearly 200 liberal organizations, strongly indorsed the report. He said: "I believe deeply that this report is right—that any weaker report would have been wrong, dangerously wrong." Wirtz praised the President and the Vice President as the "2 most effective liberals in the country." He warned that "among the enemies of the report will be those 'liberals' who read it, nod their heads gravely, think how nice it is to have pleaded guilty and then say in effect, 'O.K. It was our fault. We have apologized. Now let's shake hands and forget it.'" "I believe equally deeply that the test of integrity in responding to this report is whether it is recognized as being a call on the nation not as a government but as a people."

Health, Education & Welfare Secy.-designate Wilbur J. Cohen said at a conference of businessmen and government officials Apr. 2 that the report was a "valuable contribution." He said the report "reaffirms our national goals and ideals at a time when our greatest single task is to heal the division in our society." A week earlier, at a news conference Mar. 25, Cohen had scored the report as "over-simplified" in attributing riots to "white racism." He had scored the use of "slogans" to deal with complicated problems. He said the commission had "wholly bypassed" the problem of how to organize the disadvantaged and channel their energies toward obtaining jobs and schooling.

Sen. Harris Apr. 3 urged Gov. Otto Kerner (D., Ill.), the commission's chairman, to hold an emergency meeting of the commission to answer "erroneous criticism" and to discuss methods of implementing the recommendaitons at federal, state and city levels. By "mistaken criticism," Harris said, "I have in mind, for example, the charge made by some, who obviously had not read the report, that we condoned violence, when in fact the opposite is quite obviously the case." Kerner, vacationing in Florida, said in Miami Apr. 7: "The report apparently hasn't had much value as of today. And unless it triggers sustained national compassion and understanding, it won't be of much value in the future." Mayor John V. Lindsay of New York, the commission's vice chairman, said at a news conference in New York Apr. 10 that an emergency meeting would be held. He blamed Congressional "inertia" and a "lack of leadership" by the Administration for the outbreak of violence following the death of the Rev. Dr. Martin Luther King Jr. But Kerner said in Springfield, Ill. Apr. 11 that the commission's work had been completed and that he saw no need for an emergency meeting. Lindsay appealed to members of the New York State Congressional delegation at a breakfast meeting in Washington Apr. 24 to work toward implementing the proposals of the commission by introducing legislation for massive national housing, education and employment programs. He reiterated his belief that the commission should reconvene to focus national attention on its recommendations. Lindsay compared the commission's recommendations for additional spending for housing and jobs with the recent Congressional cutbacks in urban programs.

4 Republican Congress members Mar. 28 had introduced a

manpower bill to create 300,000 jobs as a means of implementing commission recommendations. The authors of the bill—Sens. Jacob K. Javits (N.Y.) and Winston L. Prouty (Vt.) and Reps. Charles E. Goodell (N.Y.) and Albert H. Quie (Minn.) were immediately supported by 10 other Senators and 59 House members. The bill proposed tax incentives for industry to hire and train ghetto residents. Cost of the program: $664 million in appropriations, $292 million in revenue lost through the tax incentives. Javits said at a news conference: "I feel it is noteworthy that members of the minority in Congress are willing to implement the report, while the President and members of his Administration have consistently given the cold shoulder to the findings and recommendations of the commission which was established and appointed by the Administration itself."

A pastoral letter read at all masses in St. Patrick's Cathedral in New York Mar. 10 said that the report "uncompromisingly reveals to us what we have always known and never really admitted"—"our inheritance of racial exclusion, prejudice and discrimination." The letter urged Catholics "to join with all believers in human dignity in a personal and social examination of conscience on racial attitudes in their individual, family, occupational and community living." The letter, signed by the Most Rev. John J. McGuire, administrator of the archdiocese, was reported to have been indorsed by Archbishop-designate Terence J. Cooke.

Representatives of 4 major American religious groups urged Pres. Johnson and Congress Apr. 3 to "take extraordinary action" as "a first step in the direction of implementing the [commission's] recommendations" and enact a multi-billion dollar Economic Bill of Rights for the Disadvantaged, a goal that had been sought by Martin Luther King. In their plea, the religious leaders also called on "our citizens to support the government, even in the area of taxation," and on the "private sector to accelerate its program for improving conditions under which the disadvantaged live and work. . . ." The plea was signed by the Most Rev. John F. Dearden, president of the National Conference of Catholic Bishops; Dr. Arthur S. Fleming, president of the National Council of Churches; Archbishop Iakovos, chairman of the Standing Conference of Orthodox Bishops in the Americas; and Rabbi Jacob P. Rudin, president of the Synagogue Council of America.

The bishops of the Roman Catholic Church in the U.S. Apr. 23 adopted a 2,000-word statement indorsing the commission's conclusions and calling on Catholics to "declare war" on racism in housing, education and employment. The approximately 250 bishops, attending the spring meeting of the National Conference of Catholic Bishops in St. Louis, approved a $25,000 appropriation to "Operation Connection," an interfaith group engaged in raising money from the private sector to finance black-sponsored programs in 5 American cities. According to the Rev. Albert Cleage of Detroit, one program would be to finance a campaign to elect a black mayor in Newark.

Studies Analyze Disorders

The National Advisory Commission on Civil Disorders (the Kerner commission) July 27 released several studies on the urban disturbances rocking the nation's cities. According to one of the findings, the urban riots were a form of social protest increasingly accepted by black Americans as justifiable because of conditions in the nation's ghettos. The studies, which supplemented the commission's earlier report, indicated that a significant minority of ghetto residents had participated in street violence occurring in their cities and that the rioters' behavior was greeted with ambivalence and tacit support, not condemnation, by other ghetto residents.

One study explicitly rejected the "riffraff" theory of riot participation, which held that riots were perpetrated by a small fraction of the black community composed of riffraff and outside agitators who were rejected by a majority of ghetto residents. A 2d study examined racial attitudes and reported that most Negroes, while still espousing integration, did not accept the "basic assumption of major improvement so seemingly obvious to many white Americans." A 3d study found that institutions serving the black slums were "insensitive" to the plight of ghetto residents. The latter 2 studies were financed by the Ford Foundation.

The first study, entitled "Who Riots? A Study of Participation in the 1967 Riots," was conducted by Dr. Robert M. Fogelson of the Massachusetts Institute of Technology and Dr. Robert Hill of Columbia University. The authors said that the "riffraff theory" had been widely used by police chiefs to explain the riots. According to the report, the theory was accepted by the public because it reassured most white Americans that the problems of the U.S. city could be handled without "thoroughly overhauling its basic institutions or seriously inconveniencing its white majority." Since the riots could be seen as a function of poverty rather than race, they were regarded as "peripheral to the issue of white-black relations."

To test the adequacy of the riffraff theory the researchers studied survey and census data from 10 cities. Estimates of riot participation ware based on 6 cities (Cincinnati, Dayton, Detroit, Grand Rapids, Newark and New Haven) where census maps of riot areas were available. Figures from 4 other cities (Boston, Buffalo, Plainfield and Phoenix) were used to compare data on those arrested in riots with a general profile of riot-area residents.

Although the authors did not offer an alternate "theory" of riot participation, their findings indicated that the 1967 urban riots were carried out by a "small but significant minority of the Negro population, fairly representative of the ghetto residents" and "tacitly supported by at least a large minority of the black community." They expressed the view that the riots were a "manifestation of race and racism in the United States," a reflection of and protest against the "essential conditions" of ghetto life and an "indicator of the necessity for fundamental change in American society." *Major findings of the study:*

● There was a larger number of female participants in the riots than were indicated by arrest statistics.
● Where data was available, it showed that more than ⅔ of those arrested were 18 years of age and older. A plurality of those arrested were single.
● In 7 of the 9 cities surveyed, 97% or more of those arrested were local residents.
● About ¾ of those arrested were employed.
● 40% to 90% of those arrested had prior criminal records (not necessarily convictions), but this must be weighed against estimates that 50% to 90% of the black males in the urban ghetto have criminal records.
● While an overwhelming majority of the black community deplored the violence in the riots, a majority felt that the riots would have "beneficial consequences for improving the Negro's social and economic conditions."

These findings were also supported in part by the conclusions of the 2d study, "Racial Attitudes in 15 American Cities," conducted by Profs. Angus Campbell and Howard Schuman of the University of Michigan. Campbell and Schuman found that the riots were justified but "not recommended" by most Negroes.

The authors collected data in more than 5,000 interviews of black and whites in 15 major U.S. cities. They found that most Negroes saw the riots partly or wholly as "spontaneous protests" against unfair conditions and economic deprivation. ⅓ of the whites agreed that the riots were a revolt against real grievances. ⅓ of the whites but only a very small percentage of the blacks defined the riots as "essentially criminal actions," to be suppressed by police action.

Perhaps more strongly than any other U.S. population segment,

Negroes were found to possess ideals of nondiscrimination and racial harmony. Only one black respondent in 8 said that he favored residential separatism, but a much larger percentage felt a need for more black identity or supported spokesmen associated with separatism or both. ⅓ of the black respondents saw little real change in the position of Negroes since the 1954 Supreme Court decision on school desegregation. 95% of the whites interviewed said that they were opposed to discrimination in employment, and 75% said they would support legislation to this effect. Most whites looked to established government agencies to solve urban problems.

The study on slum institutions was directed by Prof. Peter H. Rossi of Johns Hopkins University. The researchers gathered data about 6 occupational groups that served the Negro ghetto in the same 15 U.C. cities—policemen, teachers, retail merchants, welfare workers, political party workers and employers. They found that central city institutions were "insensitive" to the plight of the urban Negro. Under these conditions, they added, "ghetto alienation from the main community" was not surprising. Blacks claimed that the retail merchants charged unfair prices and sold poor quality goods. Policemen said that they were harassed by ghetto residents. Teachers were more sympathetic to the Negroes but were quick to blame poor performance on the students rather than on the school system.

(The results of a separate federally-financed study of police operations in slum precincts in Washington, Boston and Chicago were reported by the *N.Y. Times* July 5. The findings showed that 27% of the policemen studied were "either observed in misconduct situations or admitted to observers that they engaged in misconduct." One out of 10 of the policemen observed were reported to have used "improper" or "unnecessary" force. The precinct studies were part of the broad investigation of the President's Commission on Law Enforcement & Administration of Justice, but the results were not published along with the commission's report Feb. 18, 1967.)

'Unjustified Force' Charged in Newark Riot

The Governor's Select Commission on Civil Disorder in New Jersey had charged Feb. 10 that National Guardsmen and state and local police had used "excessive and unjustified force" against blacks during the Newark riot of July 1967. The commission called for a grand jury investigation into charges of corruption in the city government and recommended sweeping reforms in the city's legal, police and educational systems. The commission, headed by Robert D. Lilley, president of New Jersey Bell Telephone Co. and director of the Fidelity Union Trust Co., included 2 former New Jersey governors—Alfred Driscoll (R.) and Robert B. Meyner (D.)—and 3 Negroes.

The commission's 478-page "Report for Action" was compiled and written by Sanford M. Jaffe, the commission's executive director, and Robert B. Goldman, its deputy director. The report said: "There is no full or logical explanation for mass violence such as Newark experienced last summer." There is evidence of deteriorating conditions in the ghetto; of increasing awareness of and frustration with these conditions among its residents; of the emergence of outspoken groups that focused these feelings; and of miscalculations, insensitive or inadequate responses by established authority." "The evidence that witnesses or interviewees were able or willing to provide . . . wouldn't support a conclusion that there was a conspiracy or plan to organize the disorders."

The report said that the Newark police were neither equipped nor psychologically prepared to cope with the outbreak of violence. Newark Mayor Hugh J. Addonizio and Police Director Dominick Spina were unable to recognize the bitterness of the city's Negroes, the report said, and Addonizio was incapable of making decisions. The city administration was described as "too hesitant to request state police assistance, despite the views of high officers in the Newark Police Department that such aid was needed."

The "amount of ammunition expended by police forces was out of all proportion to the mission assigned to them," the report asserted. Police Chief Spina had testified before the commission: "I think a lot of the report of snipers was due to . . . the trigger-happy Guardsmen, who were firing at noises and firing indiscriminately sometimes, it appeared to me."

Although the Newark Police Department had said that 11 deaths were from shooting "from undetermined sources," the commission reported that: "The location of death, the number of wounds, the manner in which the wounds were inflicted, all raise grave doubts about the circumstances under which many of these people died. . . . These homicides are matters of grave concern and should be quickly and exhaustively investigated and resolved by appropriate grand juries." The commission also "strongly suggested" that policemen had engaged in senseless reprisal at the moment the disorders started to wane.

The commission made100 recommendations covering the areas of city government, police, municipal courts, housing, schools, employment, welfare, health, antipoverty and anti-riot procedures for the city. Among the commission's proposals: (1) State operation of the city public school system to end the city's "educational crisis." (2) Decentralization of the school system. (3) Abolition of the Municipal Courts and assumption by the "more politically insulated" state courts of their responsibilities. (4) The recruitment of black and Puerto Rican policemen and the promotion of qualified Negroes to positions of lieutenant and captain. (5) The appointment of a police commissioner's board "representing the total Newark community" to review complaints of police misconduct. (6) The utilization of the resources of the New Jersey business community in the hiring, training and upgrading of slum residents for jobs and the elimination of discriminatory practices in labor unions. (7) The creation by the state of a master plan for riot control. (8) The establishment of task forces to open lines of communication between City Hall and the ghetto. (9) Additional riot control training and extensive curtailment of the use of firearms. (10) Comprehensive summer jobs and recreation programs. (11) The consolidation of administration and financing of basic services such as police with the surrounding county government.

The commission said in the introduction to its report:

. . . Although violence has marked the path of many ethnic and social groups, the major issues that were in contention in those conflicts have long since been resolved. But one great issue remains unresolved: It is the place of the Negro in American society. It is this issue that almost tore the nation apart 100 years ago. It is this question that led to the Chicago riot of 1919, the Harlem riots of 1935 and 1943, and the mounting disorders . . . since World War II. In the wake of the major racial conflicts of this century, commissions like this were established. They investigated . . . and made recommendations. Many chapters in these earlier volumes read much like some in this report. Poor housing, unemployment and inferior education of Negroes figure prominently in the report on the 1919 Chicago riot, just as they do in our analysis of the conditions in Newark in 1967. The mood in our cities clearly indicates that commissions like ours will have outlived their usefulness unless action is forthcoming from their recommendations. Our disadvantaged communities must see far more tangible evidence of a commitment to change than has emerged so far, or the summer of 1967 is likely to become a prologue to tragedy, and the time for study and planning will have run out. . . .

There is a clear and present danger to the very existence of our cities. . . . The burden of responsibility weighs most heavily on those in positions of leadership, power and with control over the resources that will be needed to produce tangible results. . . . The fate of a city today is in the hands of the policeman on the beat, the landlord of a tenement building, the shop steward in the factory, the employer, the storekeeper, the social worker, the public employe behind his desk or the neighbor who will not be a neighbor. . . . We need fewer press releases from police commissioners on community relations and more respect by patrolmen for the dignity of each citizen. We need fewer speeches from employers and union leaders on equal opportunity in the future, and more flexible hiring standards now. We need more principals, teachers and guidance counselors who want their students to succeed instead of expecting them to fail. We need more social workers who respect and foster a client's pride instead of treating him as an irritant or a child. Suburban residents must understand that the future of their communities is inextricably linked to the fate of the city, instead of harboring the illusion that they can maintain invisible walls or continue to run away. Such change . . . requires the realization of the simple truth that people are a community's most valuable resource, and that to help people gain access to opportunity represents an investment likely to yield a better return than all the subsidies we now provide for scores of economic sectors in our country. . . .

If the events of last July had one effect, it was to show that we can no longer escape the issue. The question is whether we shall resort to illusion, or finally come to grips with reality. The illusion is that force alone will solve the problem. But our society cannot deliver on its promises when . . . disorder and lawlessness tear our communities apart. No group of people can better themselves by rioting. . . . Riots must be condemned. The cardinal principle of any civilized society is law and order. . . . Without it no one will succeed or endure. The primary responsibility of government toward a threatened riot or mass violence is prompt and firm action, judiciously applied and sufficient to restore peace and order. At the same time, we recognize that in the long run law and order can prevail only in conditions of social justice. Law enforcement in our country is neither designed nor equipped to deal with massive unrest. Our police establishments should not be forced into the role of armies of occupation. Therefore, reality demands prompt action to solve the long-neglected problems of our cities.

Inherent in these problems is the virus of segregation. It must be attacked at the source. It is rampant in urban bodies no longer healthy enough to fight disease of any kind and which will increasingly suffer frustration and disorder unless old and out-dated approaches are abandoned and new solutions sought in the metropolitan and regional context. . . .

Mayor Addonizio said in Newark Feb. 10 that the report "at first glance" appeared "to represent a lot of honest, hard work, with some of it off the mark but most of it reasonable and accurate, considering the confusion and complexity of the issues." (The mayor's administrative assistant, Donald Malafronte, said Feb. 11 that city officials including Addonizio had expressed shock that the commission's report had bypassed "the real issues" and instead had proposed a corruption inquiry.)

Riot-Control Action

Atty. Gen. Ramsey Clark had announced Jan. 12, in his 1967 year-end report to the President, that the Justice Department had installed a computer for its newly created Intelligence Unit to handle data on urban unrest. Asst. Atty. Gen. J. Walter Yeagley, head of the Internal Security Division, was named head of the unit.

Army Secy. Stanley R. Resor said Feb. 16 that the National Guard had been given special training and equipment to handle civil disturbances. His disclosure was made in a closed session of the Senate Armed Services Committee. Gen. Harold K. Johnson, Army chief of staff, testified that the "active Army has 7 task forces, each of brigade size, specifically earmarked for civil disturbance duty." He said the forces totaled more than 15,000 men. The *N.Y. Times* had reported Feb. 15 that the Army had established a 13-member Special Civil Disturbance Board in Dec. 1967 and that the National Guard had strengthened a 227-man section and renamed it the Special Office for Military Support to Civil Authority.

An AP survey made public Mar. 1 revealed that police throughout the nation were stockpiling weapons and recruiting civilian reserves in preparation for summer riots. Among the survey's findings:

● Detroit police had stockpiled 100 pairs of binoculars, 2,000 tear-gas grenades and 1,200 gas masks; they had ordered 25 special anti-sniper rifles, 500 carbines, 300 shotguns and 150,000 rounds of ammunition; they had recruited 600 civilian reserves.
● The Monroe County (Mich.) sheriff, with a $50,000 riot-control fund, had bought a $13,500 armored truck, 15 walkie-talkies, 100 rifles, 15,000 rounds of ammunition, 500 tear-gas canisters and flak vests.
● Tampa, Fla. police had stocked 162 shotguns, 150 bayonets, 5 sniper rifles, 25 carbines and M-1 rifles, 300 gas masks.
● Chicago had bought helicopters and was training 4 pilots. Cook County (Chicago) Sheriff Joseph I. Woods's effort to recruit 1,000 volunteers for a riot control posse for the summer had been ruled illegal Feb. 29 by a Cook County Circuit Court in the absence of an immediate emergency.
● The Los Angeles police had established 15 4-man special weapons and tactics (SWAT) teams and planned to train 30 more; a $45,000 mobile command post was bought to house the field commander in the event of a riot. The Los Angeles sheriff's office bought a surplus Army M-8 armored car and equipped it as a "rescue vehicle."
● The Newark police were testing a closed-circuit TV system.
● Philadelphia Police Chief Frank L. Rizzo placed specially trained teams with shotguns and machine guns throughout the city, prepared to establish outposts on rooftops in riot zones.

The Justice Department announced Sept. 3 that it had awarded $3.9 million for riot control to 40 states, the District of Columbia and Puerto Rico. The grants were given under the 1968 Crime Control & Safe Streets Act to provide special training and equipment for police and pay for police-community relations programs.

Police Reforms

During 1968, many of the nation's police departments instituted programs to reform police methods in ghetto communities, train police in the handling of crowds and improve the "image" of the policeman. Many of these reforms reflected recommendations of the National Commission on Civil Disorders in its summary report released Feb. 29.

Concern about police violence was voiced by many authorities, among them Dr. Nelson Watson, staff psychologist of the International Association of Chiefs of Police. Watson was quoted by the *N.Y. Times* July 7 as saying that the "very fact that police are the only group authorized by the state to use force tends to attract the occasional man who likes to use it." However, 2 other psychiatrists asserted Nov. 16 that police departments in major cities had been recruiting men shown to be better adjusted and to display better judgment than members of the general population. Drs. Margaret H. Peterson and Fred D. Strider of the University of Nebraska School of Medicine presented their views at a Chicago conference on violence attended by 1,000 psychiatrists.

In Los Angeles, where hostility to policemen was pronounced in the predominantly black Watts section of the city, the police department had instituted an intensive program to improve the police-citizen relationship. Los Angeles Police Chief Thomas Reddin said in a *N.Y. Times* interview published Nov. 18 that big city police forces had become so "motorized and mechanized" that they had lost touch with the community. "We have to find a way to humanize the policeman again," he added. One part of the Los Angeles program was based on revival of the "cop on the beat," familiar to the specific neighborhood.

The police department of Sausalito, Calif. was reported Nov. 29 to have instituted mandatory group therapy sessions in an effort to develop its staff's maturity and strength to withstand provocation.

The New York City Police Department's 28,000-member Patrolmen's Benevolent Association took advertisements in the city's 3 major newspapers May 27 to call for greater public understanding and cooperation with police. Community councils had been established in each of the city's 76 residential-area precincts to enhance the policeman's image by developing recreational and skill-training programs and providing neighborhood forums for airing grievances.

New York Mayor John V. Lindsay Aug. 4 disclosed plans under which the city's police and courts could handle up to 12,000 arrests daily in case of mass disorders. The plans were described in a 33-page report of the Mayor's Committee on the Administration of Justice Under Emergency Conditions. The procedures to be used included the rearrangement of detention and court facilities to handle large numbers of arrested persons without tying up the police. The plans were made in response to the Kerner commission's recommendations for emergency action during civil disorders.

The formation of a new police group, a 220-member Special Events Squad (SES), was announced Aug. 9 by N.Y. City Police Commissioner Howard R. Leary. The SES was trained to handle crowds gathering at demonstrations, rallies or sporting events. Another mobile crowd-control unit, the Tactical Patrol Force, had already been assigned to work in high crime areas at night.

The Washington, D.C. Police Department Aug. 12 issued guidelines for the handling of disorderly individuals and crowds by methods short of arrest. The new police rules followed the recommendations of the Kerner commission, which found that indiscriminate disorderly-conduct arrests were instrumental in touching off riots. After several incidents in which police bullets had wounded innocent persons, the Washington City Council initiated a policy restricting police use of weapons except if needed to stop an escaping suspect witnessed committing a felony. The new guidelines otherwise forbade police use of guns except in self-defense or when lives were in danger. Over the objections of Police Chief John B. Layton, the Washington City Council Dec. 3 authorized policemen to publicly air grievances against the police department.

(Addressing the U.S. Conference of Mayors in Chicago June 13, Atty. Gen. Ramsey Clark had asserted that higher police salaries were essential for "our safety and liberty." Clark said that the average rookie policeman made less than "what the government says is necessary to support a family of 4" and that "in some cities, ⅔ of the policemen have finished only the 8th grade."

(The Ford Foundation May 12 had announced grants totaling $767,800 to the New York City Police Department and the NYU School of Law for projects aimed at increased understanding between the police and community. The law school was given $600,000 for a 5-year student study of the police and criminal law. The remaining $167,800 was for the extension of a pilot project training neighborhood women as police precinct receptionists. Other Ford grants announced May 12 included $700,000 to the

Metropolitan Applied Research Center in New York to expand research and action programs in urban and minority group problems;
$100,000 to the N.Y. Urban League; $365,000 to the Northwestern
University Law School to train police legal advisers and $150,000
to the New Haven Legal Assistance Association.)

'Decline' in Summer Riots

Atty. Gen. Ramsey Clark said Oct. 3 that there was a "clear and
significant decline in the number and severity of riots and disorders
this summer." Clark's conclusion came from a comparison of statistics gather by the Civil Disturbance Information Unit of the Justice Department for the months June–Aug. 1968 with data from
former years. Clark noted, however, that riots following the death
of Dr. Martin Luther King Jr. "made Apr. 1968 the 2d worst
month of rioting in recent years."

The Justice Department data, released with Clark's statement,
showed 29 deaths recorded in 1968 summer civil disorders, compared with 87 during the summer of 1967. The National Guard
was called for assistance 6 times during the months studied and 18
times during the same period in 1967. Disturbances listed as "major
or serious" by the Information Unit dropped from 46 in 1967 to 25
in 1968. Clark said that, in his opinion, "effective police action"
accounted for much of the improvement.

In an interview July 25 Clark had said that there was less evidence of "militant agitation or conspiratorial efforts" in the outbreak
of riots in major cities than there had been in the past few years.

Housing & Job Lack Not Riot Causes

Inadequate housing could not be blamed for recent urban unrest
and riots, the National Commission on Urban Problems concluded
in a study issued Dec. 5. The report, written by Dr. Frank S. Kristof
of the New York City Housing & Development Administration, asserted that the U.S. had made "steady and unremitting progress" in
housing since the Federal Housing Act of 1949 was passed. 20½
million additional housing units had been needed in 1950. But the
need would be cut to about 10.8 million in 1970, Kristof estimated.
He urged massive federal spending to eliminate the remaining scar-
city in the next decade.

Factors Kristof listed among the causes of the urban disorders:

(a) the movement of Negroes "from a scattered and inarticulate rural status to a crowded, increasing political and socially conscious force"; (b) the difference in status between blacks (and other minority-group members) and the great majority of Americans in an affluent society.

Crash summer job and other programs for ghetto youths had little effect in preventing summer riots, according to an unpublished report entitled "From the Streets" and reported by the *Los Angeles Times* Jan. 25. The report contended that only a significant minority of ghetto youths were "very angry" and that a majority of ghetto youths were "overly content or apathetic." The report was based on Aug. 1967 interviews with 5,886 youths, mostly black, in 11 cities. The study was conducted by the TransCentury Corp., a year-old research firm in Washington under a $159,000 contract from the President's Youth Opportunities Council.

"The complex causes of urban unrest and riots are little affected by whether or not there are summer programs, good or bad," the report said. ". . . It often appears that summer programs are funded out of fear of the minority of 'angry' youths, are programmed to attract the majority of 'contented' youths and are administered in a vain attempt to 'cool' the ghetto and thus maintain the *status quo*."

POOR PEOPLE'S CAMPAIGN

Caravans Converge on Washington

The Negro-dominated Poor People's Campaign, planned by the late Rev. Dr. Martin Luther King Jr. in Aug. 1967, brought 9 caravans of poor people to Washington, D.C. beginning May 11. Demonstrations continued in Washington until late June, when the campaign in the capital ended.

The drive bore little fruit in terms of the dramatic goals asserted by its leaders, but it brought at least a promise of reform in a series of agreements negotiated with federal agencies. These included an expanded food distribution program, changes in welfare guidelines and eligibility requirements, and new provisions for participation of the poor in local operations of several government agencies.

As proposed by King, the largely black movement called for

massive lobbying by the nation's poor in Washington to pressure Congress and the Administration to enact legislation to reduce poverty. Plans were made for the encampment of thousands of participants in a canvas-and-plywood "Resurrection City U.S.A." in the capital and for massive demonstrations. Ultimately perhaps 2,500 demonstrators moved into the camp's flimsy shelters, and more than 50,000 people took part in a Solidarity Day March.

The caravans had started from various parts of the country May 2–17. They held rallies and picked up additional participants along the way to Washington.

The Rev. Walter E. Fauntroy, vice president of the District of Columbia City Council, had announced Feb. 26 that he would not yield to Congressional demands that he resign or break off with the city's black militants who were supporting the Poor People's Campaign. Fauntroy also served as Washington bureau director of King's Southern Christian Leadership Conference (SCLC). A week earlier Rep. William J. Scherle (R., Ia.) had charged that Fauntroy had "placed himself in a contradictory position, and a position which the city cannot tolerate." Fauntroy, appointed by Pres. Johnson in Sept. 1967, said: "You would have to ask the President. But I would hope that his silence means assent on this question."

King had announced in Atlanta Mar. 4 that the "nonviolent poor people's march on Washington" would begin Apr. 22 when about 30 black leaders would start the "educational phase" of the demonstration and formally call on the Administration and Congress. A "mule train" caravan of some 3,000 blacks would set out the same day for Washington from Mississippi, he said. As he toured Mississippi at the opening of a 3-week recruiting drive for the poor people's march, King announced in Grenada, Miss. Mar. 19 that he would call for "a massive outpouring of hundreds of people, white and black," in Washington June 15 for a special day of protest.

During a visit to Harlem (New York) Mar. 26, a week before he was murdered, King explained that the demonstrators would "build a shantytown in Washington" and would stay there "60 or 90 days, if necessary," to spur Congressional action. (In Newark Mar. 27, King said that the "crucial" character of the issues in the Presidential election campaign might compel him to declare publicly for a Presidential candidate. He said both Sen. Robert F. Kennedy [D., N.Y.] and Sen. Eugene McCarthy [D., Minn.] were "competent" men who offered an "alternative" to Pres. Johnson's "deadend" policies.)

An opening phase of the Poor People's Campaign began Apr. 29 when the Rev. Ralph David Abernathy, 41, who had succeeded the late King as SCLC president Apr. 9, led a "delegation of 100" (ranging at times from 130 to 150 persons), representatives of Negroes, Puerto Ricans, Mexican-Americans, American Indians and Appalachian whites, in conferences in Washington with cabinet members and Congressional leaders and presented a long list of legislative demands.

The delegates Apr. 29 met first with Agriculture Secy. Orville L. Freeman. They described the "incontestable fact" of hunger and malnutrition in the country as a "national disgrace" and then declared in a statement to Atty. Gen. Ramsey Clark: "Justice is not a reality for the black, Mexican-American, Indian and Puerto Rican poor. Discrimination in employment, housing and education not only persists but in many areas is rapidly increasing."

At a meeting with Labor Secy. W. Willard Wirtz, Abernathy said: "We ask you to eliminate programs that try to fit poor people to a system that has systematically excluded them from sharing in America's plenty. We say that the system must change and adjust to the needs of millions who are unemployed or underemployed." In testimony before the Senate Subcommittee on Manpower, Employment & Poverty Apr. 30, Abernathy called for "an immediate income maintenance program," "thousands of new units of low-income housing" and a minimum of a million jobs in the public and private sector in the coming year plus a 2d million in the next 4 years. He said: "We are tired of training programs that either screen us out by discrimination or meaningless tests, which ask our families to suffer from inadequate support while we are in training." "The most bitter mockery of all," he continued, was to discover that "either there is no job waiting at the end or that we are once again condemned to exchange our manhood for dead-end jobs which pay a boy's wages."

After meeting with State Secy. Dean Rusk May 1, Abernathy led a procession of about 50 delegates through the State Department lobby. Abernathy then told newsmen: "I think this is the most fruitful 3 days ever seen in the history of this city. The leaders here for the first time heard the cries and groans of the poor people speaking in their own language, unpolished—an outpouring from the souls of poor people. The poor are no longer divided. We are not going to let the white man put us down any more. It's not white power, and I'll give you some news, it's not black power, either. It's poor power and we're going to use it."

The National Park Service of the Interior Department May 10 issued a 37-day renewable permit to allow the campaign leaders to erect their plywood-and-canvas shantytown for 3,000 participants on a 16-acre West Potomac Park site. The campsite was about 2½ miles from the Capitol and a mile from the White House. Many Southern members of Congress had reacted adversely to the prospect of the encampment of poor in the capital. But efforts to prevent or limit the campaign were largely abortive. The House Public Works Subcommittee on Public Buildings & Grounds held hearings May 6 on 75 bills designed to limit large-scale demonstrations on federal property, to limit the chances of violence and to set bond requirements to compensate for any possible damage. In a Senate speech Apr. 26, Sen. John Stennis (D., Miss.) had called for the abandonment of the demonstration since "nothing good" would come of it. Sen. Jennings Randolph (D., W. Va.) charged in the Senate May 2 that there were "strong evidences of Communist planning and participation" in the demonstrations. Sen. John L. McClellan (D., Ark.) asked Pres. Johnson May 7 to announce, "promptly and firmly," that "the government of the U.S. in its capital city will not be subjected to intimidation." He cited "sworn" intelligence statements that "militant advocates of violence who will swarm along the marchers' routes" planned to incite rioting and looting.

The Defense Department announced May 11 that "selected troop units" had been alerted to help District of Columbia police in the event of violence. Pres. Johnson, at his news conference May 3, had announced that the government had made "extensive preparations" to meet "the possibilities of serious consequences flowing from the assemblage of large numbers over any protracted period of time in the seat of government, where there's much work to be done and very little time to do it."

The 2d phase of the campaign began May 12 when Mrs. Martin Luther King Jr. led a 12-block Mother's Day march of "welfare mothers" from 20 cities to the Cardozo High School Stadium in the center of Washington's black ghetto. Mrs. King declared at the rally, attended by 5,000 participants, that she would try to enlist the support of "black women, white women, brown women and red women—all the women of this nation—in a campaign of conscience." She stressed the need for nonviolence but admitted that it was "not an easy way, particularly in this day when violence is almost fashionable, and in this society, where violence against poor people and minority groups is routine." But, she continued, "I must remind you that starving a child is violence. Suppressing a culture is violence. Neglecting school children is violence. Punishing a mother and her family is violence. . . . Ignoring medical needs is violence. Contempt for poverty is violence. Even the lack of will power to help humanity is a sick and sinister form of violence." Mrs. King was accompanied by several white women, including Mrs. Robert F. Kennedy; Mrs. Joseph S. Clark, wife of the Democratic Senator from Pennsylvania; and Mrs. Philip A. Hart, wife of the Democratic Senator from Michigan.

The erection of the prefabricated plywood-and-canvas shelters was started May 13 when Abernathy, dressed in blue denims, drove a ceremonial nail at the dedication of "Resurrection City, U.S.A." At each stroke of the hammer about 500 black members of a "construction battalion" cried "Freedom!" Before he started, Abernathy asked Linda Aranayko, 20, a member of the Creek tribe of Oklahoma, for permission to "use this land." Abernathy said he would conduct a nonviolent protest "to arouse the conscience of the nation." He vowed to "plague the pharoahs of this nation with plague after plague until they agree to give us meaningful jobs and a guaranteed annual income." Abernathy said: "Unlike the previous marches which have been held in Washington, this march will not last a day, or 2 days, or even a week. We will be here until the Congress of the United States decide that they are going to do something about the plight of the poor people by doing away with poverty, unemployment, and underemployment in this country."

The first of the caravans had headed toward Washington May 2 after a memorial tribute to King at the Lorraine Motel in Memphis. Abernathy led a singing group of 1,500 people 3 miles through the city to the black ghetto, where 300 to 500 of them boarded buses for Marks, Miss. The marchers were greeted in Marks, one of the nation's poorest towns (median income for blacks there was a little more than $500 annually), by a crowd of 2,000 persons. They camped in an industrial park outside the town and began recruiting march volunteers.

Abernathy led about 150 persons from Marks to Edwards, Miss. to start the "Southern Caravan." The caravan traveled May 6 through Selma, where Abernathy led 1,000 marchers across the Edmund Pettus Bridge in recollection of an abortive march 3 years earlier (when demonstrators were beaten by state and local police). The Southern Caravan reached Birmingham May 8 with 400 to 500 persons. The Birmingham police charged them with marching illegally without a permit, but a threatened clash did not take place.

The 2d group consisting of about 1,000 persons and called the "Freedom Train," left Marks in 10 buses May 8. A 3d group, of 80 persons comprising the "Mule Train," left Marks May 13 in 15 mule-drawn wagons.* Other caravans, traveling by bus were: the Midwest Caravan (1,000 persons), which started from Chicago May 8; the Eastern Caravan (800 persons), which left Boston May 9 after a rally with Abernathy; the Los Angeles Caravan (175 persons), which started May 10; the San Francisco Caravan (150 persons), which left Reno, Nev. May 17; the Seattle Caravan (75 persons), which started May 17; the San Antonio Caravan (200 persons), which met the San Francisco and Los Angeles contingents in Kansas City May 19.

Troubles in Resurrection City

The Rev. Bernard Lafayette Jr., national campaign coordinator, asked the approximately 2,225 persons in caravans approaching Washington May 17 to delay their arrival in the city until May 30 to allow time to raise additional funds needed to complete the living facilities. Only 206 of the planned 600 prefabricated plywood A-frame dwelling units had been erected May 17, and 1,000 marchers were already in Washington. Lafayette said that the campaign was "in a financial crisis" with enough money only "for the next few days."

William A. Rutherford, executive director of the SCLC, had said in an interview May 11 that the SCLC had obtained about 30% of $1 million required for the campaign through June 30. The expenses included costs of medical equipment, sewage systems, electrical wiring and phone lines, food, shelters, bedding and bathing

---

*67 members and 14 wagons of the Mule Train, which at one point numbered 130 people, were arrested by state troopers in Douglasville, Ga. June 14 for traveling on a busy expressway. The charges were dropped, however, and the wagon train permitted to proceed. Gov. Lester G. Maddox said he had ordered the action to "protect their own safety and welfare, as well as the safety of motorists." The Mule Train reached Atlanta June 15 and was taken the rest of the way to Washington by train and truck. The Mule Train arrived in Washington June 25. The caravan made a 25-mile tour through the city and then returned to its camping site in Virginia. The government impounded the mules June 26 on charges that they were not being properly cared for.

facilities. Dieticians had estimated a daily $1.30 cost for meals for each participant. Another major expense, Rutherford said, was transportation.

As demonstrations got underway in Washington May 21, the Poor People's Campaign was confronted by mounting crises. The campaign seemed to suffer from lack of organization and from disunity in the staff leadership. The problems of insufficient cooking, bathing and sanitation facilities were compounded by unusually heavy rainstorms, which forced many people out of the campsite. The crisis in organization was dramatized by the appointment of an outsider, Bayard Rustin, to lead a special June 19 Solidarity Day March and his subsequent resignation June 7 following a dispute among campaign leaders over Rustin's role.

The Rev. Andrew J. Young, SCLC executive vice president, arrived in Washington May 18 and said at a news conference that reports of serious managerial and financial crises were incorrect. He said that the Rev. Lafayette had conceded that he had "goofed" "under the pressure of questioning" at a news conference. "One goof was saying that we need $3 million immediately," Young asserted. "Another was predicting that one million people will be here for the march on May 30." Young said that the $3 million cited by Lafayette might be the final cost of the entire campaign but that the current cash needs were about $84,000 to complete construction at the campsite.

The Rev. Abernathy announced May 21 the postponement of the planned massive Memorial Day demonstration to June 19. In this announcement he disclosed that Bayard Rustin, executive director of the A. Philip Randolph Institute, had been asked to organize the campaign's June 19 National Day of Support. At a May 20 SCLC staff meeting, Rustin had been asked to organize the previously planned May 30 demonstration.

300 demonstrators were barred from the House of Representatives' visitors gallery May 21 by 100 Capitol and city policemen because they did not have proper admission passes. After a 2-mile silent march from Resurrection City, the marchers, led by the Rev. Jesse K. Jackson, 26, supervisor of the shantytown, were stopped at the bottom of Capitol Hill. Jackson negotiated with police, who were willing to let the demonstrators pass in groups of 20 or less. During 10 minutes of negotiations, staff members of 4 sympathetic Democratic Congressmen—Reps. John Conyers (Mich.), Philip Burton (Calif.), Joseph Y. Resnick (N.Y.) and Benjamin S. Ro-

senthal (N.Y.)—distributed 50 gallery passes. (It was reported that the Justice Department's Community Relations Service had asked the Congressmen to provide passes to avert a threatened confrontation.) By the time 40 of the admitted marchers reached their seats, the House had adjourned.

250 welfare mothers, led by George A. Wiley, executive director of the National Welfare Rights Organization, marched to the Longworth House Office Building May 23 to "keep an appointment" with Rep. Wilbur D. Mills (D., Ark.), chairman of the House Ways & Means Committee. 150 persons gained entrance to the lobby of the building while the rest remained singing and chanting outside. The marchers were warned by police to quiet down and were barred from the building. When the demonstrators continued to sing, police began making arrests. About 18 persons were charged with violating a special statute prohibiting "unlawful assemblages" on the Capitol grounds. After receiving a call from Wiley, the Rev. Jesse Jackson rushed to the scene, negotiated with police and persuaded them to make no more arrests. The demonstrators then marched to a rally in a hearing room in the Rayburn Building. Later the demonstrators marched to Mills' home on Connecticut Avenue and arrived just minutes after Mills had left.

A bipartisan *ad hoc* committee of 30 Senators and Representatives was formed May 23 to help the marchers present their demands to the government. Sen. Edward W. Brooke (R., Mass.), chairman of the group, said: "We are against violence and disruption. We are not opposed to peaceful demonstrations within the confines of the law."

The Rev. James Bevel had announced May 22 that about 200 black youths, mostly members of Chicago and Detroit street gangs, had been sent home. "They went around and beat up on our white people," Bevel said. "They interfered with the workers and were hostile to the press. We had to get them out."

Leaders of non-black groups participating in the Poor People's Campaign May 25 bitterly denounced the treatment they had received from black leaders and members of the march. Spokesmen for American Indians, Mexican-Americans and Appalachian whites said black leaders had ignored them for the most part and militant Negroes had abused them. They said that tension had been "building up for weeks" among non-black groups but had been "played down for the sake of unity."

150 demonstrators led by Abernathy and Jackson were denied

admittance to the Agriculture Department's cafeteria by Asst. Agriculture Secy. Joseph M. Robertson May 28. Robertson demanded that before entering, the marchers pay a $292.66 bill for meals they had eaten May 27. Jackson retorted that the bill was a token of what the country owed the poor.

In what was described as a "shifting of gears," the Rev. Andrew Young announced May 31 the replacement of Jackson by the Rev. Hosea Williams as supervisor of Resurrection City. Young said that Jackson, SCLC director of Operation Breadbasket, would start work on organizing "action cadres" in various parts of the country. The groups would be called to Washington to replace demonstrators in the event of massive arrests. Young said the campsite was "pretty well settled" and would begin to be operated by the committee and its council rather than the SCLC staff.

Nearly 500 demonstrators took over an auditorium in the Department of Health, Education & Welfare (HEW) May 31 and demanded a meeting with HEW Secy. Wilbur J. Cohen. When they were told Cohen was not available, they said they would stay "until he comes to see us." Cohen appeared at 6 p.m. and made a statement indorsing a proposed uniform federal welfare system.

More than 400 demonstrators, led by a group of Mexican-Americans, staged a 7-hour camp-in on the steps of the Justice Department June 3 in protest against the "unjust arrest and indictment" of 13 Mexican-Americans on charges of conspiring to disturb the peace by leading a walk-out and boycott of 4 predominantly Mexican-American Los Angeles high schools in March. Declining to meet with the entire group, Atty. Gen. Ramsey Clark said he would see a 20-member delegation. His offer was rejected. After 7 p.m. Clark relented and agreed to meet a delegation of 100 persons the next day. A 2-hour conversation between Clark and a small group followed while the crowd outside swelled to more than 700. When Hosea Williams returned and said they had not reached agreement, the group formed a ring around the building to prevent Clark's departure. But Clark slipped out through an unwatched entrance. Clark met with the campaign delegates (25 Mexican-Americans, 15 Indians, 20 whites and 40 blacks and Puerto Ricans) June 4. They charged that "there is no justice for the poor in America." Clark gave the delegates a 15-page summary of current Justice Department actions in promoting equal opportunity in employment, education, housing and legal protection.

Speaking at a news conference in Washington June 3, Bayard

Rustin issued a "Call to Americans of Goodwill" for a massive "national mobilization" in the capital June 19 to support the Poor People's Campaign and for enactment of an economic bill of rights. Rustin urged the federal government to meet the following "immediate demands," which, he said, "are attainable even from this miserable Congress": (1) the creation of a million federally financed "socially useful career jobs in public service"; (2) 6 million new dwellings in the next 10 years; (3) repeal of "punitive welfare restrictions" in the 1967 amendments to the Social Security Act; (4) extension to farm workers of rights guaranteed in the National Labor Relations Act to organize unions and bargain collectively; (5) restoration of Congressional budget cuts for bilingual education, Head Start, summer jobs, the Economic Opportunity Act and the Elementary & Secondary Education Act. Rustin called on the President to declare a "national emergency" to meet health and food needs of the poor.

Hosea Williams denounced Rustin June 4 as "out of order" in making this policy statement. Williams said the statement was "unauthorized" and "a bunch of foolishness." He said Rustin's only responsibility was to "do some public relations work."

Rustin announced June 6 that he was suspending his activities as coordinator of the June 19 demonstration pending clarification of his role by the campaign leaders. He said he had tried to contact Abernathy for 3 days "through emissaries," telegrams and phone calls, and "I have yet to receive a call from him." "Unless by noon tomorrow, negotiations begin to give me complete authority, then I'm out," Rustin said.

Rustin resigned June 7. While Abernathy said the conflict had involved "only minor differences," it was reported that the Rustin appointment had been unacceptable to the entire campaign steering committee. The *N.Y. Times* June 8 quoted a campaign official as saying: The controversy over Rustin's appointment had forced Abernathy to "choose between mere reform within the system, as represented by Rustin, and really revolutionary change, as demanded by his people." "It was really no choice because he can't lay down the law to them."

In response to a question at a press conference Abernathy said: Among the goals that Rustin had not pressed were jobs, a guaranteed income for the unemployed, major housing and welfare reform and a call for an end to the war in Vietnam.

Abernathy announced June 7 that Sterling Tucker, 44, executive director of the Washington Urban League, had been asked to replace Rustin. (Abernathy had designated Tucker May 25 as Washington, D.C. march coordinator.) Tucker June 9 accepted the appointment. Tucker issued a new call for support with a revised list of demands on Congress and the Administration. The demands included "a lessening of war and world violence" and the establishment of "strong federal gun controls."

A revised and more specific list of objectives and proposals was issued by the campaign's leaders June 12. In contrast to the original list of 99 general demands, the 49 new "basic" demands included (1) passage of pending housing and employment bills; (2) repeal of Social Security amendments stiffening criteria for welfare payments; (3) passage of a collective bargaining bill for farm workers; (4) maintenance of current spending for poverty programs, and (5) legislation to strengthen and broaden food distribution programs.

Abernathy, speaking at a news conference June 10, had said the campaign had made "significant gains," but "not enough for us to go back to rat-infested slums where jobs do not exist." Among accomplishments he cited: the Agriculture Department had announced an agreement to "provide food in the neediest counties in this country"; the Senate had approved an amendment removing restrictions on Agriculture Department use of contingency funds; the Senate had approved an amended bill to increase low-income family housing; the Office of Economic Opportunity had decided to free $25 million for expanded programs.

About 250 demonstrators began a vigil outside the Agriculture Department building June 12 in support of demands for broader food distribution to the poor. 320 demonstrators marched from Resurrection City to the building the same day and presented the demands to Asst. Agriculture Secy. Joseph Robertson, who met them outside the building's locked gates. Robertson gave the demonstrators copies of testimony in which Agriculture Secy. Orville L. Freeman had told the House Agriculture Committee June 11 of the department's past expansion of food services and its intention to expand them further. Abernathy, denouncing Freeman's testimony, read a statement to the demonstrators and a group of sympathetic Congressmen June 13 saying: "The Secretary took some comfort from the fact that he reduced the price of food stamps to 50¢ a person for people with no income. He didn't tell the committee how a family with no income is supposed to find 50¢ per person for food stamps."

Freeman, testifying before the House Committee again June 12, conceded that he had developed a new awareness of poverty in the U.S. Testifying in support of a bill to remove the dollar ceiling from the food stamp authorization program, Freeman said that in the coming year "$100 million more than the present authorization" of $225 million would be needed. As a long-range goal, Freeman said, a food stamp program should be operating in every county and city. He estimated that such a program could cost $1½ billion annually. Freeman had earlier denied charges of the severity and extensiveness of hunger in America.

Freeman sent Abernathy June 14 a letter outlining those of the campaign's goals that were under study by the Agriculture Department. These included: (1) A family food assistance program in 1,000 of the lowest per-capita income counties; (2) review of the standards for application of the Food Stamp Act; (3) emergency supplementary food assistance programs for about 250 counties cited in a report as in need; (4) an improvement in the quality, quantity and variety of surplus foods; (5) pending the appropriation of funds by Congress, increases in free and reduced-price school lunches; (6) a review of Citizens Advisory Civil Rights Committee programs for elimination of discrimination in the department.

Vice Pres. Hubert H. Humphrey June 15 announced his support of the campaign's key demands, including an "income maintenance" program and more extensive federal welfare policies, job programs and food distribution. In a 4-page statement Humphrey, however, rejected the idea that the government should serve as the employer of last resort.

Chairman W. R. Poage (D., Tex.) of the House Agriculture Committee June 16 issued a 79-page "hunger study" that indicated there were no verified cases of starvation in the U.S. The report was based on responses of county health officers to queries from Poage. The health officials generally replied that starvation did not exist. They contended that many instances of malnutrition could be found but that this often was attributable to ignorance or local custom.

A group of welfare protesters clashed with police June 18 as they prepared to march to the home of Chairman Wilbur D. Mills (D., Ark.) of the House Ways & Means Committee to demand the repeal of restrictive welfare regulations. 9 persons were arrested. 200 demonstrators accompanied by police marched 2 miles along Connecticut Avenue and then boarded buses to Mills' home.

More than 50,000 persons, half of them white, participated in the campaign's Solidarity Day March June 19. After a one-mile walk from the Washington Monument to the Lincoln Memorial, the crowd, which briefly included Vice Pres. Humphrey and Sen. Eugene McCarthy (D., Minn.), heard speeches by Abernathy, NAACP Executive Director Roy Wilkins, United Auto Workers Pres. Walter P. Reuther, Urban League Director Whitney Young Jr. and Mrs. Martin Luther King Jr.

Abernathy declared: "We will stay in Washington and fight non-violently until the nation rises up and demands real assurance that our need will be met." "I don't care if the Department of the Interior gives us another permit to stay in Resurrection City. . . . I intend to stay here until justice rolls out of the halls of Congress and righteousness falls from the Administration, and the rough places of the government agencies are made plain and the crooked deals of the military-industrial complex become straightforward." (At a news conference June 15, Abernathy had called on the "fortunate majority" of Americans "from all regions, urban and rural, of all creeds, races and minorities, and from all economic levels and professions" to come to Washington June 19 for the Solidarity Day March. He said that the demonstration would be a "last call to save America.")

Violence erupted again June 20 when demonstrations were resumed at the Agriculture Department. (The vigil begun June 12 had been suspended June 19 for the Solidarity Day March.) Police arrested 77 persons who blocked the entrances to the building. The demonstrators then moved into the street and sat down, bringing the rush-hour traffic to a standstill. 9 persons were injured. 300 marchers threw rocks and bottles at police outside Resurrection City in the evening. The police used tear gas to disperse them.

(Press reports indicated a rising number of incidents of violence involving Resurrection City beginning June 20. A clash between 6 Resurrection City youths and city and park police was reported early June 20. Camp marshals broke up the fight and took the youths back to Resurrection City. A white visitor was shot in the knee June 23 and robbed by 4 black youths. 4 white youths visiting the camp that day were beaten by residents. Police hurled tear gas into the camp, reportedly to protect motorists who were being stoned by youths from inside the camp.)

Speaking at a news conference June 21, Abernathy challenged Pres. Johnson to explain why poverty existed in the U.S. Abernathy said that one question symbolized all the other questions he was raising: "Why does the U.S. government pay the Mississippi plantation of a U.S. Senator more than $13,000 a month not to grow food or fiber, and at the same time why does the government pay a starving child in Mississippi only $9 a month, and what are you going to do about it?"

More than 300 persons demonstrated outside the Agriculture Department June 21. 100 Mexican-Americans and Indians marched outside the Justice Department the same day while a delegation met with officials to discuss the restrictions on Indian fishing rights in the state of Washington.

Campaign in Washington Ends

As the Poor People's Campaign neared its end, Abernathy said at a news conference June 22 that the campaign would suspend demonstrations for 2 days to begin a "spiritual rededication" to non-violence. He said that the residents of Resurrection City, who had dwindled to 1,500, would remain in their shantytown in spite of the impending expiration of the Interior Department permit. (Police officials reported June 22 that the camp's population totaled 500 persons; the June 24 issue of *Newsweek* magazine reported that at its peak the camp's population had numbered 2,563.)

The camping permit for Resurrection City expired at 8 p.m. June 23. An Interior Department spokesman announced in the evening that no extension would be granted.

Abernathy led more than 300 demonstrators from Resurrection City to the Agriculture Department and the Capitol early June 24. Abernathy and 260 other demonstrators were arrested at noon for unlawful assembly on the grounds of the Capitol. At the same time, Washington police closed Resurrection City. More than 1,000 police surrounded the site while others moved in and peacefully arrested the 124 remaining residents on charges of demonstrating without a permit. By 4 p.m. Interior Department workers had begun dismantling the camp. The task was completed the following day. (Abernathy said Nov. 21 that the campaign had no intention of paying a $71,795 bill presented in August by the National Park Service for the cost of dismantling Resurrection City. Instead, he said, the campaign planned to sue the government for more than $100,000 in damages. Abernathy argued that the group had been given only a few hours notice when ordered to leave the Washington site and had had no time to restore the area.)

Violence erupted later June 24 when about 150 demonstrators who had not been arrested with the Abernathy group marched to SCLC's Washington headquarters. Gangs of black youths gathered and began smashing windows, looting stores and fighting police. The police used tear gas to disperse crowds in a 20-block area. Mayor Walter Washington announced at 8 p.m. that 450 District of Columbia National Guardsmen had been called to the city. He declared a state of emergency and imposed an 8 p.m.-to-5:30 a.m. curfew. As the violence spread, the Guard contingent was increased to 650 and then to 900 men. Mayor Washington made it clear, however, in a TV broadcast later June 24 that the unrest "should not be taken as as an indication that we are in the midst of a disorder of the magnitude of last April." Mayor Washington ended the curfew June 25 and put the Guard on standby status. It was reported that arrests between 4 p.m. June 24 and 4 p.m. June 25 totaled 316, including 106 for curfew violations.

Abernathy was sentenced to 20 days in jail June 25 for leading the unlawful assembly at the foot of Capitol Hill. Those arrested with him were given sentences ranging from 2 to 45 days. From his jail cell, Abernathy released a letter in which he called on the nation's clergy to demonstrate in Washington June 26. The letter said: "I am in jail with the poor and today I ask you the clergy to join us." The letter was distributed nationally, but fewer than 25 clergymen answered Abernathy's call. Abernathy announced June 27 that he would fast during his sentence for spiritual strength.

Abernathy announced July 16 that the Washington direct-action phase of the campaign was ended and called on the 300 demonstrators remaining to go home and await assignments for protest "on a national level." (Most of the campaigners had left Washington by the time Abernathy had been released from jail July 13 after serving his 20-day sentence.) Abernathy said that even though Congress had "failed to move meaningfully against the problem of poverty," the campaign had made major gains. He asserted that poverty would never again be ignored in the U.S. and that national attention had been turned from the question of violence to the deeper issue of "the poverty and exploitation that breed violence."

Campaign at GOP Convention

The Poor People's Campaign moved to Miami Beach Aug. 6 to make its protest visible at the Republican National Convention, then taking place there. According to the Rev. Abernathy, the

Miami Beach demonstration's purpose was to educate the GOP delegates about the campaign against poverty. The demonstrators, he declared, were "representatives of the 51st state—that of poverty."

In addition to leading a number of demonstrations at convention headquarters in the Fountainebleau Hotel, Abernathy led groups of poor people into the spectators' gallery of Convention Hall Aug. 6 and 7. Those who were unable to obtain tickets waited outside with a mule-drawn covered wagon, the symbol of the Poor People's Campaign. (Delegates Norman O. Jarvis of Washington, D.C., Ogden Reid of New York and Clarence Townes, chairman of the convention's Minorities Division, had obtained guest tickets for Abernathy and his followers.)

At a news conference Aug. 6, Abernathy lauded Gov. Nelson Rockefeller of New York as "a man with the intelligence and courage to carry out a platform to end poverty and injustice in America." In a statement all but indorsing the governor for the GOP Presidential nomination, Abernathy declared that Rockefeller "was one of the last chances for the Republican Party to really win back the black vote." Referring to Richard M. Nixon's candidacy, Abernathy said: "In my judgment, Mr. Nixon cannot bring about the type of victory for all Americans so desperately needed for the Republican Party."

Poor People's Campaign workers participated Aug. 7 in a day of demonstrations during which they visited the Miami Beach headquarters of the major candidates. The denim-clad, singing demonstrators were greeted with cheers at the Rockefeller campaign hotel but were met with counter-demonstration by Nixon supporters at Nixon headquarters. They were barred from a news conference given by Gov. Ronald Reagan of California.

PRESIDENTIAL & CONGRESSIONAL ACTION

President's Messages

Pres. Johnson Jan. 24 submitted to Congress a special message on civil rights. In the message he appealed to Congress "to complete the task it has begun" and to enact his 1967 civil rights proposals, still pending in the areas of housing, jobs, jury selection and federal protection of persons exercising their civil rights. The President made no new legislative proposals.

Johnson denounced "the voices of extremists on both sides." He emphasized the need for broad social reform. He said: "The more we grapple with the civil rights problem—the most difficult domestic issue we have ever faced—the more we realize that the position of minorities in American society is defined not merely by law, but by social, educational and economic conditions."

Johnson asked Congress for legislation: (a) "To strengthen federal criminal laws prohibiting violent interference with the exercise of civil rights"; (b) "to give the Equal Employment Opportunity Commission the authority it needs to carry out its vital responsibilities" for ending discrimination in employment; (c) "to assure that federal and state juries are selected without discrimination"; (d) "to make equal opportunity in housing a reality for all Americans."

The President spoke of "the tragedy" of the urban riots of the summer of 1967. "The prime victims of such lawlessness—as of ordinary crime—are the people of the ghettos," Johnson declared. "No people need or want protection—the effective non-discriminatory exercise of the police power—more than the law-abiding majority of slum-dwellers. Like better schools, housing, and job opportunities, improved police protection is necessary for better conditions of life in the central city today. It is a vital part of our agenda for urban America." He held that "lawlessness must be punished—sternly and promptly." "But," he added, "the criminal conduct of some must not weaken our resolve to deal with the real grievances of all those who suffer discrimination. Nothing can justify the continued denial of equal justice and opportunity to every American."

Johnson Jan. 23 had sent Congress a special message proposing a program to train and hire the hard-core unemployed. The message proposed that expenditures for this purpose be increased by 25% ($442 million)—from $1.65 billion in fiscal 1968 to $2.09 billion in fiscal 1969. A major expansion was proposed for the federal program to find, counsel and provide health and education services and job training for the chronically unemployed. It was estimated that such persons numbered a million, half of them in 50 major cities. Expenditures for this purpose, Johnson said, should rise from $210 million in fiscal 1968 to $495 million in fiscal 1969. The number of people served annually would be extended from 89,000 currently to 200,000. The target was to find jobs for

100,000 in the next 18 months and for 500,000 by mid-1971. The services were to be expanded from 76 localities to 146.

Expansion was urged also for a pilot project to provide direct subsidies to private employers undertaking programs to train and hire the chronically unemployed. Cooperating employers, to be called the Job Opportunities in Business Sector (JOBS), would sign federal contracts, and the government would defray the "extra costs" entailed by the program, including productivity losses or salary costs of promotions to make jobs available. A National Alliance of Businessmen, headed by Henry Ford 2d, chairman of the Ford Motor Co., was established to promote the program and to try to find jobs for 200,000 needy youths in the summer.

Johnson announced Feb. 24 that 60 major business executives had enlisted in the JOBS program. The announcement was made after a meeting at the LBJ Ranch in Texas with Ford Motor Co. Chairman Henry Ford 2d, Coca-Cola Co. Pres. J. Paul Austin and Ford Vice Pres. Leo C. Beebe. All 3 were active in the National Alliance of Businessmen, a group working to avert racial rioting. Ford was chairman of the alliance, Austin vice chairman and Beebe executive vice chairman. (After meeting with the President, Ford told newsmen: "It is no longer merely a matter of social justice and the principles of democracy" to solve the nation's racial problems. "Our very national unity and domestic peace are at stake." "And it is also plain that bringing these disadvantaged people out of the ghettos and into the mainstream of the American economy is a goal that can be accomplished only if business grabs the heavy end of the load.")

Housing Rights & Antiriot Bill Enacted

In what was widely regarded as a clear response to the assassination of Martin Luther King, Congress Apr. 10 completed action on a major civil rights bill prohibiting racial discrimination in the sale or rental of about 80% of the nation's housing. This 1968 Civil Rights Act also outlawed specific actions by planners of riots.

The bill had been passed by the Senate Mar. 11 after 7 weeks of debate and controversy. The vote was 71–20 (42 D. & 29 R. vs. 17 D. & 3 R.). The Senate's action was hailed by Pres. Johnson Mar. 11 as an affirmation of "our nation's commitment to human rights under law." He urged the House to approve the bill soon so that it would "be before me for signing into law."

The bill, which was then returned to the House, was a revision of a measure that had been passed by the House in 1967 as an extension of federal protection to civil rights workers and persons trying to exercise their civil rights. The Senate added sweeping open-housing and antiriot provisions during a protracted legislative struggle marked by 4 attempts to invoke cloture (shut-off of debate). The 4th cloture move was made Mar. 4 and was successful. It was the 8th time the Senate had invoked cloture since 1917, when the cloture rule had been adopted.

The open-housing provisions, added by the Senate, were effected in 3 stages: (1) Effective on enactment, it applied to federally-owned and multi-unit dwellings whose mortgages were insured or guaranteed by the Federal Housing Administration and the Veterans Administration; (2) effective Dec. 31, it applied to multi-unit dwellings and to real-estate developments (owner-occupied dwellings of 4 or less units excluded); (3) effective Jan. 1, 1970, it applied to single-family houses sold or rented through brokers (but not to homes sold by the owner without the aid of a broker). About 52.6 million housing units were affected.

As remedies, the bill authorized conciliaton attempts by the Housing & Urban Development Department. If HUD conciliation failed, federal court action could be initiated by individuals or by the Justice Department, or by the latter only to end a "pattern or practice" of resistance to the law.

The antiriot provisions made it a federal crime: (a) to travel from one state to another, or to use radio, TV or other interstate facilities with the intent to incite a riot (defined as a public disturbance involving 3 or more persons and endangering either people or property); (b) to manufacture, transport in interstate commerce or demonstrate the use of firearms, firebombs or other explosive devices intended for use in a riot or other civil disorder; (c) to obstruct firemen or policemen engaged in attempting to suppress a riot.

The Senate had also added a provision to extend to American Indians broad rights in their dealings with tribal governments, the courts and local, state and federal governments.

The Senate struggle for the strong civil rights bill was led by Sens. Philip A. Hart (D., Mich.), the bill's floor manager, Walter F. Mondale (D., Minn.), Jacob K. Javits (R., N.Y.) and Edward W. Brooke (R., Mass.).

The first key vote in the Senate debate, which began Jan. 18, occurred Feb. 6 when a Southern-backed substitute bill, sponsored by Sen. Sam J. Ervin Jr. (D., N.C.), was tabled (killed) by 54–29 vote. It would have limited federal protection of rights workers with exclusions for state activities. Up to that time, there had been an effort toward compromise between the Administration position and the Ervin proposal, favored by Senate Republican leader Everett M. Dirksen (Ill.). In the vote on tabling Ervin's substitute, Dirksen was allied with a minority (13) of Republicans against tabling. 19 Republicans voted for tabling after Sen. Thruston B. Morton (R., Ky.) reportedly convinced the Senate Republican Policy Committee, at a meeting prior to the vote, that Republicans should not be aligned with the Southern conservatives against civil rights legislation.

With the demise of the Ervin substitute, the pro-rights forces introduced the open-housing provisions.

The cloture votes that followed were taken Feb. 20 (result: 55–37, 7 short of the necessary ⅔ majority of those voting), Feb. 26 (56–36, 6 short), Mar. 1 (59–35, 4 short) and Mar. 4 (65–32, exactly the ⅔ majority necessary for passage).

In the meantime, there was movement toward a strong open-housing provision. The movement was marked by a change in Dirksen's position from opposition to support, although the support was balanced afterwards by a move for restrictions. After declaring Feb. 19 against cloture, Dirksen, who opposed the open-housing provision as written, joined Senate Democratic (majority) leader Mike Mansfield (Mont.) in offering to table the open-housing provision. Mansfield considered it "unrealistic" to hope to win passage of the rights bill with the provision. But the Senate voted 58–34 (simple majority required) against tabling the provision.

Dirksen shifted Feb. 26 to support for "some form of open housing" and said he would vote for cloture if a "satisfactory compromise is worked out." By Feb. 27 he had moved to support a compromise including strong open-housing provisions. He offered Feb. 28 a compromise calling for an end to discrimination in the sale and rental of about 80% of the nation's housing. The original Administration proposal would have embraced about 97% of housing. With few Senators on the Senate floor Feb. 29, however, Dirksen obtained consent to add several restrictions, one of which would provide exemption for single-family, owner-occupied homes financed by the FHA or Veterans Administration. Sen. Howard W. Baker (R., Tenn.), Dirksen's son-in-law, also offered Feb. 29 an amendment to bar brokers from discrimination but to permit a homeowner the right to refuse to sell to a Negro sent by a broker. Together, the revisions would have provided exemptions for all single-family, owner-occupied homes; the Senate rejected the Baker proposal by a 48–43 vote Mar. 5.

The Senate voted 48–45 Mar. 7 to grant exemption for owners of 3 houses in transactions without a broker, but a series of weakening amendments was rejected Mar. 8. A 61–19 vote ratified the procedure to substitute the compromise bill, encompassing about 80% of all housing, for the original rights bill pending since Jan. 15. An owner-occupied dwelling of up to 4 families capacity was exempted if the owner rented or sold rooms while occupying part of the dwelling himself. Another exemption was provided for religious organizations and private clubs on housing used for their own purposes.

The bill's antiriot provision was added Mar. 5 by 82–13 vote. It was sponsored by Sens. Strom Thurmond (R., S.C.) and Frank J. Lausche (D., O.), who paced the aisle crying "I want an antiriot bill." Later Mar. 5, the Senate accepted by 48–42 vote an amendment to provide store owners and their employes with federal protection during riots and, by 52–37 vote, an amendment to exempt police, National Guard and Army personnel from prosecution under the bill for actions taken during a riot.

The gun-control provision, offered by Sen. Russell B. Long (D., La.), was accepted Mar. 6 by 72–23 vote.

The provision for barring bias in Indian dealings was approved Mar. 8 by 81–0 vote.

In the final day's Senate debate Mar. 11, Dirksen, criticized by conservatives for abandoning his original position, said: "I apologize to no one for what I have done"; the states, which should determine the issue of open housing, had begun action on it 10 years ago but only 21 had open housing laws today; "how long must we wait for the other 29 states? 15 years? 20 years? Mr. President, this free land cannot wait that long."

In the aftermath of Martin Luther King's assassination, the House passed the measure by 250–171 vote Apr. 10. Pres. Johnson called the House action "a victory for every American" after "a long, tortuous and difficult road."

The President signed the measure Apr. 11 in the East Room of the White House. Some 300 guests, including Congressional and civil rights leaders, attended the signing ceremony. In a statement delivered at the ceremony, Johnson said: He had transmitted the open-housing message to Congress in Apr. 1966; at that time "few in the nation . . . believed that fair housing would in our time become the unchallenged law of this land." But "now at long last this afternoon its day has come." The assassination of King had "outraged" the nation, but "America is also outraged at the looting and burning that defiles our democracy." "We all know that the roots of injustice run deep, but violence cannot redress a solitary wrong or remedy a single unfairness." "The only real road to progress is through the process of law."

After the bill had reached the House, Republican leader Gerald R. Ford (Mich.) had sought to have the bill sent to a joint conference with the Senate. Ford expressed support for open housing Mar. 14 after having opposed such legislation in 1966. But he favored an exemption to permit real-estate brokers to discriminate in the sale or rental of single-family housing on the owners' request.

An attempt to put the bill before the House by unanimous consent was blocked Mar. 14, and the bill was referred to the House Rules Committee. The House Democratic leadership sought to have the committee vote on acceptance of the Senate amendments, but the committee Mar. 19 voted, 8–7 to delay action on the bill until Apr. 9.

Following King's assassination Apr. 4, there was a surge of demand for action on civil rights. By Apr. 9, with Congress members shaken by the widespread riots and with troops ringing the Capitol, the committee voted 9–6 to clear the bill for House consideration without change and with debate limited to one hour. 2 committee members—Reps. John B. Anderson (R., Ill.) and B. F. Sisk (D., Calif.)—switched their votes from their Mar. 19 position to gain clearance for the measure. Earlier Apr. 9 the committee had voted, 8–7, to defeat a move to send the bill to conference with the Senate; Anderson joined 7 Democrats to bar the move.

A new effort to send the bill to conference was made during House debate Apr. 10 but was defeated by 229–195 vote (152 D. & 77 R. vs. 106 R. & 89 D.), and the measure was passed the next day.

OEO Investigated

An Office of Economic Opportunity (OEO) program to train Chicago street gang youths and place them in jobs came under attack in Senate Permanent Investigations subcommittee hearings beginning June 20. Sen. John J. McClellan (D., Ark.), chairman of the subcommittee, said June 20 that the hearings were to determine whether the OEO had allowed members of the rival Blackstone Rangers and East Side Disciples to take full control of the $927,341 program in order to "buy peace" on Chicago's South Side.

The main target of the hearings was OEO's connection with the Blackstone Rangers, described as perhaps the biggest and best-organized youth gang in the U.S. Formed in 1960 by 30 Blackstone Ave. youths for protection against other gangs, the Rangers had grown to an estimated 1,500 to 8,000 members, aged 12 to 25, in the city's predominantly black Woodlawn area. Led by a president, a vice-president and "the mains," a 21-member executive board, the Rangers had conducted a series of battles over the years with the Disciples, a smaller coalition of black street gangs. Years of unsuccessful attempts to turn the gang organizations to constructive purposes led to the June 1, 1967 funding of what OEO officials called the "high risk" job-training program involving the Rangers and Disciples. The idea for the program was attributed largely to Jerome S. Bernstein, an OEO official who had been fired, allegedly for political reasons.

Under the OEO program, 4 job-training centers were set up, and trainees enrolled in the program received $45 a week to attend classes. Rangers president Eugene (Bull) Hairston, 24, and vice president Jeff (Angel, or Black Prince) Fort were paid $500 a month as teachers and leaders of the project. Federal funding of the training centers ended in May 1968, and a request for $1 million to continue the project was pending before the OEO when the Senate investigation began.

Winston P. Moore, Cook County Jail superintendent, testified June 20, the first day of the hearings, that the gangs were a "black Mafia" being trained in organized crime. Sen. McClellan noted that several of the gang members who had received federal funds had been charged with felonies. (Hairston had been convicted May 29 on charges of soliciting a 14-year-old to commit murder.) Chicago Police Cmndr. William B. Griffin told the subcommittee July 1 that crime had increased in the Woodlawn area because the gangs, which police had managed to "splinter" into controllable groups, had united again after the OEO project began. He charged that local authorities connected with the program had refused to cooperate with the police.

The most spectacular testimony of the hearings came from a former gang leader who had not been enrolled in the OEO project.

George (Watusi, or Mad Dog) Rose, 23, said June 21 that the First Presbyterian Church, one of the project training centers, had been used by the Rangers to store weapons and marijuana and to hold parties, all with the knowledge of the church's white pastor, the Rev. John K. Fry, 44. He said that Fry also counseled the gang in an extortion racket that cost South Side merchants up to $8,000 a week. (Under private grants totaling $88,000, the church had provided the Rangers with counseling, food and lodging when needed and legal advice.)

Fry denied Rose's testimony when he answered the charges before the subcommittee June 24. He said that weapons had been stored in the church under an arrangement with the Chicago police to "disarm" the Rangers. He added that police had broken the agreement and had raided the church. Answering charges that OEO funds went to support the Ranger treasury, he said that some "voluntary" contributions had been made out of OEO stipends and that the money had been used for "broadly humanitarian purposes." (OEO Director Bertrand Harding June 23 condemned the subcommittee for relying on testimony by Rose, an ex-convict. In a statement on the charges, he said that the "apparent eagerness of some to accept the uncorroborated statements of a Chicago hoodlum, who was never a participant in the program, raises questions about their own credibility.") Lt. Edward L. Buckney, commander of Chicago's Gang Intelligence Unit, told the Senators July 3 that "if the Rangers were divorced from the First Presbyterian Church . . . , the police could very well deal with them on the street."

Testimony Sept. 5 centered on charges that through documents forged by the Rangers, OEO funds had been diverted from their specified purpose. McClellan said that the evidence did not show "positively where the money went" but that there was a "strong suspicion" it had been used for criminal activities. Public testimony was interrupted Sept. 6 when OEO officials turned over to the subcommittee confidential reports that they had refused to release earlier because they contained unverified data. McClellan had recessed the hearings so that the documents could be reviewed in closed meeting.

Sen. Harry F. Byrd Jr. (D., Va.), a member of the Labor & Public Welfare Committee, had said Sept. 3 that the committee had delayed action on Harding's nomination as OEO director pending word that the Chicago job-training program would not be continued.

Harding said in a letter dated Aug. 21 that the experiment "was not successful in its major objectives" and would not be renewed. He said Oct. 10 that a similar project in Wilmington, Del. also would receive no further OEO funds. He asserted, however, that both projects had been creative attempts "to salvage the hard-core alienated youths in our city slums" and had been worth their cost even if they failed.

Sen. Charles H. Percy (R., Ill.) July 9 had praised the black president of the Woodlawn Organization, which had coordinated the project. Percy said that the Rev. Arthur Brazier had acted with "courage, guts and determination" and that he hoped others would not be discouraged from continuing such projects. Fry said Aug. 3 that he believed that the Chicago program would be continued through private contributions even if federal funds were cut off.

Johnson's Record

Addressing 2,000 supporters of the National Urban League in New York Nov. 19, Pres. Johnson reviewed his Administration's achievements in civil rights legislation and sketched his views on the future challenge of equal rights. The President spoke at an Equal Opportunity Awards dinner.

Johnson specifically cited among the achievements of the past 5 years the Civil Rights Act of 1964, the Voting Rights Act of 1965 and the Fair Housing Act of 1968. But he said that "we are nowhere in sight of where we must be before we can rest." He said that the immediate future posed 4 requirements: to raise Negro income from its current level of 60% of that of whites; to change the conditions of the one American family in 3 currently below the poverty line; to find jobs for the one teenager in 4 who was unemployed; and to cut the nonwhite infant mortality rate, currently 3 times that of the white population.

The President said Dec. 6 that after he left office he would hope to encourage the new administration "to recognize our shortcomings and inadequacies" in the field of civil rights. Johnson made his remarks in Washington on accepting the first Achievement Award of the United Negro College Fund. The fund's president, Dr. Stephen Wright, said that Johnson had earned the titles "Education President" and "Civil Rights President."

POLITICS & PUBLIC SERVICE

Nixon Elected President

Republican ex-Vice Pres. Richard M. Nixon was elected President of the U.S. Nov. 25 and his running mate, Maryland Gov. Spiro T. Agnew, was elected Vice President in an election in which the Vietnam War was the dominant issue but in which civil rights and racial problems were major topics of dispute. They defeated Vice Pres. Hubert H. Humphrey, the Democratic Presidential candidate, and Sen. Edmund S. Muskie (Me.), Democratic Vice Presidential nominee.

Nixon and Agnew ran on a 1968 Republican Party platform, adopted at the GOP National Convention in Miami Beach Aug. 7, that contained these statements and planks relating to civil rights or the conditions of Negroes:

. . . Millions of Americans are caught in the cycle of poverty—poor education, unemployment or serious underemployment, and the inability to afford decent housing. . . .

. . . We must bring about a national commitment to rebuild our urban and rural slum areas. . . .

. . . We must bring about quality education for all.

We must assure every individual an opportunity for satisfying and rewarding employment.

We must attack the root causes of poverty and eradicate racism, hatred and violence.

We must give all citizens the opportunity to influence and shape the events of our time. . . .

. . . A peaceful, reunified America, with opportunity and orderly progress for all—these are our overriding domestic goals. . . .

. . . In many areas poverty and its attendant ills afflict large numbers of Americans. Distrust and fear plague us all. Our inner cities teem with poor crowded in slums. Many rural areas are run down and barren of challenge or opportunity. Minorities among us—particularly the black community, the Mexican-American, the American Indian—suffer disproportionately.

Americans critically need—and are eager for—new and dynamic leadership. We offer that leadership—a leadership to eradicate bitterness and discrimination—responsible, compassionate leadership that will keep its word—leadership every citizen can count on to move this nation forward again, confident, reunited, and sure of purpose. . . .

For today and tomorrow, there must be—and we pledge—a vigorous effort, nationwide, to transform the blighted areas of cites into centers of opportunity and progress, culture and talent. . . .

The need is critical. Millions of our people are suffering cruelly from expanding metropolitan blight—congestion, crime, polluted air and water, poor housing, inadequate educational, economic and recreational opportunities. This continuing decay of urban centers—the deepening misery and limited opportunity of citizens living there—is intolerable in America. We promise effective, sustainable action enlisting new energies by the private sector and by governments at all levels. We pledge: . . .

● Energetic, positive leadership to enforce statutory and constitutonal protections to eliminate discrimination;

● Concern for the unique problems of citizens long disadvantaged in our total society by race, color, national origin, creed, or sex. . . .

. . . We will vigorously implement the Republican-conceived home-ownership program for lower income families and also the Republican-sponsored rent certificate program. Economic incentives will be developed to attract private industry and capital to the low-cost housing market. By reducing interest rates through responsible fiscal and monetary policy we will lower the costs of homeownership, and new technologies and programs will be developed to stimulate low-cost methods of housing rehabilitation. . . .

Americans are acutely aware that none of these objectives can be achieved unless order through law and justice is maintained in our cities. Fire and looting, causing millions of dollars of property damage, have brought great suffering to home owners and small businessmen, particularly in black communities least able to absorb catastrophic losses. The Republican Party strongly advocates measures to alleviate and remove the frustrations that contribute to riots. We simultaneously support decisive action to quell civil disorder, relying primarily on state and local governments to deal with these conditions.

America has adequate peaceful and lawful means for achieving even fundamental social change if the people wish it. We will not tolerate violence! . . .

Lawlessness is crumbling the foundations of American society.

Republicans believe that respect for the law is the cornerstone of a free and well-ordered society. We pledge vigorous and even-handed administration of justice and enforcement of the law. We must re-establish the principle that men are accountable for what they do, that criminals are responsible for their crimes, that while the youth's environment may help to explain the man's crime, it does not excuse that crime.

We call on public officials at the federal, state and local levels to enforce our laws with firmness and fairness. We recognize that respect for law and order flows naturally from a just society; while demanding protection of the public peace and safety, we pledge a relentless attack on economic and social injustice in every form. . . .

The birthplace of American opportunity has been in the classrooms of our schools and colleges. From early childhood through the college years, American schools must offer programs of education sufficiently flexible to meet the needs of all Amercans—the advantaged, the average, the disadvantaged and the handicapped alike. . . .

To treat the special problems of children from impoverished families, we advocate expanded, better programs for pre-school children. We will encourage state, local or private programs of teacher training. The development and increased use of better teaching methods and modern instruction techniques such as educational televison and voluntary bilingual education will continue to have our support. . . .

This nation must look to an expanding free enterprise system to provide jobs. Republican policies and programs will encourage this expansion. To qualify for jobs with permanence and promise, many disadvantaged citizens need special assistance and job training. We will enact the Republican-proposed Human Investment Act, offering tax credits to employers, to encourage such training and upgrading A complete overhaul of the nation's job programs is urgent. . . .

. . . Welfare and poverty programs will be drastically revised to liberate the poor from the debilitating dependence which erodes self-respect and discourages family unity and responsibility. We will modify the rigid welfare requirements that stifle work motivation and support locally operated children's day-care centers to free the parents to accept work. Burdensome administrative procedures will be amplified, and existing programs will be revised so that they will encourage and protect strong family units.

The nation must not blink the harsh fact—or the special demands it places upon us—that the incidence of poverty is consistently greater among Negroes, Mexican-Americans, Indians and other minority groupings than in the population generally.

An essential element of economic betterment is the opportunity for self-determination—to develop or acquire and manage one's own business enterprise. This opportunity is bleak for most residents of impoverished areas. We endorse the concept of state and community development corporations. These will provide capital, technical assistance and insurance for the establishment and renewal of businesses in depressed urban and rural areas. We favor efforts to enable residents of such areas to become owners and managers of businesses and, through such agencies as a Domestic Development Bank, to exercise economic leadership in their communities.

Additionally, we support action by states, with federal re-insurance, to help provide insurance coverage for homes and small businesses against damage and fire caused by riots.

We favor maximum reliance on community leaders utilizing the regular channels of government to provide needed public services. One approach is the Republican-sponsored Community Service Corps which would augment cooperation and communication between community residents and the police.

In programs for the socially and economically disadvantaged we favor participation by representatives of those to be served. The failure so to encourage creative and responsible participation from among the poor has been the greatest among the host of failures of the War on Poverty. . . .

. . . The plight of American Indians and Eskimos is a national disgrace. Contradictory government policies have led to intolerable deprivation for these citizens. We dedicate ourselves to the promotion of policies responsive to their needs and desires and will seek the full participation of these people and their leaders in the formulation of such policies. Inequality of jobs, of education, of housing and of health blight their lives today. We believe the Indian and Eskimo must have an equal opportunity to participate fully in American society. Moreover, the uniqueness and beauty of these native cultures must be recognized and allowed to flourish.

. . . The strengthening of citizen influence on government requires a number of improvements in political areas. For instance, we propose to reform the electoral college system, establish a nationwide, uniform voting period for Presidential elections, and recommend that the states remove unreasonable requirements, residence and otherwise, for voting in Presidential elections. We specifically favor representation in Congress for the District of Columbia. We will work to establish a system of self-government for the District of Columbia which will take into account the interests of the private citizens thereof, and those of the federal government.

We will support the efforts of the Puerto Rican people to achieve statehood when they freely request such status by a general election, and we share the hopes and aspirations of the people of the Virgin Islands who will be closely consulted on proposed gubernatorial appointments. . . .

The Democratic platform, adopted in Chicago Aug. 28, contained these statements and planks concerning civil rights and the condition of Negroes:

. . . Democrats in the Presidency and in the Congress have led the fight to erase the stain of racial discrimination that tarnished America's proudly announced proposition that all men are created equal.

We knew that racial discrimination was present in every section of the country. We knew that the enforcement of civil rights and general law are indivisible. In this conviction, Democrats took the initiative to guarantee the right to safety and security of the person, the right to all the privileges of citizenship, the right to equality of opportunity in employment, and the right to public services and accommodations and housing. For example:

● Because of the Civil Rights Act of 1964, all men born equal in the eyes of their Creator are by law declared to be equal when they apply for a job, or seek a night's lodging or a good meal.
● Because of the Voting Rights Act of 1965, the right to the ballot box—the right on which all other rights depend—has been reinforced by law.
● Because of the Civil Rights Act of 1968, all families will have an equal right to live where they wish. . . .

. . . For the first time in history, a nation is able to rebuild or replace all of its substandard housing, even while providing housing for millions of new families. This means rebuilding or replacing 4.5 million dwelling units in our urban areas and 3.9 million in rural areas, most in conditions of such dilapidation that they are too often dens of despair for millions of Americans.

Yet this performance is possible in the next decade because of goals and programs fashioned by Democratic Presidents and Democratic Congresses in close partnership with private business. The goal is clear and pressing—"a decent home and a suitable living environment for every American family," as set forth in the 1949 Housing Act by a Democratic Congress and Administration. To achieve this goal in the next 10 years:

● We will assist private enterprise to double its volume of homebuilding, to an annual rate of 2.6 million units a year—a 10-year total of 26 million units. This is the specific target of the history-making Housing & Urban Development Act of 1968.
● We will give the highest priority to federally assisted homebuilding for low-income families with special attention given to ghetto dwellers, the elderly, the physically handicapped, and families in neglected areas of rural America, Indian reservations, territories of the United States and migratory worker camps. All federal subsidy programs—whether in the form of public

housing, interest rates at 1%, rent supplements or direct loans—will be administered to favor these disadvantaged families. . . .

● Above all we will work toward the greatest possible freedom of choice—the opportunity for every family, regardless of race, color, religion, or income, to choose home ownership or rental, high-rise or low-rise, cooperatives or condominiums, detached or town house, and city, suburban or country living. . . .

. . . We of the Democratic Party believe that a nation wealthy beyond the dreams of most of mankind—a nation with a twentieth of the world's population, possessing half the world's manufactured goods—has the capacity and the duty to assure to all of its citizens the opportunity for the full measure of the blessings of American life. For the first time in the history of the world, it is within the power of a nation to eradicate from within its borders the age-old curse of poverty. Our generation of Americans has now made those commitments. It remains to implement and adequately fund the host of practical measures that demonstrate their effectiveness and to continue to devise new approaches.

We are guided by the recommendations of the National Advisory Commission on Civil Disorders concerning jobs, housing, urban renewal, and education on a scale commensurate with the needs of the urban ghettos. We are guided by the report of the Commission on Rural Poverty in tackling the equally compelling problems of the rural slums.

Economic growth is our first antipoverty program. The best avenue to an independent, confident citizenry is a dynamic, full-employment economy. Beyond that lie the measures necessary to assure that every American, of every race, in every region, truly shares in the benefits of economic progress.

Those measures include rehabilitation of the victims of poverty, elimination of the urban and rural slums where poverty is bred, and changes throughout the system of institutions that affect the lives of the poor.

In this endeavor, the resources of private enterprise—not only its economic power but its leadership and ingenuity—must be mobilized. We must marshal the power that comes from people working together in communities —the neighborhood communities of the poor and the larger communities of the city, the town, the village, the region.

We support the community action agencies and their programs, such as Head Start, that will prevent the children of the poor from becoming the poor of the next generation. We support the extension of neighborhood centers. We are committed to the principle of meaningful participation of the poor in policy-making and administration of community action and related programs. . . .

. . . We acknowledge with concern the findings of the report of the bipartisan National Advisory Commission on Civil Disorders, and we commit ourselves to implement its recommendations and to wipe out, once and for all, the stain of racial and other discrimination from our national life. "The major goal," the Commisson wrote: "is the creation of a true union—a single society and a single American identity." A single society, however, does not mean social or cultural uniformity. We are a nation of many social, ethnic and national groups. Each has brought richness and strength to America.

The Civil Rights Act of 1964 and the Voting Rights Act of 1965, all adopted under the vigorous leadership of President Johnson, are basic to America's long march toward full equality under the law.

We will not permit these great gains to be chipped away by opponents or eroded by administrative neglect. We pledge effective and impartial enforcement of these laws. If they prove inadequate, or if their compliance provisions fail to serve their purposes, we will propose new laws. In particular, the enforcement provisions of the legislation prohibiting discrimination in employment should be strengthened. This will be done as a matter of first priority.

We have also come to recognize that freedom and equality require more than the ending of repression and prejudice. The victims of past discrimination must be encouraged and assisted to take full advantage of opportunities that are now opening to them.

We must recognize that for too long we have neglected the abilities and aspirations of Spanish-speaking Americans to participate fully in American life. We promise to fund and implement the Bilingual Education Act and expand recruitment and training of bilingual federal and state employees.

The American Indian has the oldest claim on our national conscience. We must continue and increase federal help in the Indian's battle against poverty, unemployment, illiteracy, ill health and poor housing To this end, we pledge a new and equal federal-Indian partnership that will enable Indian communities to provide for themselves many services now furnished by the federal government and federal sponsorship of industrial development programs, owned, managed and run by Indians. We support a quick and fair settlement of land claims of Indians, Eskimo and Aleut citizens of Alaska.

. . . In the decaying slums of our larger cities, where so many of our poor are concentrated, the attack on poverty must embrace many interrelated aspects of development—economic development, the rehabilitation or replacement of dilapidated and unsafe housing, job training and placement, and the improvement of education, health, recreation, crime control, welfare, and other public services.

As the framework of such an effort, we will continue to support the Model Cities program under which communities themselves are planning and carrying out the most comprehensive plans ever put together for converting their worst slum areas into model neighborhoods—with full participation and leadership by the neighborhood residents themselves. The Model Cities program will be steadily extended to more cities and more neighborhoods and adequately financed.

The resources and leadership of private enterprise must be marshalled in the attack on slums and poverty, and such incentives as may be essential for that purpose we will develop and enact.

Some of the most urgent jobs in the revival of the inner city remain undone because the hazards are too great and the rewards too limited to attract sufficient private capital. To meet this problem, we will charter a new federal banking structure to provide capital and investment guarantees for urban projects planned and implemented through local initiative—neighborhood development corporations, minority programs for self-employment, housing development corporations, and other urban construction and planning operations. We will also enact legislation providing tax incentives for new business and industrial enterprises in the inner city. Our experience with aid to small business demonstrates the importance of increased local ownership of business enterprises in the inner city. . . .

. . . Every American in need of work should have opportunity not only for meaningful employment, but also for the education, training, counselling, and other services that enable him to take advantage of available jobs.

To the maximum possible extent, our national goal of full employment should be realized through creation of jobs in the private economy, where 6 of every 7 Americans now work We will continue the Job Opportunities in the Business Sector (JOBS) program, whch for the first time has mobilized the energies of business and industry on a nationwide scale to provide training and employment to the hardcore unemployed. We will develop whatever additional incentives may be necessary to maximize the opportunities in the private sector for hardcore unemployed. . . .

. . . For those who cannot obtain other employment, the federal government will be the employer of last resort, either through federal assistance to state and local governments or through federally sponsored projects. . . .

. . . Education is the chief instrument for making good the American promise. It is indispensable to every man's chance to achieve his full potential. We will seek to open education to all Americans.

We will assure equal opportunity to education and equal access to high-quality education. Our aim is to maintain state-local control over the nation's educational system, with federal financial assistance and help in stimulating changes through demonstration and technical assistance. New concepts of education and training employing new communications technology must be developed to educate children and adults.

Every citizen has a basic right to as much education and training as he desires and can master—from preschool through graduate studies—even if his family cannot pay for this education.

We will marshal our national resources to help develop and finance new and effective methods of dealing with the educationally disadvantaged—including expanded preschool programs to prepare all young children for full participation in formal education, improved teacher recruitment and training programs for inner city and rural schools, the Teacher Corps assistance to community controlled schools to encourage pursuit of innovative practices, university participation in research and operation of school programs, a vocational education system that will provide imaginative new ties between school and the world of work, and improved and more widespread adult education programs. . . .

The Democratic National Committee had taken action Jan. 8 to persuade Southern states to include Negroes in the delegations to the National Convention. The committee, meeting in Chicago, had approved and publicized a statement affirming its "understanding" that any state party sending a delegation to the convention "undertakes to assure that voters in the state, regardless of race, color, creed or national origin, will have the opportunity to participate fully in party affairs."

In the Alabama primaries May 7, Democrats elected to the

party's National Convention a delegation that included Negroes for the first time. Of 9 black candidates, 2 who ran unopposed won.

While campaigning for the Republican Presidential nomination, Nixon had said in Washington Apr. 19, at a luncheon of the American Society of Newspaper Editors, that "the most important thing" for the Negro was "dignity—and dignity doesn't come from government doles but when private enterprise gets into the ghetto and when those who live in the ghetto get into private enterprise." Nixon said in a CBS radio address Apr. 25: The nation's racial problems required "a new approach . . . oriented towards more black ownership, black pride, black jobs, black opportunity and, yes, black power, in the best, the constructive sense of that often misapplied term." "What most of the militants are asking is not separation but to . . . have a share of the wealth and a piece of the action." "For too long, white America has sought to buy off its own sense of guilt with ever more programs of welfare, of public housing, of payments to the poor, but not for anything except for keeping out of sight; payments that perpetuated poverty and that kept the endless, dismal cycle of dependency spinning from generation to generation." What was needed were "bridges between the underdeveloped and developed segments of our society—human bridges, economic bridges, bridges of understanding and help." "We need incentives to private industry to make acceptable the added risk of ghetto development and of training the unemployed for jobs. Helping provide these incentives is the proper role of government. Actually doing the job is not—because industry can do it better."

In an NBC radio address May 2, Nixon proposed programs of tax incentives and guaranteed loans to break "the dismal cycles of despair and dependency" in the slums. Direct tax credits or accelerated depreciation would be extended to businesses willing to put offices or plants in urban areas, he said. Low-cost capital loans would go to black businessmen unable to find long-term financing.

In Medford, Ore. May 14, Nixon indicated "compassion" for the Poor People's Campaign but said "the economic crisis of 1968 has ruled out any massive new transfusion of federal funds into programs for the poor." He reiterated his stand that "black capitalism" would raise the Negro economically. But a multi-billion-dollar "freedom budget" for the poor "is not the road to bring people out of poverty," he said.

Nixon said in a CBS radio broadcast in Chicago May 16 that a "new alignment" in U.S. political forces had "already [become] a new majority" and would "affect the future of all Americans for generations to come." The new alignment, he said, consisted of: (1) long-time Republicans who advocated individual freedom and enterprise and opposed "centralized and domineering" government; (2) the "new South," freed from "racist appeal" or one-party voting habits and progressing with "resurgent private enterprise"; (3) the "black militant" advocating black private enterprise and opposing "handouts or welfare"; (4) the "new liberal" seeking participatory democracy, "more personal freedom and less government domination."

After his nomination, Nixon Aug. 9 rejected a campaign based on appeals to white "backlash" against black unrest. "It's not so much backlash," he said, "as it is decent people trying to fight their way up. They don't want to be mean. They don't want to hate." He also said: "When I finish this campaign, Negroes are going to know that my heart is in the right place and they are going to respect me."

Nixon's initial post-nomination campaign appearance, in a motorcade through the streets of Chicago Sept. 4, drew an enthusiastic and orderly crowd estimated to total 450,000 persons. One of the participants in the motorcade was Sen. Edward W. Brooke (R., Mass.), the only black member of the U.S. Senate, who told a crowd at the end of the route that Nixon would "unite the country, black and white as well."

In a speech at a B'nai B'rith convention in Washington Sept. 8, Nixon avoided attacking his rival, Humphrey, although Humphrey, in an address earlier Sept. 8 to the same group, had charged Nixon and 3d-party candidate George C. Wallace with attempting to exploit fears aroused by the civil rights issue. Nixon confined himself to remarks about his views on law and order. "When an individual talks about the necessity for order, or law and order, people think it is a code word for racism," Nixon said. "But order without progress is tyranny. You cannot have order without progress in a free society."

In a TV interview shown in North and South Carolina Sept. 12, Nixon expressed approval of a Supreme Court decision upholding school desegregation but reservations about some of the methods used to enforce it. "When you go beyond" the decision that "said . . . we would not have segregation," he declared, "and say that it is the responsibility of the federal government and the federal courts to, in effect, act as local school districts in determining how we carry that out, and then to use the power of the federal treasury to withhold funds or give funds in order to carry it out, then I think we are going too far.   In my view, that kind of activity should be very scrupulously examined and in many cases I think should be rescinded."   The use of federal power "to force a local community to carry out what a federal administrator or bureaucrat may think is best for that local community is a doctrine that is a very dangerous one," he said.

At a press conference in Anaheim, Calif. Sept. 17, Nixon elaborated his statement against the use of federal funds to enforce school desegregation.   He said he was not against withholding federal funds from school districts "where a freedom-of-choice plan is a subterfuge for segregation." He opposed withholding the funds "to achieve integration in a positive way," such as busing.   "I do not believe that education is served by taking children who are 2 or 3 grades behind and busing them across to another district," he declared. Nixon contended that Democratic policies would keep Negroes as "a separate colony" dependent on federal grants while his own policies would bring them into the "main stream" of the American system.   He said he did not interpret "law and order" as a code phrase for racism inasmuch as blacks would be the chief beneficiaries of domestic order just as they had been the chief victims of anarchy.

Nixon Sept. 21 visited the Progress Plaza Shopping Center in a predominantly Negro area of North Philadelphia and conferred with the Rev. Leon Sullivan, a neighborhood leader.   Sullivan called the $2 million center "the largest black-owned and black-operated" retail establishment in the country.   Sullivan told Nixon: "I don't want a handout.   I want a handup."   Nixon replied: "You will get it from either of us.   I make that promise for Humphrey."

In his first campaign trip after announcing his candidacy for the Democratic Presidential nomination, Humphrey had pledged before an African Methodist Episcopal Church group in Philadelphia May 2 to work for "a new and complete national commitment to human rights."   He said the nation must solve problems such as hard-core unemployment and "rats and roaches and rotten houses" in slums. He called for implementation of the recommendation of the commission on civil disorders and for black ownership of businesses in black communities.   "One sure way of preventing destruction of property is making sure the people own it," he said.

At Kent (O.) State University May 3, Humphrey replied to a Negro student leader who voiced disillusionment with the American dream. Humphrey said "the whole basic reason for democracy" and its "moral justification" was "man and his relationship to his God." "I'm proud to say I'm a soul brother," he said. "I have a soul, too. I believe in human brotherhood." He said he had known Dr. Martin Luther King Jr., who "believed in the American dream" and asked only an education for his children and their acceptance "on the basis of merit, not on the basis of race."

Humphrey suggested May 14 that whites owning businesses in Negro areas take in black partners, who should be eligible for loans from either federal or private sources at "low and even subsidized" rates. Speaking to a Negro audience attending the convention of the African Methodist Episcopal Zion Church in Detroit, Humphrey asked: "If we can loan money to people we never met at low interest rates with repayment extended over 40 years, why can't we be as considerate to someone at home?"

Humphrey declared in a July 11 statement that the public must become more involved in the national decision-making process. "There must be new channels of communication with the President for those persons previously excluded from meaningful participation in our national life because of race, poverty, geography or modern technology and industrialization," he added. "Councils of Citizens" should be established to advise the President and cabinet officers on legislation and administrative regulations before they are drafted. "Neighborhood Councils of Citizens" could perform the same function in cities and rural areas.

Humphrey said in a July 20 position paper: Although self-help is important, the U.S. should also have legislation to permit "the maximum practicable public investment" to help Negroes and other minorities get started in business. "A country that subsidizes multi-million-dollar corporations to explore outer space won't be 'buying off the Negro' if it contributes to his setting up a business in the inner city." Tax incentives should be provided to stimulate private investments in Negro businesses. The private sector would provide most of the capital for developing black business in the slums; his proposed national urban development bank would play a relevant role in financing such activity.

Humphrey was booed off the stage by black militants at a rally in a Negro section of Los Angeles July 27, but he said July 28: "I am going to come to black communities whenever I have the chance. I am not going to be driven away."

Humphrey said in a talk to the National Association of County Officials in Washington July 27 that "the overwhelming majority of Americans want law and order and progress." Rioting and violence "must not only be deplored and condemned, but those of us entrusted with the responsibility must see that it is stopped," he declared. "There is no progress in destruction."

Humphrey declared Sept. 8 that the Republican Party had chosen "to join forces with the most reactionary elements in American society" "to exploit the fears and tensions that grip significant portions of our people." Humphrey said that Nixon was "no racist" and actually was "a fair and just man," but that the Republicans had adopted a campaign policy of "openly" competing with 3d-party candidate George C. Wallace "for the votes of people who at very best want to put the brakes on our progress toward full opportunity." Humphrey made the remarks in a speech at the B'nai B'rith convention in Washington. While "there has been historic progress" in social programs, Humphrey told the convention, and although this progress had been "too slow" and "very late," it had come "in a lawful and nonviolent way." Now, he said, the nation had reached "a crossroads" and the coming election presented it with a "hazardous" and "fateful" choice. Riots, rumors and racism "divide and frighten the people," he said. "Burning, looting and white and black terrorism make headlines." "The choice is simply this," he said: "Shall we—as a nation—move forward toward one society of opportunity and justice or shall we abandon this commitment out of fear and prejudice and move instead toward a fractured and separated society—black against white, rich against poor, comfortable against left-out?" "The movement for equal rights must now change," he declared. The "new objective" must be "to build real equality, especially in the city slums and pockets of rural poverty."

The National Committee of Inquiry, a group of nearly 1,000 prominent Negroes formed to make recommendations to black voters, refused Oct. 13 to indorse Humphrey for President. Some 100 members met in Gary, Ind. and passed a resolution urging blacks to vote Nov. 5 only "for candidates who show respect for black people." The committee included moderate and militant black leaders such as Mrs. Martin Luther King Jr., the Rev. Ralph D. Abernathy and Stokley Carmichael. At a news conference Oct. 14 with Gary Mayor Richard G. Hatcher, Rep. John Conyers Jr. (D., Mich.), temporary chairman of the committee, said that it would support Humphrey only if he took an unequivocal stand against the Vietnam War and made convincing pledges to help solve black problems. Hatcher said that the group had hoped to come out with a definite Presidential indorsement. He mentioned a Humphrey speech on law and order as one factor that prevented even a qualified indorsement of Humphrey.

Shortly after his nomination for Vice President, Agnew Aug. 9 had expressed concern about criticism of his civil rights stand. Agnew said: He was disturbed about a confusion between civil rights and civil disobedience. "To me, civil rights means the right of any citizen, regardless of race, creed or color, to enjoy the protection of our constitution, to be immune from racial discrimination, to have equal job opportunities, to be able to house his family in any neighborhood he chooses to, and to have equal access to public accommodations." "I don't know how these rights, which I admit and deplore have been denied to some people, have anything to do with civil disobedience." How can one say "that a person who is against civil disorder is against civil rights? . . . I don't think the 2 have anything to do with each other."

Beginning his first full week of campaigning in Seattle, Wash. Aug. 19, Agnew said " a man can be totally pro-civil rights and totally against civil disobedience." In Detroit Aug. 21 he told delegates to the Veterans of Foreign Wars convention: "You know how strongly I feel about the absolute necessity for respect of law, but that's not the whole answer. With law and order must come justice and equal opportunity. Law and order must mean to all of our people the protection of the innocent, not to some the cracking of black skulls."

In Grand Rapids, Mich. Aug. 24, where he was introduced to the Republican State Convention by Gov. George Romney (R., Mich.), Agnew said: "When we win, we're just liable to bring back into American life a lot of things that the devotees of the so-called 'new politics' consider dull—dull things like patriotism, . . . incentive, . . . a respect for law and a concern for a greater justice for all Americans." "In fact, things could become so dull that some little old ladies in tennis shoes might not need them any longer to evade the criminals on city streets and might go back to wearing high heels."

At the Oshkosh, Wis. airport Sept. 4, Agnew said the term "law and order" was used by George Wallace "as a hatchet," by Humphrey "as a shield against criticism of the sluggish Administration of which he is part," and by Nixon "as a pledge, not maliciously, not defensively, but as a commitment to logic and as a commitment to America." "Without law," he said, "there can be no civil rights for any American. Without order we can have no social progress. Without law and order we have social suicide."

Agnew was criticized repeatedly for using the phrase "law and order." But Agnew Sept. 10 rejected an appeal by Sen. Edward W. Brooke (R., Mass.) to say "order with justice" in place of "law and order," which Brooke, himself black, identified as "an unfortunate code word" suggesting hard-line repression of demonstrators, especially Negroes. In a speech Sept. 15 in Norridge, a Chicago suburb, Agnew said the "law-and-order" issue "very possibly will decide the 1968 election." Agnew declared:

"Law and order comes when government makes up its mind that the people and the Constitution, not the mob, will rule America." "Anarchy is not the answer, nor is rioting the inalienable right of any citizen." The Administration had failed "to maintain order" and "to make law meaningful." "When the people feel more action is to be gained by going to the streets rather than to the courts, something is wrong. And when mob violence is rewarded, something is wrong." "For violence rewarded breeds further violence, and perpetual violence ultimately will produce its own brutal counter-reaction. Continuous confrontation could very well transform our free states into police states. Right now, the greatest threat to our civil rights comes from those who abuse our civil liberties."

"We shall establish clear and unequivocal guidelines as to what constitutes peaceful confrontation and what is deliberate provocation." "In restoring rightful authority we must not establish authoritarian government. The balance of democracy is a delicate one, and the preservation of this balance is the first duty of citizen and government alike."

"We will not tolerate violence, nor will we tolerate the vicious conditions of poverty and prejudice that create violent men. We will use the law vigorously as the only weapon to achieve social justice." "We shall open the channels of redress so government can respond with speed and strength to legitimate grievances. We are ready to put all the influence and resources of our society on the line for the man who for too long has had society's foot on his neck. And we are not going to allow any man to prey upon passion or prejudice to destroy our society."

At a meeting of the American Political Science Association in Washington Sept. 5, Agnew had favored a "thinning out" of slum populations, without complusion. Rural migrants could be encouraged to settle in non-urban areas by increased economic opportunities, he said. New satellite cities, with a balanced mix of housing and industry, could be created to surround the inner city. Cities would not be "completely fit for human habitation until discrimination in housing, employment and education has become as extinct as slavery," Agnew held. The emphasis should be on "helping minority group members to become managers and owners of businesses in the ghettos and to become homeowners." There should be a "national strategy" to create jobs, housing, schools and a welfare system that "provides decently for those who must be supported by society but gives to others incentive and opportunity to become self-supporting."

Agnew asserted at Cleveland airport Sept. 8 that the U.S. "was not such a bad country to live in, and we want to keep it the way it is and not make it a comfortable place for criminals." He said that the way to correct discrimination was "through the ballot box and the courts and not through anarchy and violence."

Agnew insisted in a talk at Euclid Beach Park Sept. 8 that "civil disobedience can't be condoned when it interferes with civil rights of others, and most often it does." At a Chicago news conference Sept. 13, Agnew opposed nonviolent civil disobedience campaigns such as the Negro sit-in movement in the South in the 1950s. While the movement had protested "inequities," he conceded "you can't condone it, because it leaves to the judgment of an individual whether he shall obey a law."

Muskie had said in Chicago Aug. 29, shortly after his nomination: The racial problem was one of "engaging the confidence" of the Negroes and the poor and of encouraging their "maximum participation" in society and politics. The Negro and the poor must understand that they would not gain "instant success" but must "have patience."

Other Candidates

One of the candidates for the Democratic Presidential nomination had been Sen. Robert F. Kennedy (Mass.). A slate of delegates pledged to Kennedy won the District of Columbia Democratic primary May 7 over 2 slates backing Vice Pres. Humphrey. The Kennedy slate was headed by the Rev. Channing E. Phillips, a Negro, who was also elected as District of Columbia Democratic National Committeeman. His running mate, Mrs. Flaxie M. Pinkett, also a Negro, was elected District of Columbia National Committeewoman. The regular party organization was represented by a slate headed by incumbent National Committeeman E. Franklin Jackson, a black minister. His slate had supported Pres. Johnson but switched to Humphrey after Johnson had withdrawn from the campaign.

Robert F. Kennedy was assassinated just after he won Cali-

fornia's Democratic Presidential primary June 4 and the state's 172
Democratic National Convention delegate votes. Kennedy re-
ceived 46% of the total Democratic vote. Sen. Eugene J. Mc-
Carthy (D., Minn.) received 42%. Kennedy's victory was attrib-
uted to a heavy vote for him from minority groups—Negroes and
Mexican-Americans—and from labor.

The California campaign had included a TV "debate" between
Kennedy and McCarthy over the ABC network June 1. In the debate, McCarthy advocated "a new Bill of Rights" providing a massive housing program for ghetto dwellers, some dispersion from
ghettos and interim programs "if there is a threat of violence before
we get around to doing the things that have to be done." Programs aimed only at improving the ghetto might produce "a kind
of *apartheid*," he said. "We need to get a distribution of the races
throughout our society." Kennedy favored "moving people out of
the ghetto" but said: "We have to do something for them there."
"When you say you are going to take 10,000 black people and
move them into Orange County . . . , putting them in suburbs where
they can't afford the housing, where their children can't keep up
with the schools, and where they don't have the schools or the jobs,
it's just going to be catastrophic. I don't want to have them
moved." McCarthy June 2 accused Kennedy of having "injected
scare tactics into the campaign" by his comment about moving
blacks into Orange County (a conservative area south of Los Angeles). McCarthy called the remark "a crude distortion of my
proposals" that could "increase suspicion and mistrust among the
races."

McCarthy, campaigning for the nomination, had asserted in
Omaha Apr. 2 that "we have the moral strength to see to it that 15
million Negroes can become full participants in the good life of
America." Campaigning in New Haven and Hartford, Conn., Mc-
Carthy said it was time to "release the colonial nation" of Negroes
in the U.S. and to guarantee that everyone "receives an income proportionate to his dignity as a person." He told a Boston University
audience Apr. 11 that Negroes in America were "mired in a cycle
of poverty" and that sweeping measures would have to be undertaken "to effect a reconciliation" between the races. "Just as
American Negroes are wearying of the demeaning conditions and
the racist attitude which have now brought rioting to our cities,
white Americans are tired of the riots these conditions cause," Mc-
Carthy declared. The nation "longs for reconciliation," which
"will come only with an Administration which is prepared to com-

mit itself to massive programs of correction"—a minimum income
"for all Americans," federally-subsidized programs to "assure that
no citizens will be deprived of health care for lack of funds" and to
"upgrade the education of our adults who are trapped in the poverty syndrome," a "massive" building program "to bring within
reach of low and moderate income families" some 6 million housing units.

McCarthy appeared June 20 before the National Newspaper
Publishers Association representing 72 of the largest Negro publi-
cations in the country. He told the publishers that power and responsibility must be "democratically shared" if urban, poverty and
racial problems were to be solved, and the sharing was "not going
to be painless for America."

McCarthy said at the Colorado State Democratic Convention
in Ft. Collins July 13 that the poor should be given some responsibility for managing welfare and other programs aimed at helping
the poor. The government should try "placing real confidence in
the poor themselves, and real money in local action programs in
which they play a leading part." McCarthy said at a rally in Detroit July 27 that "it is time for a new Administration to address itself to the condition of powerlessness. For the fact is that poverty
is no accident. Black people are poor because they are powerless
and powerless because they are black." "It is time to release the
black people and the poor people from bondage." At the rally in
Detroit Tiger Stadium, McCarthy won the indorsement of the Rev.
Albert Cleage, Detroit black militant leader. Cleage said: "Black
power is the only issue I'm concerned about."

McCarthy said in an 800-word position paper on urban problems July 28: If he were elected President, he would spend "a substantial part of the $30 billion [a year] now going to Vietnam" to
solve the problems of the cities. A minimum income should be
provided for "those unable to work," and the welfare system should
be abolished. "Black power and white power" should be given to
local communities and the poor. A "massive job creation program"
should be started with (a) "tax incentives to private enterprise, encouraging them to locate in areas of unemployment," and (b)
"state, local and federal public works so that those now unemployed
will have jobs that make a real contribution to the community."

McCarthy added in a position paper on Negro unemployment,
released in Washington Aug. 13: "We will not meet our urban crisis
until we solve the problem of ghetto unemployment. We must pro-

vide permanent work. We must provide work with room for further advancement. If the private sector cannot produce the jobs necessary, the government must be the employer of the last resort." "We must stimulate the private sector to create new jobs on an unprecedented scale. And we must see to it that the private sector produces new kinds of jobs in new environments." "We call . . . for a new employment policy for the ghetto—to create new jobs, and new kinds of jobs for the poor of our inner cities. Such a new policy must summon the resources and commitment of the public and private sectors alike. And it may move immediately to guarantee full access for the unemployed in 4 critical areas": " access to job markets," "access to job information," "access to job skills" and "overcoming racial discrimination." "Tax credits should be keyed to increased income for the subemployed. The size of the businessman's tax credits should depend on his success at raising the earnings of the unemployed for an extended period above a specified minimum level, and at raising the earnings of the menially employed above their average income in the past. Businessmen must have an incentive to use on-the-job training to help move people from the category of the subemployed to more desirable job classifications."

McCarthy proposed Aug. 14, in a position paper on housing: Enough housing should be built each year to actually meet the goal of 6 million for the next 5 years recommended by the National Advisory Commission on Civil Disorders. Federal funds should be provided liberally on the local level. Aid should be made in the form of block grants, and basic decisions on specific projects should be delegated to the individual cities. "Federal funds should be made available to the agencies—public and private—that are currently engaged in promoting fair housing. Priority should go to those agencies working at the metropolitan level."

McCarthy said Aug. 17, in a speech to a predominantly black audience of 2,000 at a meeting of Operation Breadbasket in Chicago's South Side: Americans should not be surprised when blacks protest and demonstrate against "discrimination and repression." "You cannot, for 200 years, talk about equality and not provide it without expecting at some point for people to protest and demonstrate. You cannot talk about the gross national product without having 10 to 20 million living in poverty asking 'What about us?' "

McCarthy's candidacy was indorsed Aug. 7 by Julian Bond, black member of the Georgia Legislature.

Sen. George S. McGovern (S.D.), also seeking the Democratic

Presidential nomination, said at an airport news conference in New York Aug. 12 that he considered "racism at least as great a threat to the nation as the war in Vietnam." McGovern said in a speech before the National Press Club in Washington Aug. 15: An extensive federal commitment was necessary to eradicate slums and calm racial tension. "Empty-headed cries for law and order" carried an "undertone of racism that only aggravates the lawlessness and discontent." "Law and order without justice is a very hollow slogan. Hitler did a pretty good job of preserving law and order." "The next President of the United States will either deal creatively and energetically with our troubled cities or he will preside over 4 years of unprecedented violence and confusion." Civil rights laws must be enforced so that Negroes could escape from the ghettos as nonblack ethnic groups had done in the past. The slums must be rehabilitated, not only by private-public enterprises, but by "extensive federal assistance" and reconstruction of some of the basic institutions that had contributed to the sense of hopelessness in the slums.

Gov. Ronald Reagan of California, a "favorite-son" candidate for the Republican Presidential nomination, had said in an interview in Washington June 23: "We are a compassionate people" and it was a "fallacy" that the Poor People's Campaign was necessary "to arouse the national conscience." The campaign's leadership had "deluded" and "victimized" the poor by leading them to believe the Congress could end poverty, if it wanted to, by a new law or program. If the leadership of the campaign refused to close Resurrection City when its federal permit expired, it should "be moved out." Militant black leaders had "something else in mind" than progress for the black people and were "aligned with causes in which they are preaching insurrection and overthrow of a system." The militants were harming the black cause by obscuring the "tremendous progress" made by blacks in recent years and the more favorable attitude taken toward Negroes by the white community.

In support of New York Gov. Nelson A. Rockefeller's candidacy for the Republican Presidential nomination, a group dubbed Black Independents & Democrats for Rockefeller announced its formation July 15. The group included both moderate and militant Negroes, among them former CORE head James Farmer; Omar Ahmed, an associate of the late Malcolm X; Dr. Benjamin Watkins, honorary "mayor of Harlem"; New York City Transit Authority Secy. Lloyd Peterson; and Mrs. Arthur C. Logan, a member of the board of directors of the Southern Christian Leadership Conference.

The group said it was backing Rockefeller "because we believe he is a reasonable man" and none of the other potential candidates deserved black support.

9 Blacks Elected to U.S. House

The elections Nov. 5 brought victory to a record number of black candidates—9, all Democrats—for seats in the U.S. House of Representatives. The previous high was 7 during the Reconstruction years 1873-4. 6 of the black Representatives were incumbents: Adam Clayton Powell (N.Y.), John Conyers Jr. (Mich.), William L. Dawson (Ill.), Charles C. Diggs Jr. (Mich.), Augustus F. Hawkins (Calif.) and Robert N. C. Nix (Pa.). The 3 black newcomers were Mrs. Shirley Chisholm (N.Y.) of Brooklyn, who defeated James Farmer, ex-chairman of CORE; Louis Stokes (O.) of Cleveland, brother of Cleveland's first Negro mayor, Carl B. Stokes; and William L. Clay (Mo.) of St. Louis.

Black civil rights leader Charles Evers, 45, had led 6 white segregationist opponents in a special election Feb. 27 for Mississippi's 3d District Congressional seat. John Bell Williams had held the seat for 21 years prior to his election as governor. Evers did not get a majority vote, and Charles H. Griffin, 41, former administrative aide to Williams and 2d leader in the Feb. 27 vote, defeated Evers by a 2-1 margin in the run-off election Mar. 12.

Blacks & the Armed Forces

The Defense Department July 10 reported a sharp decrease in armed forces re-enlistments in 1967, with re-enlistments of blacks showing a greater drop than re-enlistments of whites. 1967 re-enlistment rates (1966 figures in parentheses): Army—blacks 31.7% (66.5%); whites 12.8% (20%). Marine Corps—blacks 15.9% (19.5%); whites 9.7% (10.5%). Navy—blacks 22.5% (24.7%); whites 16.7% (17.6%). Air Force—blacks 26.9% (30%); whites 17.3% (16%).

The Defense Department Oct. 1 reported a decrease in the number of Negro combat deaths in Vietnam. Of the 25,616 U.S. soldiers killed between Jan. 1, 1961 and June 30, 1968, blacks accounted for 13.7%, or .4% less than the 14.1% recorded up to Dec. 31, 1967. Negro combat deaths 1961-6 had accounted for 16% of the total. Negro combat fatalities in 1967 had totaled

12.7% of the 9,378 Americans slain in the Vietnam fighting that year.

Of the 629,729 U.S. servicemen involved in the war in Vietnam as of June 30 (including American troops stationed in Thailand and aboard U.S. vessels off the North Vietnamese coast), blacks constituted 10½%, or .7% more than the 9.8% of Dec. 31, 1967.

The Defense Department had drawn up the special studies on the Negro role in the Vietnamese war following charges by some black leaders that black servicemen were carrying a heavier proportionate burden than whites.

41 black soldiers were court-martialed at Ft. Hood, Tex. Oct. 25–Dec. 7 for refusing to disperse during a demonstration Aug. 24 against possible riot duty at the Democratic National Convention in Chicago. 29 were found guilty, and 12 were cleared. Prison terms ranged from 3 months to 4 years at hard labor.

At least 316 Negroes were added to the nation's 4,080 local draft boards during 1967, the Selective Service System reported Jan. 13. At the end of 1966, 278 blacks were serving on local boards; by Nov. 30, 1967 there were 594 Negroes on local boards, and officials estimated Jan. 13 that the number had already passed 600. The increase was attributed both to the personal appeals made by the Selective Service System director, Lt. Gen. Lewis B. Hershey, to Southern governors and to the more than 1,500 vacancies created by a provision of the 1967 draft law that required all local board members 75 years of age or with 25 years of service to retire. The 594 black members constituted 3.8% of the 17,264 local board members. (Negroes comprised 11% of the U.S. population.) In mid-1966, 1.3% of draft board members were black; 1.8% were Puerto Rican, Mexican-American, Oriental and American Indian. In Mississippi and Alabama no increases were reported. In Louisiana, however, the number of black board members increased from none to 33, and in Arkansas the number rose from none to 35.

HOUSING & THE CITIES

States & Cities Ban Housing Bias

Several state and city open-housing laws were adopted in 1968, particularly after the signing of the 1968 Civil Rights Bill Apr. 11. Among state and local open-housing law developments:
• Voters in Flint, Mich. approved a fair-housing ordinance Feb. 21

by a 30-vote margin (the vote, according to a 2-day recount Mar. 4–5: 20,170 to 20,140). Margaret Fisher, information director for the National Council against Housing Discrimination, said that it was the first time an antidiscriminatory housing measure had been won through popular vote.

• The first statewide open-housing law in the South became law in Kentucky Mar. 27 after nearly a year of demonstrations in Louisville. The ordinance, which Gov. Louie B. Nunn allowed to become law without his signature, did not apply to sales made by the owner without an agent, to rentals in buildings with few units if the owner either had lived in the building or rented directly to tenants or to transactions by religious or charitable institutions.

• Gov. John H. Chafee of Rhode Island Apr. 6 signed a bill permitting civil court suits against landlords accused of discrimination.

• A law to prevent discrimination by real estate agents and lending institutions was adopted by the Seattle City Council Apr. 19. The ordinance carried an emergency clause to make it effective immediately.

• The City Council of Kansas City Apr. 19 adopted a law designed to match open-housing provisions of the federal bill.

• In Milwaukee, the scene of 200 consecutive nights of demonstrations against housing discrimination, the city Common Council Apr. 30, by 15–4 vote, adopted an open-housing ordinance that exempted only rentals in owner-occupied duplexes. Mayor Henry M. Maier had asked the council to pass an ordinance modeled on the federal bill. Plans to hold an open-housing referendum (in which it was assumed that open housing would be defeated) had been enjoined Mar. 5 by Federal Judge Robert E. Teban.

• The Chicago City Council July 11 adopted a law, proposed by Mayor Richard J. Daley, that banned discrimination by anyone selling or renting housing. The ordinance expanded a 1963 open-housing law directed against discriminatory practices by real estate brokers.

The Annual Governors Conference in Cincinnati July 24 adopted a "declaration of conscience" supporting the eradication of racial bias in a number of activities, including "the purchase, sale and rental of real estate." The declaration was sponsored by Gov. George Romney (R., Mich.).

Government Action Vs. Housing Discrimination

The Justice Department July 22, in its first suits under the fair-housing section of the 1968 Civil Rights Act, charged that 3 subdivisions in Baton Rouge, La. discriminated against blacks who wanted to buy homes. The suits filed in U.S. District Court in New Orleans, were against builders and sellers in Sherwood Forest Place, Drusilla Place and Jefferson Terrace.

The first indictment under the section was returned in federal court in Brooklyn (New York City) Dec. 6. The man indicted was Donald Feise, 19, a Marine charged with setting fire to a neighbor's house in West Babylon, N.Y. because it was going to be sold to a Negro.

The first government desegregation suit against a public housing agency was settled Dec. 7. A consent order signed by the Justice Department and by the Little Rock, Ark. Housing Authority required that the authority desegregate its housing projects. A Housing & Urban Development Department spokesman said Dec. 7 that "in all likelihood" the authority would receive a $132,000 Model Cities grant that had been withdrawn after the Justice Department filed the suit Nov. 21.

Defense Secy. Clark M. Clifford announced June 20 that a Pentagon rule that servicemen may not rent housing from owners who discriminate against members of the armed forces would be enforced nationwide after July 31. He said procedures would be established to give a serviceman immediate legal advice in case of housing discrimination.

Responding to a May 27 complaint by the New York City Commission on Human Rights, the Metropolitan Life Insurance Co. July 18 announced plans to increase the number of black and Puerto Rican tenants in 3 of the company's New York City apartment developments. The commission had charged that some racial and ethnic groups had been systematically excluded from the company's "white" properties and, therefore, applied only at Metropolitan Life's "black property" in Harlem. The new plans were part of an agreement worked out by the company and the commission. The New York Urban League's Operation Open City called the agreement a "sell-out" by William H. Booth, chairman of the commission, and charged July 27 that Metropolitan Life had done nothing to implement its plans.

High Court Bars Property Bias

In a landmark 7–2 decision, the U.S. Supreme Court ruled June 18 that racial discrimination was prohibited in all sales and rentals of residential and other property. The decision was based on an almost-forgotten 1866 law that, according to the court, provided that "all citizens of the United States shall have the same right, in every state and territory, as is enjoyed by white citizens thereof to inherit, purchase, lease, sell, hold, and convey real and personal property."

The decision was handed down on a suit brought by Joseph Lee Jones, a black bail bondsman from St. Louis, and his wife against the owners of the Paddock Woods subdivision in suburban St. Louis. Jones claimed that their offer to buy a homesite had been refused because he was a Negro. A Federal District Court and the U.S. Court of Appeals for the 8th Circuit previously had dismissed the case, the latter holding that neither the 1866 law nor the Constitution forbade racial discrimination by private owners in real estate transactions.

Justice Potter Stewart wrote the high court's majority opinion, stating that the 1866 act "bars all racial discrimination, private as well as public, in the sale or rental of property, and that the statute, thus construed, is a valid exercise of the power of Congress to enforce the 13th Amendment." In accord with Stewart were Chief Justice Earl Warren and Justices Hugo L. Black, William J. Brennan Jr., William O. Douglas, Abe Fortas and Thurgood Marshall. Dissenting were Justices John M. Harlan and Byron R. White, both of whom argued that the 1968 Civil Rights Act made the court's ruling "academic."

In several respects the court's action went beyond the 1968 law, which specifically exempted from its provisions those private homeowners who did not sell through a real estate broker and did not advertise their discrimination. The 1968 law also exempted certain operators of rooming houses and religious organizations. In addition, the 1968 law applied only to residential rentals and sales, while the court's action banned racial discrimination in business and personal, as well as residential property transactions.

Urban Plans & Programs

Gov. Nelson A. Rockefeller of New York proposed Apr. 18 that $150 billion be invested in the next decade "to save and rebuild" the nation's cities. The funds would come from public and private sources—$60 billion from private capital attracted by "a wide range of incentives" for "massive redevelopment" of slums; $60 billion from self-liquidating bonds issued by state and local agencies for construction of self-supporting facilities, such as universities, hospitals and middle-income housing; $30 billion from state and local "full faith and credit bonds," with some form of federal support, for self-supporting projects such as schools, parks and mass transportation. Rockefeller proposed the program in a speech before the American Society of Newspaper Editors in Washington.

The creation of an Urban Institute, an independent but government-supported center devoted to the problems of the nation's cities, was announced by the White House Apr. 26. Asst. Health-Education-Welfare Secy. William Gorham, 37, was elected president of the institute by the 15-member board of trustees; Vice Chairman Arjay Miller of the Ford Motor Co. was elected chairman of the board. Pres. Johnson's intention of establishing the institute had been first announced in a Mar. 1967 Presidential message to Congress on urban and rural poverty. Meeting with the institute's trustees at the White House Apr. 26, Johnson said he hoped the institute would "give us the power through knowledge to help solve the problem that weighs heavily on the hearts and minds of all of us—the problem of the American city and its people." "We know today only how much we do not know about the cities," he said. The institute, patterned on the Rand Corp., would be engaged in (1) the study of problems such as housing, transportation and employment and their interrelationships, and proposals for their solutions; (2) the evaluation of the effectiveness of federal, state and local programs to meet these problems; (3) the gathering of data from the currently "splintered and fragmented" sources and the researching of urban problems in order to provide organizations such as Urban Coalition with useful information to implement their programs.

A number of Ford Foundation grants were made during 1968 for programs in the nation's black ghettos:

● The New Detroit Committee, a group of Detroit's business, labor and community leaders headed by Joseph L. Hudson Jr., had announced Jan. 4 that 2 Ford matching grants of $100,000 had been awarded to the Federation for Self-Determination, headed by a black-power advocate, the Rev. Albert B. Cleage Jr., and to the Detroit Council of Organizations, headed by a moderate, the Rev. Roy A. Allen. The only condition for the grants, Hudson said, was that "an interlink, an intercommunication device, be set up among the federations submitting proposals." Cleage said Jan. 5 that his group would not accept the conditions of the grant and was severing all relations with the New Detroit Committee. Cleage said: "The first local effort for carrying out a new trend toward forming a labor-industry government coalition has failed for the same reason that previous efforts have not succeeded"; "whites have

tried to absorb blacks paternalistically and then on terms set by whites."
Allen announced Jan. 25 that his organization had voted unanimously to accept the Ford grant.

● The foundation Jan. 5 granted $230,000 to the Southern Christian Leader-
ship Conference to train black ministers in urban leadership in such fields
as education, housing, employment, business opportunities, voter registration,
welfare and political processes.

● The foundation Mar. 7 announced 23 grants totaling $3.2 million to help
a variety of antipoverty programs. The largest grant, $520,000, went to the
Negro Industrial & Economic Union of Cleveland to expand a program to
stimulate black business ownership and investment. The Bedford-Stuyvesant
Development & Service Corp. in Brooklyn (New York City) was awarded
$400,000 to supplement an earlier $350,000 grant to expand planning for
renewal of the area. $508,500 was given to the Citizens Crusade Against
Poverty to train community development workers.

● The foundation Apr. 24 announced a $350,000 grant to States Urban Ac-
tion, headquartered in Washington, which provided technical aid to state governments involved in urban reform.

● The foundation Apr. 24 announced a $100,000 grant to the city of Gary,
Ind. (population: 178,000, 55% black) to help finance a program of municipal reform. Mayor Richard C. Hatcher, the city's first black mayor, announced that with an additional $30,000 in federal aid and $20,000 in contributions from business groups, the city would hire experts in the areas of
housing, public safety, personnel and fiscal planning. The foundation, in
announcing its grant, said that Gary was oppressed by the classic problems
of municipal government: the city had no taxing or other home-rule powers,
no civil service system, low salary scales and inefficient municipal organization.

The Ford Foundation announced Sept. 28 that it would invest
an estimated $10 million in ventures aiding the poor and land con-
servation rather than in investments offering a higher financial return. Announcing the plan, Ford Foundation Pres. McGeorge
Bundy declined to estimate what percentage of the Ford portfolio,
currently valued at more than $3 billion, might eventually be shifted
to social investment. He said that initially $10 million would be
earmarked for this purpose. Priority was to be given to black
business development, integrated housing projects and the purchase
of land for aesthetic and recreational purposes.*

---

* Bundy had pledged Feb. 17 that the foundaton would work to eliminate
anti-Negro prejudice even if it meant supporting advocates of black separatism. In the preface to the foundation's annual report, Bundy said that
while the foundation would support all "Negro leaders of good will and
peaceful purpose," ultimately Negroes could not "stand aside from American
life as a whole." "There is only one bar and bench, only one system of
government, only one national marketplace, and only one community of
scholars," he said. "Our great general institutions—unions and universities,
businesses and bureaucracies—will have to be open to all." The racial crisis
was the "first of the nation's social problems," Bundy said, and "the deep

The purchase of a 7-acre urban renewal area in St. Louis by an all-Negro businessmen's group had been announced Feb. 9 by the St. Louis Land Clearance Authority. The $689,000 project was to build a commercial development to serve residents of a nearby housing project.

Protestant, Roman Catholic and Jewish leaders announced in New York Mar. 14 the formation of Operation Connection and pledged $10 million to it to be used by black groups in 5 urban centers in their efforts to achieve full equality. The only condition of the pledge of funds was that it would not be used to support violent activities. The project was announced by the Right Rev. John E. Hines, presiding bishop of the Protestant Episcopal Church, Rabbi Abraham Heschel of the Jewish Theological Seminary of America, the Rev. Albert Cleage Jr., pastor of the Central Congregational Church in Detroit and president of the Federation for Self-Determination, and Rabbi Marc Tanenbaum of the American Jewish Committee. Hines and Cleage were named co-chairmen of Operation Connection. Cleage said: "If this fails, then Roman Catholics, Jews and Protestants might as well close shop. The problem of the black community is powerlessness. We are facing the most distressing situation in the history of our country, and if the black community is ignored by the church and the synagogue, then the whole program will turn out to be a farce." The program's only goal, Cleage emphasized, was "power for the black community." Heschel agreed: "It is clear that we have failed to help the black community develop a sense of power. We must stop thinking of the Negro community as recipients, but as participants."

A group of black Boston businessmen received a federal commitment of $996,000 Mar. 20 to undertake a housing rehabilitation project in the city's black ghetto.

The Most Rev. John J. Wright, bishop of Pittsburgh, announced Mar. 23 that the Pittsburgh Catholic diocese had pledged 10% of its annual $100,000 income to the Interfaith Housing Corp.

---

corrosiveness of white prejudice requires honest recognition" as being the "most powerful single enemy" to Negro progress. This prejudice could "consume those who think themselves immune to it," or "could masquerade as kindness, sympathy, and even support," Bundy warned. He said "the cause of the American Negro has nourished the self-righteousness of generations of white men who never troubled to understand how destructive it can be to make the uplifting of others the means of one's own self-esteem." "So where this foundation finds means of attacking it [anti-Negro prejudice], we will adopt them," he pledged.

to help fight the problems of slum housing. Wright, in announcing the gift, condemned racism as "the vicious heresy" and said the gift represented "part of our permanent commitment to the battle against ignorance, error, human inadequacy and unrealized human dignity."

Vice Pres. Hubert H. Humphrey announced in Washington Apr. 26 that 6 businesses had agreed to invest a total of $52.1 million for the construction of plants that would provide jobs for 2,400 unemployed slum residents in the predominantly black Bedford-Stuyvesant section of Brooklyn (New York City) and in Los Angeles. The federal government would contribute $6.9 million to the program. The companies involved were: Advance Hudson Mounting and Finishing Co., Inc.; Campu-Graphics, Inc.; Day Pac Industries, Inc.; Torite Enterprises, Inc.; Udico Corp. and Sahagen Industries, Inc.

The National Economic Growth & Reconstruction Organization (NEGRO) opened a Washington branch office Apr. 29. Speaking at opening ceremonies, Dr. Thomas W. Matthew, head of the $3 million non-profit corporation, said that the group would start a women's dress factory in the building. The group had already begun to operate bus lines in the Watts section of Los Angeles and a general hospital in New York.

The establishment of the Baltimore Community Investment Co., a profit-making company that would lend high-risk capital to potential black businessmen, was announced in Baltimore May 9.

The New York Urban Coalition, a group of about 150 business, labor, religious and civil rights leaders, pledged nearly $1½ million May 19 for 3 economic development corporations designed to aid existing businesses and promote new ones in the city's slums. Coalition Pres. Saul Wallen announced that $500,000 was being provided for a management-assistance corporation and $600,000 for a 2d corporation designed to help small businesses obtain long-term loans without collateral. The 3d corporation would be given $250,000 to $500,000 to provide high-risk loans for new businesses in slum areas.

NAACP Executive Director Roy Wilkins reported July 18 that black-controlled financial institutions had joined forces in a program to stimulate more Negro financing of city housing and business loans. They had already allocated nearly $5 million in mortgage loan commitments and deposits to 4 Negro companies. $4.2 million of the total went to the Bank of Finance in Los Angeles.

A bipartisan group of 26 Senators July 24 introduced a bill to encourage the formation of community-controlled profit-making corporations in poor neighborhoods. Under the plan, which was not enacted during 1968, the federal government would match funds raised through the sale of stock—often in denominations as small as 10¢—with "seed money." Supporters estimated that only about $2 billion in federal funds would be involved. James Farmer, ex-director of CORE, and Roy Innis, CORE's current director, appeared at a joint press conference with 4 of the Senate sponsors and promised to support the measure. The 4 major sponsors were Sen. Gaylord Nelson (D., Wis.), Fred R. Harris (D., Okla.), Charles H. Percy (R., Ill.) and Jacob K. Javits (R., N.Y.). At a meeting to discuss the plan Dec. 14 several key black spokesmen expressed concern that the bill, the Community Self-Determination Act, might result in the abandonment of existing federal antipoverty efforts. Clarence Mitchell Jr., Washington director of the NAACP, said that the bill might be used to let private industry "off the hook." He said that private industry should not insist on government incentives before providing jobs for the poor.

Small Business Administrator Howard Samuels, speaking before the Virginia Bankers Association in Richmond Dec. 5, noted that minorities "do not participate in the ownership of American business." He said that minorities made up 15% of the population but "probably own no more than . . . 1% of the nation's 6 million businesses." Samuels cited the situation in Washington, D.C., where more than half the population was Negro but where Negroes owned only 2,000 of the 28,000 private businesses.

(A gift of parish property worth $680,000 had been announced Feb. 28 by the Most Rev. Fulton J. Sheen, bishop of Rochester, N.Y. The property, he said, was to go to the federal government with the stipulation that it be used for housing the poor. After sharp protest from Roman Catholic clergymen and laymen, however, the cancellation of the gift was announced Mar. 3. This Ash Wednesday gift of St. Bridget's parish, which included 1½ acres of land, a church, a rectory and a school in the predominantly black and Puerto Rican section of downtown Rochester, was offered, Sheen said, "not because the property was not needed—for it is, indeed—but rather in order that through a sacrificial gift the diocese might alleviate the plight of the needy." Housing & Urban Development Secy. Robert C. Weaver, in a letter dated Jan. 29, had said the gift was "excellent, feasible and most desirable." He said that his staff would act "so as to achieve the maximum effect in inducing other assistance through private and public sources for the upgrading of the area and the welfare of its inhabitants and to establish it as a model which can be duplicated." But parishioners marched in protest against the gift outside Sheen's headquarters Mar. 1. The pastor of St. Bridget's, the Rev. Francis H. Vogt, called the gift a "mistake" and said his parishioners were "just sick" about it. Then, without explanation, Vogt told his parishioners at the noon mass Mar. 3 that the gift was being canceled.)

(The *Manhattan Tribune,* a new weekly newspaper covering New York City's Upper West Side and Harlem, went on sale Nov. 13 for 10¢ a copy. Published by William F. Haddad, a Board of Education member and a director of the Urban Coalition, and Roy Innis, national director of CORE, the paper had a staff equally divided between Negroes and whites. Haddad, a white, said that they hoped to bridge the gap between the "frustrated, angry black community and the frightened white community.")

'Apartheid Society' Feared

The National Commission on Urban Problems released July 17 a study warning that if current trends continued, "America by 1985 would be well on the road towards a society characterized by race stratification along racial and economic lines as well as geographic separation." The report was based on projections of population figures by demographers Patricia Leavy Hodge and Philip M. Hauser of the University of Chicago. The projections indicated that by 1985 central cities would have 10 million more nonwhites (a 94% increase) and the suburbs 53.9 million more whites (a 104% increase). The report said: "The projections vividly portray the geographic fulfillment and the fears expressed by the President's Commission on Civil Disorders—that the American society is becoming an *apartheid* society."

SCHOOLS

Desegregation Lags

Figures released by the Health, Education & Welfare (HEW) Department May 27 showed that only about 14% of the black pupils in 11 Southern states were attending desegregated schools at the beginning of the 1967–8 school year. According to a *N.Y. Times* report May 25, HEW had been claiming a total of about 18%. The figures showed a decline in rate of improvement, but HEW officials said that there had been a redefinition of a "desegregated school." Before 1967–8, schools were considered desegregated if 5% of the pupils were white. Since 1967–8, enrollment had to be at least 50% white for the school to be defined as "desegregated." Before the fall of 1967, HEW figures for percentage of integration in Southern schools had doubled each year since the application of the 1964 Civil Rights Act: from 3.2% in 1964 to 6.5% in 1965 and 12.5% in 1966.

Among other assessments of school desegregation progress in the North and South:

• In an interview in the *Washington Post* Aug. 8, HEW Secy. Wilbur J. Cohen said that integration in northern schools might be a generation away and that efforts in the meantime should be directed towards better schools in ghetto neighborhoods.

• The Southern Regional Council, an Atlanta-based, biracial group organized in 1944 to promote racial equality, said in a report released Oct. 15 that there had been "a deplorable degree of failure" in desegregating Southern schools in 1967. The council noted that its 1965 and 1966 reports had been "guardedly optimistic" but that currently there was "virtually no reason" to say that things would improve.

• The *Washington Post* Nov. 10 quoted retiring U.S. Education Commissioner Harold Howe 2d, 50, as saying that progress in the integration of public schools, North and South, had been "minimal." He said that the U.S. was still faced with a school system divided along racial lines. "Some 85% of Negro youngsters in the South still go to almost fully segregated schools," he declared, and "in the North the picture's very much the same." Howe dismissed as campaign rhetoric Pres.-elect Richard Nixon's statements that he would not use federal funds to force integration.

The public schools of Washington, D.C., reopened Sept. 4, had a Negro enrollment of 93.6%, compared with 92.3% in 1967.

Government Demands Northern Desegregation

The Department of Health, Education & Welfare Mar. 18 had issued a policy statement extending its school-desegregation guidelines to Northern schools. The statement said it was the "affirmative duty" of every school system to eliminate racial segregation and discrimination. It called for the elimination of inferior services and facilities in schools attended by blacks or other minority groups. HEW cited as examples of unequal treatment: overcrowded classes, facilities and activities; assignment of fewer, less-qualified teachers; lower per-pupil expenditures; inadequate textbooks, equipment and buildings; less adequate courses and extracurricular activities.

The HEW statement called for the elimination of factors other than housing patterns that caused segregation. The statement said: "While these policies don't require the correction of imbalance resulting from private housing patterns, neither the policies nor Title VI bars a school system from reducing or eliminating racial imbalance in its schools." The statement recommended the reorganization of entire school systems, the closing of predominantly black schools or the assignment of students by geographic attendance zones.

The policy statement also called for the completion of the desegregation of Southern schools by the start of the 1969–70 school year.

HEW ordered the Union, N.J. school system Oct. 14 to comply with the 1964 Civil Rights Act and desegregate Jefferson elementary school by Dec. 14. A *N.Y. Times* report Dec. 5 called the order HEW's first major "crackdown" on school segregation in the North. It said Middletown, O. was the 2d Northern community to get such an order from HEW.

The Justice Department Apr. 25 had filed, in U.S. District Court in Chicago, its first desegregation suit against a Northern school system. It charged discrimination in faculty and staff assignment in suburban South Holland School District 151 of Cook County, Ill. The department alleged in its suit that District Supt. Charles Watts and the members of the district's board of education had assigned, with few exceptions, the 69 white and 33 black faculty and staff members to elementary schools attended solely or predominantly by members of their race. 800 of the district's 2,670 pupils were black. Of the 6 schools, 2 in the suburb of Phoenix were almost all black, one in Harvey and 3 in South Holland were all white. Atty. Gen. Ramsey Clark said that the department had received a written complaint from a parent of black children attending school in the district. The district officials, notified of the complaint, failed to act on it. The suit asked the court to "enjoin discrimination on the basis of color in operation of the school district" and to enjoin school officials "from failing to adopt a plan for the desegregation of the faculty and the staff in the school district." The suit was the 157th filed by the Justice Department under the 1964 Civil Rights Act.

The Justice Department broadened its case against the South Holland district by charging May 27 that students as well as faculty members were segregated. The complaint charged that the district had "drawn and maintained . . . boundaries and created new school facilities to promote and preserve" racial segregation. After a 10-day hearing Federal District Judge Julius J. Hoffman, 73, in Chicago July 8 ordered the district to desegregate its faculties and students. (The district's school superintendent, Dr. Thomas E. van Dam, reported Sept. 22 that enrollment was 10% less than expected in the 6 elementary schools affected by the court-ordered desegregation plan. In an interview reported by the *N.Y. Times* Sept. 23, the superintendent said that transfer records showed that most of the missing pupils were white and had enrolled in private schools.)

(A much-debated plan to move 573 black elementary school pupils by bus from overcrowded ghetto schools on Chicago's South Side to predominantly white schools on the West Side of the city was met with resistance when put into effect Mar. 11. The plan was a compromise voted by the school board Mar. 4. A previous plan that involved the bussing of 1,035 black children had been rejected by the board Feb. 28 after hearings and demonstrations. In protest against the new plan, white students boycotted 9 West Side schools Mar. 4–5. When bussing started Mar. 11, a fire bomb was thrown through the window of one of the schools, causing little damage, and groups of white mothers demonstrated at the doors of the schools.)

The 2d desegregation suit filed by the Justice Department against a Northern school system was settled out of court Aug. 6 when Indianapolis public school authorities agreed to integrate faculties in the city's elementary schools. The Justice Department had filed the suit May 29.

New York State Education Commissioner James E. Allen Jr. June 14 had ordered the total integration of Mount Vernon, N.Y. schools by a bussing plan that would group elementary school pupils by age rather than by neighborhood. After demonstrations and protests by white residents joined by a few Negroes, the city board of education appealed Oct. 11 to the State Supreme Court for a re-

versal of Allen's decision.   Allen's order had followed the failure
of a plan for desegregation by means of a consolidation of elementary schools.

'Freedom of Choice' Found Inadequate

In 3 unanimous decisions May 27, the U.S. Supreme Court ruled
that "freedom of choice" desegregation plans in the South were inadequate if they did not bring about integration as well as other
plans would.   Allowing children of all races to choose their schools,
a plan practiced in 9 out of 10 Southern communities, tended to
perpetuate segregation, the court said.   Justice William J. Brennan's
majority opinion said: "The burden on a school board today is to
come forward with a plan that promises realistically to work, and
promises realistically to work now."   He added, "We do not hold
that 'freedom of choice' can have no place in such a plan.   Rather,
all we decide today is that in desegregating a dual system a plan
utilizing 'freedom of choice' is not an end in itself."

The decision was the court's first detailed review of the means
used to carry out its 1954 school desegregation ruling and was restricted to those Southern and border states which had officially-
segregated school systems at that time.   The 3 cases were appeals
brought by black parents in New Kent County, Va., Gould, Ark.
and Jackson, Tenn.   In each case, a U.S. Court of Appeals had held
that existing desegregation plans were adequate on the ground that
racial separation by private choice was not unconstitutional.

The Supreme Court Dec. 9 affirmed a May 31 U.S. District
Court ruling that a 1963 South Carolina law granting tuition aid to
students between the ages of 6 and 20 to attend private, non-
parochial schools was unconstitutional.   The state law had provided
student grants equal in amount to the per-capita cost of public education in the state.

The Justice Department Feb. 12 had filed suit in the U.S. District Court in Jackson, Miss. on charges that Franklin County, Miss.
operated 2 12-grade schools to perpetuate racial segregation and
that students of the all-black school received inferior educational
opportunities and facilities.   Under a 1965 "freedom-of-choice"
desegregation plan, the county operated a dual school system.   Only
7 of the county's 1,125 black students chose to attend the traditionally all-white school in the 1967–8 school year; none of the 1,150
white students selected the all-black school.   According to the com-

plaint, the high-school grades in both schools "have too few students to meet generally acceptable educational standards."

The Justice Department Feb. 14 filed 2 suits in the U.S. District Court in Macon, Ga. against the boards of education of Baldwin and Crisp Counties. The department alleged that each county had failed to take adequate steps under "freedom-of-choice" desegregation plans to end dual school systems based on race. Each county, the suit contended, maintained inferior educational opportunities and facilities for Negro students. A similar Justice Department suit was filed in the federal court in Savannah Feb. 15 against the Screven County board of education.

A 3-judge federal court in Montgomery, Ala. Oct. 14 ordered 19 Alabama school districts to abide by an Aug. 28 order to 78 districts and adopt zoning, consolidation or pairing desegregation plans if they could not demonstrate the effectiveness of existing "freedom of choice" plans. Judges Richard Rives, Frank M. Johnson Jr. and H. Hobart Grooms affirmed, however, that they thought "freedom of choice" was "the most feasible method to be used in this state."

A 3-judge federal panel in Shreveport, La. Nov. 14 upheld "freedom of choice" desegregation for 31 school districts in the state and dismissed a Justice Department motion favoring geographical zoning plans for the districts.

In a dispute involving "freedom of choice," 21 Chesterfield County, S.C. public schools were closed on the county school board's orders Sept. 7 following protests against a school desegregation plan calling for a unitary system. Negroes had boycotted Pageland area 7th and 8th grades since school had opened Aug. 27 because of failure to comply with the original desegregation plan, under which the area's 7th and 8th grades would all go to a Petersburg school. White pupils had threatened to boycott the schools if the board did not restore the "freedom-of-choice" system of desegregation. The school board reopened the schools Sept. 12–16 under a "freedom-of-choice" plan. School-pairing plans had been dropped as a result of white boycotts of the schools in Newberry and Denmark, S.C. and a threatened boycott in Columbia. In protest against the reversal of the pairing plan, Negroes boycotted the schools in Denmark until Sept. 16, when they returned to school under a compromise providing a revised "freedom-of-choice" plan. An organization named Citizens for Freedom of Choice had been formed in Columbia in August to work for this form of dual system, and membership spread quickly throughout South Carolina.

In what was reported to be the first such action in the South, parents of white pupils went to court Nov. 26 to seek greater desegregation in public schools. Parents of 63 pupils filed a motion in Federal District Court in Little Rock, Ark. to challenge the Little Rock school zoning plan on the ground that it would "entrench" and "mirror the lines of the presently existing pattern of racially segregated" housing and thereby foreclose "forever, the possibility of a nonracial, unitary school system." The school board had adopted the plan by 5–2 vote Nov. 15 and had filed it with Federal Judge Gordon E. Young, who had ordered the board to discontinue its "freedom-of-choice" plan.

U.S. District Judge Frank Johnson Jr. in Montgomery, Ala. Feb. 24 had ordered Montgomery to end its dual school system and to integrate schools, classes and faculties.

The U.S. 5th Circuit Court of Appeals in New Orleans Dec. 12 ordered that every all-Negro school in its district "must be integrated or abandoned by the commencement of the next school year." The ruling was made in an opinion that refused to reconsider a District Court ruling that a Walton County, Ga. school be desegregated.

The U.S. 4th Circuit Court of Appeals had ruled in Richmond, Va. Feb. 8 that the Asheboro, N.C. school system had violated the rights of 9 Negro teachers who had lost their jobs because their pupils had been transferred to white schools. The appeals court, reversing a lower court ruling, ordered that 2 teachers be rehired and that 3 receive financial compensation.

New York Teachers' Strike

3 teachers' strikes called by the 55,000-member AFL-CIO United Federation of Teachers (UFT) paralyzed New York City's public school system beginning Sept. 9, the start of the fall term. The strikes did not end until Nov. 19. 50,000 teachers and a million pupils were kept out of classes for 36 of the first 48 scheduled school days in a school decentralization battle with strong racial overtones. Classes were conducted at a few schools where teachers and parents crossed the UFT picket lines.

The dispute centered on the Ocean Hill-Brownsville School Demonstration District in Brooklyn, an experimental unit involving 8 schools with more than 8,000 pupils, most of them black and Puerto Rican, and about 500 teachers, the majority of them white. The Ocean Hill-Brownsville district was one of 3 special units set up in July 1967 by the New York City Board of Education as an experiment in school decentralization. The purpose of the project, financed by a Ford Foundation planning grant,* was to test community control of neighborhood schools. The other 2 units were East Harlem's I.S. (Intermediate School) 201 and 5 schools in the "2 Bridges" area of the City's Lower East Side.

The union teachers held that their professional positions were threatened by the local control exerted by the Ocean Hill-Brownsville governing Board. They demanded protection against harassment and arbitrary dismissal. The governing board charged collusion between the teachers' union and the central Board of Education in trying to prevent effective community control of their schools.

The dispute that led to the strikes had begun in May when the local governing board provoked a confrontation with the central education establishment by summarily dismissing 13 teachers and 6 administrators from 6 schools in the Brooklyn demonstration unit. Only one of those dismissed was black, and one was Puerto Rican. District Administrator Rhody McCoy, 45, said that the 19 educators were trying to "sabotage" the experiment. Since the governing board had not cited specific charges in the dismissals, the Board of Education termed the ousters illegal, and the UFT charged that the dismissed teachers had been deprived of "due process."

The governing board was composed of 16 elected members—5 representing the community, 7 representing parents, 3 teachers and one from Brooklyn College, who was known as the "university representative." They indicated in a newsletter sent to parents in the district that they had not been given any real power to control their schools and that "we have been used as a buffer between the power structure and you, our brothers and sisters."

The confrontation set off a series of disturbances in the district, including boycotts by pupils and teachers, demonstrations and mounting friction between the governing board and the teachers' union. Mrs. Elaine Rooke, president of the parents' association at the district's J.H.S. (Junior High School) 271, emphasized that the boycott of students was being run by community parents, not by the governing board. Hand-lettered sign in front of the school May 11 read: "We want to control our schools," "We want our children educated" and "Closed by PTA."

---

* Supplemental grants totaling $46,000 had been announced by the Ford Foundation Feb. 15 for the 3 projects. The foundation had already awarded $135,000 in the summer of 1967 to underwrite the costs of planning the projects.

Before adjourning May 25 the New York State Legislature, pressured to adopt a citywide decentralization program, adopted a compromise plan after heavy lobbying by both the UFT and advocates of community control. The legislation enlarged the Board of Education from 9 to 13 members to allow Mayor John V. Lindsay to appoint a bloc of prodecentralization members. The enlarged board Sept. 4 adopted a short-range plan, authorized by the Legislature, that gave substantial operating power to the 30 regular and 3 experimental local school boards. The plan was approved Oct. 17 by the state Board of Regents.

UFT Pres. Albert D. Shanker, 40, warned Aug. 16, after the Board of Education's proposals were announced, that there might be a citywide strike if decentralization could not be achieved without "destroying the rights of teachers."

The UFT struck on the opening day of school, Sept. 9, in protest against the refusal of the Ocean Hill-Brownsville Governing Board to reinstate 10 of the teachers dismissed in May. A trial examiner, Francis Ellis Rivers, 75, a black member of the State Board of Mediation, had cleared the teachers of charges of sabotaging community control or doing unsatisfactory work. The UFT also demanded that union teachers who had stayed out of the district's schools several days in May in support of their dismissed colleagues be allowed to return to class. The Ocean Hill-Brownsville Governing Board had replaced these teachers with about 350 recruits, many in their 20s and many without much classroom experience.

After a 2-day strike, union members returned to work Sept. 11 when the Board of Education agreed to reinstate the 10 teachers. The union struck again Sept. 13 on the ground that the governing board had failed to honor the agreement by not admitting the teachers. The governing board said that it was the community residents who had barred their return.

The schools were reopened Sept. 30 under an agreement for the teachers to return to Ocean Hill-Brownsville under the surveillance of union and Board of Education observers. But the district's J.H.S. 271 was ordered closed temporarily because of clashes between supporters of the governing board and police.

The governing board was suspended by the Board of Education Oct. 6, and McCoy and 7 of the district's 8 principals were relieved of their duties Oct. 8 for disobeying orders to reinstate the teachers. Superintendent of Schools Bernard Eugene Donovan, 57, Oct. 11

ordered the reopening of J.H.S. 271 and the return of the 7 principals "under my direct supervision."

The 3d teachers' strike, which lasted for 5 weeks, began Oct. 14. The union charged that members had been terrorized and threatened with death at J.H.S. 271. A series of proposals offered by Mayor Lindsay and by State Education Commissioner James E. Allen Jr. failed to mollify the union, and Gov. Nelson A. Rockefeller said Oct. 30 that he was considering calling a special session of the Legislature to break the deadlock.

After 27 hours of negotiation with representatives of Lindsay, UFT Pres. Shanker presented a strike settlement plan at a stormy meeting of the union delegate assembly Nov. 17. Shanker hastily adjourned the meeting because, he said later, he feared that the delegates might not recommend the settlement. Union members voted overwhelmingly Nov. 18, however, to go back to school.

The settlement agreement reinstated the transferred teachers and gave authority over the Ocean Hill-Brownsville district to a state trustee, Herbert F. Johnson, 61, an associate state commissioner of education. It provided for the continued suspension of the district governing board and the removal of 3 principals appointed by the board. The UFT had charged that the appointment of the 3 principals, Louis Fuentes, William H. Harris and Ralph Rogers, had been irregular and that the 3 had been among those who had tried to force union teachers out of the district.

Although new disturbances were threatened in Ocean Hill-Brownsville, union teachers returned to class without major incident Nov. 19, and the 3 principals left peacefully to accept temporary reassignment.

A New York Civil Liberties Union report released Oct. 10 supported the Ocean Hill-Brownsville Governing Board's charge that the UFT and the Board of Education wanted to prevent effective community control. The report said that the UFT had used " 'due process' as a smokescreen to obscure its real goal, which is to discredit decentralization and sabotage community control." It charged that the Board of Education had attempted to "scuttle the experiment in Ocean Hill-Brownsville by consistently refusing to define the authority of the local governing board."

A letter that the former acting president of the Board of Education, Mrs. Rose Shapiro, had sent May 16 to Mayor Lindsay denied the charge that the governing board's powers were not defined. The letter said that the real issue was "the refusal of the governing board to accept the maximum powers and duties legally provided."

UFT spokesman Dan Sanders said Oct. 10 that the Civil Liberties Union report was "a very shabby piece of research designed to support a predetermined conclusion." He said that the union did support decentralization "into large enough districts that would provide a measure of integration and would not allow a small group of extremists to take over." Sanders' statement reflected a fear of UFT members, more than 90% of them white, that their jobs would be threatened by local control in ghetto areas. Ocean Hill-Brownsville officials pointed out, however, that 70% of the new teachers hired by the district governing board were white.

The fear of black anti-Semitism was voiced by UFT members (more than half of the city's teachers were Jewish). Anonymous, anti-Semitic literature attacking the teachers had been distributed during the dispute. 40% of the teachers hired at J.H.S. 271 by the local governing board, however, were Jewish.

NYU Ousts Hatchett

A major controversy developed at New York University over the employment and subsequent dismissal of black militant John F. Hatchett as director of the university's new Martin Luther King Jr. Afro-American Student Center. Hatchett, who had been ousted from his position as a substitute school teacher in Harlem after taking pupils to a memorial program for Malcolm X, was appointed to the NYU post July 24 and fired Oct. 10.

NYU's appointment of Hatchett touched off a vehement debate when it was noted that he had been the author of an article charging that black pupils were being "mentally poisoned" by "Jews who dominate and control the educational bureaucracy of the New York public school system." The article had appeared in the *Afro-American Teachers Forum* the previous winter, and it had been characterized as "black Nazism" in a joint statement issued Feb. 29 by the American Jewish Committee, the Catholic Inter-Racial Council and the Protestant Council of the City of New York.

NYU Pres. James M. Hester had announced Aug. 10 that Hatchett would be retained in his post on the basis of a plan suggested by ex-Supreme Court Justice Arthur Goldberg and Federal Judge Constance Baker Motley. Goldberg and Mrs. Motley, a trustee of NYU, had been asked by Hester to devise a solution to the problem. The substance of the plan called for strengthening the organization of the center, in part, by appointing Judge Motley as chairman of its board. As part of the agreement, Hatchett agreed to a statement in which he recognized "the problem his article has aroused" and committed himself "wholeheartedly to directing the center in keeping with the traditional policies" of NYU.

Hatchett was fired Oct. 10 after he had told a group of 700 students Oct. 8 that Vice Pres. Hubert H. Humphrey, Richard M. Nixon and Albert Shanker, president of the United Federation of Teachers, were "racist bastards." The dismissal resulted in a week-long "strike" by some white and black students during which university operations were only slightly disrupted, although 2 buildings and Hester's office were occupied by striking students.

(NYU, the U.S.' largest private university, had approximately 42,000 students, of whom some 2,000 were black.)

Black Students

Although warned by the Health, Education & Welfare Department May 29 that it might be violating the 1964 Civil Rights Act, Northwestern University (Evanston, Ill.) agreed Oct. 8 to provide black students with separate housing. Other steps announced by Ronald J. Hines, university vice president, included an agreement to recruit black students and to provide more scholarships for Negroes, courses in Afro-American studies and a counselor to work with black students.

A *N.Y. Times* survey had shown May 13 that in spite of a concerted effort to enroll more Negro freshmen, Ivy League colleges (and the 7 parallel women's colleges) had fallen short of their goals. While the colleges accepted as many as 200% (at Princeton) more black students than in 1967, it turned out that frequently the same student was being accepted by more than one school. Another problem: scholarship aid was not sufficient to let students from low-income families accept admissions.

Albert H. Bowker, chancellor of the City University of New York, described plans Aug. 2 to triple the school's black and Puerto Rican enrollment by 1969 by guaranteeing to admit the top 100 students from 60 public academic high schools, the 100 top students from large non-public academic schools and 20% of the graduates from smaller private schools.

The Defense Department and the U.S. Office of Education asked 150 colleges and universities Sept. 4 to provide college places for veterans who came from poverty areas and to attempt an experiment similar to one in which Webster College (near St. Louis) recruited

44 men before their Army discharge for a 2½-year teacher-training program.

Yale University, following a recommendation made by a faculty-student committee headed by Prof. Robert A. Dohl and including 4 student members of the university's Black Student Alliance, announced Dec. 12 that it would offer a BA degree in Afro-American studies.

NSA Dispute Over 'Racism'

The 21st annual congress of the National Student Association (NSA) was held at Kansas State University in Manhattan, Kan., Aug. 17–26. It was marked by dissension over "racism" and accord on the need for immediate reform in universities and political institutions.

Black students, represented on only 10 to 15 of the 366 delegations attending the conference, walked out of a meeting Aug. 20 following the defeat of a motion to discuss "white racism" before other convention business was handled. The convention voted that night to suspend one member of the all-white University of Alabama delegation and to seat a black delegate in his place; following the vote, most of the Alabama delegation left the congress Aug. 21. More than 20 of the major universities, including the Universities of Chicago, Maryland and California at Berkeley, challenged their own right to vote on the basis that they represented "white racism institutions" and white racist student bodies. Outgoing NSA Pres. Edward Schwartz criticized the convention's handling of the race question. "We should admit that this congress is racist," he said, "but we should go further and do productive work in preparation for next year's congress to make it nonracist. We shouldn't pass unproductive *ex post facto* indictments of the University of Alabama or of our white Northern selves." The conference was in its 5th day before credentials issues were settled and it could take official action.

In order to make better use of students' political influence, the NSA voted Aug. 22 to amend its constitution and allow the formation of a separate organization to lobby for legislative change.

The conference approved resolutions calling for the abolition of the draft, the legalization of marijuana and the adoption of the demands of the 3d World Commission, a coalition of black, Mexican-American and Puerto Rican students.

Other Developments

The Ford Foundation Feb. 21 announced grants totaling more than $3 million to help strengthen and develop predominantly Negro colleges. The grants included $1,107,225 for Tuskegee Institute (Tuskegee, Ala.) and $875,770 to Hampton Institute (Hampton, Va.) for general development in the next 3 years. Other predominantly black colleges received grants to improve their business administration practices and to broaden educational services and programs. The new grants brought to more than $28 million the grants given by the foundation to aid Negro higher education since 1963.

The National Education Association, holding its annual convention in Dallas, Tex., July 2–6, won a public apology from the city July 5 after a Dallas tavern had refused July 3 to serve First Secy. Mooki Vitus Molapo, 31, of the Lesotho embassy. The U.S. State Department also apologized to the Lesotho embassy. Mrs. Elizabeth D. Koontz, who took office as the 1,000,000-member NEA's first black president, proposed July 6 that the NEA sponsor a "high-level conference" of people with wide knowledge and differing opinions "to come to grips with selected major issues" in education.

4 Negro boys entered previously all-white Girard College in Philadelphia Sept. 11 after a battle dating to the 1950s against the exclusion of non-whites at the privately financed 120-year-old elementary and secondary school. The school had agreed to accept Negroes after a May 20 U.S. Supreme Court ruling that let stand a Mar. 7 lower court order that the school admit qualified black boys. The Mar. 7 decision by the U.S. 3d Circuit Court of Appeals upheld a July 5, 1967 order by a federal judge. The state had argued against the appeal on the ground that the 14th Amendment forbidding exclusion because of race was applicable because Girard was a tax-exempt institution and because its trustees were appointed by the state. Girard had argued that its support came entirely from a private trust and that none of its trustees had "governmental status."

EMPLOYMENT

EEOC Reports Job Bias

A report released by the Equal Employment Opportunity Commission (EEOC) Jan. 15 showed that in 1966 Negroes comprised about 18% of New York City's population but had only 8.8% of all jobs of reporting companies and only 2.9% of the white-collar jobs. (The 1964 Civil Rights Act had required companies with 100 or more employes or those with 50 or more with federal contracts of $50,000 or more to file employment reports with the EEOC. The law was extended June 2, 1967 to companies with 50 or more employes.) The report was released at the start of 4 days of hearings in New York.

The EEOC study of the financial industry showed that blacks comprised 6.7% of the white-collar employes in the city's banking industry and 5.9% of the insurance industry's white-collar workers, while Puerto Ricans made up 10% of the city's population but provided only 5.1% of the white-collar workers in banking and 2.8% in insurance. (The EEOC, however, noted "dramatic increases" in the employment of blacks by the largest bank and insurance firms in 1967.) Of the 1,282 professional employes in 21 law firms surveyed, there was only one Negro and one person with a Spanish name. The percentage of Negro white-collar workers in the city's 9 largest banks ranged from 2.2% to 9% of the total. In the city's 20 top brokerage firms the percentage of Negro white-collar workers ranged from .4% to 9.2%.

In a sampling of 100 major New York-based corporations (at least 500 employes in each company's headquarters offices, total assets of $116 billion, 15.8% of the gross national product), the EEOC found that only 2.6% of the white-collar positions were held by blacks. The commission report said that "in Negro white-collar utilization, the 100 corporations as a group have worse records than banks, insurance companies, brokerage firms, broadcasting companies, and newspaper, book and periodical publishers"; they had "a record in Negro white-collar employment only about half as good as the nation as a whole."

The EEOC Jan. 16 released a survey showing that Negro white-collar employment in the communications industry ranged from a high of 3.9% in radio and TV to a low of 2½% in advertising agencies. Puerto Ricans held 2½% of the white-collar jobs in book publishing and only .9% in radio and TV. Reporting to the commission Jan. 17 on hiring practices in the communications industry, Charles B. Markham, EEOC director of research and reports, said: "Even though employers in the communications industries do not provide a major proportion of total white-collar jobs in New York City, these employers have a place of awesome influence in the nation, and it is they who can most readily establish the intellectual climate for significant social changes." "It is not clear that the communications industry has accepted this responsibility." (The Office of Communication of the United Church of Christ announced in New York Feb. 25 that it had received $160,000 from the Ford Foundation to fight discrimination against Negroes on radio and TV.) *

In testimony before the commission Jan. 16, David Rockefeller, president of the Chase Manhattan Bank, said "business can and must assist in every possible way," but "the basic drive and determination to succeed must come from within the Negro and Spanish-American communities themselves." He reported that 23% of the 15,000 metropolitan Chase Manhattan employes were members of minority groups. Ralph H. Skinner, an Eastern Airlines vice president, told the commission Jan. 16 that of 816 pilots stationed in New York, only one was black; of 703 stewardesses, 42 were blacks; of 416 clerical workers, 14 were black and 13 were Spanish-American.

At the conclusion of the hearings Jan. 18, EEOC Chairman Clifford L. Alexander Jr. said at a news conference: "If future intentions were gauged by the past standard of performance, it would mean that Negroes and Puerto Ricans would probably be waiting until the year 2164 for a democracy to say what he or she shall have"; banks and insurance companies had done a "good job" in hiring minority workers, particularly as clerks, but "the minority hiring situation" in the communications industry "is much worse than I expected." Alexander said the EEOC would hold hearings in "about a year" to see whether the companies that had promised action had carried out their pledges.

Unions to Recruit Black Trainees

The executive board of the AFL-CIO Building & Construction Trades Department announced in Bal Harbour, Fla. Feb. 13 that the presidents of 18 international building trades unions with a total membership of 3½ million members had agreed to actively recruit

---

* The Ford Foundation Jan. 5 had announced a $522,000 grant to the National Catholic Conference for Interracial Justice to expand an interdenominational program, Project Equality. The latter program, designed to eliminate racial discrimination in employment, would be run in cooperation with the Metropolitan Applied Research Center in N.Y. City.

Negroes for apprenticeship program and to provide training to qualify them.

The terms of the proposals had been set forth in a Feb. 1 letter
from Building & Construction Trades Department Pres. C. J. Hag-
gerty to Labor Secy. W. Willard Wirtz. The letter said the unions
had offered a plan of "public-private cooperation" as "a means of
recognizing and meeting social responsibilities in full and voluntary
support of government efforts to eliminate, once and for all, [racial]
discrimination."

The unions agreed: (1) to foster "programs of recruitment of
qualified applicants from the Negro population and other minority
groups" and "programs for special attention to deficiencies affecting
the full qualification of Negro and other minority group applicants,
if such exist, and remedy the same if practical"; (2) "to counsel and
urge . . . affiliates to consider appropriate means whereby suitable
minority candidates may be recruited"; (3) "to recommend that
apprenticeship programs, sponsored or co-sponsored by . . . local
unions, disseminate full information concerning program entrance
and necessary qualifications, not only to the Bureau of Apprenticeship & Training, but also to one or more sources of potential minority candidates within the community"; (4) "to recommend that
affiliate local unions and joint apprenticeship committees explore
mutual problems with appropriate organizations directly representative of minority groups within the community"; (5) to promote the
"maximum utilization of responsible civil rights organizations willing to join in a cooperative effort to effect this proposal with full
recognition for the necessity for industry to formulate its requirements for employment and entry in the trade."

NAACP Labor Director Herbert Hill charged Feb. 16 that the
statement was simply one more in a long series of public relations
gestures in which the building trades unions successfully provide a
public relations cover to continue their widespread anti-Negro practices." In a speech to the annual Civil & Human Rights conference
of the National Education Association in Washington, Hill said:
The letters "provide for no sanctions, establish no timetables, create
no enforcement apparatus" and thereby substitute "voluntary compliance for civil rights law enforcement" although it was an "incon-
trovertible fact" that voluntary compliance "does not work." "The
building and construction trades unions, together with the AFL-
CIO, have once again used their political power to secure an im-

munity from the enforcement of civil rights laws and executive orders."

Bias Charged

The Anti-Defamation League of B'nai B'rith reported Jan. 16 that 87% (338) of 388 private employment agencies checked in 6 major U.S. cities disregarded federal, state and local antidiscrimination laws. They accepted orders calling for a "white gentile" or "white Protestant" secretary. The survey was made in New York, Los Angeles, Phoenix, Atlanta, Chicago and Miami.

The Justice Department Feb. 7 filed suits in the U.S. District Court in Los Angeles against Local 250 of the Steamfitting & Industrial Pipefitting Division of the Steamfitters Union and in the U.S. District Court in Indianapolis against Local 73 of the Plumbers & Pipe Fitters union on charges of employment discrimination against Negroes. The suit said that while each union controlled "a substantial portion of the employment opportunities in its geographical and occupational area," there were no Negroes in the 3,000-member Steamfitters local or in the 400-member Plumbers & Pipe Fitters Local, and neither local had any black apprentices.

Speaking at a House committee hearing presided over by Rep. William F. Ryan (D., N.Y.), Herbert Hill, NAACP labor director, accused the government Dec. 5 of "directly subsidizing racial discrimination." He said that the Office of Federal Contract Compliance had been "timid" about enforcing cancellation provisions against companies guilty of job discrimination. Hill proposed that the office be transferred from the Labor Department to the Justice Department to block the influence of "bigoted labor unions."

ORGANIZATIONS & PERSONALITIES

'Black United Front' Formed

About 100 black leaders representing some 20 organizations held a secret meeting in Washington, D.C. Jan. 9 and formed a coalition "Black United Front" to organize Negroes in the nation's capital. The meeting, held at the New School for Afro-American

Thought, had been called by Stokely Carmichael,* ex-chairman of the Student Nonviolent Coordinating Committee (SNCC); the press was barred. The conferees selected a steering committee whose members included leaders of "moderate" civil rights groups such as the Washington Urban League as well as "militant" leaders of black nationalist groups. Among them were reported to be the Rev. Walter E. Fauntroy, City Council vice chairman and local representative of the Southern Christian Leadership Conference; Sterling Tucker, executive director of the Washington Urban League; C. Sumner Stone, ex-editor of the Washington *Afro-American*; and black-power champion Nathan Hare, who had been dismissed by Howard University as a sociology professor.

Signs of tension between the moderate and militant elements soon began to appear. Whitney M. Young Jr., executive director of the National Urban League, said Jan. 10 that "if Stokely wants to run this, we won't hold still for it. If he is trying to establish himself as a leader of leaders, we won't go for it." The Committee of 100 Ministers, a group of black clergymen, said Jan. 13 that it was "unalterably opposed" to what it described as "an unholy alliance" of radicals and moderates. The statement said: "We do not intend to lend support to or follow anyone who wants the U.S. defeated in its foreign efforts or advocates violence as a weapon of social advance."

Carmichael appeared in Washington Jan. 14 on the WOL radio program "Speak Up" and said in response to a listener's telephoned question: "The black man cannot be concerned with America. He must be concerned with people first . . . , and people is the opposite of what America stands for. The first thing we should do is to understand how we have been divided by the white man. Then we should move in and take over the institutions in our community . . . , police, welfare, school board and stores from the local 5-and-10 to the industrial complexes in Watts."

Carmichael told newsmen Jan. 17 that he had chosen Washington as the base for organizing blacks because "Washington represents the clearest contradictions of black and white in America. Yet, it is the capital of this country. Washington must begin to represent to people around the world what this country is all about."

The Washington Urban League, the city's largest civil rights

---

* Carmichael married South African singer Miriam Makeba, 35, in April.

organization, announced Jan. 17 that its board of directors had unanimously agreed to "defer" joining the Black United Front. But Sterling Tucker, the local chapter's executive director, said the league would "continue to explore the possibility" that the coalition would draft a program "compatible with the principles of the Urban League."

H. Carl Moultrie, president of the Washington chapter of the NAACP, said Jan. 17 that he had been instructed by the NAACP national board not to become involved in any movement that included Carmichael.

In late June the Black United Front accused the Southern Christian Leadership Conference (SCLC) of triggering disturbances during a demonstration in Washington June 24 and of allowing the black community to suffer police violence as a result. In a 6-page manifesto, the front charged that SCLC had failed to involve local Negroes in the Poor Peoples' Campaign. C. Sumner Stone said that 21 board members had approved the manifesto unanimously June 25. The Rev. Fauntroy, an SCLC representative on the board, said he had not been informed of the meeting and called the manifesto "unfortunate."

A coalition of 9 representatives of Washington Negro organizations July 17 indorsed a Black United Front resolution that described the slaying of Washington policemen as "justifiable homicide" and condemned the city's police department. (A *Washington Post* report Aug. 23 said that the Black United Front had become increasingly militant and ascribed its rising extremism to the background efforts of Stokely Carmichael.) In a simultaneous move, the Baptist Ministers Conference of the District of Columbia & Vicinity backed Fauntroy and repudiated the front resolution.

The front Aug. 13 proposed the formation of a Black Survival League to "teach black people how to protect themselves against police brutality."

2,269 NAACP delegates met in Atlantic City June 24–29 for the organization's 59th annual convention, which served as a forum for a struggle between "old guard" and "Young Turk" forces to determine the association's policies and programs. The dispute culminated in 2 walk-outs by "Young Turk" and youth delegates. Developments were further complicated by the arrival June 27 of Sen. Eugene McCarthy (D., Minn.) against the wishes of NAACP Executive Director Roy Wilkins, who accused him of "intruding and meddling" in NAACP affairs. The convention took place while

McCarthy was campaigning for the Democratic Presidential nomination.

The young dissidents, who had formed a National Committee to Revitalize the NAACP, headed by Chester I. Lewis, 39, a Wichita, Kan. lawyer, had established separate headquarters at a Negro-owned motel. The group (composed of urban Northerners and generally supported by Northerners from the college and youth division) had sent each of the 1,175 NAACP chapters literature arguing that the NAACP's traditional methods of depending heavily on legislation and black and white cooperation were no longer effective.

A 5-point Young Turk resolution proposed by Fred Crockett, chairman of the Illinois delegation, was defeated June 24 by 432–288 vote. It called for the establishment of NAACP committees to study: black survival, economic and political power in the ghettoes, the need for emphasis on Afro-American culture, the revitalization of the NAACP, and Afro-American and non-white world affairs.

3 Young Turk resolutions were rejected by voice vote June 25. Offered by Chester Lewis (who was ruled out of order by Dr. L. H. Holman, convention chairman), they proposed that: NAACP delegates be sent to Washington to support the Poor People's Campaign; the name of the organization's Springarn Medal be changed to the name of one of several black civil rights heroes; Sen. Fred R. Harris (D., Okla.), co-sponsor of Vice Pres. Hubert Humphrey's Presidential campaign, be barred from speaking because his presence would imply an indorsement by the association. The attack on Harris was rejected by Wilkins, who said the invitation had been extended before Harris had joined Humphrey's campaign and because of his civil rights record.

Although Wilkins said a McCarthy visit was "in direct violation of the organization's non-partisan position on political candidates," McCarthy came to Atlantic City and held a reception for delegates.

The 2 walkouts of Young Turks and youth delegates took place June 28 and 29 on the same issue—the rejection of their request (proposed by Gerald Taylor, 19, of New York) that they be authorized to form an autonomous organization with the right to conduct their own financial, public relations and operational affairs.

Immediately after the June 29 walkout, the remaining old guard delegates approved and submitted to the board of directors resolutions proposing: (a) a weeklong boycott in which all American Negroes would avoid "nonessential buying at businesses which are not black-owned," (b) the reseating of Adam Clayton Powell in Congress, (c) the exemption of Cassius Clay from the draft and the return of his heavyweight title, (d) opposition to the use of Chemical Mace, (e) a UN-supervised cease-fire in Vietnam, (f) the closing of NAACP bank accounts with the Chase Manhattan Bank because of that bank's support of South Africa and (g) a guaranteed annual income. Another resolution supported a concept of "black power" that would promote Negro economic, political and cultural advancements with white participation.

The board of directors, without specifically mentioning the Young Turk faction, "repudiated" the dissidents June 29 by resolving that "the historic principles of the association should be and are hereby reaffirmed, the recently encountered pressures to abandon democratic processes are rejected, and the sowers of discord and dissension and advocates of threats and terror within our ranks are repudiated." But Dr. Eugene T. Reed, a board member and a Young Turk spokesman, said he had not approved the resolution. Instead, he said, "the people indicted by this resolution are the people who now control the board of directors."

Reed later sent an angry letter of resignation to Wilkins. He charged that convention leaders had tried to silence dissident voices and that the association did not work for the benefit of the mass of Negroes. The board accepted Reed's resignation Sept. 9 although he sought to withdraw the letter before the board could approve it.

Chester Lewis had resigned July 13 as president of the NAACP's Wichita branch and as legal counsel of the Kansas State Conference of the NAACP.

The NAACP board of directors Oct. 14 dismissed Lewis M. Steel, 31, white associate counsel to the organization, because he had written an article, published in the *N.Y. Times Magazine* the previous day, critical of the Supreme Court's civil-rights decisions. The entire NAACP legal staff resigned Oct. 28 in protest against the board's ouster of Steel.

In announcing Steel's dismissal, the NAACP board said that it considered Steel's article "an indefensible rejection of much of the organization's major effort over the past 60 years." The article, "Nine Men in Black Who Think White," had accused the Supreme Court of having "struck down only the symbols of racism" while permitting the survival of "white supremacy" in the U.S.

Robert L. Carter, who had been NAACP general counsel for 24 years, announced his resignation and that of his 8-man staff at a news conference Oct. 28. He said that his staff's contribution to the civil-rights struggle had been possible only because they had refused to be bound by "traditional thinking and traditional concepts" and that the "tragic absurdity of this entire situation is that the board insists that its lawyers conform to its kind of orthodoxy." (It was announced Dec. 15 that Carter had been appointed a fellow at the Urban Center of Columbia University.)

4 NAACP officials, including Chairman William H. Booth of the New York City Commission on Human Rights, filed suit in New York State Supreme Court to have Steel reinstated. The court ruled Dec. 20 that the NAACP had been within its rights to fire Steel. According to a *N.Y. Times* report Nov. 24, the organization was suffering a crisis due to the ouster, and Roy Wilkins had admitted that "the national office is operating under considerable tension" because of the controversy.

The Rev. James E. Groppi, 38, who had led a successful Milwaukee open housing campaign beginning in Aug. 1967, resigned Nov. 15 as adviser to the Milwaukee Youth Council of the NAACP. He said he wanted to "devote more time to militant social action involvement" within his parish of the St. Boniface Roman Catholic Church.

Crisis, the official publication of the NAACP, urged black leaders to speak out "loud and clear" against "a small minority of black extremists who are . . . espousing apartheid, racism including anti-Semitism, intimidation and violence." The editorial, "Time to Speak Up," was published in the November issue of *Crisis.* It said that, partly because of the emphasis of the news media, extremists had been accepted as "the authentic voices of the Negro community," and that the moderate majority should speak out against the "merchants of hate and violence."

In an interview published in the *N.Y. Times* Dec. 29, Wilkins defended the NAACP against critics who had denounced it as traditionalist and irrelevant to the needs of most Negroes. He said that the association was beginning a "new thrust of additional services to the urban ghetto and an appeal to the young people."

Wilkins had told the NAACP's membership corporation in New York Jan. 8 that NAACP membership had decreased 3% in 1967. Total paid membership declined from 441,139 in 1966 to 427,434 in 1967, and NAACP operating income declined in the same period from $1,474,311.63 to $1,460,877.65. Wilkins attributed the membership "fluctuation" to "the uncertainty induced by violence, the punitive mood of Congress, the confusing and provocative statements of a wide variety of individuals and organizations and the frustrations induced by the overwhelming problems of the central cities." Wilkins also said: "In the face of pleas from a President and of rumblings from the ghettos, Congress has either hamstrung remedial legislation or has starved the emerging bits and pieces of it with sharply cut appropriations."

At a closed afternoon meeting Jan. 8, Wilkins and these principal NAACP officers were reelected: Kivie Kaplan, president; Bishop Steven G. Spottswood, board chairman; Jesse H. Turner, vice chairman; Alfred Baker Lewis, treasurer; Dr. Harry Greene, assistant treasurer. 5 new NAACP board members were elected: William Booth of New York, Charles Johnson of Seattle, Robert Wright of Des Moines, Emmett J. Douglas of New Roads, La. and Shirley Harrington of Jackson, Miss.

In its annual report, released June 23, the NAACP disclosed that its annual net income had risen from $2,228,127.27 to $2,632,-559.14 and that Negro membership accounted for 76.6% of the general operating fund.

CORE Moves Toward Militancy

A change in the leadership of the Congress of Racial Equality (CORE) preceded the organization's 26th national convention, held July 3–7 in Columbus, O. CORE National Director Floyd McKissick, 46, announced June 25 that he would take a leave of absence for medical reasons and that Roy Innis, 34, would become acting director July 8. On the opening day of the convention, Innis said that his major job would be to "tighten up" the structure of the organization; he said that local chapters, currently a "group of autonomous baronies," would have to be brought under the control of the national office so that the organization could move in a single direction.

During the convention, however, a group of dissidents July 7 rejected national leadership and walked out. Sol Herbert, chairman of the Bronx (New York City) chapter, said July 8 that 6 chapters would form a new organization and than 12 or 13 other CORE groups were considering similar actions. Herbert and Robert C. Carson, chairman of the Brooklyn (New York City) chapter, charged that national CORE had become mired in paper work and political maneuvering and had "done nothing for black people in the last year or 2."

In a move for "black unity," Roy Wilkins, NAACP executive director, and Whitney M. Young Jr., director of the National Urban League, had been invited to address the CORE convention. Wilkins' appeal for cooperative efforts was received politely by convention delegates July 5. When Young addressed the meeting July 6, he indorsed a black-power concept that emphasized "control of one's destiny and community affairs." During a long, standing ovation following Young's speech, many delegates called out: "The brother's come home," welcoming what they considered the league's departure from its traditionally moderate position.

Black nationalist resolutions calling for indorsement of the principle of a nation-state for Negroes in the U.S. or in Africa and for creation of black protection agencies were tabled when the convention recessed July 7. After reconvening, CORE Sept. 16 adopted a new constitution that advocated black nationalism and barred white membership in the organization. Innis was elected permanent national director, and Wilfred Ussery was reelected national chairman.

Urban League Plans Ghetto Drive

Delegates of the National Urban League July 31 approved a "new thrust" program designed to develop black economic, social and political power in the nation's ghettos. The delegates' action took place in New Orleans during the league's 58th annual convention, held July 29 to Aug. 1. Sterling Tucker, director of the organization's Washington, D.C. chapter, was chosen to lead the new $2 million program, called a "constructive black power" effort by the league's executive director, Whitney M. Young Jr.

Members of a group called the Black Youth for Progress invaded the meeting July 31 to demand representation in the league's leadership and the adoption of a list of youth proposals for the "new thrust." Young told Gerald Williams, the group's spokesman, that the success of the new program would depend on young people.

Young announced Aug. 29 that 3 black students who had been active in a league summer program in city slums had been elected to the organization's board of directors. This was the first time that students had been elected to the board.

Plans for "new thrust" projects in 21 communities, funded by organizations including the Ford and Rockefeller foundations, were announced by Young Dec. 9. He said that the league eventually would have 93 such programs. Young pointed out that the "new thrust" drive represented a change in emphasis for the league from service to community action programs. He added that the organization would retain a biracial approach.

SCLC Reaffirms Nonviolent & Biracial Policies

The Southern Christian Leadership Council (SCLC) held its 11th annual conference Aug. 14–18 in Memphis, Tenn., the site of the assassination of Martin Luther King Jr., the organization's founder. The convention pledged SCLC to remain a nonviolent and biracial organization, but the Rev. Ralph D. Abernathy, who had succeeded King as SCLC president, warned Aug. 15 that it would no longer be a peacemaker in U.S. racial disputes. He referred to his recent role as a pleader against violence in Miami during the Republican National Convention and said: "Do not expect us to be your babysitters, America." Despite rumors of dissatisfaction with Abernathy's leadership, the delegates unanimously elected him president of the organization Aug. 16.

(Abernathy was arrested Sept. 10 along with his 2 top aides, the Rev. Andrew Young and Hosea Williams, and 70 demonstrators who were trying to block emergency garbage pickups in Atlanta. The demonstration was in support of that city's strike of some 800 sanitation workers, most of them black.)

SNCC-Black Panther Accord Fails

An alliance formed Feb. 19 by the Student Nonviolent Coordinating Committee (SNCC) and the Black Panther Party broke up in the wake of a stormy July meeting of the 2 militant groups in New York City when, according to the Sept. 20 *Washington Post*, Panther members drew guns on former SNCC Chairman James Forman.

SNCC leaders also reportedly voted to "terminate" their relationship with Stokely Carmichael, 27, a former SNCC national chairman, who had refused to give up his position as Panther "prime minister." In a letter informing him of his expulsion, Carmichael was charged with "engaging in a power struggle both within and outside of the organization." Philip Hutchings, head of the organization, credited Carmichael Aug. 22, however, with "tremendous strides in the fight for black liberation."

(Gunfire was exchanged Sept. 8 behind the SNCC Washington office in the apparent culmination of a dispute between the committee's local head, Lester McKinnie, and other Negro militants. McKinnie said that the trouble started Sept. 4 when 3 men whom he identified as Black Panthers demanded that he turn over the office to them. Panther leader Eldridge Cleaver said that there were no Panthers in Washington at the time and other SNCC members also said that the Panthers were not involved. A New York SNCC official said Sept. 14 that the Washington branch was being taken over by the national office because "the situation called for strict management.")

Hutchings, 26, had been elected at the group's annual staff meeting in Atlanta in June to succeed H. Rap Brown as national leader of SNCC. Brown did not seek reelection. Hutchings said July 9 that SNCC would seek to form a political party "defined by black people." He said that the activities of the party would be determined by the needs of individual communities and that its emphasis would be on black power in the U.S. and an end to "racism, capitalism and imperialism" worldwide.

A SNCC official in Atlanta, Donald Stone, announced Nov. 27 that an alliance had been formed between SNCC and the National Black Liberators to ward off "mounting repressions facing black communities."

Black Panthers

Since its formation in Oct. 1966 by Huey P. Newton and Bobby Seale in Oakland, Calif., the militant Black Panther Party had become part of the national Negro movement. Its membership had swelled from a few hundred to several thousand persons with chapters in major U.S. cities. National interest in the Black Panthers was generated by the trial and conviction of Newton for manslaughter and by the Presidential candidacy of Eldridge Cleaver, Panther "minister of information." Violent confrontations between Panthers and police officers had occurred in California, New York and New Jersey. Charging police harassment and brutality, Panther leaders had issued repeated calls to Negroes to arm themselves for a struggle for liberation.

Newton, 26, was convicted of manslaughter Sept. 8 in the Oct. 28, 1967 fatal shooting of Oakland Patrolman John Frey, 23. Newton was sentenced Sept. 27 to 2–15 years imprisonment. The prosecution had asked for a verdict of first-degree murder. Oakland's Alameda County Courthouse, where the 7-week trial took place, was the scene of extensive "free Huey" demonstrations during the early days of the trial. 2,500 sympathizers marched on the courthouse July 15 when the trial began after 11 delays. Officials searched spectators and newsmen for weapons before they were allowed to enter the courthouse. (A "free Huey Newton" rally took place in Chicago's Lincoln Park Aug. 27 during the Democratic National Convention.)

In addition to the murder charge, Newton had been indicted for assault with a deadly weapon against patrolman Herbert Heanes, 25, who was wounded in the arm, and on charges of kidnaping a black motorist, Dell Ross, near the scene of the shooting. (Newton had been shot in the abdomen by Heanes during the gun battle.)

Deputy prosecutor Lowell Jensen questioned Heanes on the 1967 shooting at the opening of the prosecution's case Aug. 5. According to Heanes, he had joined Frey shortly after Frey had stopped a car identified as a Panther-owned vehicle. The driver, whom Heanes identified as Newton, was told by Frey that he was under arrest. Shots were then exchanged, and Heanes fired at Newton. Heanes was wounded and Frey killed in the exchange of gunfire. The prosecution tried to establish that Frey had stopped the car because warrants had been issued against it for 2 unpaid traffic tickets.

Under cross-examination by defense attorney Charles R. Garry, Heanes admitted Aug. 6 that he did not remember seeing Newton with a gun in his hand. Heanes denied Garry's suggestions that he was the one who had shot Frey. Another prosecution witness, Henry Grier, 40, a Negro, testified Aug. 7 that he had seen Newton shoot Frey. Garry pointed out discrepancies between Grier's initial statement to the police and his testimony in court. The defense tried to show Aug. 19 that it had been too dark for Grier to make an accurate identification. The prosecution submitted ballistics evidence Aug. 14 in an effort to show that the bullets that killed Frey had not come from Heanes' gun.

The kidnaping charge against Newton was dropped Aug. 20 after Ross, a prosecution witness and the alleged victim, claimed to have suffered a loss of memory about the incident.

Garry said July 25 that the defense intended to show that the "police instigated and plotted the incident that brought Huey Newton here." He established that the Oakland Police Department had distributed a list identifying cars driven by Panthers and that Newton's car was on the list. Garry presented evidence of the atmosphere of conflict between the police and the black community.

Defense witnesses testified Aug. 19 that Frey had harassed and threatened several Negroes with his gun.

Newton took the stand Aug. 22 to deny that he had shot Frey. Most of his testimony was his explanation of his resentment against white society. In his summation Sept. 4, Garry called Newton a "selfless man" who found himself charged with murder because of his leadership of the black cause.

The jury, which elected its only black member as foreman, arrived at a guilty verdict after 4 days of deliberation. After sentencing, Newton was removed temporarily to the California Medical Facility at Vacaville Sept. 27.

Eldrigde Cleaver, 33, author and 1968 Presidential candidate of the Peace & Freedom Party, was sought as a parole violator on a fugitive warrant issued Nov. 27 in San Francisco. It was widely speculated that Cleaver had left the U.S. Nov. 28 for Montreal, where an international conference of antiwar militants was under way. A federal warrant for Cleaver's arrest was issued Dec. 10. Cleaver had been free on parole after serving 9 years of a 14-year sentence on a 1958 conviction for assault with intent to kill. He had been rearrested Apr. 6 after being wounded in a Panther shootout with Oakland police. (Panther member Bobby Hutton was killed in the shooting.) Cleaver's parole was immediately rescinded.

Cleaver was released June 12 on $50,000 bail by order of Superior Court Judge Raymond J. Sherwin, who criticized the cancellation of parole. Sherwin said that the cancellation had stemmed not from a failure of Cleaver's "personal rehabilitation" but from his "undue eloquence in pursuing political goals . . . offensive to many of his contemporaries." The State District Court of Appeals in San Francisco ruled Sept. 27 that Sherwin had acted beyond his authority in the case. This ruling was upheld by the California Supreme Court Nov. 20 when it refused to hear an appeal by Cleaver. U.S. Supreme Court Justice Thurgood Marshall Nov. 26 denied a request for a stay to prohibit officials from taking Cleaver into custody. The fugitive warrant was issued after Cleaver failed to surrender as ordered Nov. 27. He had said Nov. 24 that his only alternative was to "get out of the country."

A vigil was begun Nov. 24 outside of Cleaver's San Francisco home by demonstrators who said they would remain "until Eldridge is no longer in danger at his home." Cleaver's wife Kathleen said Nov. 26 that the Panthers would prevent her husband's imprisonment "by any means necessary."

Cleaver had been nominated for President by the Peace & Free-

dom Party Aug. 18 by a 3–1 vote over his major rival, comedian
Dick Gregory, at the party's convention in Ann Arbor, Mich.
Cleaver's campaign platform called for "the immediate withdrawal
of U.S. troops from Vietnam." The more than 200 convention
delegates reflected their party's alliance with the Black Panthers by
supporting "the right of armed self-defense" by "the oppressed peoples in America." Cleaver told newsmen in New York City Oct. 11
that the purpose of his campaign was to "lay the base for a revolutionary movement that will unite black . . . and white radicals."
(In popular vote tabulations Nov. 7, with 96% of U.S. precincts
reporting, Cleaver had polled 28,005 votes and Gregory had received 48,953 votes.)

A faculty invitation to Cleaver to give a series of 10 lectures at
Berkeley campus of the University of California had touched off a
battle involving the university, the State Board of Regents and Gov.
Ronald Reagan. The lectures, proposed by the Student Center for
Participant Education and approved by the faculty Board of Educational Development, were to have been part of an experimental
sociology course. Reagan led the opposition to Cleaver's appearance at Berkeley, denouncing him Sept. 17 as "an advocate of racism and violence." The Board of Regents, in a compromise move
Sept. 20, refused to bar Cleaver's appearance but said that he could
give one guest lecture instead of the series planned. The regents
also censured the faculty board for having "abused a trust" in setting up the course. At a mass meeting on the Berkeley campus
Sept. 24, 2,000 students voted unanimously to demand that the
regents rescind their restrictions on the Cleaver lectures. The Berkeley faculty, at an Oct. 3 meeting of the Academic Senate, voted
668–114 to repudiate the regents' move as an "intolerable" interference with academic freedom. Berkeley Chancellor Roger W.
Heyns Oct. 7 cleared the way for Cleaver to appear by making a
lecture hall available for the series as a "student-sponsored, noncredit" course. Cleaver was given a standing ovation by the 250 to
300 students who gathered to hear his first lecture entitled "The
Roots of Racism." His lecture was described as "moderate" and
"scholarly" in tone.

2 Oakland policemen had been dismissed and jailed Sept. 10
after firing more than 12 bullets into the headquarters of the Black
Panthers and a neighboring restaurant. No one was injured. Police
Chief Charles Gain said that the 2 police officers, Richard V. Williams, 28, and Robert W. Rarrell, 26, had been drinking on duty

during the early morning incident. The shots seemed to have been aimed at an enlarged picture of Huey Newton in a window of the Panthers' headquarters. The incident occurred only 2 days after Newton's conviction in the death of a policeman.

Black Panther Reginald Forte, 19, and policeman Daniel Wolke, 22, were injured in an exchange of gunfire in Berkeley Nov. 13. The shooting began after Forte's car had been stopped for a traffic violation. Forte and his companions, John L. Sloan, 32, and William Kitt, 21, surrendered and were booked for attempted murder.

Police Lt. Dermott Creedon, Sgt. Robert Flynn and Inspector Michael O'Mahoney were wounded Nov. 19 in a San Francisco gunfight with 8 Negroes whose panel truck had been stopped in connection with a service station robbery. The truck bore a sign reading "The Black Panther Black Community News Service." The policemen were injured when 3 Negroes, identified as William Lee Brent, 47, Wilford M. Holiday, 35, and Samuel Napier, 30, allegedly jumped from the truck and opened fire. A grand jury Dec. 2 voted to indict Brent and Holiday in connection with the shooting.

Conflicts between Black Panthers and New York City policemen led to an incident in which police allegedly attacked 8 or 9 Panthers and a few white sympathizers in a hallway of the Brooklyn Criminal Court building Sept. 4. The assault was made by more than 150 white men, many of whom were identified as off-duty policemen who were in civilian dress and had come to attend a hearing for 3 Panthers arrested Aug. 21 for assaulting a policeman. The attack was made by whites who could not find seats in the courtroom. Swinging blackjacks, shouting "Wallace, Wallace" and proclaiming themselves "the white tigers," they converged on the small group of Panthers when they appeared in the hallway near the courtroom. Brooklyn Panther Chairman David Brothers said later that he had been kicked more than 20 times.

A number of those attacked required medical treatment for scalp wounds and other injuries.

No arrests were made in the courthouse case, but Mayor John Lindsay ordered Police Commissioner Howard R. Leary later that day to make a complete investigation of the incident. At least 2 of the policemen allegedly involved were members of the Executive Board of the Law Enforcement Group (LEG) of New York, a dissident group of young, right-wing policemen. Police Department investigators said later that they did not believe that the LEG had specifically ordered its members to attend the hearing, but Norman Frank, spokesman for the city's Patrolmen's Benevolent Association, said Sept. 12 that he had seen a notice urging policemen to show up in court Sept. 4. He said that the notice bore the name of Lt. Leon Laino, founder of the LEG. LEG officials consistently denied having instigated the attack. The LEG had been organized in August to voice the resentment of a group of policemen against Criminal Court Judge John F. Furey, who was alleged to have allowed Black Panthers to misbehave in his courtroom.

The Black Panther Party filed suit in U.S. District Court in New York Sept. 10 to obtain injunctions forbidding police to harass Panthers and asking for community control of the police. An attorney for the Panthers, Gerald B. Lefcourt, said Sept. 12 that recent arrests of members of the party indicated that police planned "a general roundup of the Panthers."

New Jersey Black Panthers and police exchanged accusations over 2 incidents—the machine-gunning of a Jersey City police station Nov. 29 and a firebomb attack on the Newark Panther headquarters Dec. 1. Jersey City Police Sgt. John Gerraghty said that Panther members were suspected of the shooting in retaliation for the Nov. 28 arrest on weapons charges of 7 Newark Negroes identified as Panthers. 3 members of the Panther party were arrested Dec. 5 in connection with the machine-gun attack. Panther spokesman Anthony Kaiser contended Dec. 1 that the bombing of the party's headquarters was in response to the attack on the Jersey City precinct house. Carl C. Nichols, 36, the party's chief organizer in New Jersey, and 2 other Panther members were injured when the bombs exploded outside their store-front office. The victims said that the bombs were hurled by 2 men in "police-type" uniforms. Newark Deputy Police Chief Kenneth Melchior said Dec. 1 that any link between the 2 incidents was "pure speculation."

3d Black Power Conference

The Rev. Dr. Nathan Wright, chairman of the organizing committee of the 3d National Conference on Black Power, said on the opening day of the conference in Philadelphia Aug. 29 that white newsmen would be barred from its sessions because of allegedly distorted stories printed after the 1967 conference in Newark. During the 4-day conference some 4,000 delegates approved more than 100 proposals that had been prepared to formulate black-power programs in areas such as economics, politics and education.

Among the resolutions adopted unanimously Sept. 1 were proposals supporting the organization of a national black party for "progressive and radical social change," immediate unilateral withdrawal of the U.S. from Vietnam, draft resistance by black youths, creation of an urban Negro army for self-protection, community control of schools in black neighborhoods and the takeover of "all businesses in the black community by any means necessary."

'Black Government' Conference

Black separatists met in Detroit Mar. 30–31 for a National Black Government Conference sponsored by the Malcolm X Society to "set up an independent black government" in 5 Southern states and to write a "black declaration of independence." The society's chairman, Milton R. Henry, announced Mar. 30 that the conference had voted to affirm "the principle that we are not citizens of the United States." The conferees Mar. 31 adopted resolutions establishing a Republic of New Africa to be set up in the South, demanding cash reparations from the U.S. for the slavery era and choosing Robert F. Williams, a black militant currently living in Peking, as president of the proposed republic.

Rap Brown Convicted

Outgoing Chairman H. Rap Brown of the Student Nonviolent Coordinating Committee (SNCC) was convicted in federal court in New Orleans May 22 on one count of violating the Federal Firearms Act. He was sentenced to 5 years in prison and fined $2,000. A jury of 3 white men, 6 white women and 3 Negro women found Brown guilty of carrying a .30-caliber carbine on a plane trip from New Orleans to New York Aug. 18, 1967 while under indictment. He was found not guilty of violating the firearms act during a flight from New York to New Orleans 2 days earlier because he was not aware he was under an arson indictment in Maryland when he carried the gun across state lines.

U.S. District Judge Lansing Mitchell imposed the maximum sentence. Before the sentence was pronounced, defense attorney William M. Kunstler of New York urged that sentence be suspended because of "the horrendous gap between white and black people in this country," and a 2d defense attorney, Howard Moore, an Atlanta Negro, urged Mitchell not to "engage in genocide of black people."

Brown was released on $15,000 bond.

Brown had been arrested by federal agents and local police in New York Feb. 20 on a New Orleans bench warrant for alleged violation of court-imposed travel restrictions. He was also served with a warrant to appear in Richmond to show cause why bail there should not be revoked for similar reasons. Brown, who had addressed black-power rallies in Oakland, Calif. Feb. 17 and in Los Angeles* Feb. 18, had been released on $15,000 bail in New Orleans Sept. 8, 1967 with permission to move freely between New York and Atlanta and to meet 15 speaking engagements on specific dates around the country. The California rallies had not been among those approved. Brown had been released on $10,000 personal recognizance bond in Richmond, Va. Sept. 18, 1967. The terms of the Richmond release restricted Brown to the Southern District of New York—Manhattan and the Bronx.

During a hearing in New Orleans Feb. 21 Brown was arrested on a new charge of threatening FBI agent William H. Smith Jr., a Negro, and his family. In the charge Brown was quoted as telling Smith: "We'll get you. You better get your hat cause I'm going to beat you back to the Coast. We better not find out where your house is. If you have any kids we'll get them too." Before the arrest Judge Mitchell had increased Brown's bail to $50,000. A U.S. Commissioner required another $50,000 bond on the intimidation charge. (Brown pleaded not guilty to the intimidation charge Mar. 13.)

Federal marshals took Brown to Richmond Feb. 22. Federal Judge Robert R. Merhige Jr. ruled Feb. 23 that Brown had violated the travel restrictions of his bond. He ordered him to pay the $10,000 immediately, and ordered him returned to New Orleans.

Brown was released on $30,000 bond from New Orleans prison Apr. 6 but immediately arrested again by federal officials and taken to Virginia for extradition to Maryland. (The extradition order was issued Apr. 9.) At the federal reformatory in Petersburg, Va., Brown Apr. 8 agreed to end a partial fast he had begun Feb. 28 in protest against the $100,000 bond set for his release on federal charges in New Orleans; the bail had already been reduced to $30,000 Mar. 13 by the U.S. 5th Circuit Court of Appeals.

---

* At the Los Angeles rally Brown proposed that any assassination of Negro leaders be followed by coordinated, "selected, protracted and swift retribution on police stations and power plants."

Brown's efforts to avoid extradition to Maryland were rejected in Richmond Apr. 10 by U.S. District Judge Robert R. Merhige Jr., who turned down a petition for a federal hearing on questions raised by the rejection of the petition. The U.S. 4th Circuit Court of Appeals in Richmond Apr. 11 rejected Brown's *habeas corpus* petition and refused his demand for release on bond while he fought the Maryland extradition move. Judge Merhige Apr. 15 ordered Brown extradited to Maryland. Brown's chief counsel, William Kunstler, had requested the implementation of the extradition order because, he said, "in view of Mr. Brown's health, we'd be far better off to go back to Maryland and ask for bond."

Brown was released on $10,000 bond in Cambridge, Md. Apr. 18 after 8 weeks in various state and federal prisons for bond violations. The terms of the bail limited Brown to New York and New Orleans, but he was permitted to enter Maryland to consult with his lawyers on his pending trial.

The Virginia Supreme Court Mar. 2 had upheld the legality of Brown's July 26, 1967 arrest in Alexandria, Va. Brown's attorney had contended that the arrest had violated Brown's constitutional rights against unreasonable search and seizure.

A 35-page memo, prepared for the National Advisory Commission on Civil Disorders and leaked to the press Mar. 4, had blamed overreaction by white local officials to a "revolutionary" speech by Brown for the racial violence in Cambridge, Md. during the summer of 1967. The report said: "Brown was more a catalyst of white fears than of Negro antagonisms, the disturbance more a product of white expectations than of Negro initiative." "To the extent that Brown encouraged anybody to engage in precipitous or disorderly acts, the city officials are clearly the ones he influenced most. Indeed, the existence of a riot existed for the most part in the minds of city officials. . . ." Brown's speech was "unequivocally militant, radical and revolutionary." But the triggering incident was a sheriff firing a shotgun without warning and wounding Brown. Cambridge Police Chief Brice G. Kinnamon "went on an emotional binge in which his main desire seems to have been to kill Negroes." "The response to Brown's exhortations were not universally favorable, with some Negroes in attendance being very much turned off by his strident and militant stance." (The memo was prepared by a team of social scientists headed by Dr. Robert Shellow, assistant deputy director for research at the National Institute of Mental Health. Alvin A. Spivak, information director of the commission, said that

it "was only a raw memo . . . never passed upon by the commission
. . . [and] based on limited information.")

Adam Clayton Powell

Adam Clayton Powell Jr., 59, who had been barred from his
seat in the U.S. House of Representatives Mar. 1, 1967, returned
to New York City Mar. 22 and surrendered to Sheriff John J. Mc-
Closkey on criminal contempt-of-court charges. He was released
on parole by State Supreme Court Justice Arthur Markewich.
Powell had been living in self-imposed exile in Bimini, the Bahamas
since his exclusion from Congress. Raymond Rubin, lawyer for
Mrs. Esther James, 71, who had won a defamation suit against
Powell, won a court order Mar. 25 for a hearing on whether Powell's parole should be revoked and Powell should be jailed. Rubin
contended that Powell had returned to Harlem in violation of a
parole granted in Puerto Rico. Justice Markewich Mar. 27 upheld
Powell's parole.
The 3-judge U.S. Court of Appeals in Washington had refused
Feb. 28 to intervene in Powell's effort to regain his seat in Congress.
In a sermon in Harlem's Abyssinian Baptist Church, of which
he was pastor, Powell told an enthusiastic congregation Mar. 24
that nonviolence was no longer an effective means of achieving civil
rights. He said black leadership had been assumed by "a new breed
of cats." Powell was surrounded by a group of black nationalist
"karate-trained" bodyguards—"Adam's Commandos"—whom he
described as "the wave of the future." He ordered a stained-glass
window depicting a white Jesus replaced with one showing Jesus as
black.
Powell had made a speaking tour of California Jan. 8–13. After
flying to Los Angeles Jan. 8, Powell had taken a walking tour of the
Watts section Jan. 9. He addressed 7,000 students at the University
of California at Los Angeles Jan. 10, then 5,000 at San Diego State
College Jan. 11 and 7,000 at the University of California in Berkeley Jan. 12. Powell Jan. 12 canceled engagements at San Francisco
State College and Stanford University because, he said, he "didn't
feel up to it," but the next day he taped a TV interview for broadcast. Powell told Negroes in Watts Jan. 9: "History is going to
record that the 2d Civil War and the beginning of the black revolution was born here." At UCLA Jan. 10 Powell said that "black
power is the saving grace of the U.S." and "is basically a drive for
immediacy." He challenged white students "to join the black revo-

lution." At the San Diego airport Jan. 11, Powell told reporters that the purpose of his trip was "to awaken white young people to the thrust of the black revolution and to the realization that all the old generation is finished." He told white students at San Diego State Jan. 11 that they were leaderless, and "whether you like it or not black people have leaders": "We have our Stokely, Rap and Floyd McKissick and the 'old man of the sea,' Adam Clayton Powell."

Powell told reporters in San Francisco Jan. 13 that the Rev. Dr. Martin Luther King Jr. had told him that he (Powell) was "the only one who can save the situation among the black people in the United States."

Trials & Other Developments

LeRoi Jones, 34, Negro poet and playwright, was sentenced in Newark, N.J. Jan. 4 to 2½ to 3 years in prison and fined $1,000 for illegal possession of firearms during the July 1967 Newark riots. Also sentenced with Jones were Charles McCray, 33, to 12 months in jail, 6 months probation and a $500 fine, and Barry Wynn, 24, to 9 months in jail, 9 months probation and a $250 fine. While out of jail on bail pending an appeal, Jones was convicted in Newark Nov. 26 of using loud and abusive language to police officers in a Newark bank Oct. 4. He was sentenced to 60 days in jail.

The Rev. James E. Groppi, white Roman Catholic priest who led Milwaukee's open housing demonstrations, was convicted by a Milwaukee jury Feb. 9 of having resisted arrest Aug. 31, 1967. County Judge F. Ryan Duffy Jr. Feb. 12 gave Groppi a 6-month prison sentence but stayed the sentence and put Groppi on 2 years' probation. Duffy also fined Groppi $500.

Negro militants Herman B. Ferguson, 46, and Arthur Harris, 22, members of the Revolutionary Action Movement (RAM), were convicted in New York June 15 on charges of conspiracy to murder moderate Negro leaders Roy Wilkins of the NAACP and Whitney Young Jr. of the National Urban League. Ferguson and Harris were sentenced Oct. 3 to prison terms of 3½ to 7 years each. But State Supreme Court Justice Joseph M. Conroy ruled Oct. 17 that there was "reasonable doubt" that the 2 defendants had received a fair trial, and he authorized their release on bail. Conroy's ruling was based on the fact that the prosecutor had mentioned, in the jury's presence, the assassination of Sen. Robert F. Kennedy (D., N.Y.).

An all-white jury in Hattiesburg, Miss. Mar. 15 convicted Cecil Victor Sessum of first degree murder for his part in the firebomb death of Negro leader Vernon F. Dahmer Sr. Jan. 10, 1966. Sessum was sentenced to imprisonment for life. During his trial, the state charged that the attack on Dahmer was a Ku Klux Klan plot conceived because of Dahmer's efforts to encourage Negroes to register to vote. William I. Smith, an admitted Klan member also convicted in the case, received a life term July 19. Ex-Klan member Billy Roy Pitts, who pleaded guilty to both murder and arson, was sentenced to life in prison, and Lawrence Byrd was given a 10-year term Nov. 8. Mistrials were declared in the murder trials of Henry Edward DeBoxtel Mar. 21, Charles Clifford Wilson July 28 and James F. Lyons Nov. 14. In each case the jurors could not agree on a verdict. The trial for arson of former Ku Klux Klan leader Sam H. Bowers Jr., had ended in a deadlock May 17 with 11 jurors voting guilty and one voting not guilty. Pitts, a key state witness in the trial, had testified May 15 that Bowers had given the orders to firebomb Dahmer's house and kill him if possible. Bowers was arrested on murder charges Nov. 18.

A jury of 8 Negroes and 4 whites in U.S. District Court in Vicksburg, Miss. Nov. 13 ordered 3 white men and the White Knights of the Ku Klux Klan to pay $1,021,500 in damages to relatives of Ben Chester White, a Negro murdered June 10, 1966. The jury in the civil case awarded the maximum amount of actual and punitive damages asked after Judge Harold Cox directed the judgment for the plaintiff and ruled that the 3 defendants were responsible for "the dastardly act." The 3 defendants had been charged with murder by the state. Ernest Avants, 37, had been acquitted by a Circuit Court jury, and a mistrial had been declared in the case against James L. Jones, 58. Claude Fuller, 48, had not been tried. Ex-Klan leader Sam H. Bowers Jr. and other Klan officers, named in the civil suit had been dismissed by Cox as defendants.

The Rev. Charles Billups was shot and killed during an apparent robbery in Chicago Nov. 7. Billups, an executive of a grocery store chain, had come to Chicago in 1963 at the request of the late Rev. Dr. Martin Luther King Jr. and had helped organize Operation Breadbasket, a Southern Christian Leadership Conference drive to get more Negroes employed in ghetto businesses.

BOSTON Globe (newspaper)—272
BOSTON University—252, 357
BOWERS Jr., Sam Holloway—204-5, 207, 210, 408
BOWIE State College (Bowie, Md.)—252-3
BOWKER, Albert H.—382
BOYCOTTS—57, 127, 158, 164, 169, 172, 248, 252-3, 266, 376
BOYD, J. D.—250
BRADDOCK, Pa.—231
BRADFORD, John—185
BRADLEY, John J.—252
BRADLEY, Russell—85
BRANDEIS University (Waltham, Mass.)—250
BRANIGIN, Gov. Roger D.—73, 201
BRAZIER, Rev. Arthur—341
BREATHITT, Gov. Edward T.—178
BREEDEN, Rev. James P.—47
BREITENEICHER, Joseph—55
BRENNAN Jr., Justice William J.—115, 167, 365, 375
BRENNER, Dr. Joseph—187
BRENT, William Lee—401
BRIDGEMEN, Paul—228
BRIDGETON, N.J.—231
BRIGGS, Ephraim E.—156
BROKERAGE Firms (employment)—385
BROOKE, Sen. Edward W. (R., Mass.)—102, 109, 114, 117, 191, 224, 278, 304, 324, 335, 350, 355
BROOKS, Fred—92
BROOKS, Judge Henry F.—179
BROTHERHOOD of Railroad Trainmen—158
BROTHERS, David—401
BROWN v. Board of Education (court case)—138
BROWN, Andrew—236
BROWN, Judge Bailey—145
BROWN, Benjamin—82-3
BROWN, Rev. de Forest—269
BROWN, Ewart—258
BROWN, H. (Herbert Geroid) Rap—54, 71, 91-2, 107, 118, 123, 129, 155, 255, 397. Arrests and charges—38-42; conviction pro-

ceedings—403-6; extradition efforts—404-5. Oratory preceding violence—37-44
BROWN, Harrison—144
BROWN, J. F.—45
BROWN, Judge John R.—134
BROWN, Ray—12
BROWN University (Providence, R.I.)—253
BROYHILL, Rep. Joel T. (R., Va.)—77
BROZEN, Yale—149
BUCKNEY, Edward L.—340
BUFFALO, N.Y.—48-50, 157, 204, 231, 308
BUILD Unity, Integrity, Liberty & Dignity (BUILD)—48
BUNCHE, Ralph J.—197
BUNDY, McGeorge—367-8
BURCH, Dr. Reynold E.—10
BUREAU of Labor Statistics—165-6
BURNS, James W.—137, 174
BURRAGE, Olen L.—205
BURTON, Rep. Philip (D., Calif.)—323
BYRD Jr., Sen. Harry F. (D., Va.)—340
BYRD Sr., Lawrence—210, 408
BYRD, Sen. Robert C. (D., W.Va.)—99
BYRNE, Brendan—9

C

CAIRO, Ill.—50-1
CALIFORNIA—167, 181, 357, 406-7. Fair Employment Practices Commission—158
CALIFORNIA, University of—406. Berkeley campus violence—251, 383, 400, 406. Santa Barbara campus—264
CALIFORNIA Packing Co.—57
CALL To Americans of Goodwill—326
CALLAGHAN, James T.—6
CALVERT, J. R.—75-6
CAMBRIDGE, Md.—37-9, 91, 405
CAMDEN, N.J.—156, 250
CAMPBELL, Alvin—272
CAMPBELL, Angus—308
CAMPBELL, Arnold—272